ORIGINAL STORY **NAGARU TANIGAWA** MANGA **GAKU TSUGANO**

CHARACTER DESIGN:
NOIZI ITO

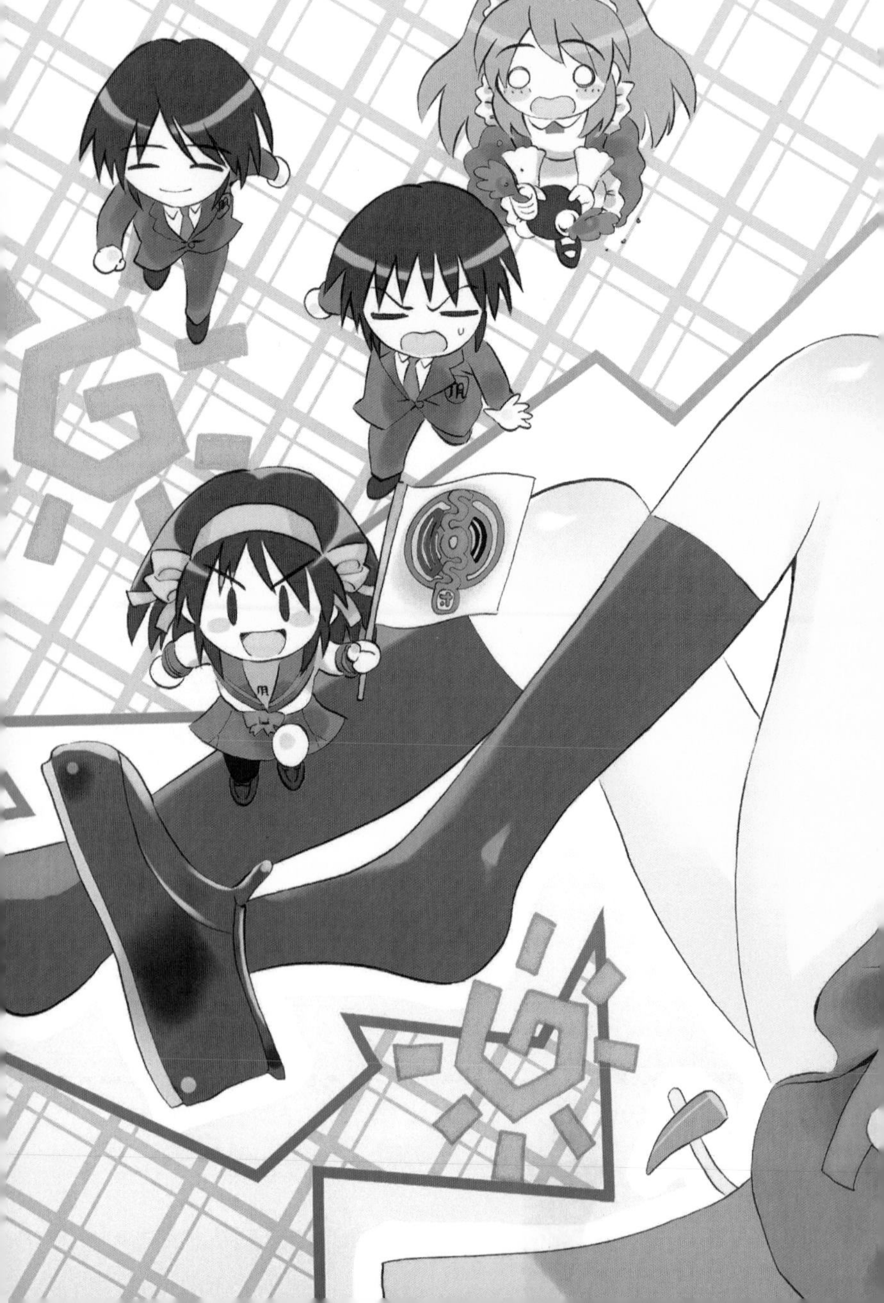

CONTENTS

To you

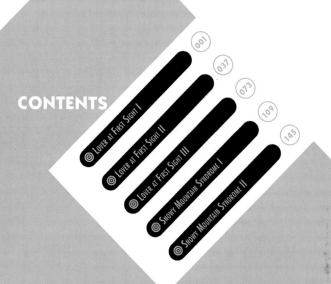

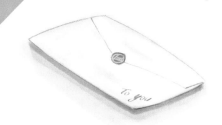

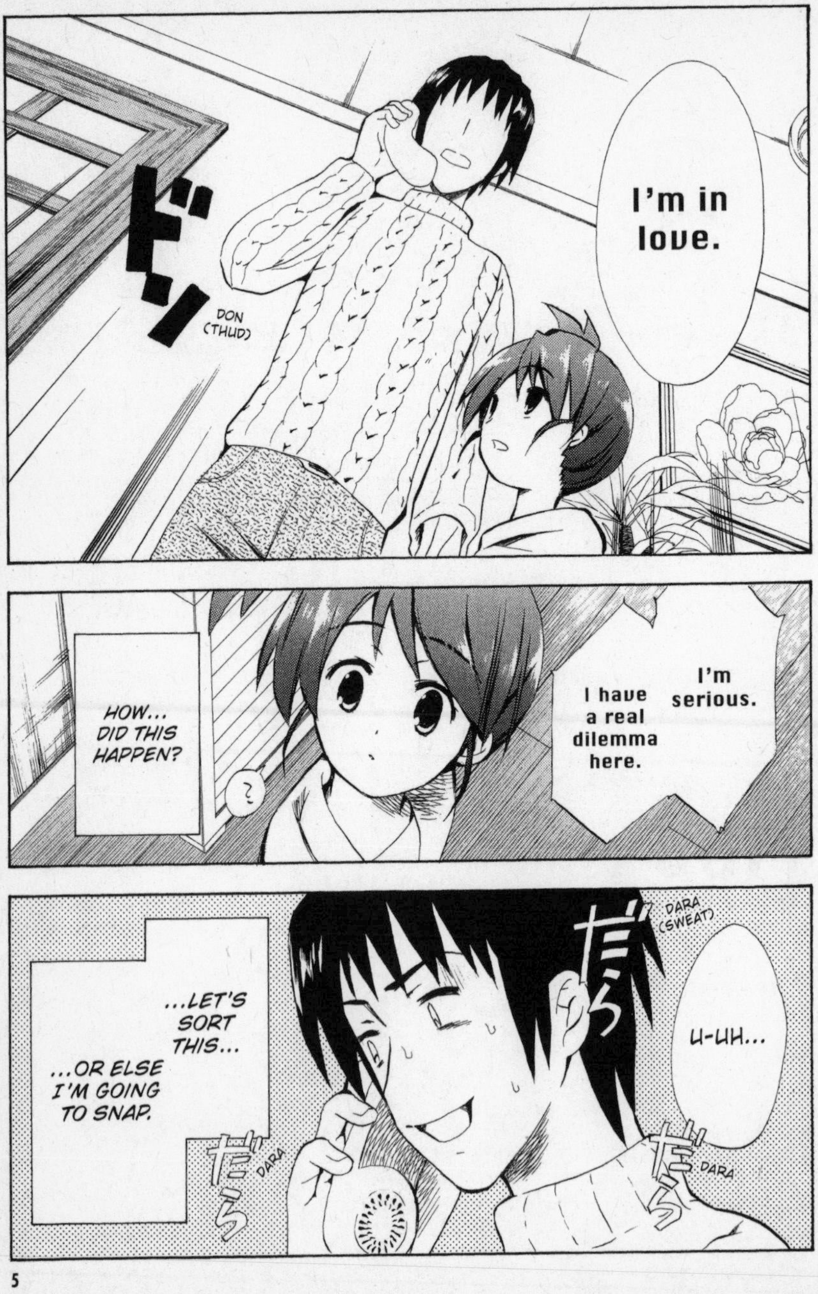
I'm in love.
ドン
DON (THUD)
I'm serious.
I have a real dilemma here.
HOW... DID THIS HAPPEN?
?
だら
DARA (SWEAT)
U-UH...
だら
DARA
...LET'S SORT THIS...
...OR ELSE I'M GOING TO SNAP.
だら
DARA

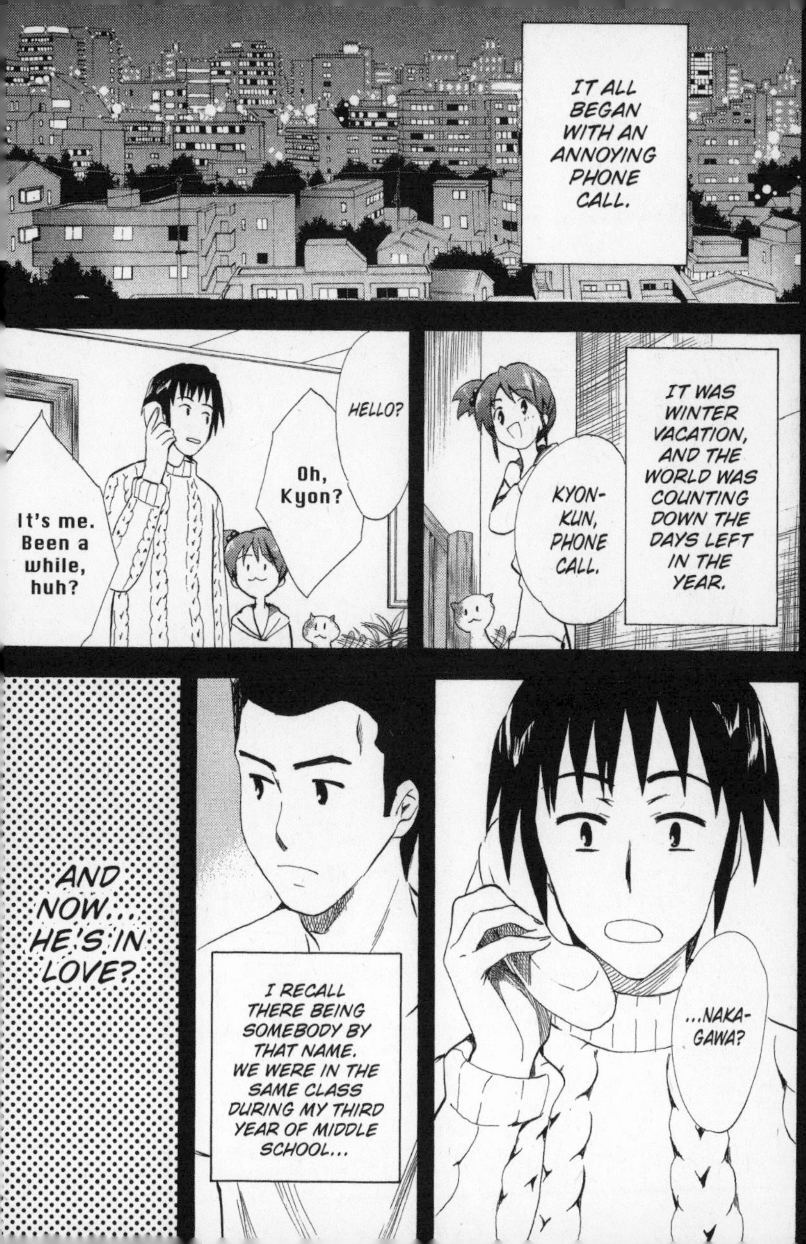
IT ALL BEGAN WITH AN ANNOYING PHONE CALL.
IT WAS WINTER VACATION, AND THE WORLD WAS COUNTING DOWN THE DAYS LEFT IN THE YEAR.
KYON-KUN, PHONE CALL.
HELLO?
Oh, Kyon?
It's me. Been a while, huh?
...NAKA-GAWA?
I RECALL THERE BEING SOMEBODY BY THAT NAME. WE WERE IN THE SAME CLASS DURING MY THIRD YEAR OF MIDDLE SCHOOL...
AND NOW... HE'S IN LOVE?

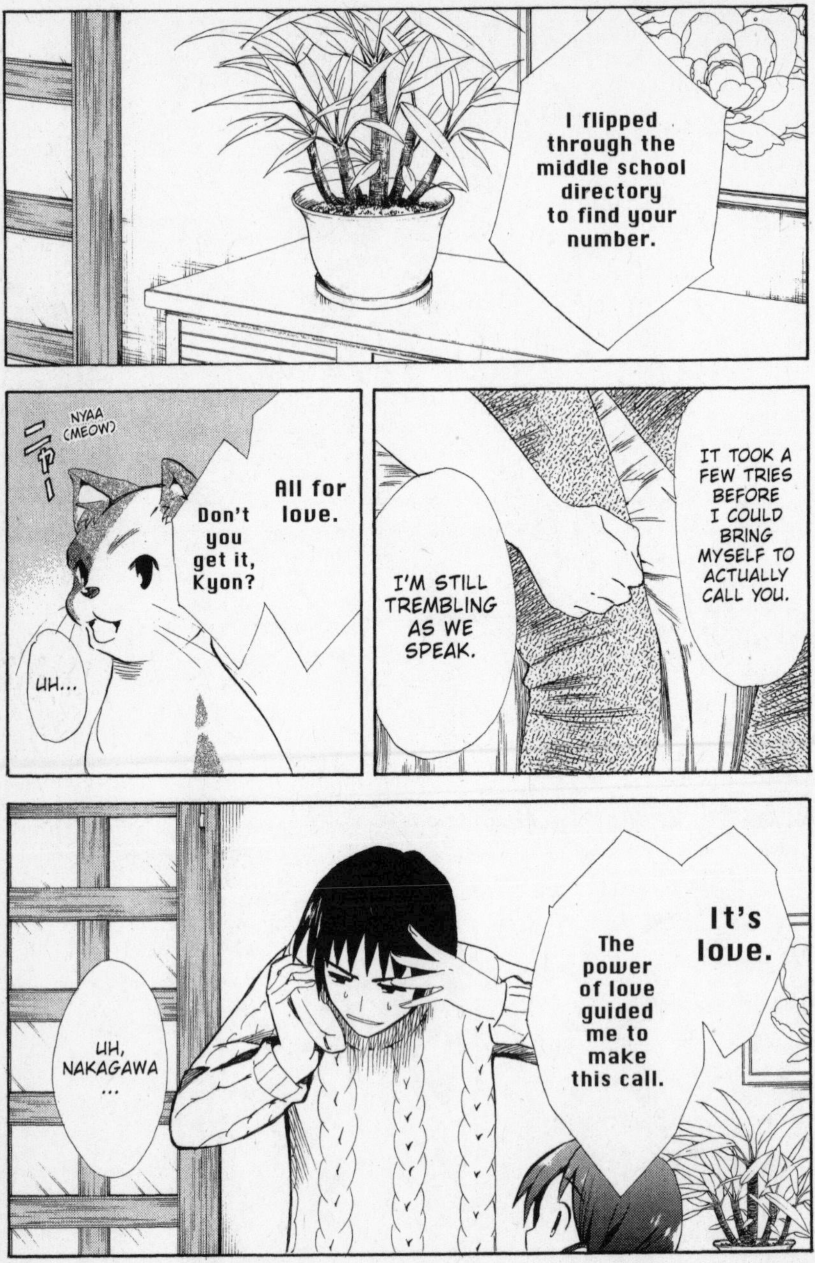
I flipped through the middle school directory to find your number.
IT TOOK A FEW TRIES BEFORE I COULD BRING MYSELF TO ACTUALLY CALL YOU.
I'M STILL TREMBLING AS WE SPEAK.
All for love.
Don't you get it, Kyon?
NYAA (MEOW)
UH...
It's love.
The power of love guided me to make this call.
UH, NAKAGAWA ...

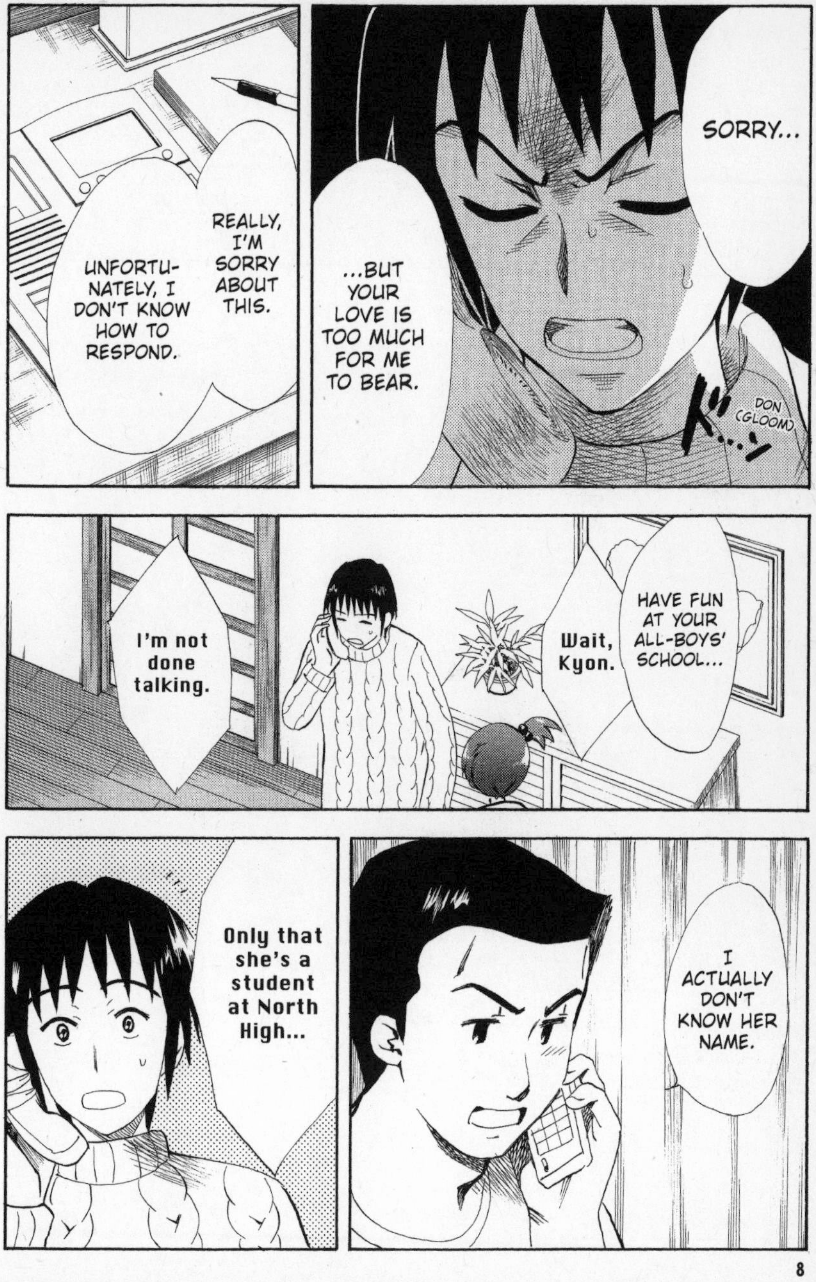
SORRY...
...BUT YOUR LOVE IS TOO MUCH FOR ME TO BEAR.
DON (GLOOM)
REALLY, I'M SORRY ABOUT THIS.
UNFORTUNATELY, I DON'T KNOW HOW TO RESPOND.
HAVE FUN AT YOUR ALL-BOYS' SCHOOL...
Wait, Kyon.
I'm not done talking.
I ACTUALLY DON'T KNOW HER NAME.
Only that she's a student at North High...

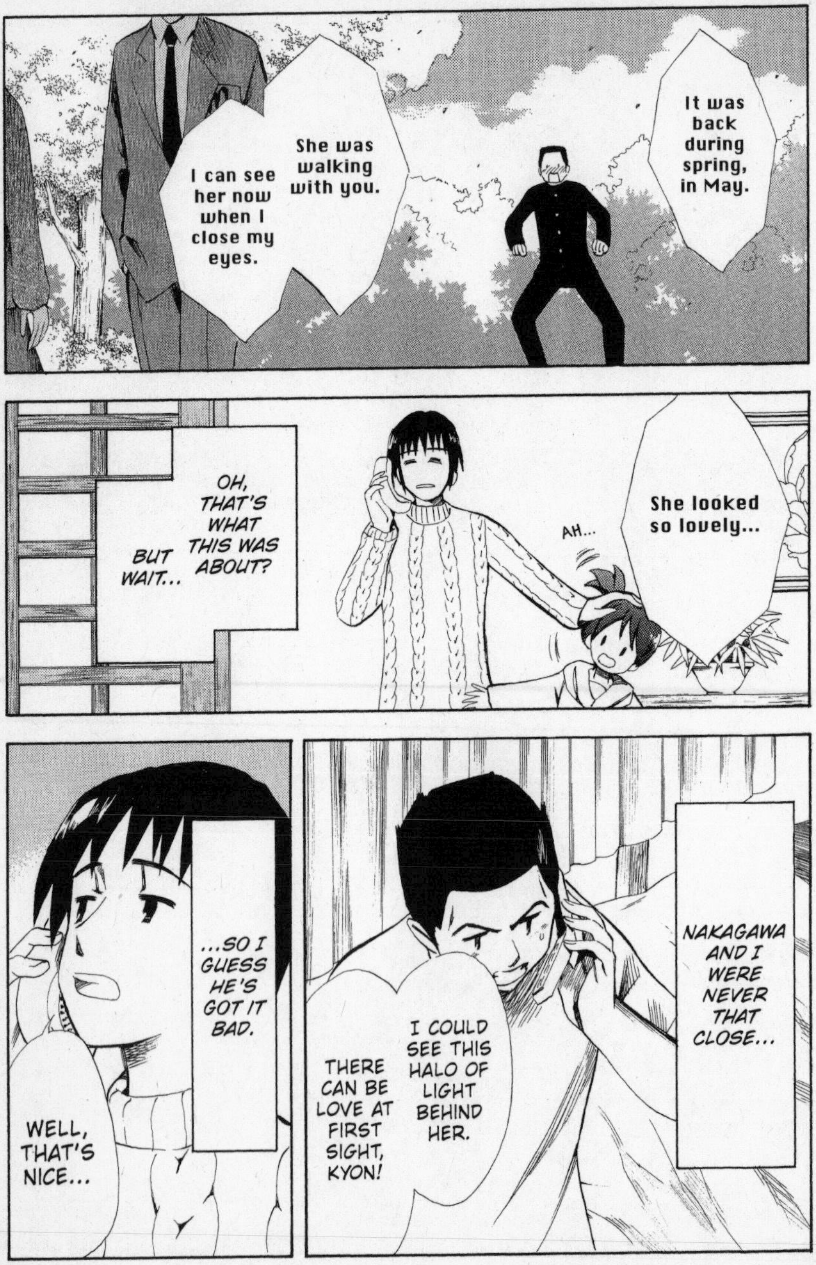
It was back during spring, in May.
She was walking with you.
I can see her now when I close my eyes.
She looked so lovely...
AH...
OH, THAT'S WHAT THIS WAS ABOUT?
BUT WAIT...
NAKAGAWA AND I WERE NEVER THAT CLOSE...
I COULD SEE THIS HALO OF LIGHT BEHIND HER.
THERE CAN BE LOVE AT FIRST SIGHT, KYON!
...SO I GUESS HE'S GOT IT BAD.
WELL, THAT'S NICE...

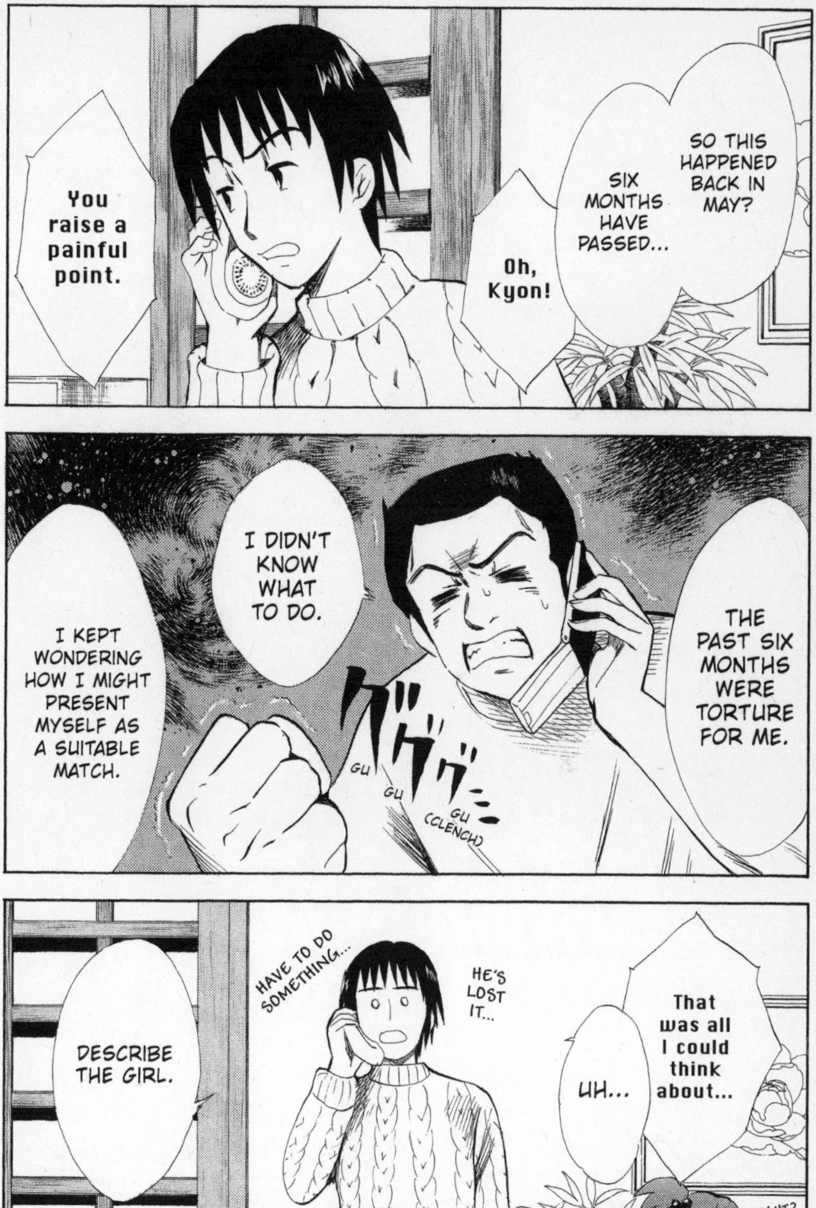
SO THIS HAPPENED BACK IN MAY?
SIX MONTHS HAVE PASSED...
Oh, Kyon!
You raise a painful point.
THE PAST SIX MONTHS WERE TORTURE FOR ME.
GU GU GU (CLENCH)
I DIDN'T KNOW WHAT TO DO.
I KEPT WONDERING HOW I MIGHT PRESENT MYSELF AS A SUITABLE MATCH.
RIGHT?
RIGHT?
That was all I could think about...
UH...
HE'S LOST IT...
HAVE TO DO SOMETHING...
DESCRIBE THE GIRL.

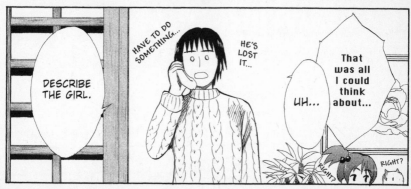

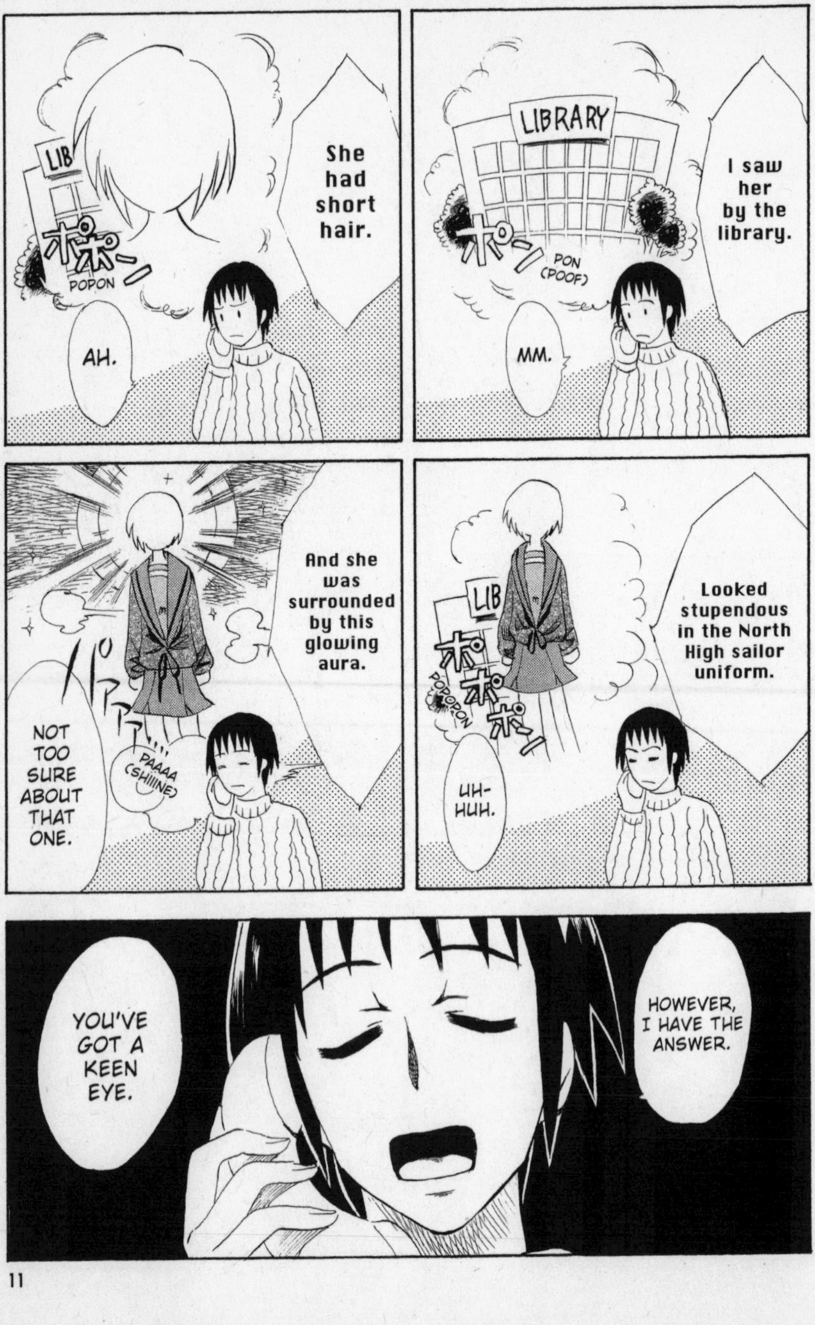
LIBRARY
I saw her by the library.
PON (POOF)
MM.
LIB
She had short hair.
POPON
AH.
LIB
Looked stupendous in the North High sailor uniform.
POPOPON
UH-HUH.
And she was surrounded by this glowing aura.
PAAAA (SHIIINE)
NOT TOO SURE ABOUT THAT ONE.
HOWEVER, I HAVE THE ANSWER.
YOU'VE GOT A KEEN EYE.

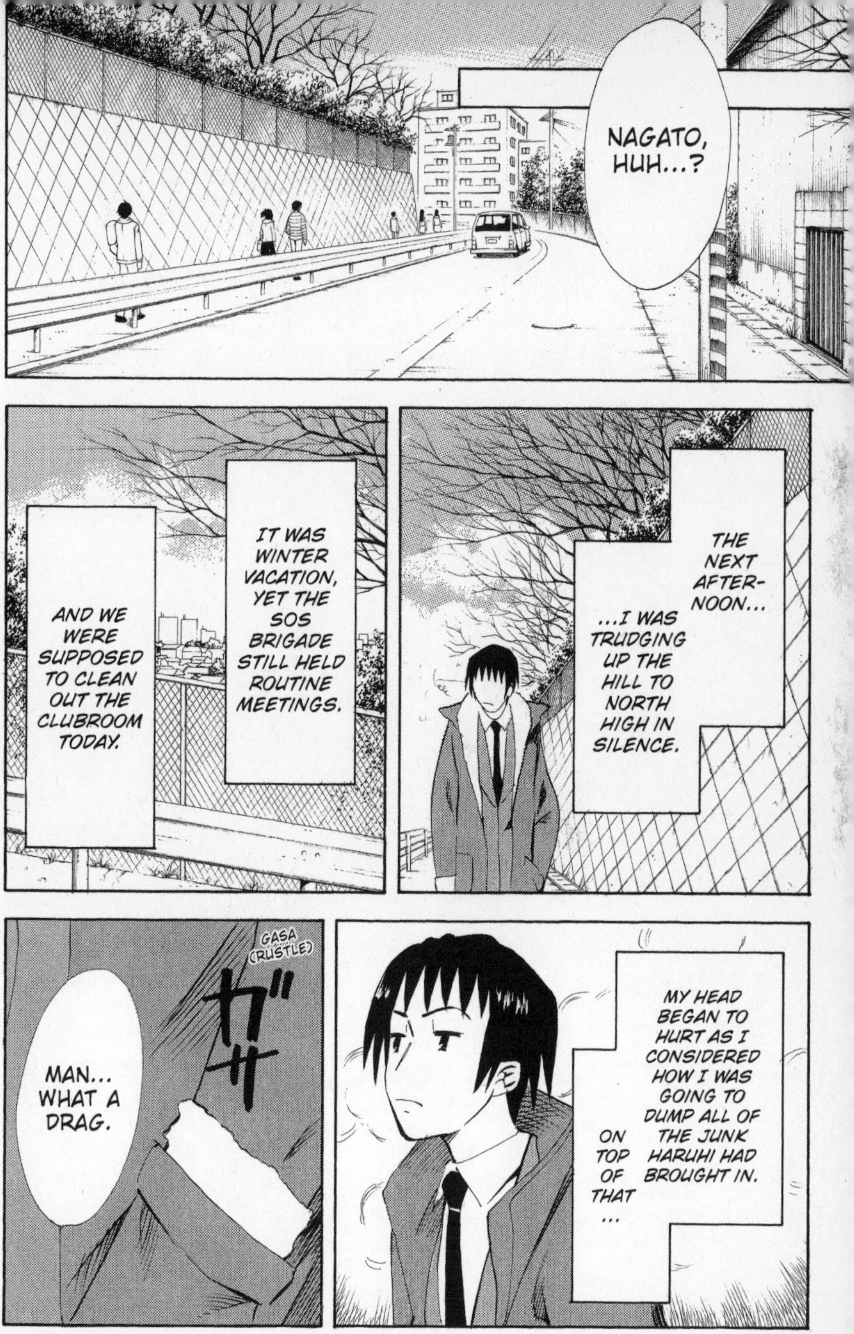
NAGATO, HUH...?
THE NEXT AFTER-NOON...
...I WAS TRUDGING UP THE HILL TO NORTH HIGH IN SILENCE.
IT WAS WINTER VACATION, YET THE SOS BRIGADE STILL HELD ROUTINE MEETINGS.
AND WE WERE SUPPOSED TO CLEAN OUT THE CLUBROOM TODAY.
MY HEAD BEGAN TO HURT AS I CONSIDERED HOW I WAS GOING TO DUMP ALL OF THE JUNK HARUHI HAD BROUGHT IN.
ON TOP OF THAT ...
GASA (RUSTLE)
ガサ
MAN... WHAT A DRAG.

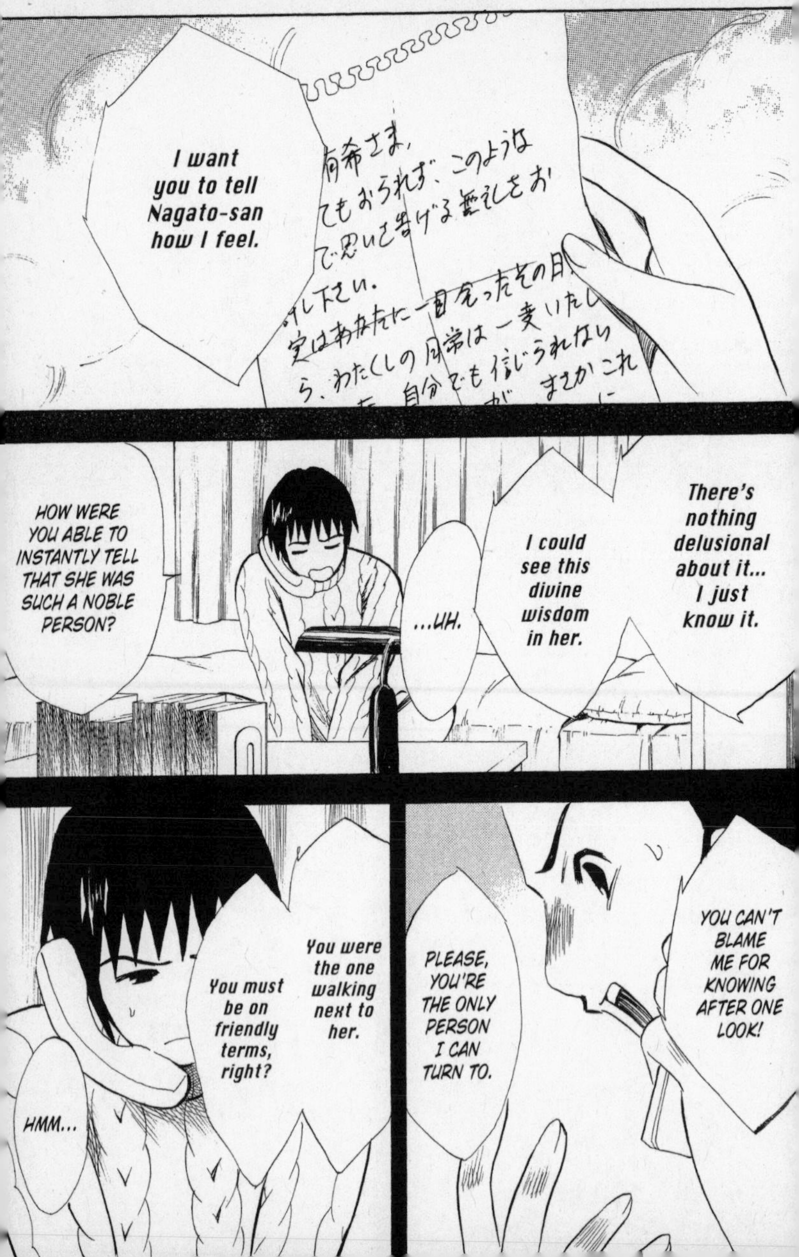
I want you to tell Nagato-san how I feel.
有希さま、
てもおられず、このような
で思いを告げる無礼をお
実はあなたに一目会ったその日
ら、わたくしの日常は一変いたし
There's nothing delusional about it... I just know it.
I could see this divine wisdom in her.
...UH.
HOW WERE YOU ABLE TO INSTANTLY TELL THAT SHE WAS SUCH A NOBLE PERSON?
YOU CAN'T BLAME ME FOR KNOWING AFTER ONE LOOK!
PLEASE, YOU'RE THE ONLY PERSON I CAN TURN TO.
You were the one walking next to her.
You must be on friendly terms, right?
HMM...

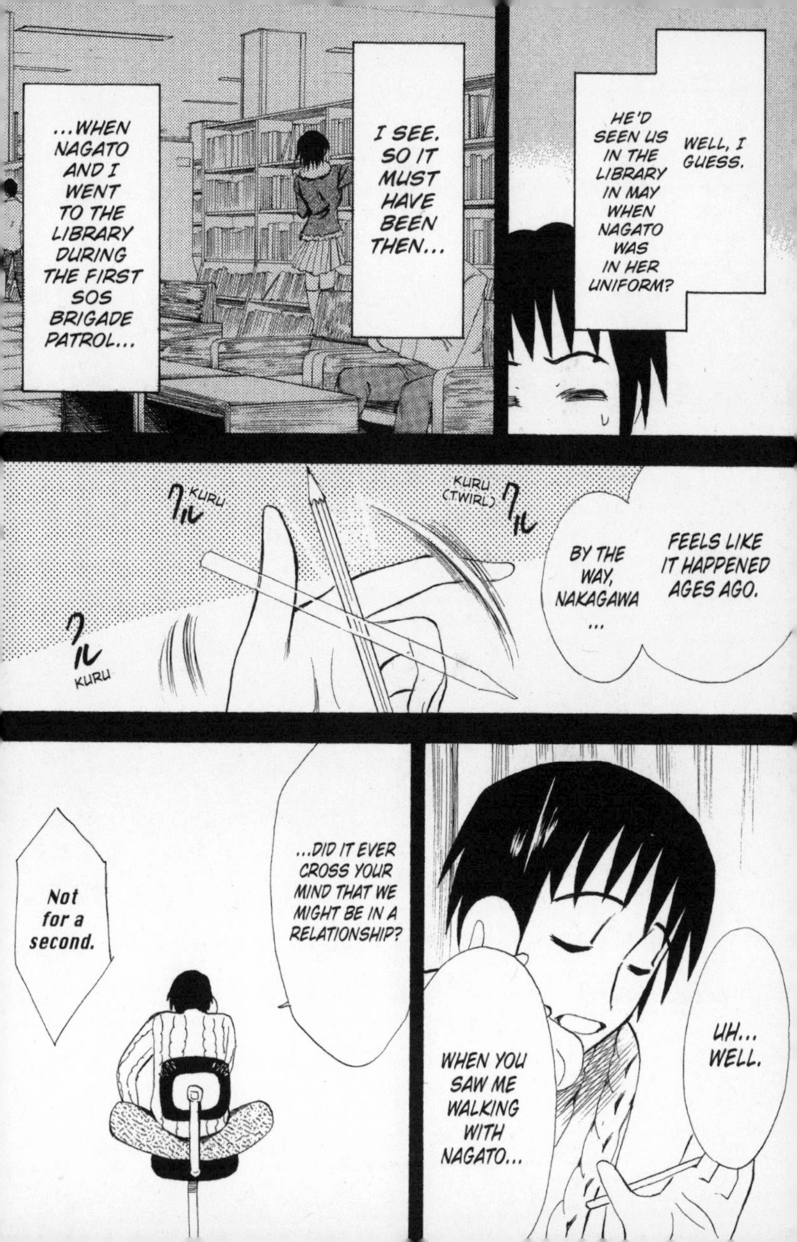

WELL, I GUESS.
HE'D SEEN US IN THE LIBRARY IN MAY WHEN NAGATO WAS IN HER UNIFORM?
I SEE. SO IT MUST HAVE BEEN THEN...
...WHEN NAGATO AND I WENT TO THE LIBRARY DURING THE FIRST SOS BRIGADE PATROL...
FEELS LIKE IT HAPPENED AGES AGO.
BY THE WAY, NAKAGAWA...
KURU (TWIRL)
KURU
KURU
UH... WELL.
WHEN YOU SAW ME WALKING WITH NAGATO...
...DID IT EVER CROSS YOUR MIND THAT WE MIGHT BE IN A RELATIONSHIP?
Not for a second.

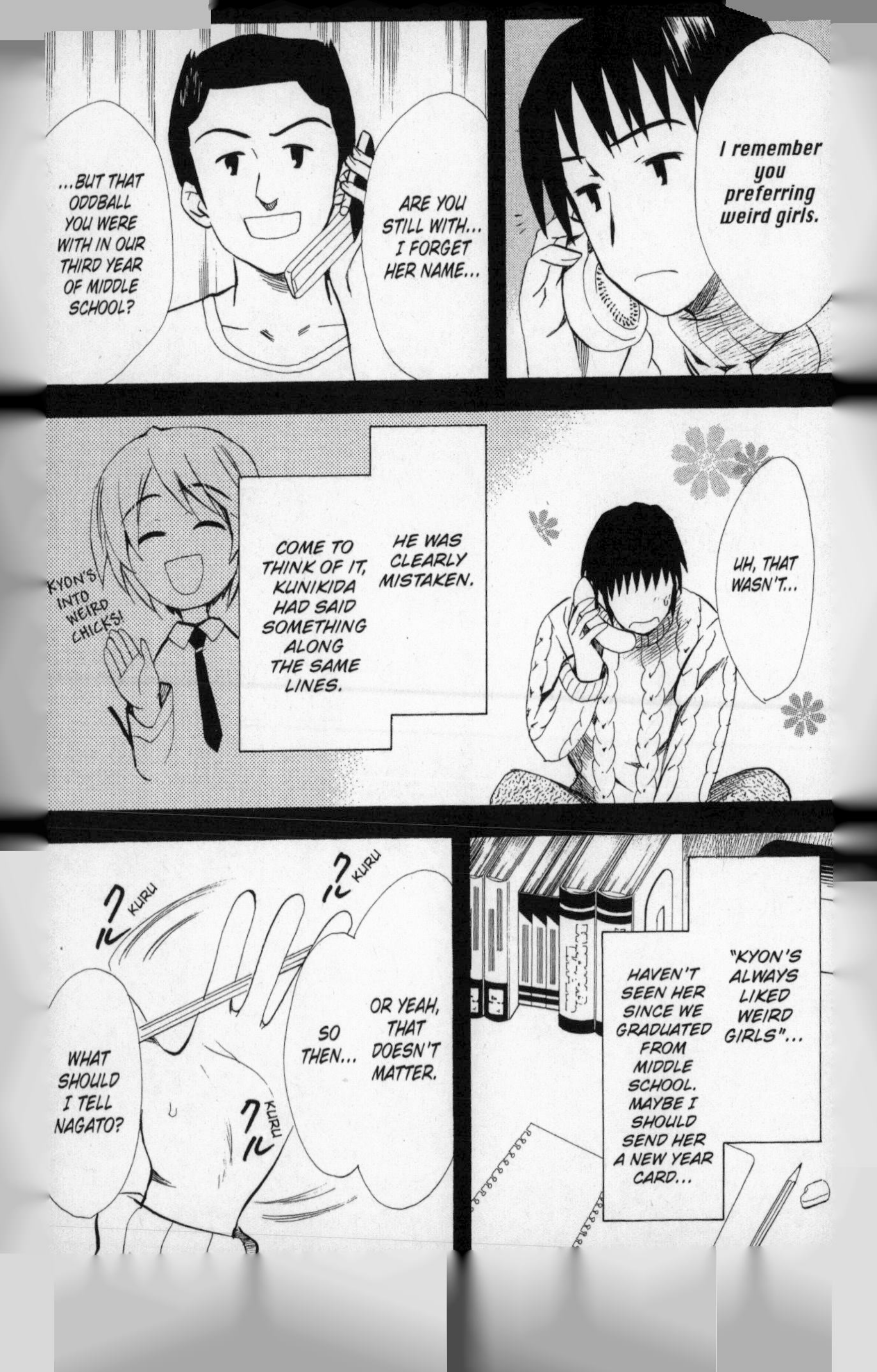
I remember you preferring weird girls.
ARE YOU STILL WITH... I FORGET HER NAME...
...BUT THAT ODDBALL YOU WERE WITH IN OUR THIRD YEAR OF MIDDLE SCHOOL?
UH, THAT WASN'T...
HE WAS CLEARLY MISTAKEN.
COME TO THINK OF IT, KUNIKIDA HAD SAID SOMETHING ALONG THE SAME LINES.
KYON'S INTO WEIRD CHICKS!
"KYON'S ALWAYS LIKED WEIRD GIRLS"...
HAVEN'T SEEN HER SINCE WE GRADUATED FROM MIDDLE SCHOOL. MAYBE I SHOULD SEND HER A NEW YEAR CARD...
クル KURU
OR YEAH, THAT DOESN'T MATTER.
SO THEN...
クル KURU
クル KURU
WHAT SHOULD I TELL NAGATO?

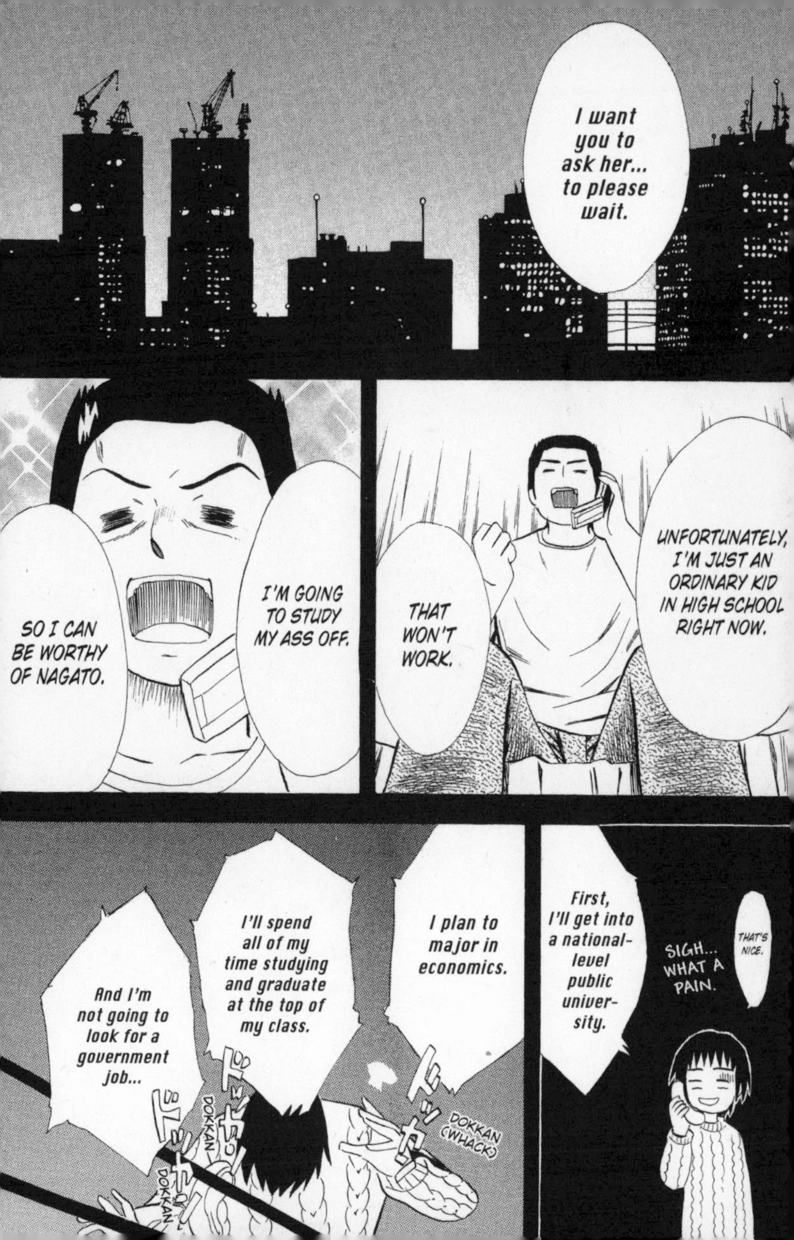
I want you to ask her... to please wait.
UNFORTUNATELY, I'M JUST AN ORDINARY KID IN HIGH SCHOOL RIGHT NOW.
THAT WON'T WORK.
I'M GOING TO STUDY MY ASS OFF.
SO I CAN BE WORTHY OF NAGATO.
THAT'S NICE.
SIGH... WHAT A PAIN.
First, I'll get into a national-level public university.
I plan to major in economics.
DOKKAN (WHACK)
I'll spend all of my time studying and graduate at the top of my class.
DOKKAN
And I'm not going to look for a government job...
DOKKAN

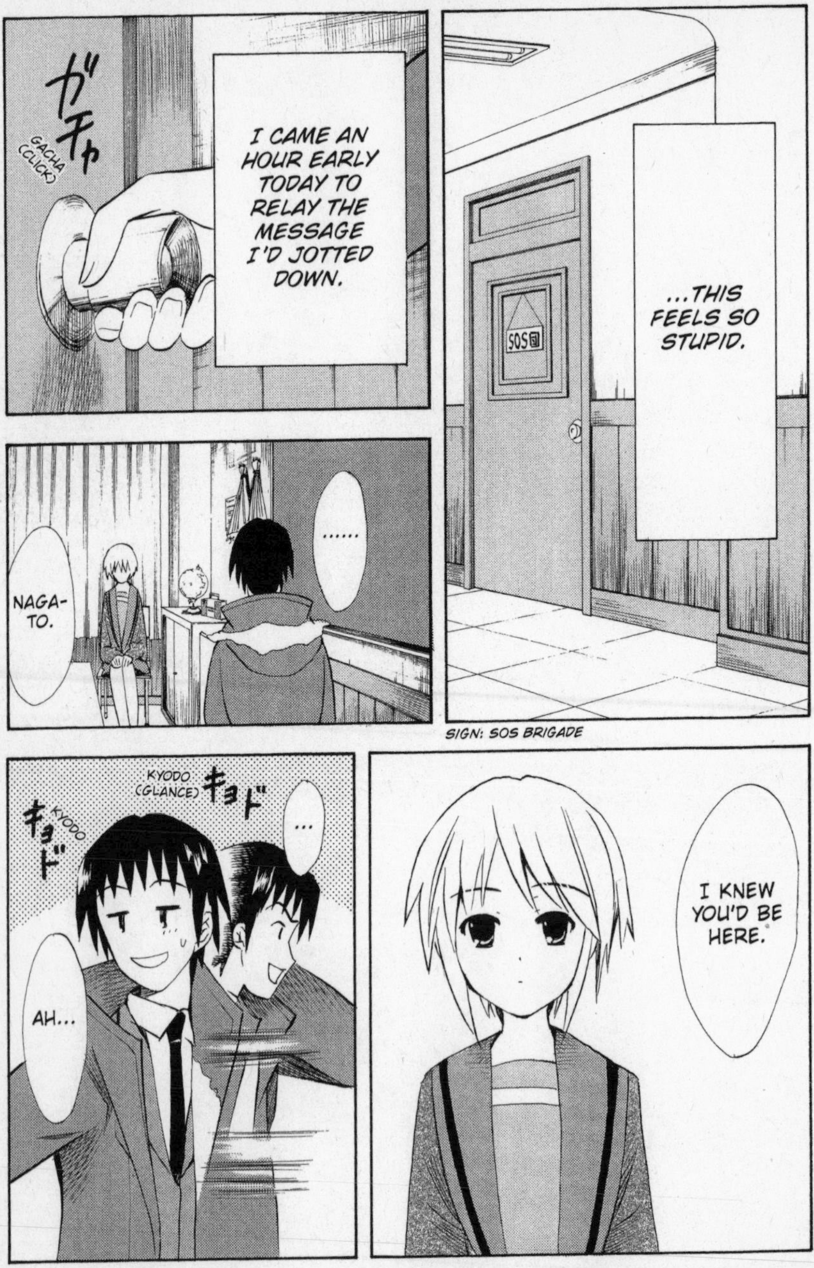
...THIS FEELS SO STUPID.
SIGN: SOS BRIGADE
ガチャ
GACHA (CLICK)
I CAME AN HOUR EARLY TODAY TO RELAY THE MESSAGE I'D JOTTED DOWN.
......
NAGA-TO.
I KNEW YOU'D BE HERE.
KYODO (GLANCE) キョド
...
キョド KYODO
AH...

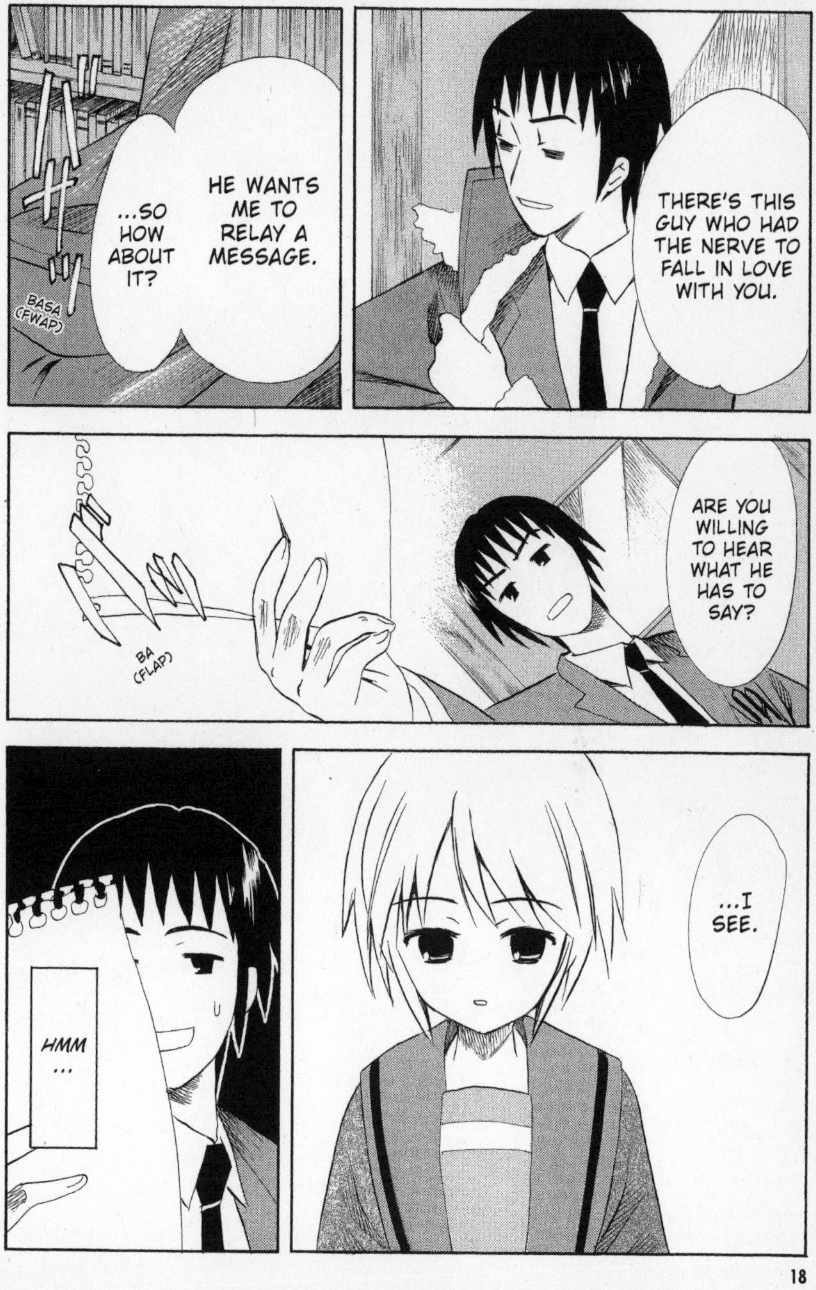
THERE'S THIS GUY WHO HAD THE NERVE TO FALL IN LOVE WITH YOU.
HE WANTS ME TO RELAY A MESSAGE.
...SO HOW ABOUT IT?
BASA (FWAP)
ARE YOU WILLING TO HEAR WHAT HE HAS TO SAY?
BA (FLAP)
...I SEE.
HMM ...

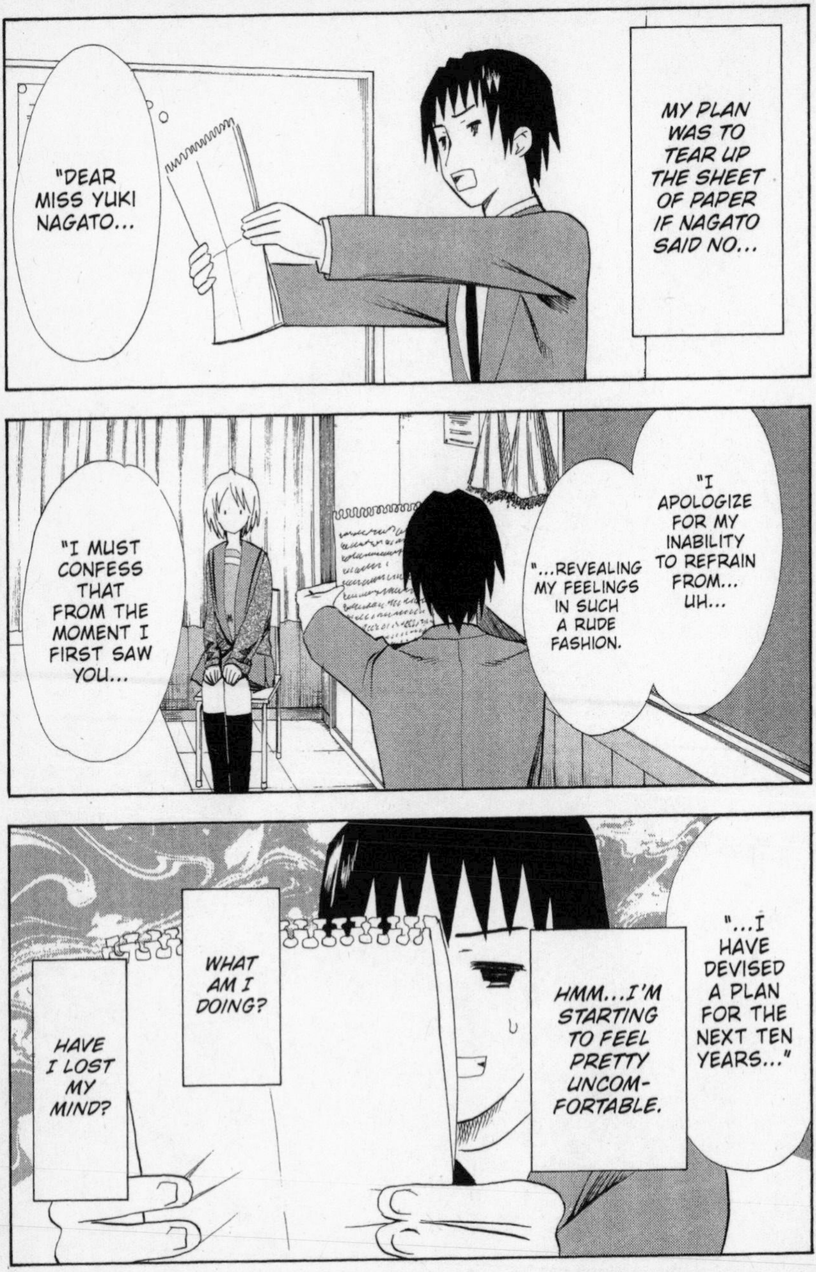
MY PLAN WAS TO TEAR UP THE SHEET OF PAPER IF NAGATO SAID NO...
"DEAR MISS YUKI NAGATO...
"I APOLOGIZE FOR MY INABILITY TO REFRAIN FROM... UH...
"...REVEALING MY FEELINGS IN SUCH A RUDE FASHION.
"I MUST CONFESS THAT FROM THE MOMENT I FIRST SAW YOU...
"...I HAVE DEVISED A PLAN FOR THE NEXT TEN YEARS..."
HMM...I'M STARTING TO FEEL PRETTY UNCOM-FORTABLE.
WHAT AM I DOING?
HAVE I LOST MY MIND?

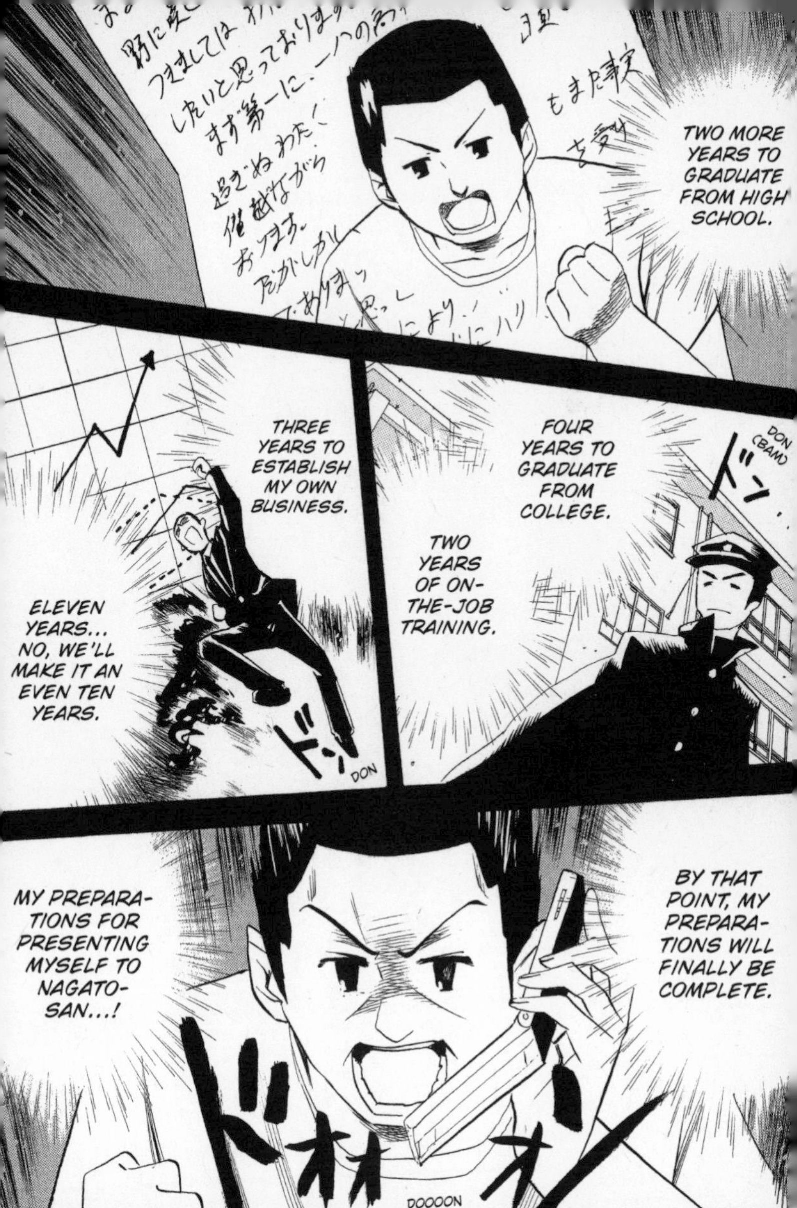
TWO MORE YEARS TO GRADUATE FROM HIGH SCHOOL.
FOUR YEARS TO GRADUATE FROM COLLEGE.
ドン
DON (BAM)
TWO YEARS OF ON-THE-JOB TRAINING.
THREE YEARS TO ESTABLISH MY OWN BUSINESS.
ELEVEN YEARS... NO, WE'LL MAKE IT AN EVEN TEN YEARS.
ドン
DON
BY THAT POINT, MY PREPARATIONS WILL FINALLY BE COMPLETE.
MY PREPARATIONS FOR PRESENTING MYSELF TO NAGATO-SAN...!
ドオオオン
DOOOON (BOOOOM)

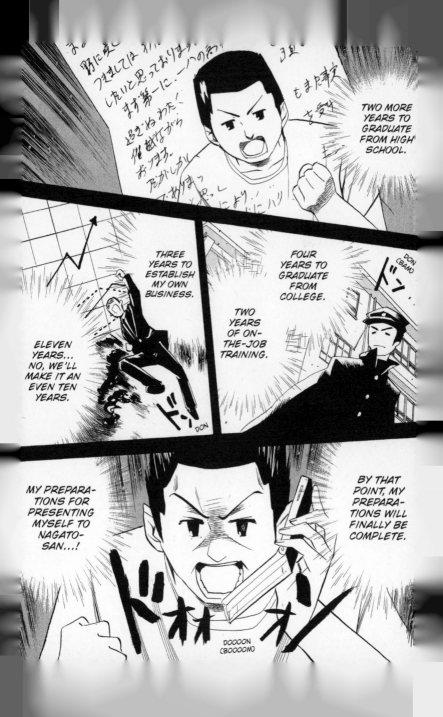

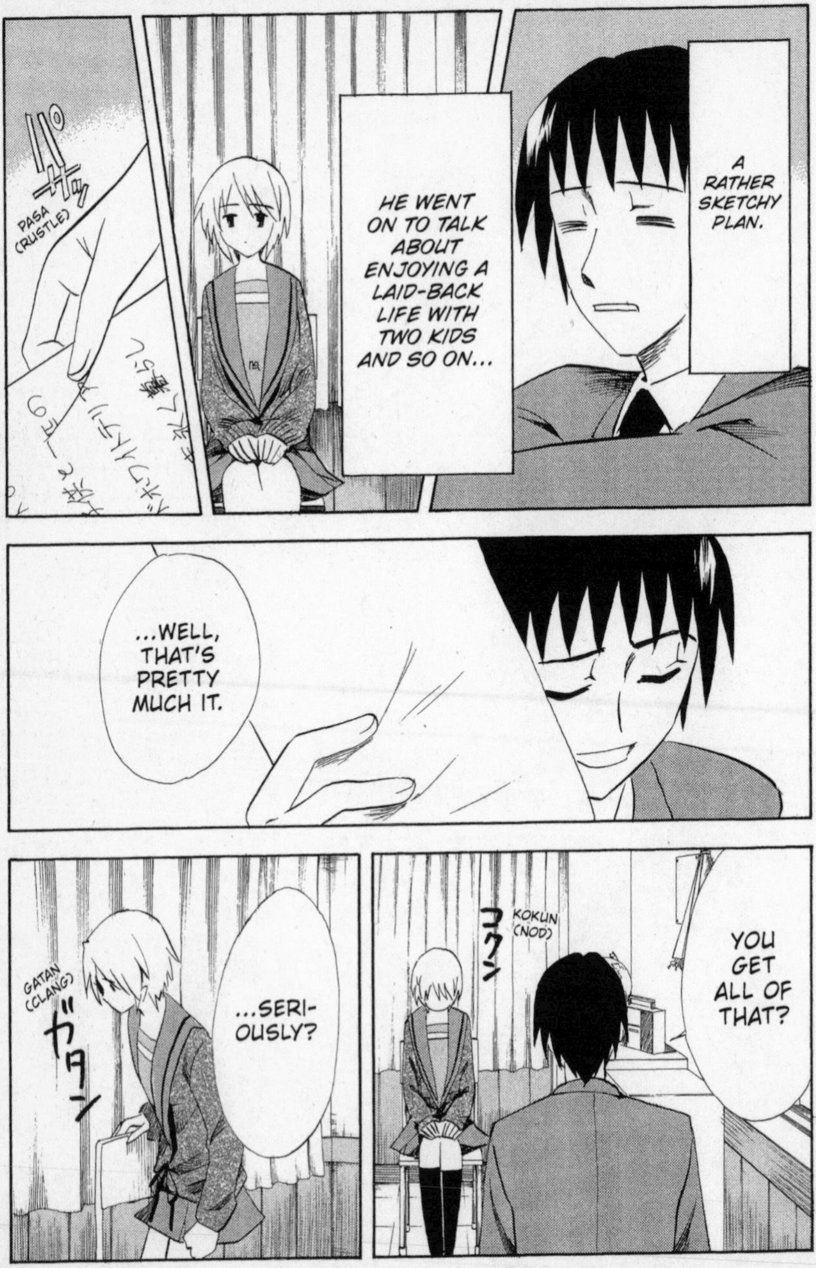
A RATHER SKETCHY PLAN.
HE WENT ON TO TALK ABOUT ENJOYING A LAID-BACK LIFE WITH TWO KIDS AND SO ON...
パサッ
PASA (RUSTLE)
...WELL, THAT'S PRETTY MUCH IT.
YOU GET ALL OF THAT?
コクン
KOKUN (NOD)
...SERI-OUSLY?
ガタン
GATAN (CLANG)

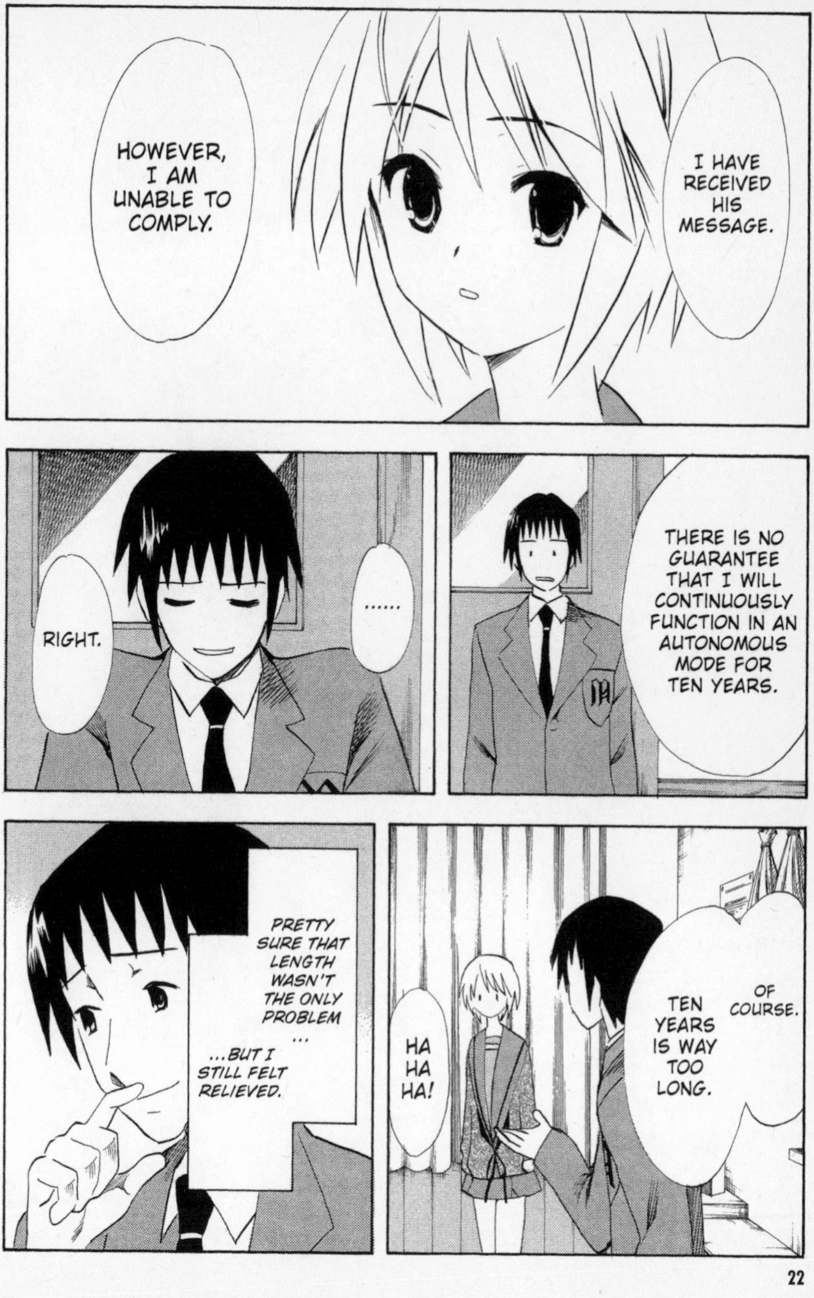
I HAVE RECEIVED HIS MESSAGE.
HOWEVER, I AM UNABLE TO COMPLY.
THERE IS NO GUARANTEE THAT I WILL CONTINUOUSLY FUNCTION IN AN AUTONOMOUS MODE FOR TEN YEARS.
....
RIGHT.
OF COURSE.
TEN YEARS IS WAY TOO LONG.
HA HA HA!
PRETTY SURE THAT LENGTH WASN'T THE ONLY PROBLEM...
...BUT I STILL FELT RELIEVED.

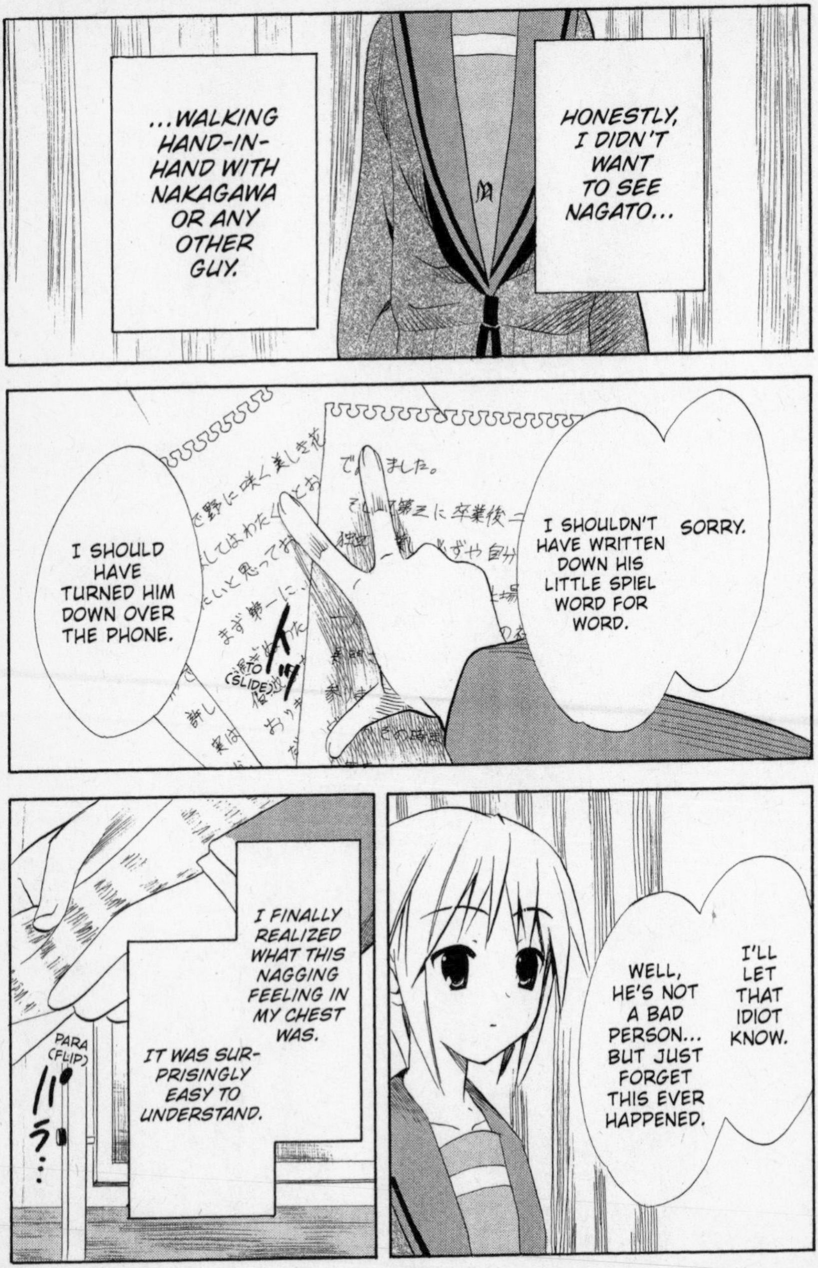
HONESTLY, I DIDN'T WANT TO SEE NAGATO...
...WALKING HAND-IN-HAND WITH NAKAGAWA OR ANY OTHER GUY.
SORRY.
I SHOULDN'T HAVE WRITTEN DOWN HIS LITTLE SPIEL WORD FOR WORD.
I SHOULD HAVE TURNED HIM DOWN OVER THE PHONE.
TO (SLIDE)
I'LL LET THAT IDIOT KNOW.
WELL, HE'S NOT A BAD PERSON... BUT JUST FORGET THIS EVER HAPPENED.
I FINALLY REALIZED WHAT THIS NAGGING FEELING IN MY CHEST WAS.
IT WAS SURPRISINGLY EASY TO UNDERSTAND.
PARA (FLIP)

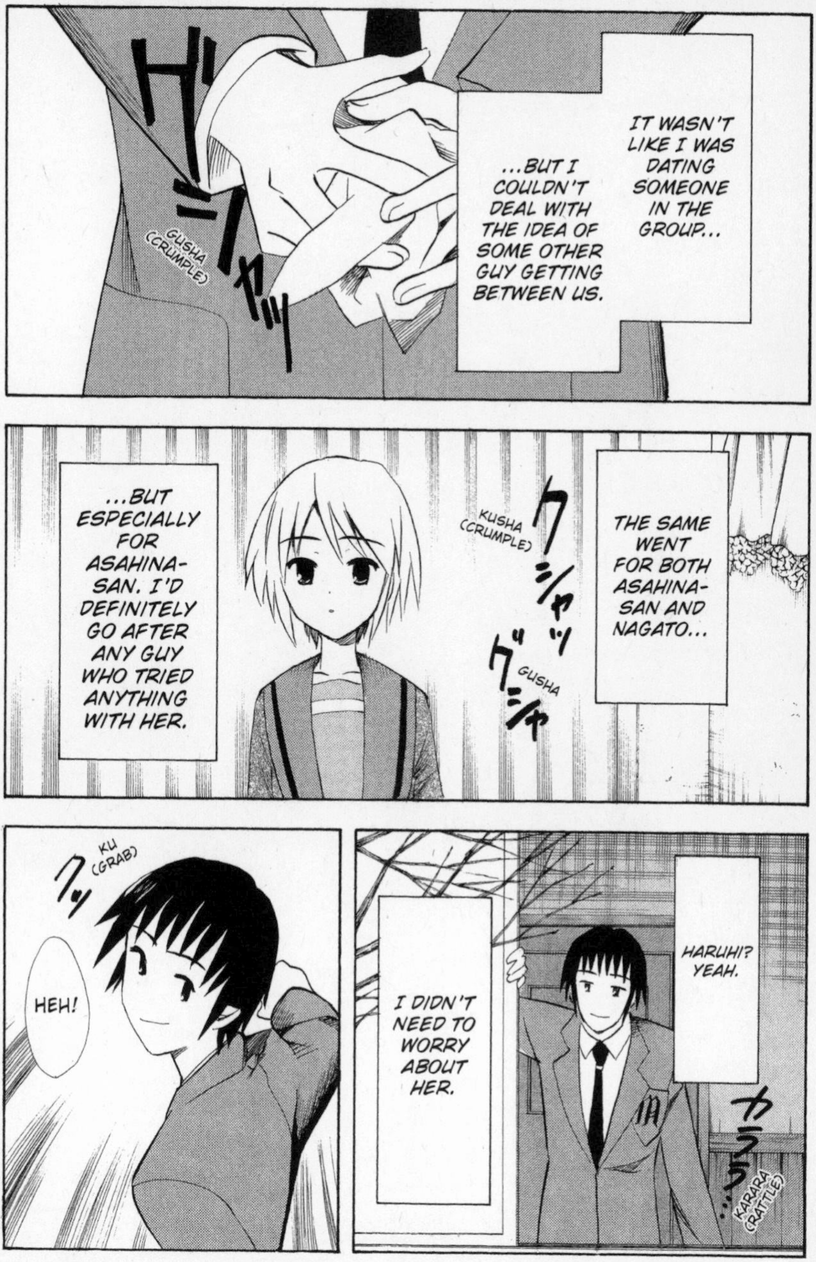
IT WASN'T LIKE I WAS DATING SOMEONE IN THE GROUP...
...BUT I COULDN'T DEAL WITH THE IDEA OF SOME OTHER GUY GETTING BETWEEN US.
GUSHA (CRUMPLE)
THE SAME WENT FOR BOTH ASAHINA-SAN AND NAGATO...
KUSHA (CRUMPLE)
GUSHA
...BUT ESPECIALLY FOR ASAHINA-SAN. I'D DEFINITELY GO AFTER ANY GUY WHO TRIED ANYTHING WITH HER.
HARUHI? YEAH.
I DIDN'T NEED TO WORRY ABOUT HER.
KARARA (RATTLE)
KU (GRAB)
HEH!

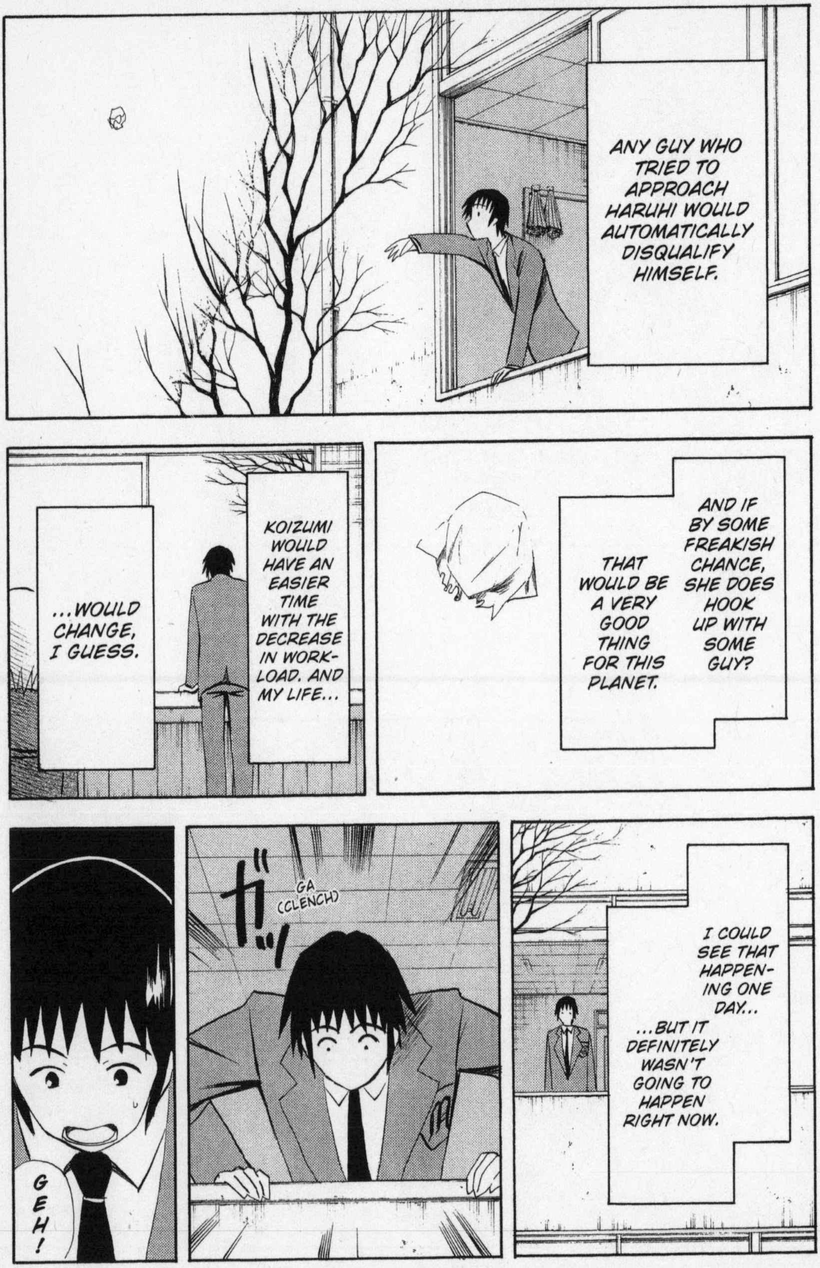
ANY GUY WHO TRIED TO APPROACH HARUHI WOULD AUTOMATICALLY DISQUALIFY HIMSELF.
AND IF BY SOME FREAKISH CHANCE, SHE DOES HOOK UP WITH SOME GUY?
THAT WOULD BE A VERY GOOD THING FOR THIS PLANET.
KOIZUMI WOULD HAVE AN EASIER TIME WITH THE DECREASE IN WORK-LOAD. AND MY LIFE...
...WOULD CHANGE, I GUESS.
I COULD SEE THAT HAPPEN-ING ONE DAY...
...BUT IT DEFINITELY WASN'T GOING TO HAPPEN RIGHT NOW.
GA (CLENCH)
GEH!

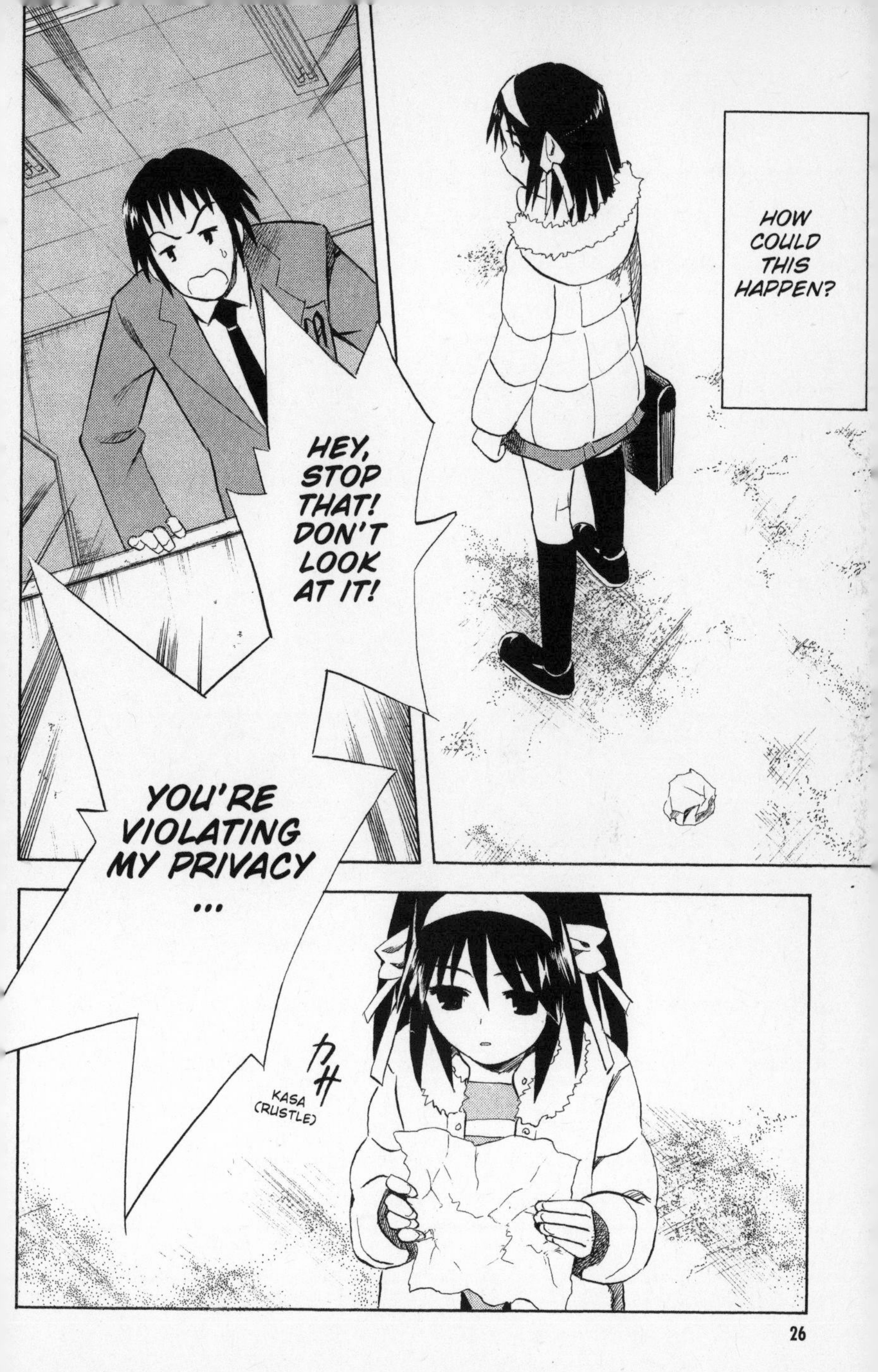
HOW COULD THIS HAPPEN?
HEY, STOP THAT! DON'T LOOK AT IT!
YOU'RE VIOLATING MY PRIVACY ...
カサ
KASA (RUSTLE)

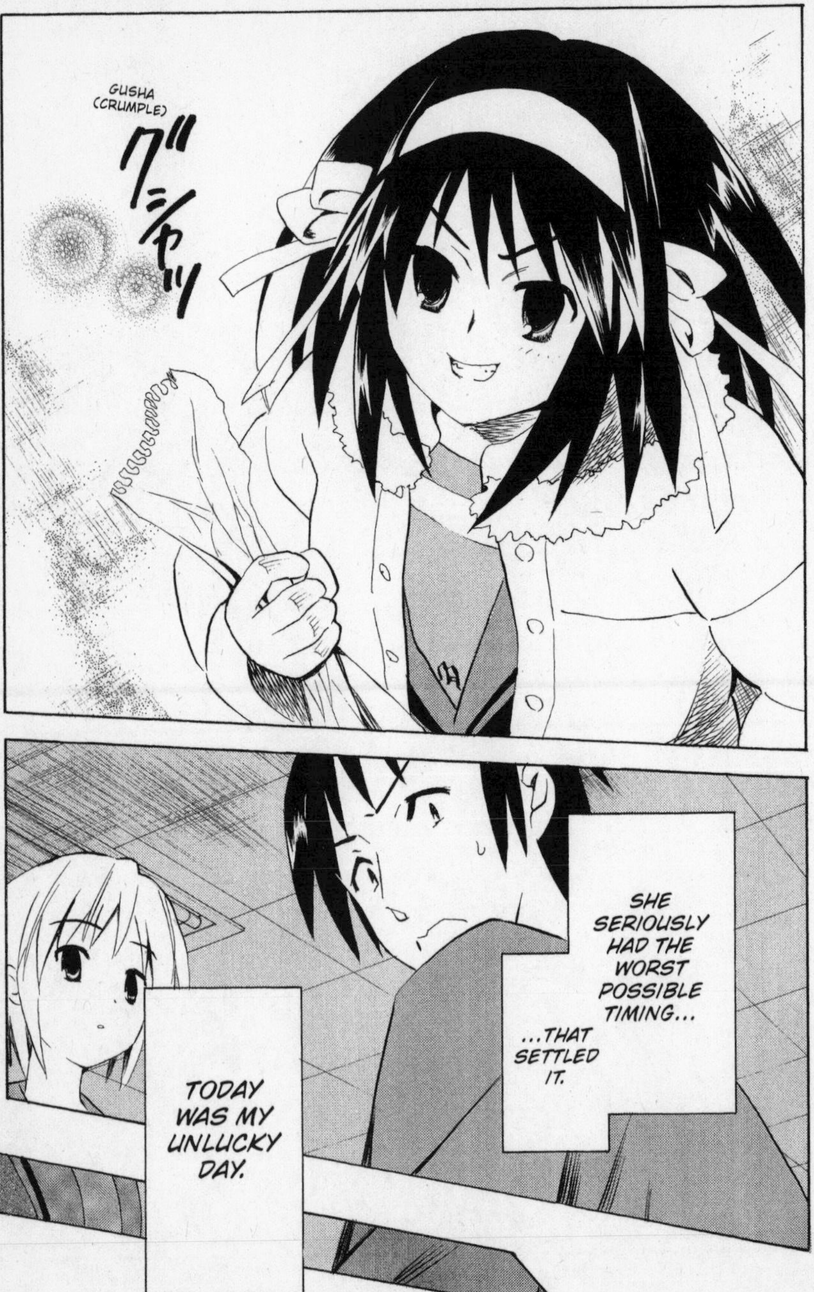
GUSHA (CRUMPLE)
グシャッ
SHE SERIOUSLY HAD THE WORST POSSIBLE TIMING...
...THAT SETTLED IT.
TODAY WAS MY UNLUCKY DAY.

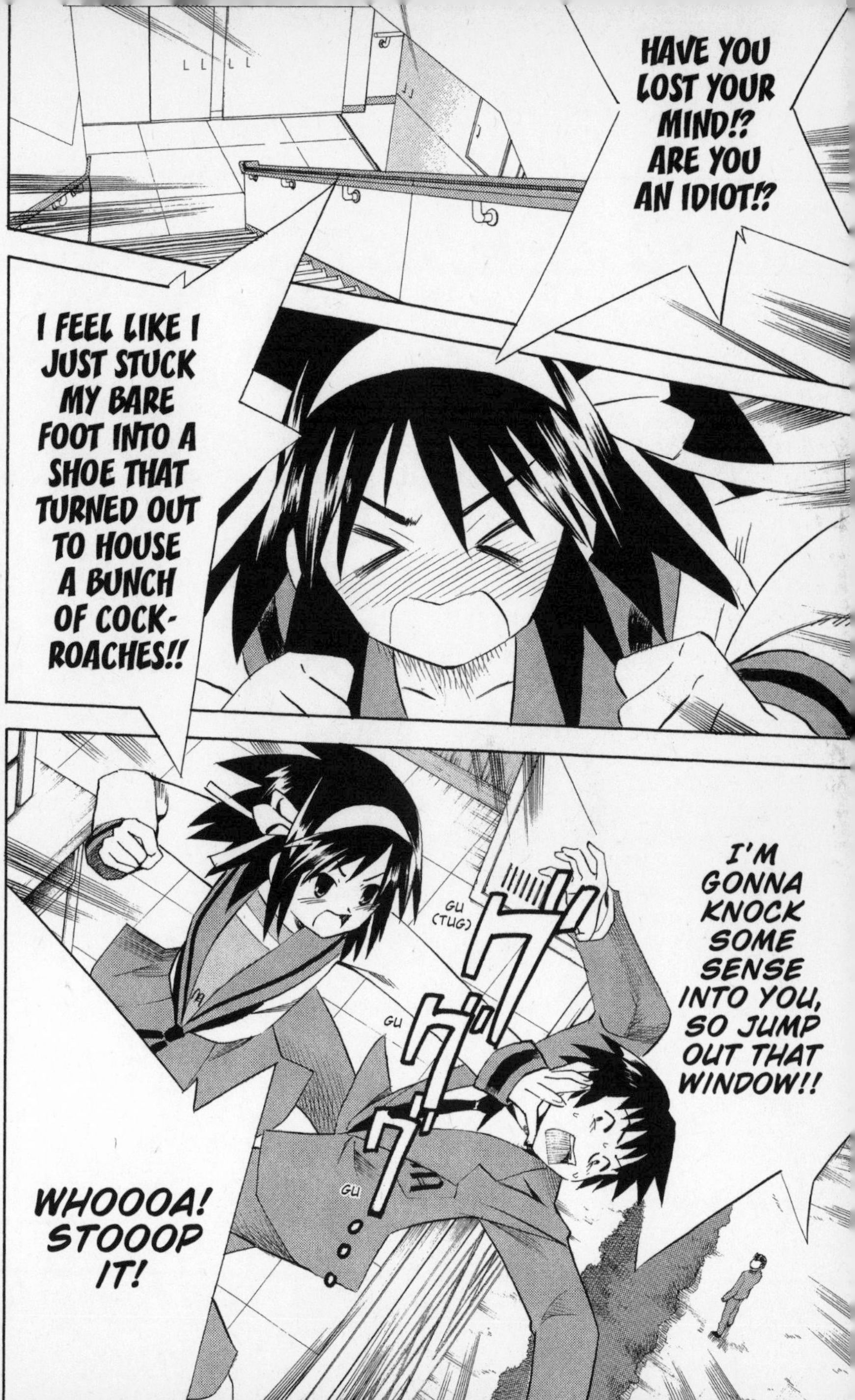
HAVE YOU LOST YOUR MIND!? ARE YOU AN IDIOT!?
I FEEL LIKE I JUST STUCK MY BARE FOOT INTO A SHOE THAT TURNED OUT TO HOUSE A BUNCH OF COCK-ROACHES!!
I'M GONNA KNOCK SOME SENSE INTO YOU, SO JUMP OUT THAT WINDOW!!
GU (TUG)
GU
GU
WHOOOA! STOOOP IT!

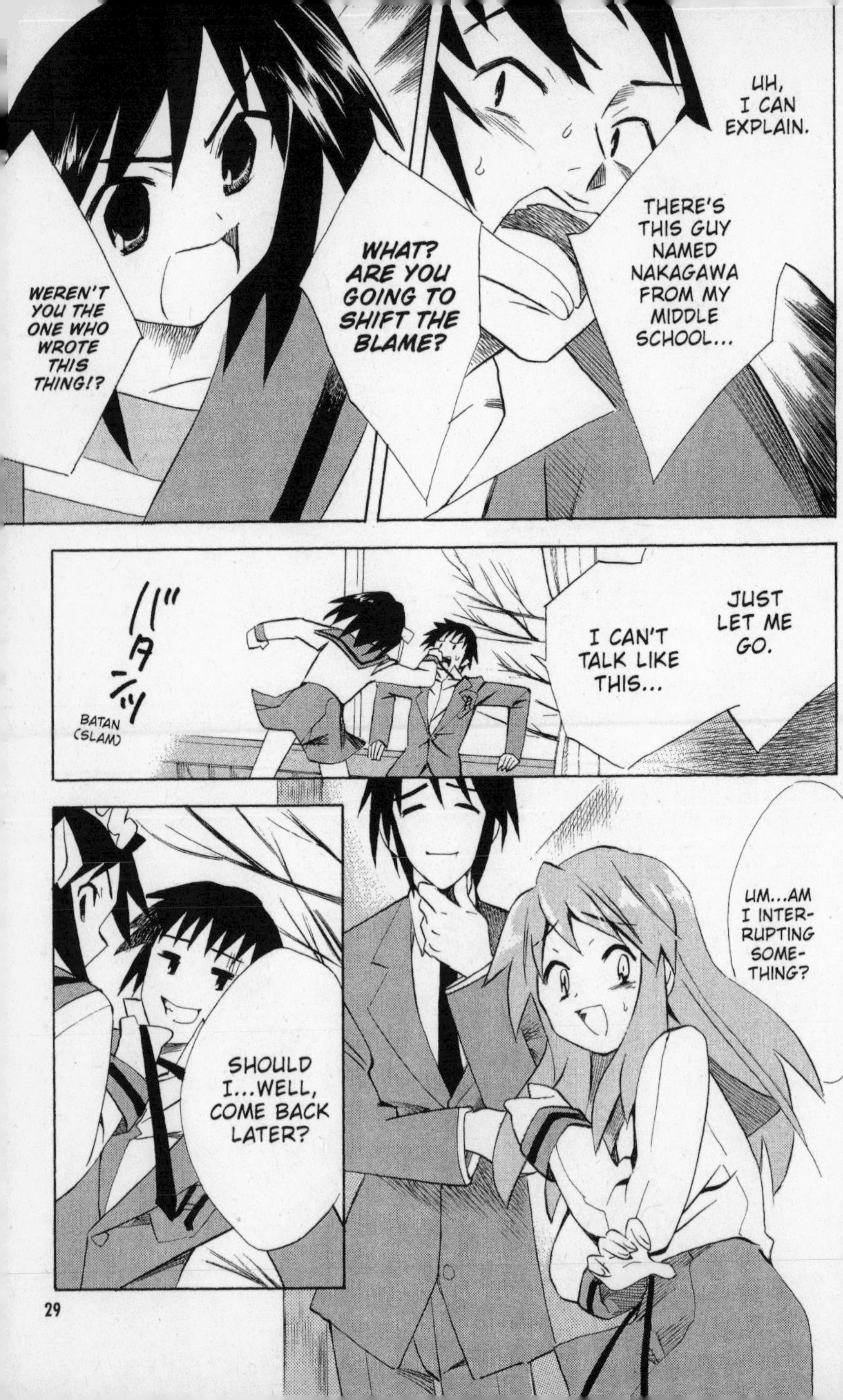
UH, I CAN EXPLAIN.
THERE'S THIS GUY NAMED NAKAGAWA FROM MY MIDDLE SCHOOL...
WHAT? ARE YOU GOING TO SHIFT THE BLAME?
WEREN'T YOU THE ONE WHO WROTE THIS THING!?
JUST LET ME GO.
I CAN'T TALK LIKE THIS...
バタンッ
BATAN (SLAM)
UM...AM I INTERRUPTING SOMETHING?
SHOULD I...WELL, COME BACK LATER?

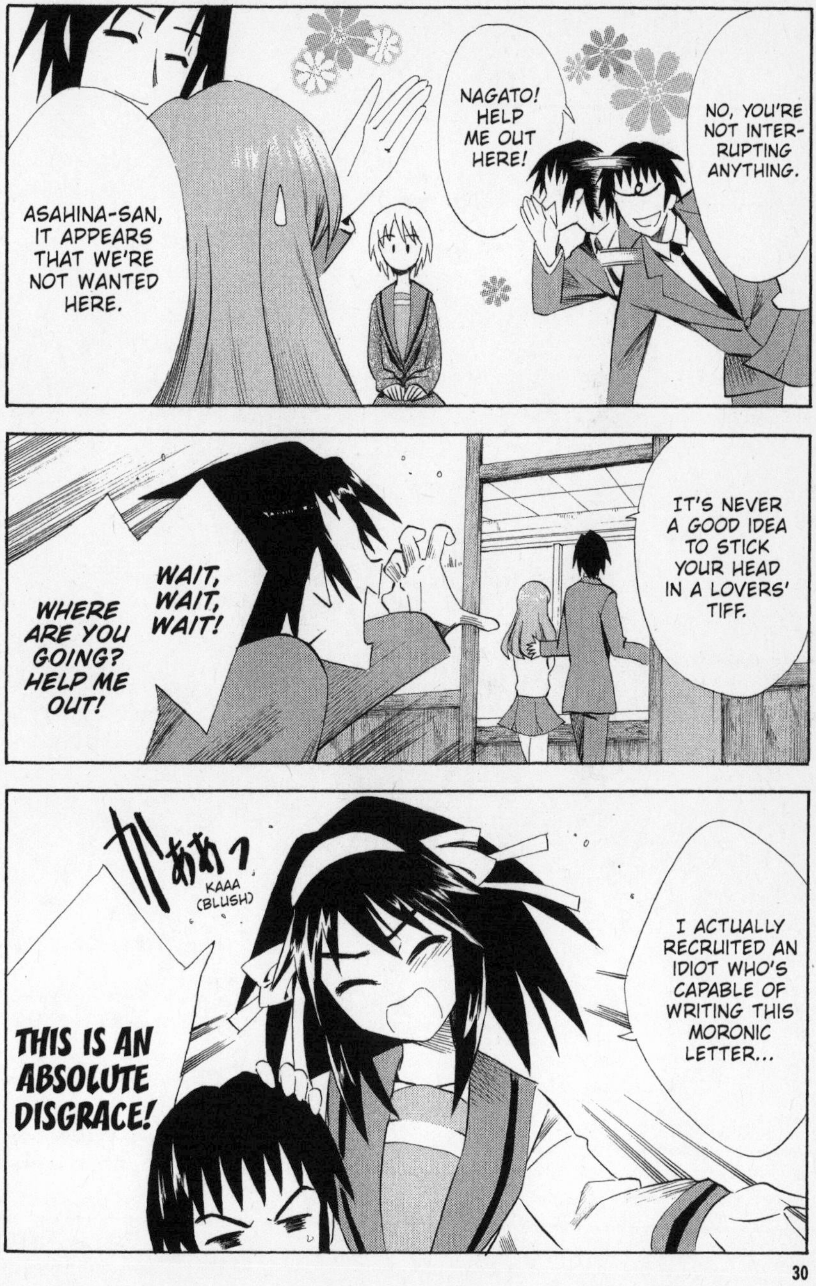
NO, YOU'RE NOT INTER-RUPTING ANYTHING.
NAGATO! HELP ME OUT HERE!
ASAHINA-SAN, IT APPEARS THAT WE'RE NOT WANTED HERE.
IT'S NEVER A GOOD IDEA TO STICK YOUR HEAD IN A LOVERS' TIFF.
WAIT, WAIT, WAIT!
WHERE ARE YOU GOING? HELP ME OUT!
I ACTUALLY RECRUITED AN IDIOT WHO'S CAPABLE OF WRITING THIS MORONIC LETTER...
KAAA (BLUSH)
THIS IS AN ABSOLUTE DISGRACE!

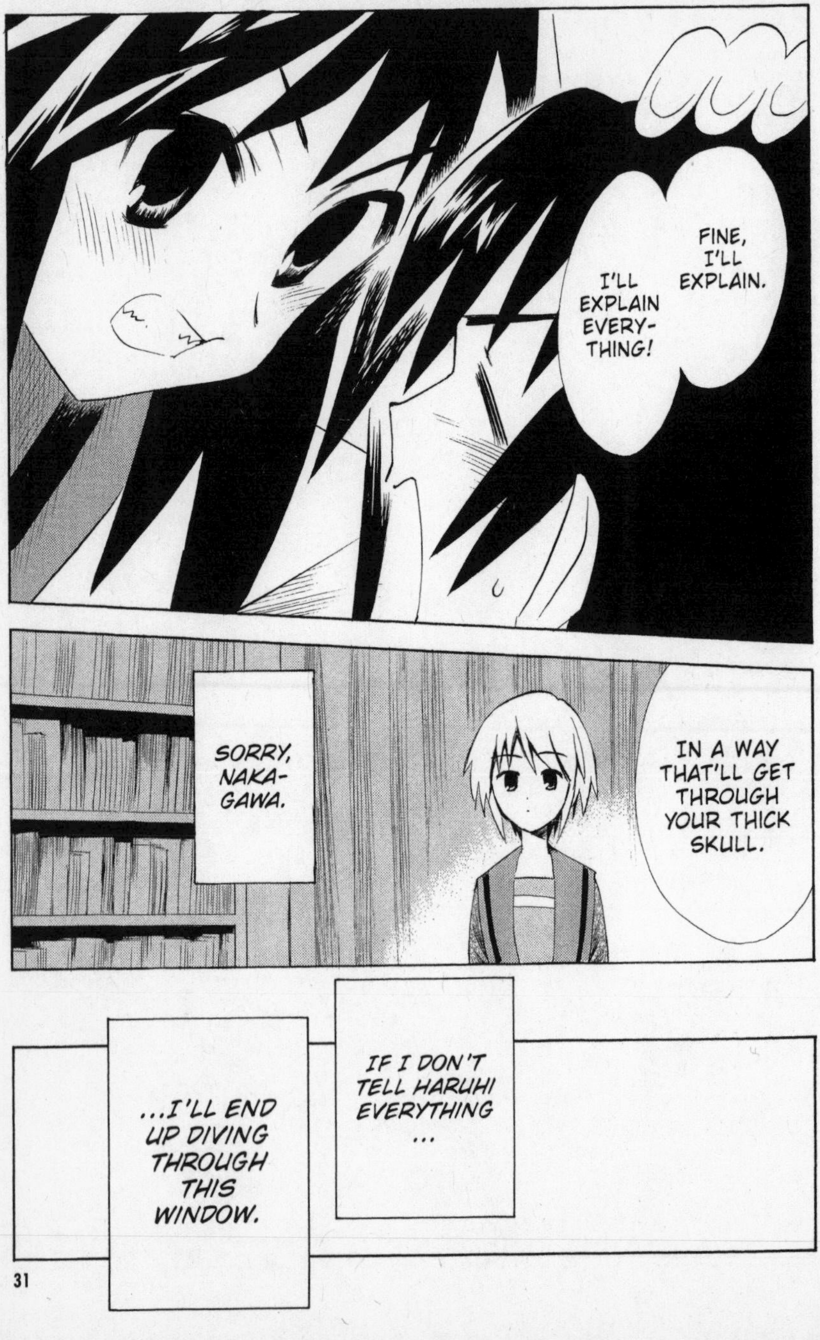
FINE, I'LL EXPLAIN.
I'LL EXPLAIN EVERY-THING!
IN A WAY THAT'LL GET THROUGH YOUR THICK SKULL.
SORRY, NAKA-GAWA.
IF I DON'T TELL HARUHI EVERYTHING ...
...I'LL END UP DIVING THROUGH THIS WINDOW.

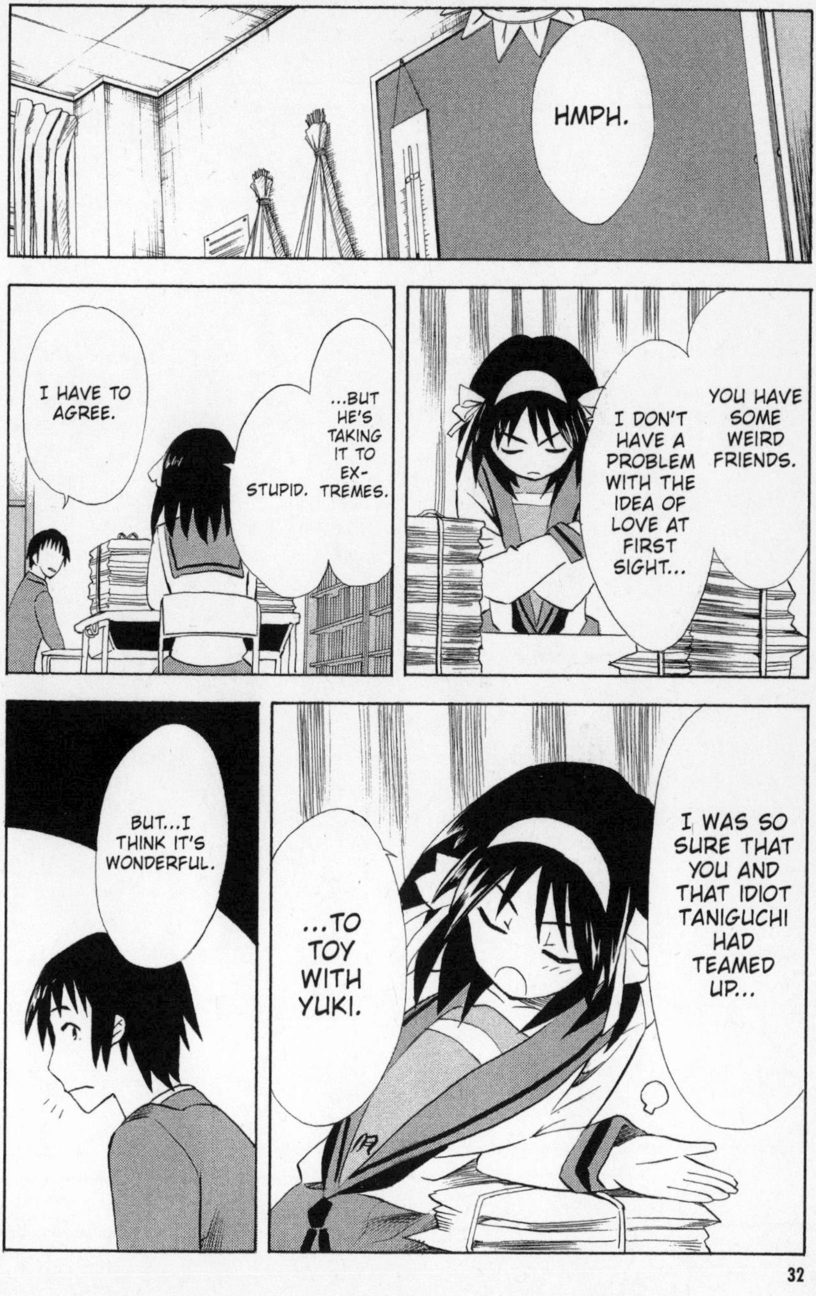
HMPH.
YOU HAVE SOME WEIRD FRIENDS.
I DON'T HAVE A PROBLEM WITH THE IDEA OF LOVE AT FIRST SIGHT...
...BUT HE'S TAKING IT TO EX-TREMES.
STUPID.
I HAVE TO AGREE.
I WAS SO SURE THAT YOU AND THAT IDIOT TANIGUCHI HAD TEAMED UP...
...TO TOY WITH YUKI.
BUT...I THINK IT'S WONDERFUL.

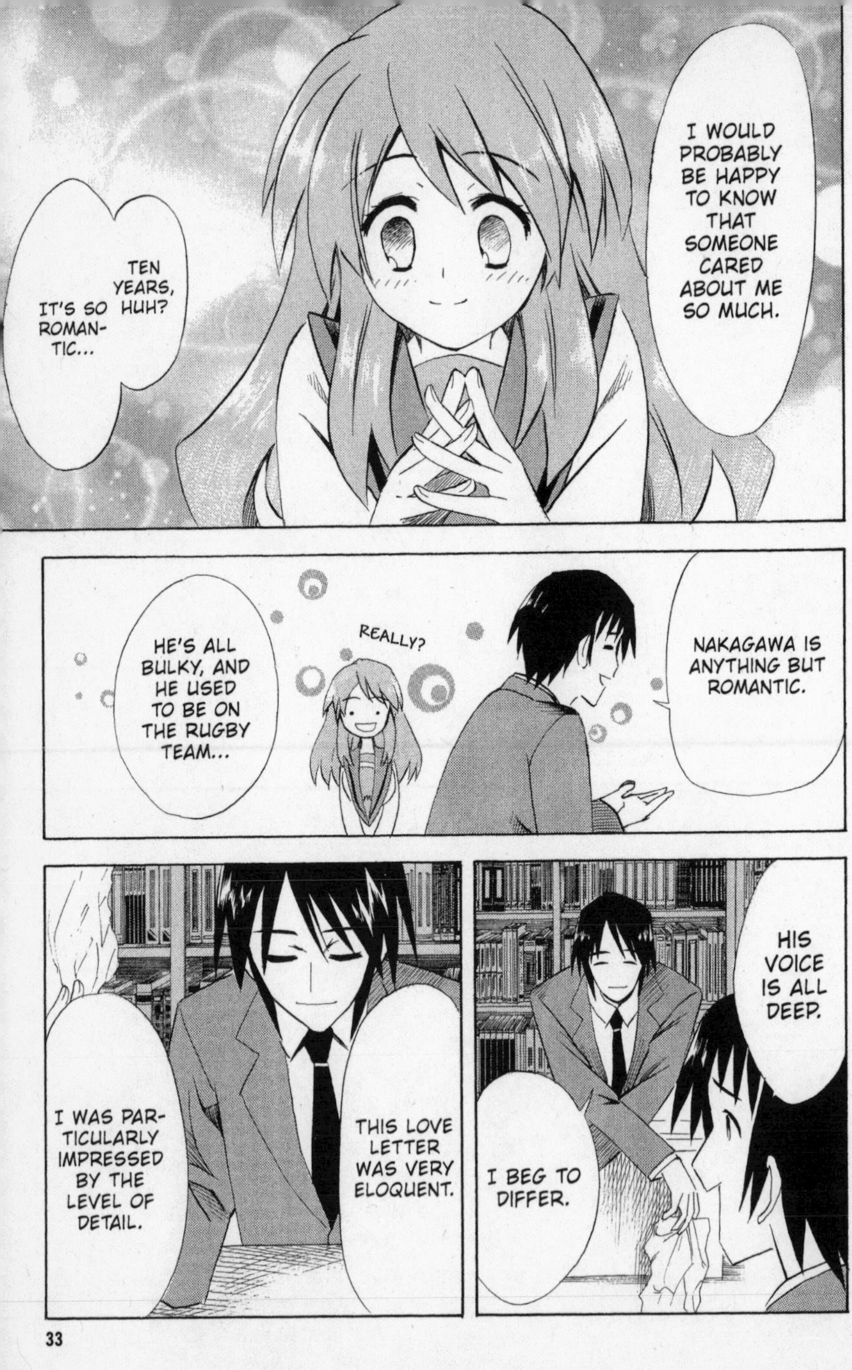
I WOULD PROBABLY BE HAPPY TO KNOW THAT SOMEONE CARED ABOUT ME SO MUCH.
TEN YEARS, HUH?
IT'S SO ROMAN-TIC...
NAKAGAWA IS ANYTHING BUT ROMANTIC.
REALLY?
HE'S ALL BULKY, AND HE USED TO BE ON THE RUGBY TEAM...
HIS VOICE IS ALL DEEP.
I BEG TO DIFFER.
THIS LOVE LETTER WAS VERY ELOQUENT.
I WAS PAR-TICULARLY IMPRESSED BY THE LEVEL OF DETAIL.

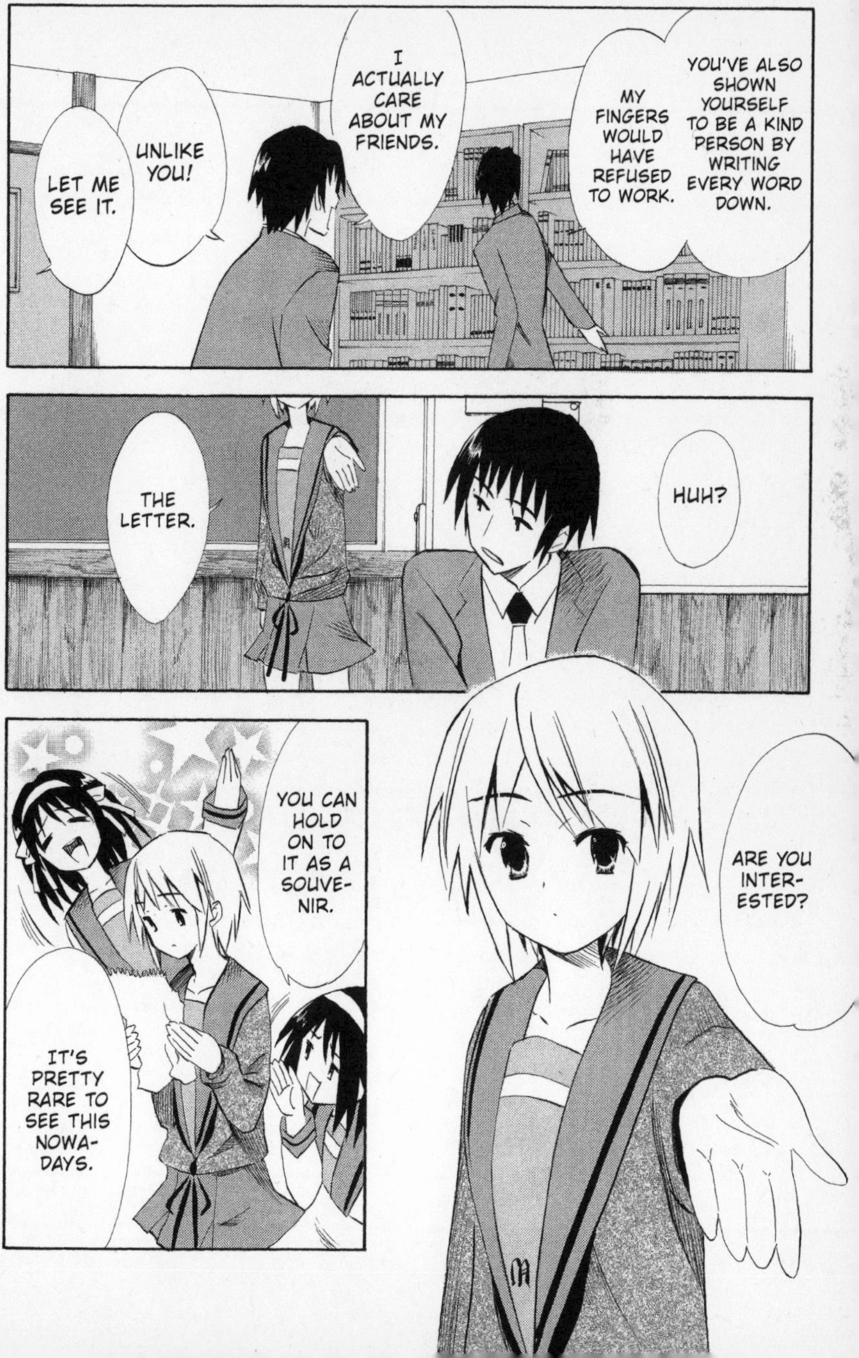
YOU'VE ALSO SHOWN YOURSELF TO BE A KIND PERSON BY WRITING EVERY WORD DOWN.
MY FINGERS WOULD HAVE REFUSED TO WORK.
I ACTUALLY CARE ABOUT MY FRIENDS.
UNLIKE YOU!
LET ME SEE IT.
HUH?
THE LETTER.
ARE YOU INTER-ESTED?
YOU CAN HOLD ON TO IT AS A SOUVE-NIR.
IT'S PRETTY RARE TO SEE THIS NOWA-DAYS.

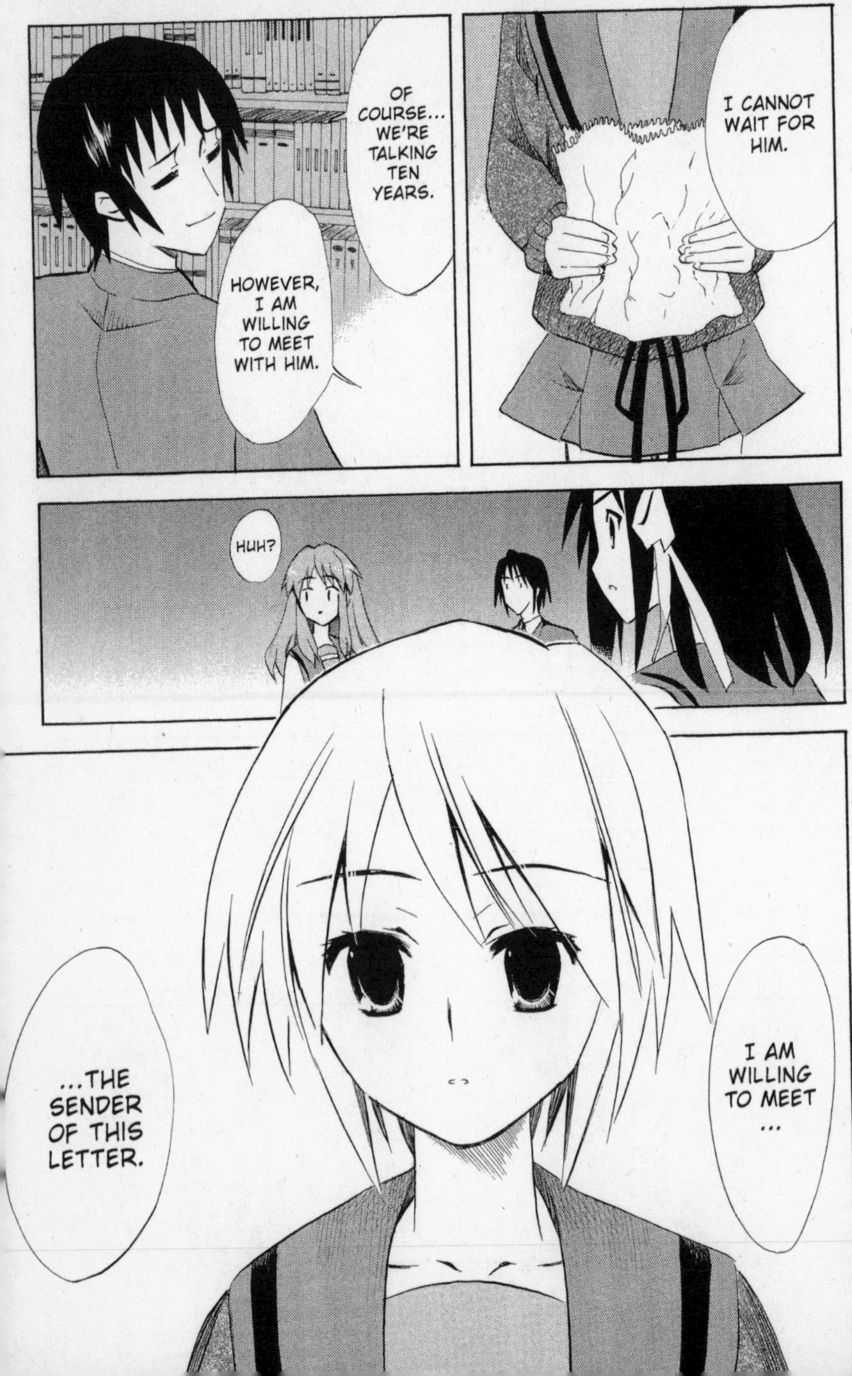
I CANNOT WAIT FOR HIM.
OF COURSE... WE'RE TALKING TEN YEARS.
HOWEVER, I AM WILLING TO MEET WITH HIM.
HUH?
I AM WILLING TO MEET ...
...THE SENDER OF THIS LETTER.

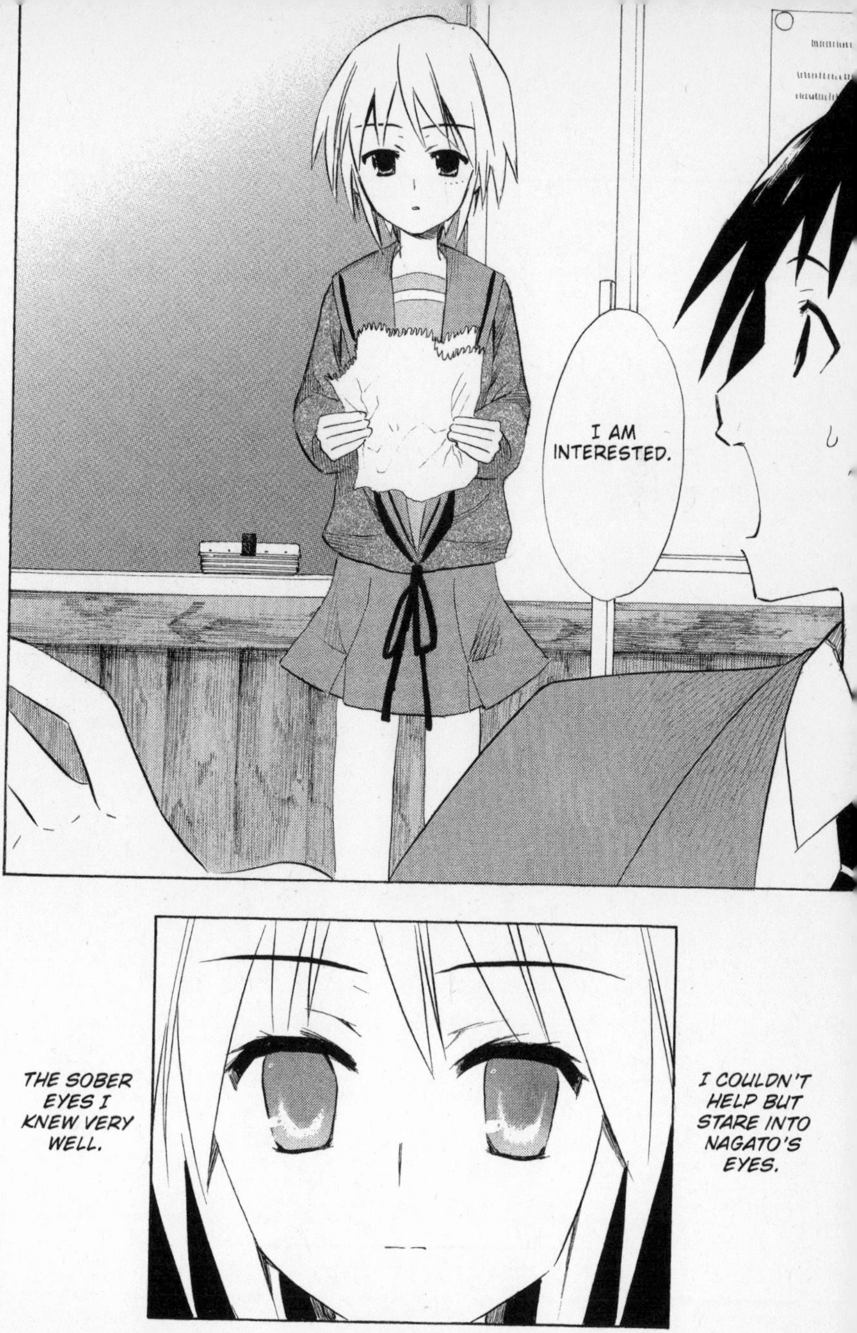
I AM INTERESTED.
I COULDN'T HELP BUT STARE INTO NAGATO'S EYES.
THE SOBER EYES I KNEW VERY WELL.

Lover at First Sight I : END

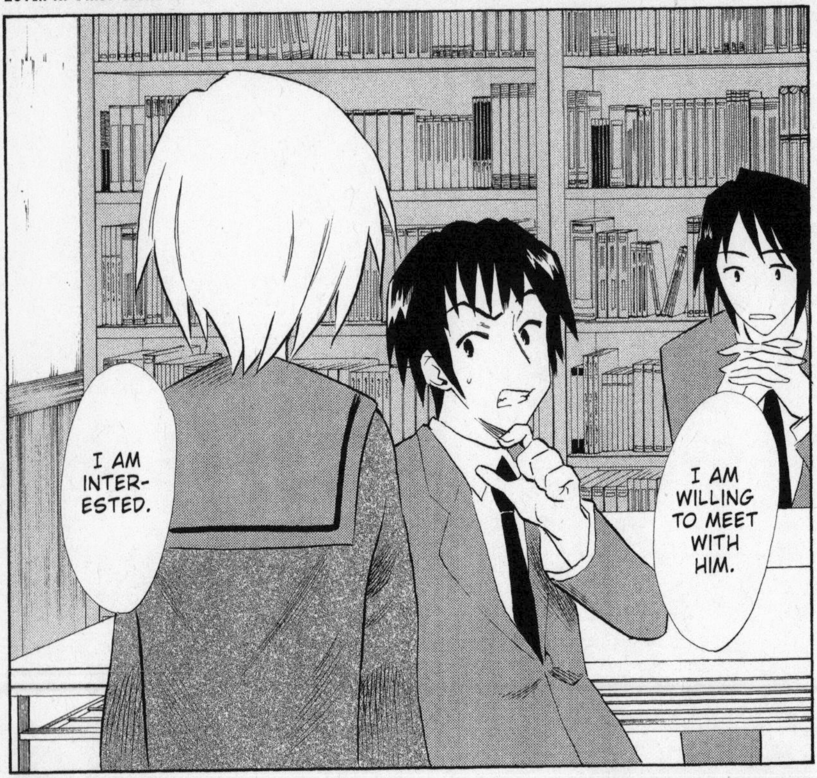
I AM WILLING TO MEET WITH HIM.
I AM INTER-ESTED.

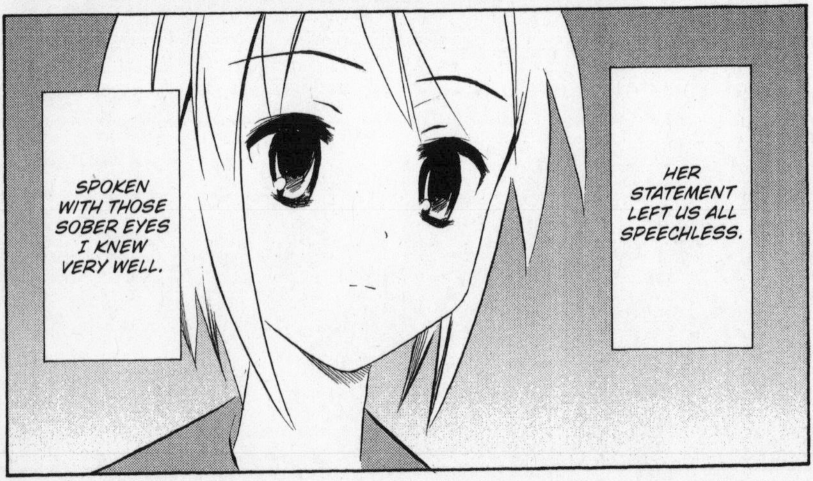
HER STATEMENT LEFT US ALL SPEECHLESS.
SPOKEN WITH THOSE SOBER EYES I KNEW VERY WELL.

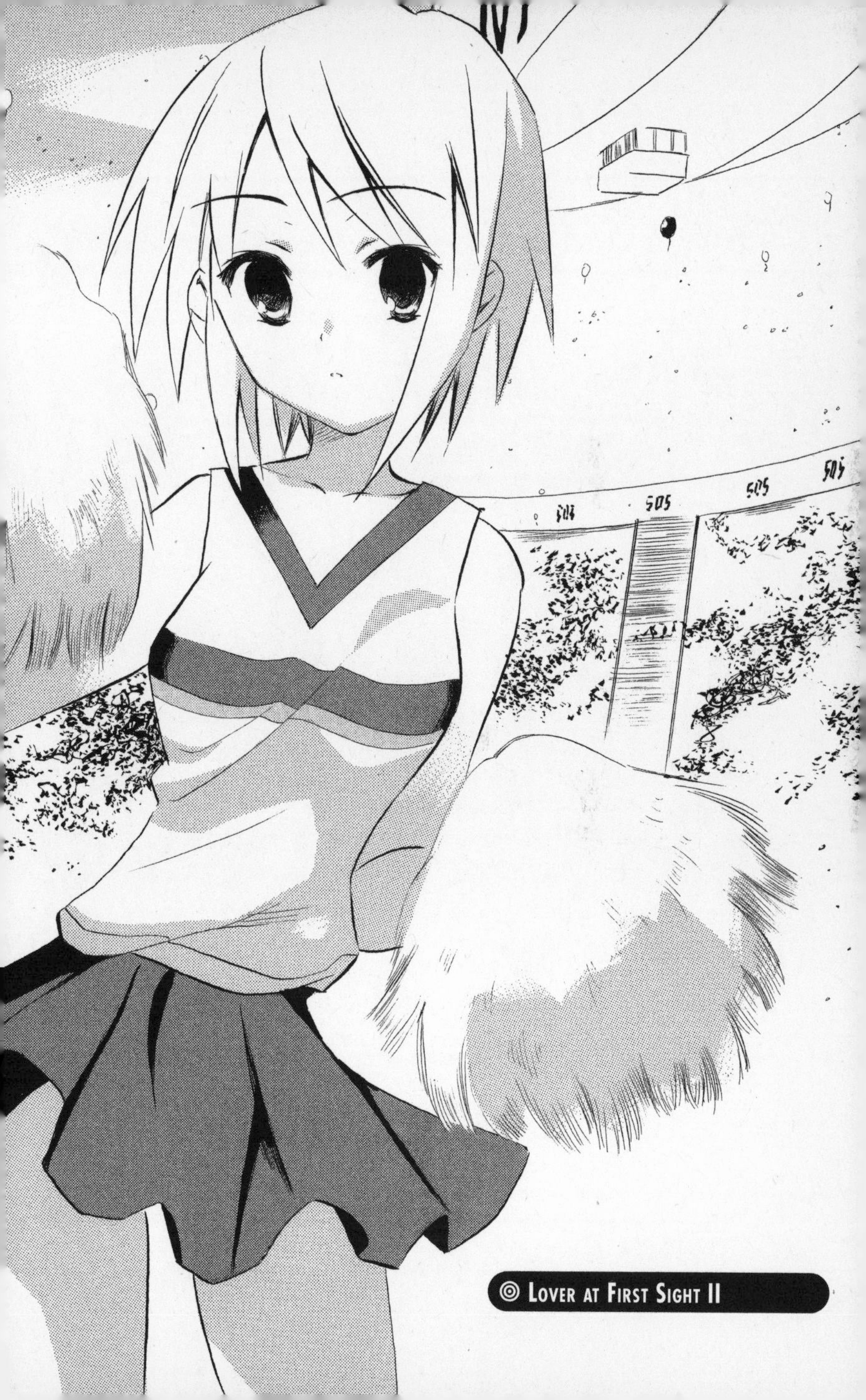

◎ Lover at First Sight II

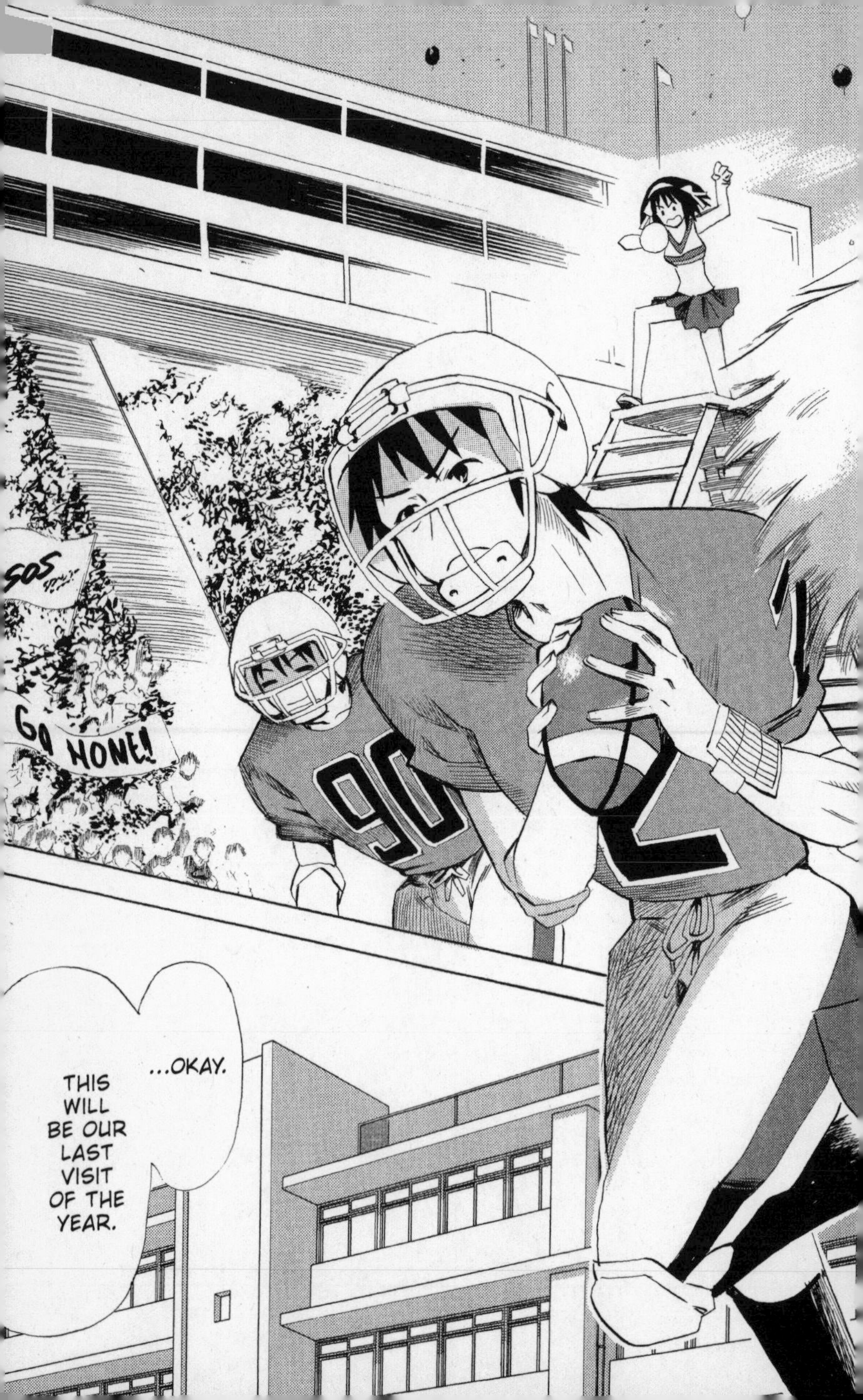
SOS
GO HONE!
...OKAY.
THIS WILL BE OUR LAST VISIT OF THE YEAR.

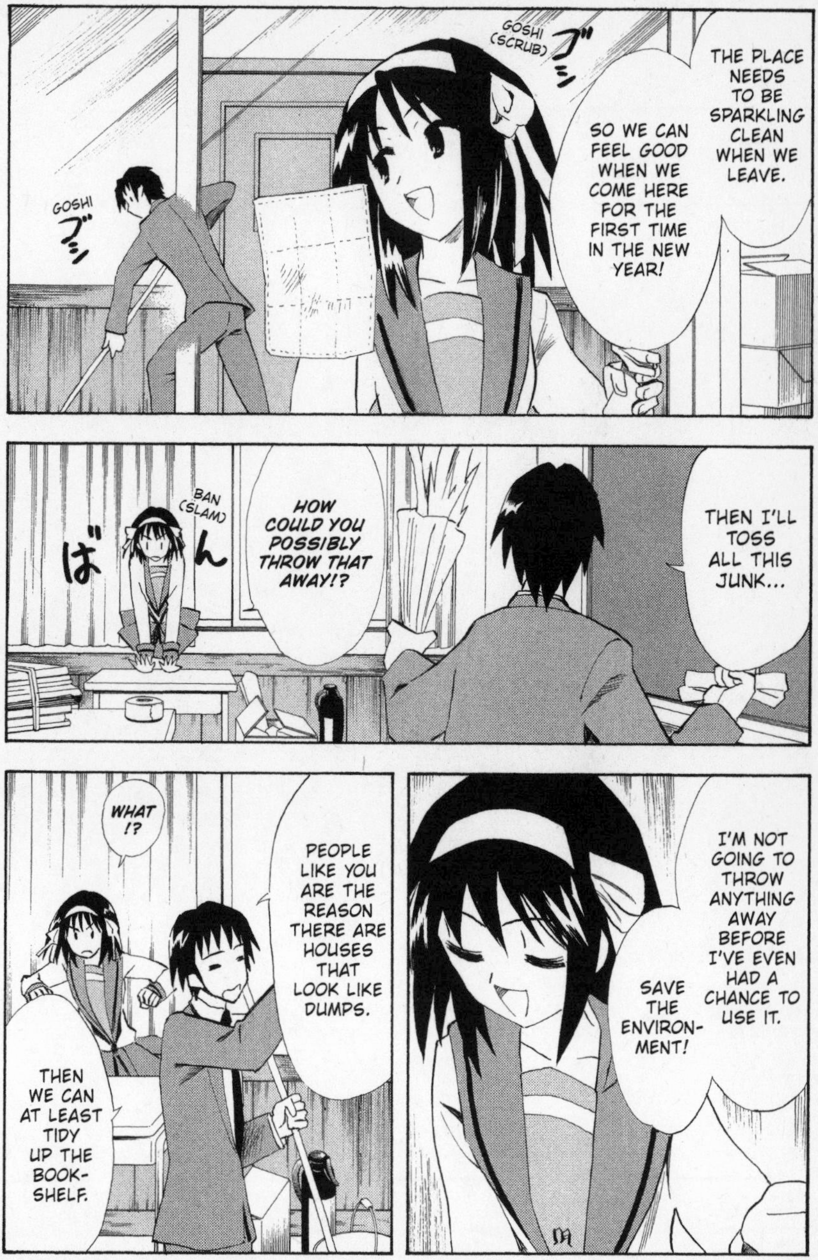

GOSHI (SCRUB) ゴシ
GOSHI ゴシ
THE PLACE NEEDS TO BE SPARKLING CLEAN WHEN WE LEAVE.
SO WE CAN FEEL GOOD WHEN WE COME HERE FOR THE FIRST TIME IN THE NEW YEAR!
THEN I'LL TOSS ALL THIS JUNK...
HOW COULD YOU POSSIBLY THROW THAT AWAY!?
BAN (SLAM) ばん
I'M NOT GOING TO THROW ANYTHING AWAY BEFORE I'VE EVEN HAD A CHANCE TO USE IT.
SAVE THE ENVIRONMENT!
PEOPLE LIKE YOU ARE THE REASON THERE ARE HOUSES THAT LOOK LIKE DUMPS.
WHAT!?
THEN WE CAN AT LEAST TIDY UP THE BOOK-SHELF.

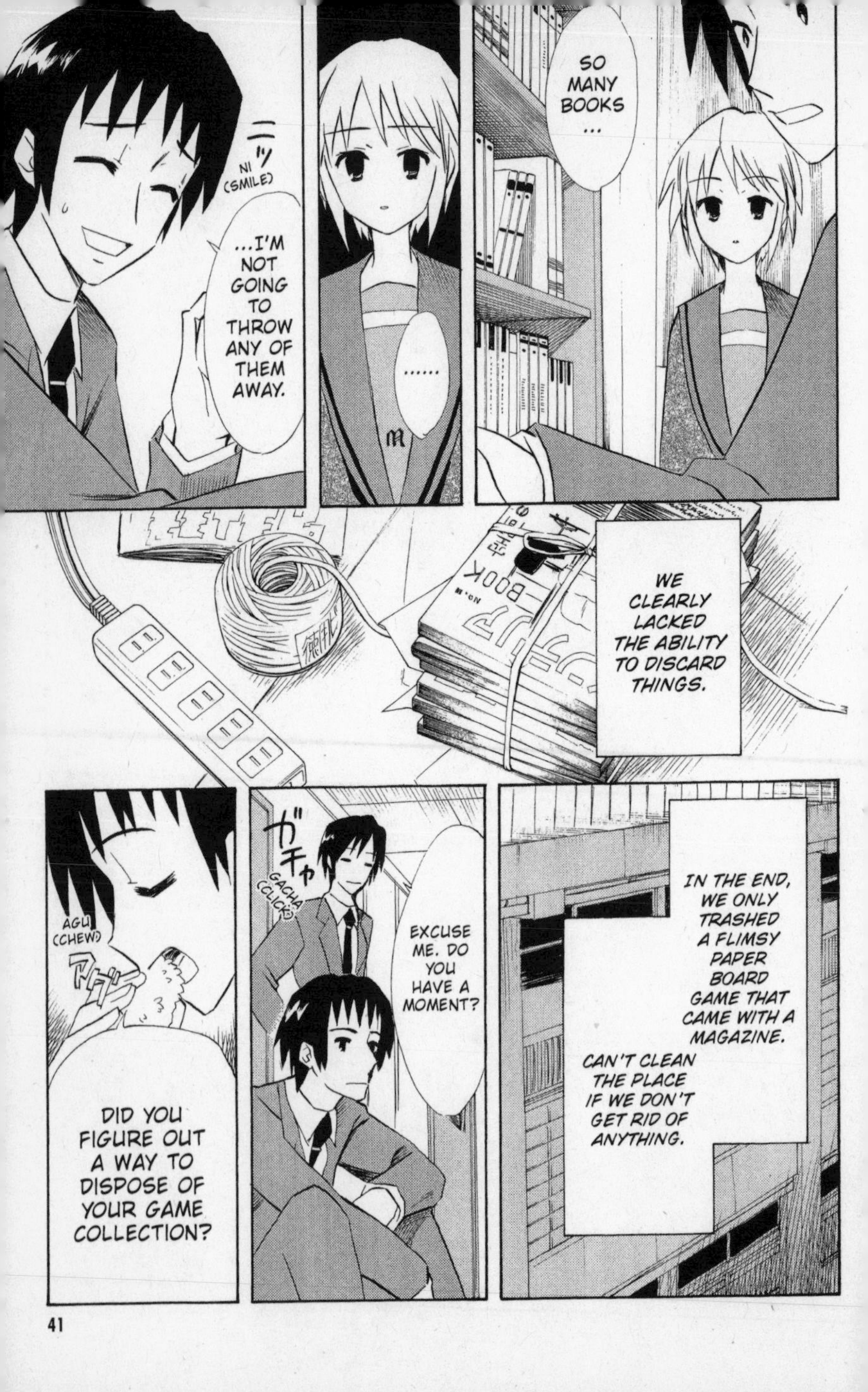
SO MANY BOOKS ...
......
NI (SMILE)
...I'M NOT GOING TO THROW ANY OF THEM AWAY.
WE CLEARLY LACKED THE ABILITY TO DISCARD THINGS.
IN THE END, WE ONLY TRASHED A FLIMSY PAPER BOARD GAME THAT CAME WITH A MAGAZINE.
CAN'T CLEAN THE PLACE IF WE DON'T GET RID OF ANYTHING.
GACHA (CLICK)
EXCUSE ME. DO YOU HAVE A MOMENT?
AGU (CHEW)
DID YOU FIGURE OUT A WAY TO DISPOSE OF YOUR GAME COLLECTION?

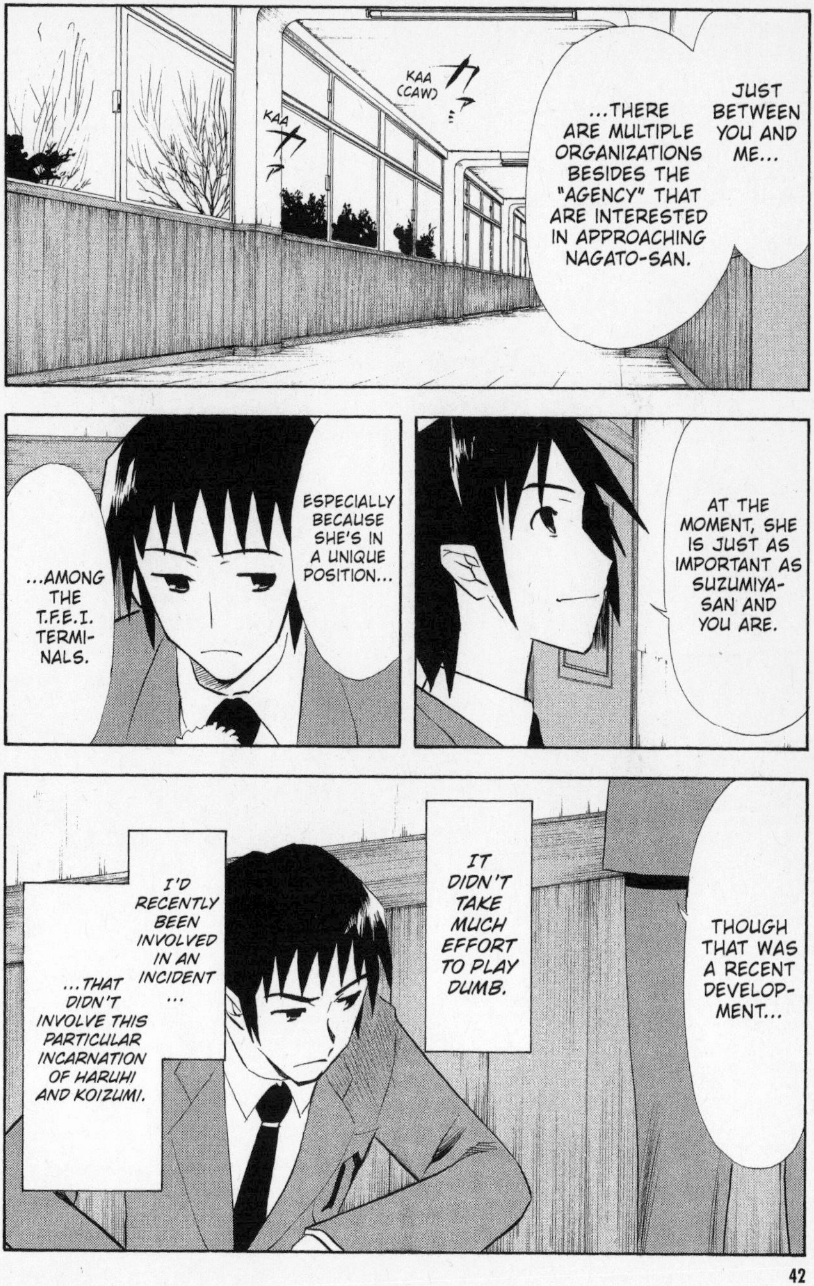
JUST BETWEEN YOU AND ME...
...THERE ARE MULTIPLE ORGANIZATIONS BESIDES THE "AGENCY" THAT ARE INTERESTED IN APPROACHING NAGATO-SAN.
KAA (CAW)
KAA
AT THE MOMENT, SHE IS JUST AS IMPORTANT AS SUZUMIYA-SAN AND YOU ARE.
ESPECIALLY BECAUSE SHE'S IN A UNIQUE POSITION...
...AMONG THE T.F.E.I. TERMINALS.
THOUGH THAT WAS A RECENT DEVELOPMENT...
IT DIDN'T TAKE MUCH EFFORT TO PLAY DUMB.
I'D RECENTLY BEEN INVOLVED IN AN INCIDENT...
...THAT DIDN'T INVOLVE THIS PARTICULAR INCARNATION OF HARUHI AND KOIZUMI.

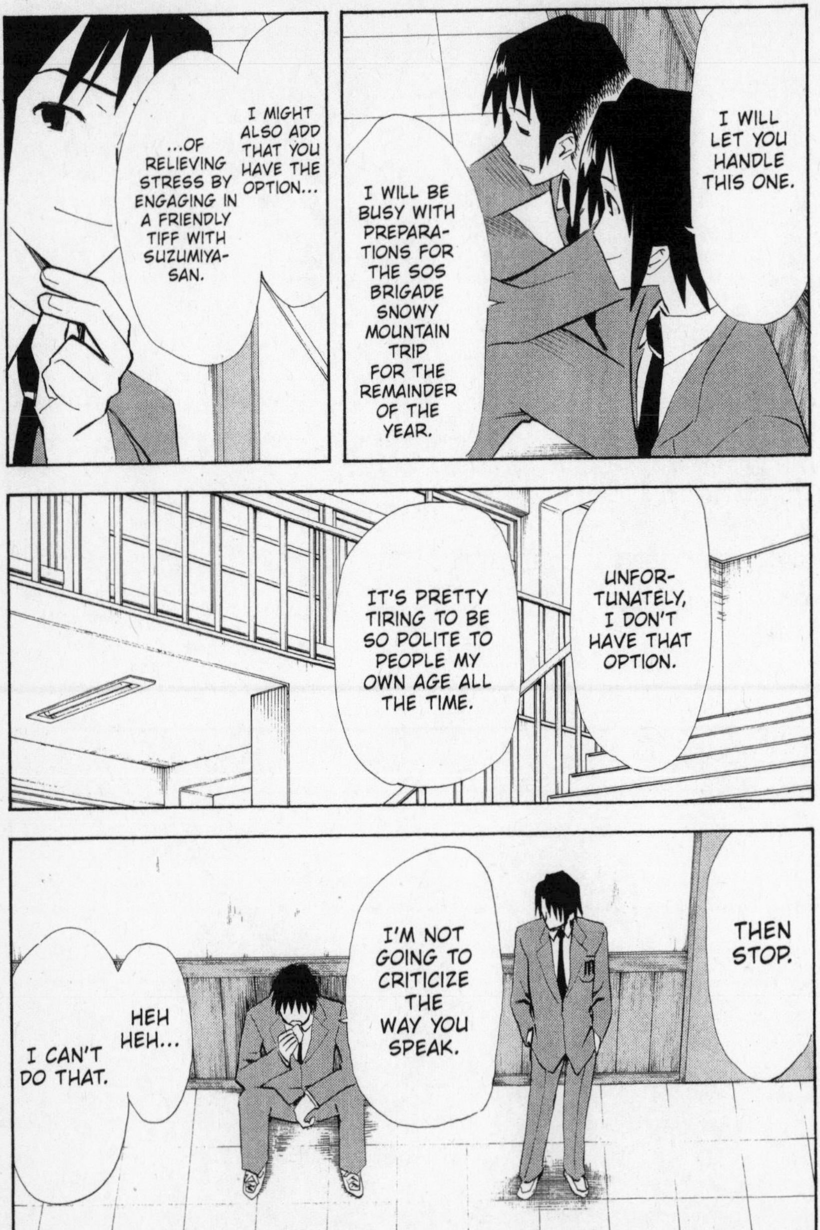
I WILL LET YOU HANDLE THIS ONE.
I WILL BE BUSY WITH PREPARATIONS FOR THE SOS BRIGADE SNOWY MOUNTAIN TRIP FOR THE REMAINDER OF THE YEAR.
I MIGHT ALSO ADD THAT YOU HAVE THE OPTION...
...OF RELIEVING STRESS BY ENGAGING IN A FRIENDLY TIFF WITH SUZUMIYA-SAN.
UNFORTUNATELY, I DON'T HAVE THAT OPTION.
IT'S PRETTY TIRING TO BE SO POLITE TO PEOPLE MY OWN AGE ALL THE TIME.
THEN STOP.
I'M NOT GOING TO CRITICIZE THE WAY YOU SPEAK.
HEH HEH...
I CAN'T DO THAT.

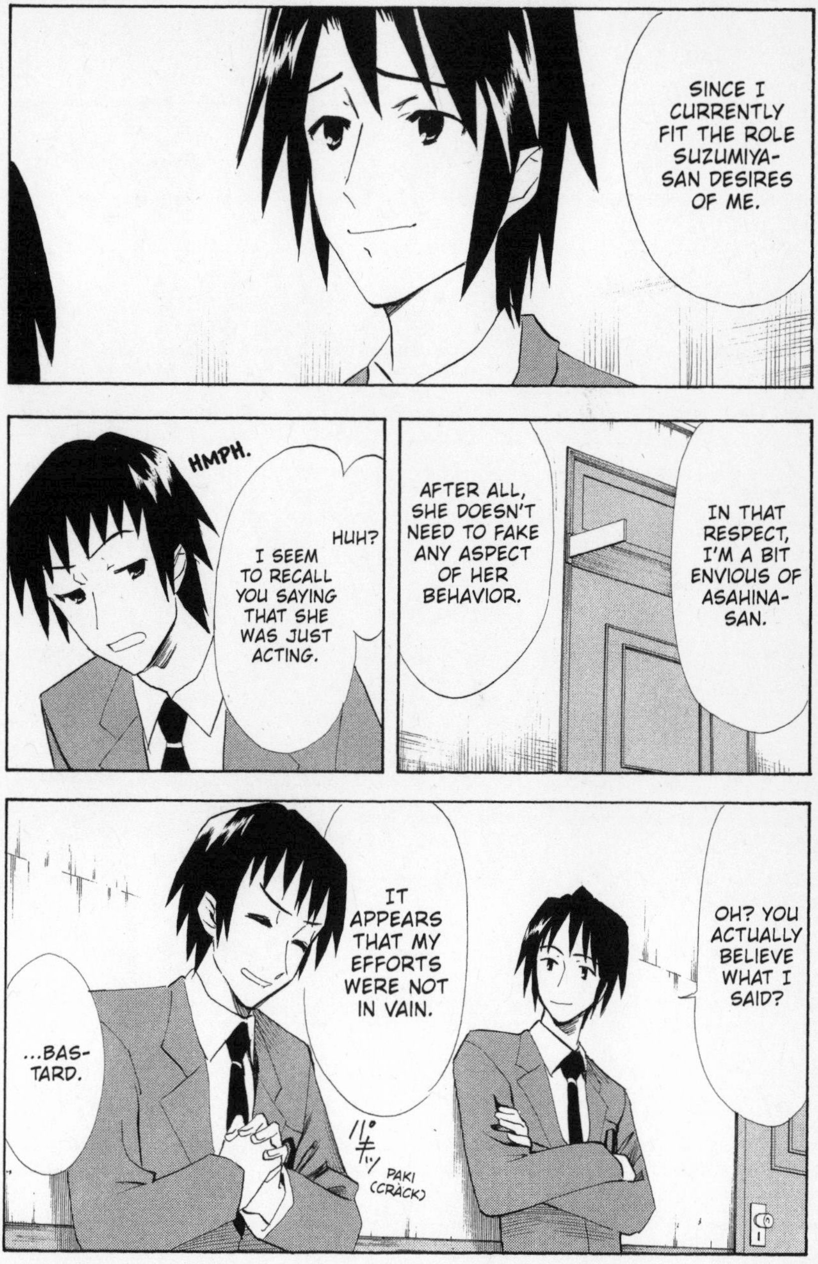
SINCE I CURRENTLY FIT THE ROLE SUZUMIYA-SAN DESIRES OF ME.
IN THAT RESPECT, I'M A BIT ENVIOUS OF ASAHINA-SAN.
AFTER ALL, SHE DOESN'T NEED TO FAKE ANY ASPECT OF HER BEHAVIOR.
HUH? I SEEM TO RECALL YOU SAYING THAT SHE WAS JUST ACTING.
HMPH.
OH? YOU ACTUALLY BELIEVE WHAT I SAID?
IT APPEARS THAT MY EFFORTS WERE NOT IN VAIN.
パキッ
PAKI (CRACK)
...BAS-TARD.

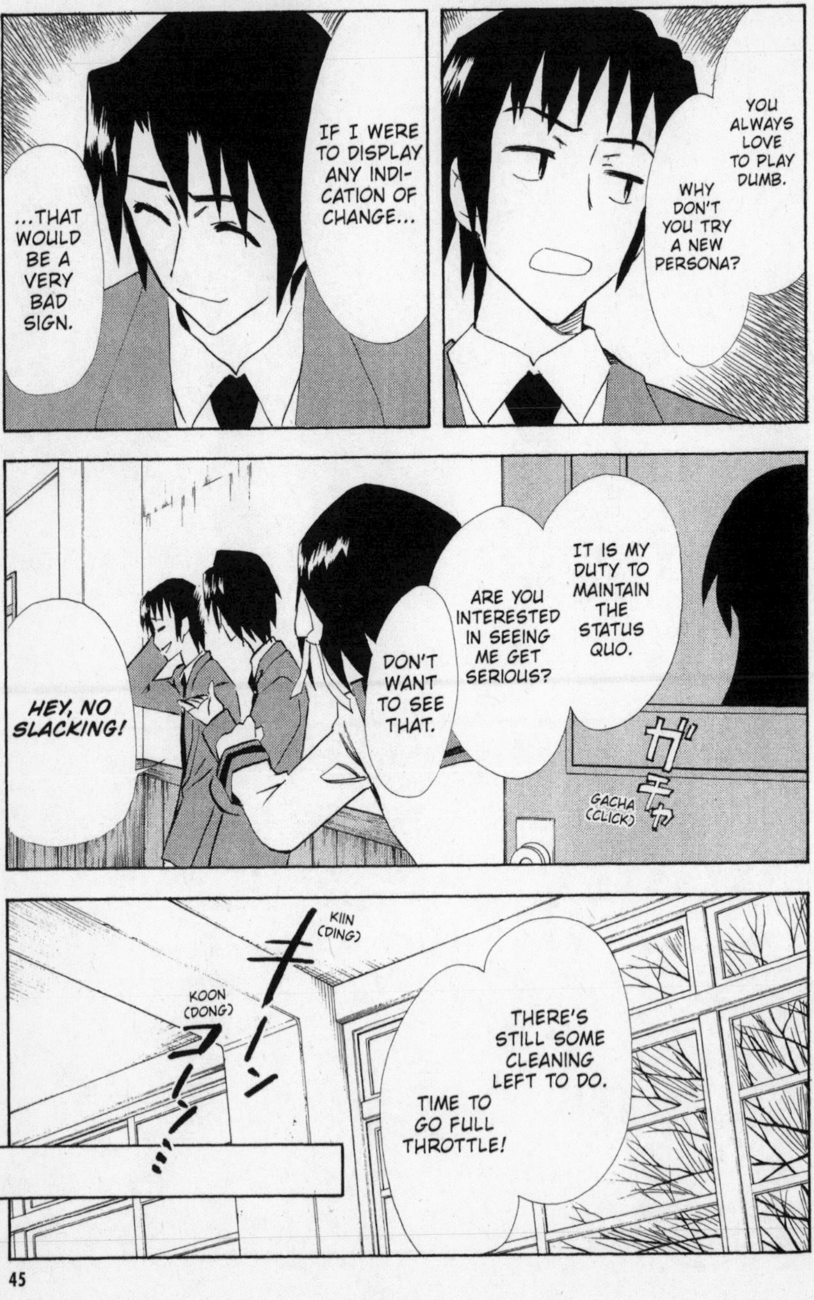
YOU ALWAYS LOVE TO PLAY DUMB.
WHY DON'T YOU TRY A NEW PERSONA?
IF I WERE TO DISPLAY ANY INDICATION OF CHANGE...
...THAT WOULD BE A VERY BAD SIGN.
IT IS MY DUTY TO MAINTAIN THE STATUS QUO.
ARE YOU INTERESTED IN SEEING ME GET SERIOUS?
DON'T WANT TO SEE THAT.
GACHA (CLICK)
HEY, NO SLACKING!
THERE'S STILL SOME CLEANING LEFT TO DO.
TIME TO GO FULL THROTTLE!
KIIN (DING)
KOON (DONG)

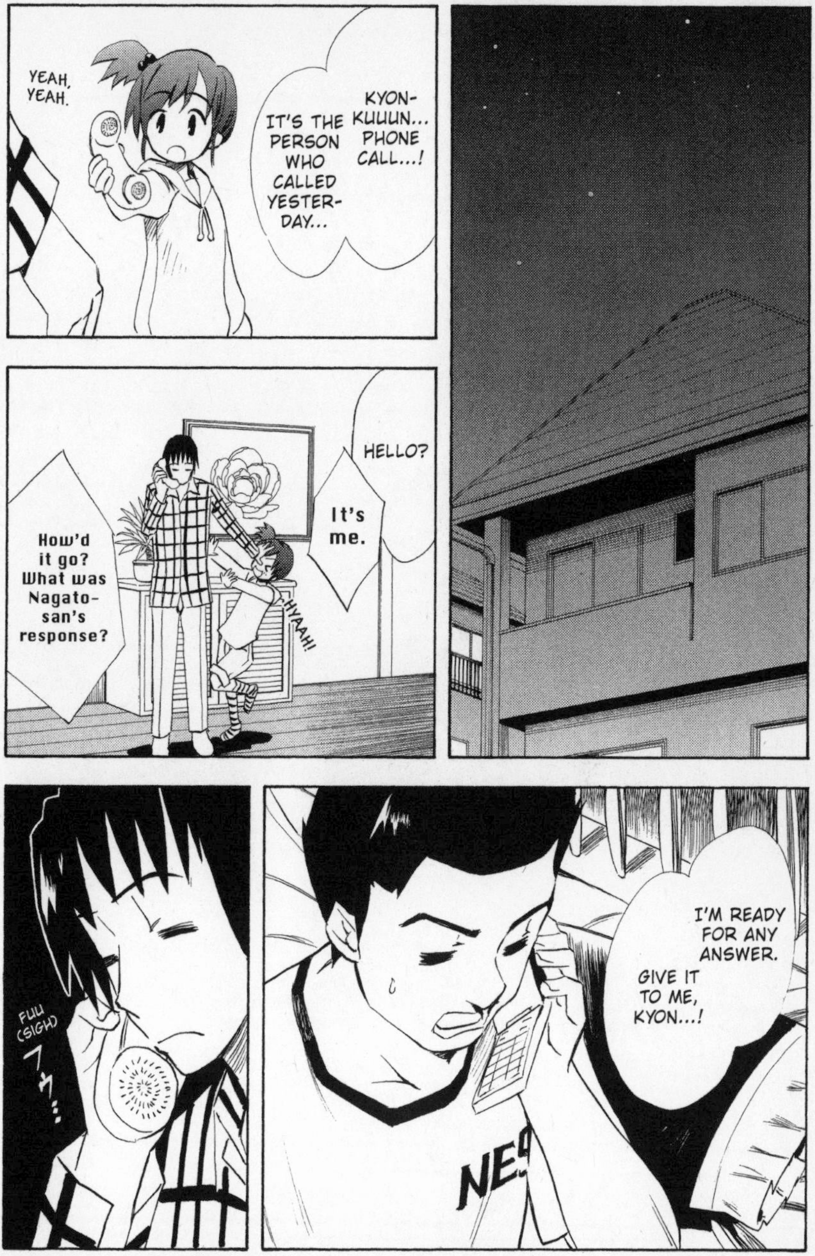
KYON-KUUUN... PHONE CALL...!
IT'S THE PERSON WHO CALLED YESTER-DAY...
YEAH, YEAH.
HELLO?
It's me.
How'd it go? What was Nagato-san's response?
HYAAH!
I'M READY FOR ANY ANSWER.
GIVE IT TO ME, KYON...!
FUU (SIGH)

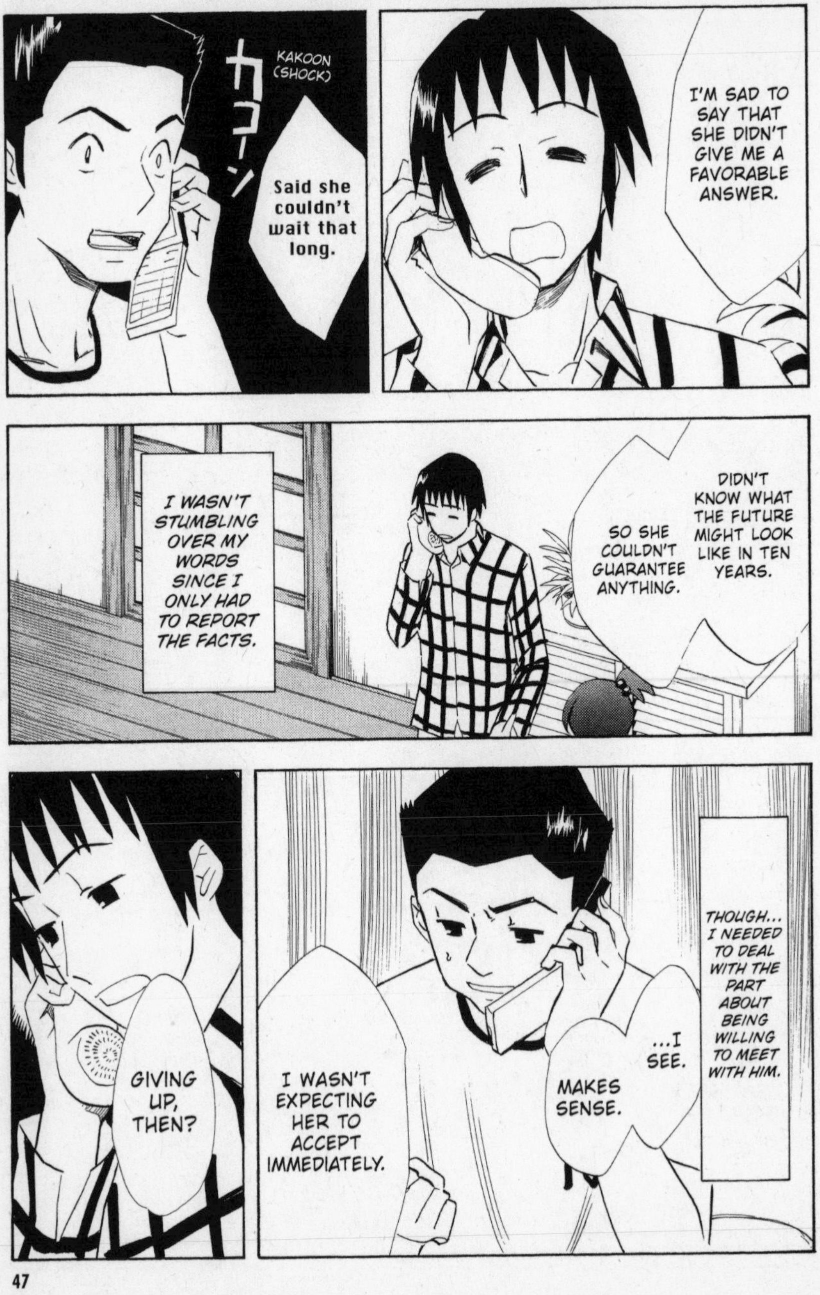
I'M SAD TO SAY THAT SHE DIDN'T GIVE ME A FAVORABLE ANSWER.
カコーン
KAKOON (SHOCK)
Said she couldn't wait that long.
DIDN'T KNOW WHAT THE FUTURE MIGHT LOOK LIKE IN TEN YEARS.
SO SHE COULDN'T GUARANTEE ANYTHING.
I WASN'T STUMBLING OVER MY WORDS SINCE I ONLY HAD TO REPORT THE FACTS.
THOUGH... I NEEDED TO DEAL WITH THE PART ABOUT BEING WILLING TO MEET WITH HIM.
...I SEE.
MAKES SENSE.
I WASN'T EXPECTING HER TO ACCEPT IMMEDIATELY.
GIVING UP, THEN?

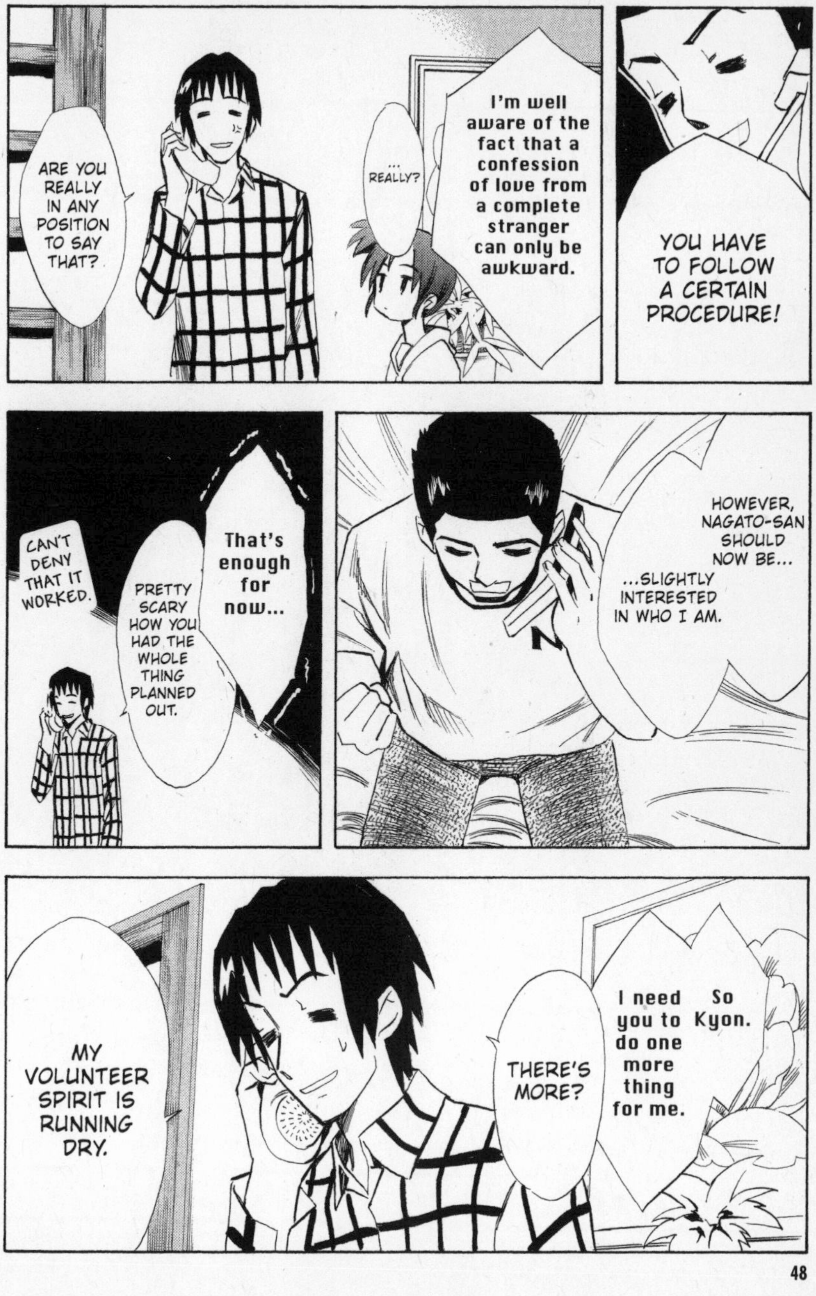
YOU HAVE TO FOLLOW A CERTAIN PROCEDURE!
I'm well aware of the fact that a confession of love from a complete stranger can only be awkward.
... REALLY?
ARE YOU REALLY IN ANY POSITION TO SAY THAT?
HOWEVER, NAGATO-SAN SHOULD NOW BE...
...SLIGHTLY INTERESTED IN WHO I AM.
That's enough for now...
PRETTY SCARY HOW YOU HAD THE WHOLE THING PLANNED OUT.
CAN'T DENY THAT IT WORKED.
So Kyon.
I need you to do one more thing for me.
THERE'S MORE?
MY VOLUNTEER SPIRIT IS RUNNING DRY.

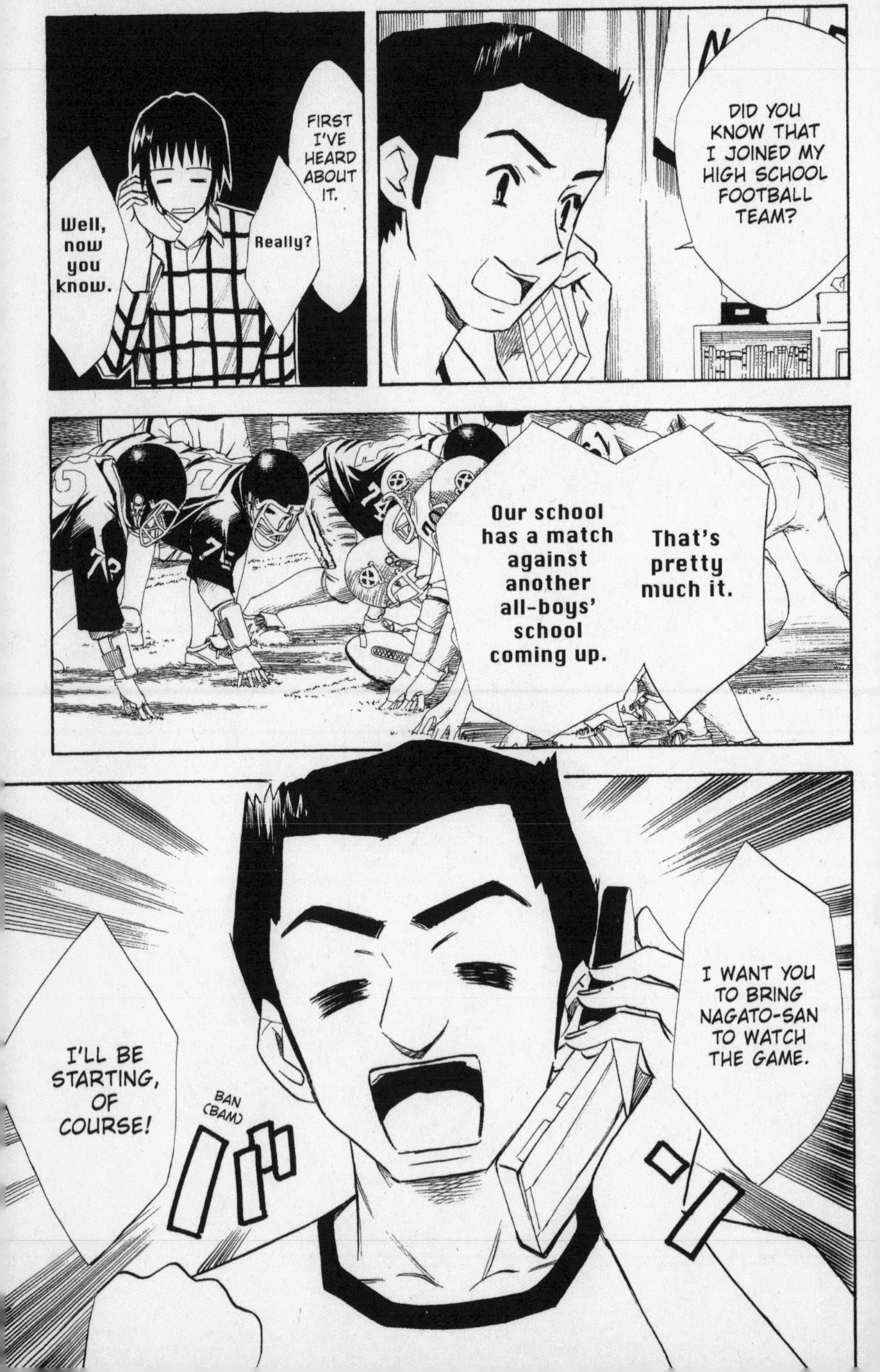

DID YOU KNOW THAT I JOINED MY HIGH SCHOOL FOOTBALL TEAM?
FIRST I'VE HEARD ABOUT IT.
Really?
Well, now you know.
That's pretty much it.
Our school has a match against another all-boys' school coming up.
I WANT YOU TO BRING NAGATO-SAN TO WATCH THE GAME.
I'LL BE STARTING, OF COURSE!
BAN (BAM)

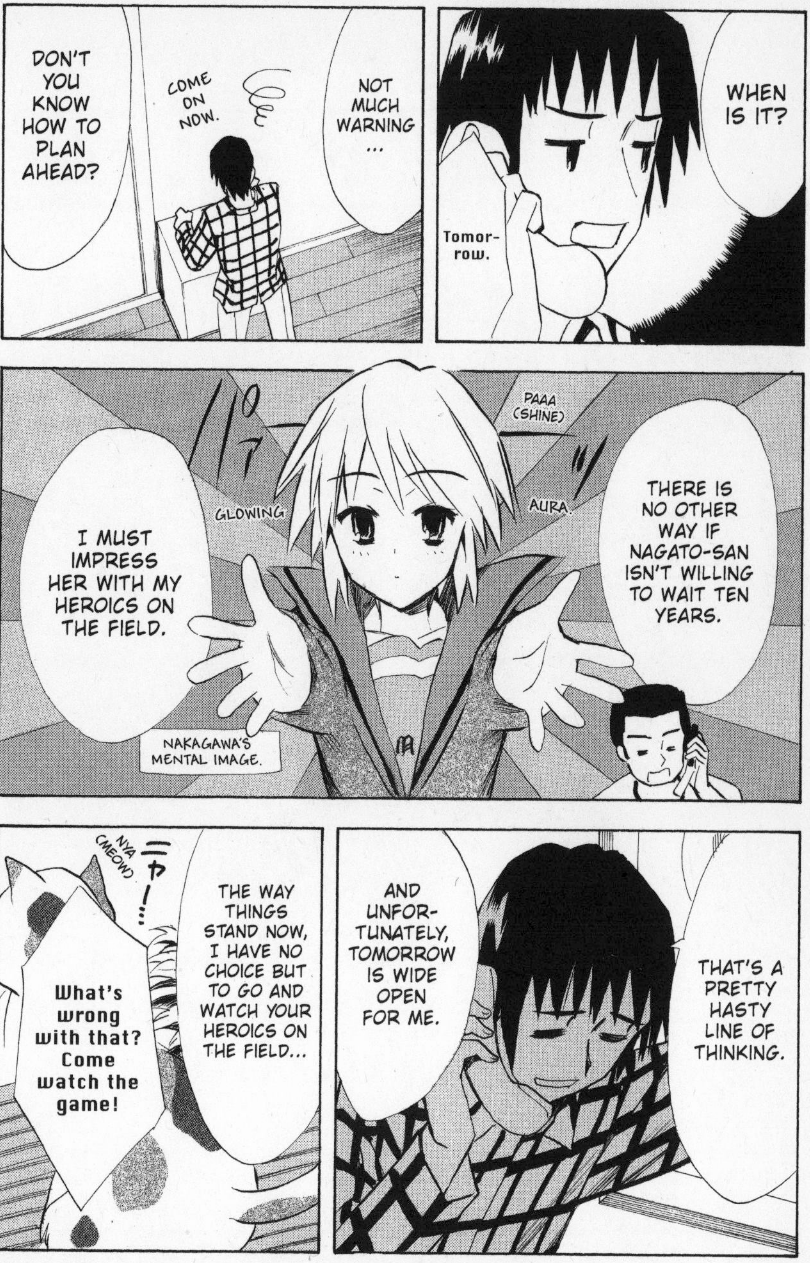
WHEN IS IT?
Tomorrow.
NOT MUCH WARNING...
COME ON NOW.
DON'T YOU KNOW HOW TO PLAN AHEAD?
PAAA (SHINE)
THERE IS NO OTHER WAY IF NAGATO-SAN ISN'T WILLING TO WAIT TEN YEARS.
AURA.
GLOWING
I MUST IMPRESS HER WITH MY HEROICS ON THE FIELD.
NAKAGAWA'S MENTAL IMAGE.
THAT'S A PRETTY HASTY LINE OF THINKING.
AND UNFORTUNATELY, TOMORROW IS WIDE OPEN FOR ME.
THE WAY THINGS STAND NOW, I HAVE NO CHOICE BUT TO GO AND WATCH YOUR HEROICS ON THE FIELD...
NYA (MEOW)
What's wrong with that? Come watch the game!

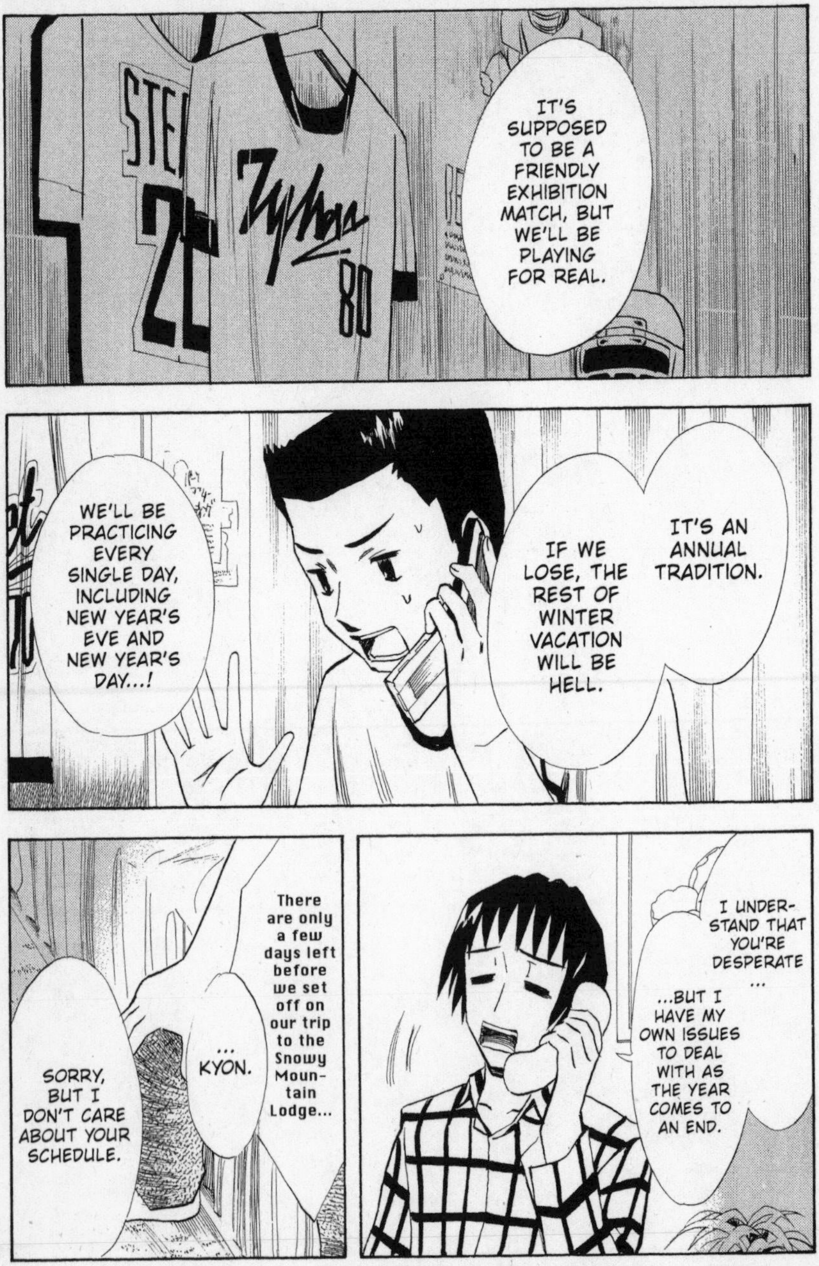
IT'S SUPPOSED TO BE A FRIENDLY EXHIBITION MATCH, BUT WE'LL BE PLAYING FOR REAL.
IT'S AN ANNUAL TRADITION.
IF WE LOSE, THE REST OF WINTER VACATION WILL BE HELL.
WE'LL BE PRACTICING EVERY SINGLE DAY, INCLUDING NEW YEAR'S EVE AND NEW YEAR'S DAY...!
I UNDER-STAND THAT YOU'RE DESPERATE ...
...BUT I HAVE MY OWN ISSUES TO DEAL WITH AS THE YEAR COMES TO AN END.
There are only a few days left before we set off on our trip to the Snowy Moun-tain Lodge...
... KYON.
SORRY, BUT I DON'T CARE ABOUT YOUR SCHEDULE.

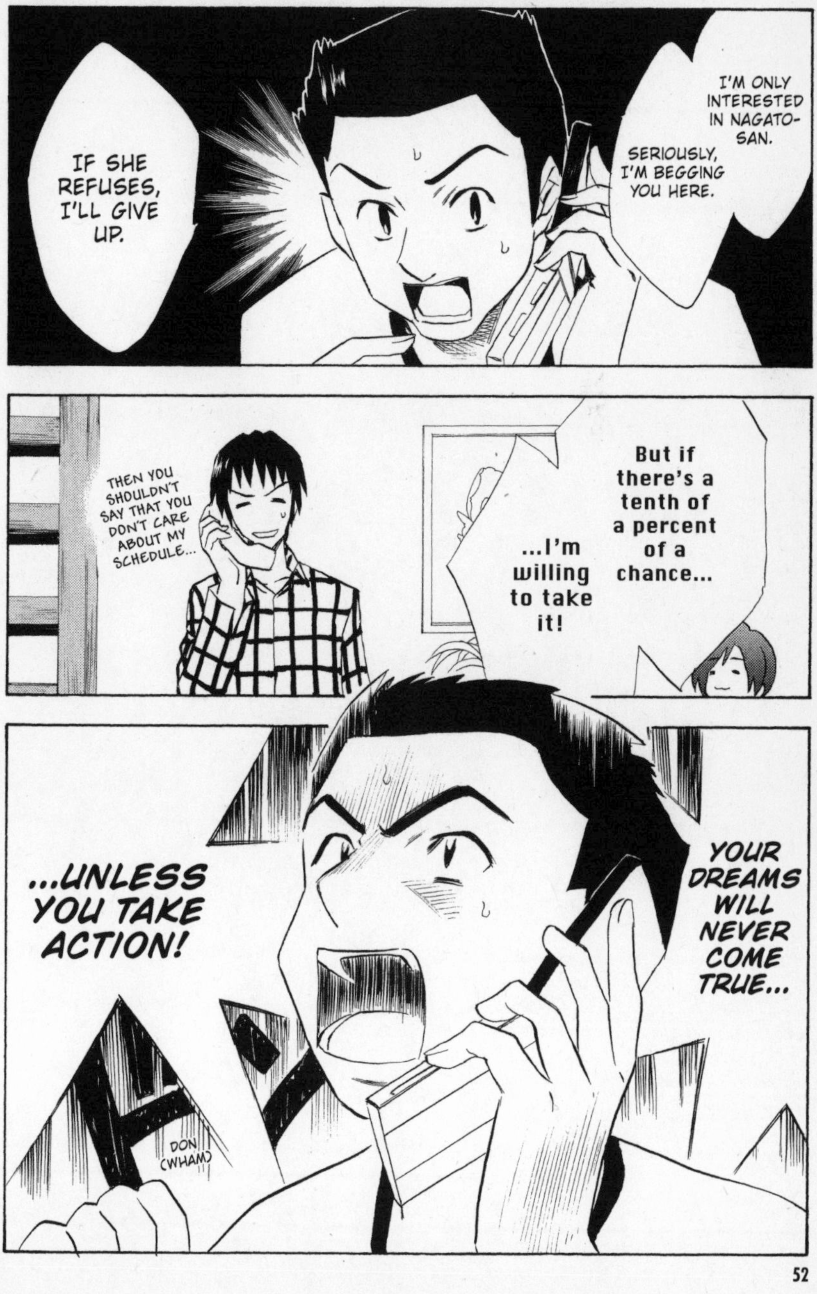
I'M ONLY INTERESTED IN NAGATO-SAN.
SERIOUSLY, I'M BEGGING YOU HERE.
IF SHE REFUSES, I'LL GIVE UP.
But if there's a tenth of a percent of a chance...
...I'm willing to take it!
THEN YOU SHOULDN'T SAY THAT YOU DON'T CARE ABOUT MY SCHEDULE...
YOUR DREAMS WILL NEVER COME TRUE...
...UNLESS YOU TAKE ACTION!
DON (WHAM)

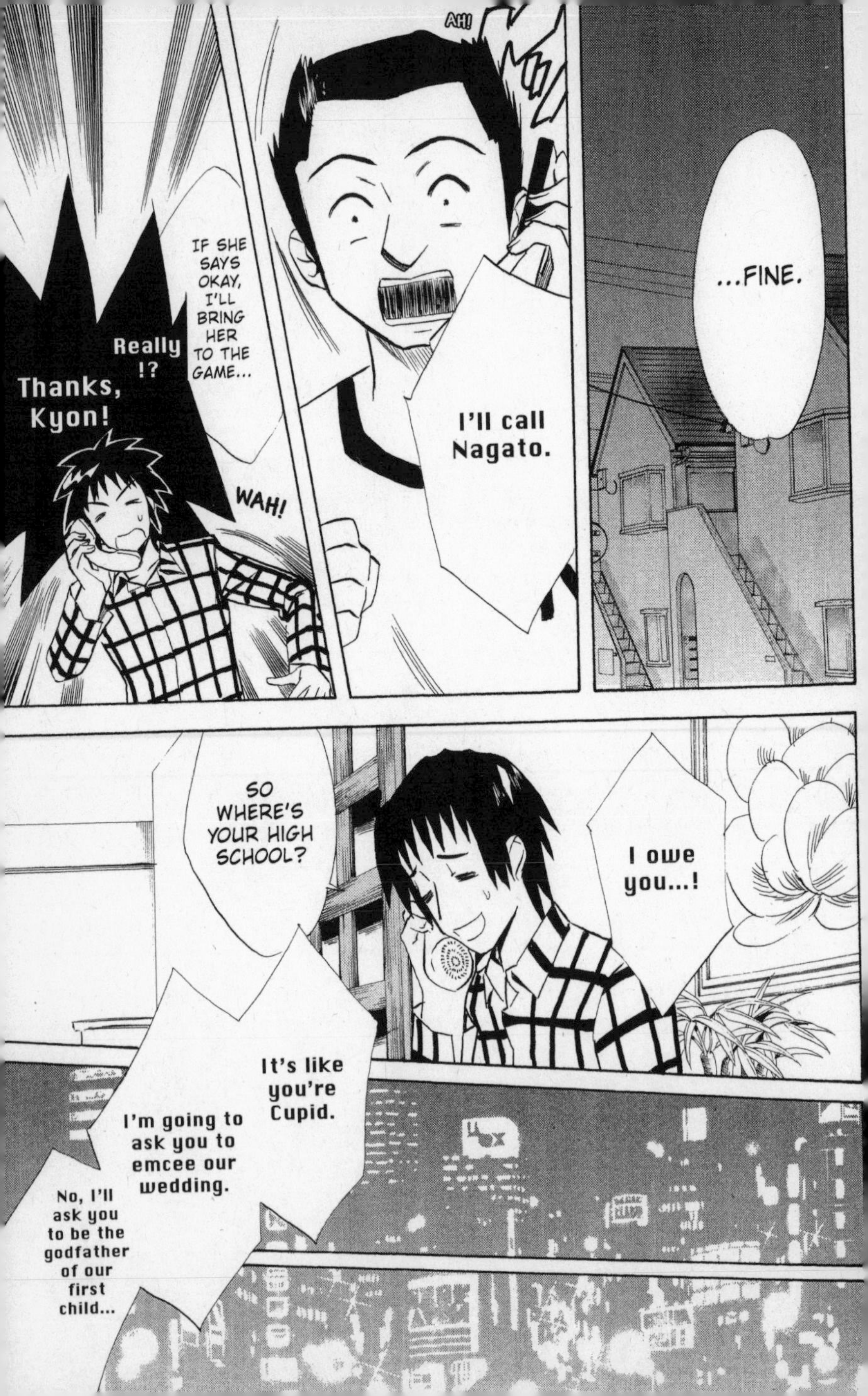
...FINE.
AH!
I'll call Nagato.
IF SHE SAYS OKAY, I'LL BRING HER TO THE GAME...
Really!?
Thanks, Kyon!
WAH!
I owe you...!
SO WHERE'S YOUR HIGH SCHOOL?
It's like you're Cupid.
I'm going to ask you to emcee our wedding.
No, I'll ask you to be the godfather of our first child...

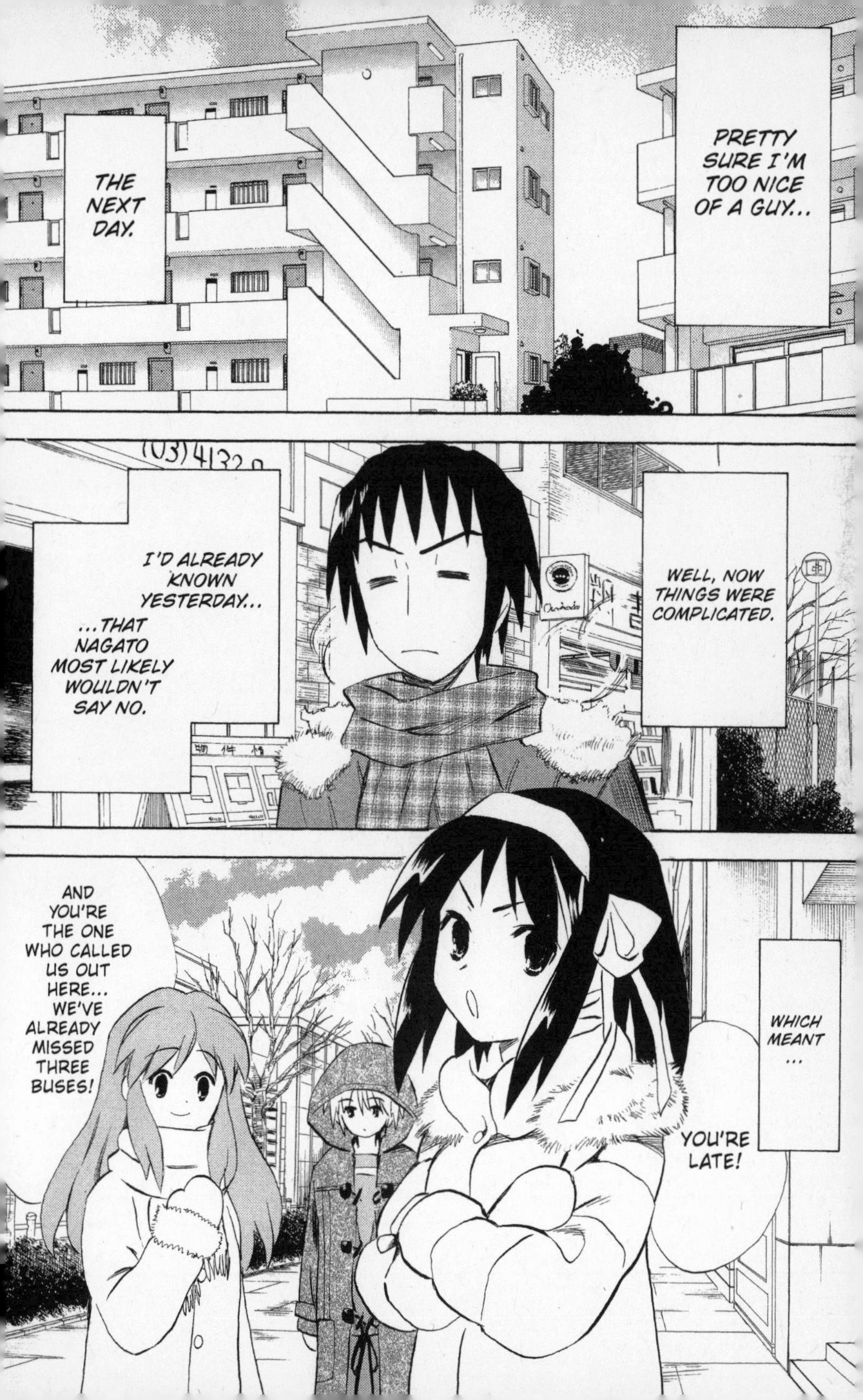
PRETTY SURE I'M TOO NICE OF A GUY...
THE NEXT DAY.
WELL, NOW THINGS WERE COMPLICATED.
I'D ALREADY KNOWN YESTERDAY...
...THAT NAGATO MOST LIKELY WOULDN'T SAY NO.
WHICH MEANT ...
YOU'RE LATE!
AND YOU'RE THE ONE WHO CALLED US OUT HERE... WE'VE ALREADY MISSED THREE BUSES!

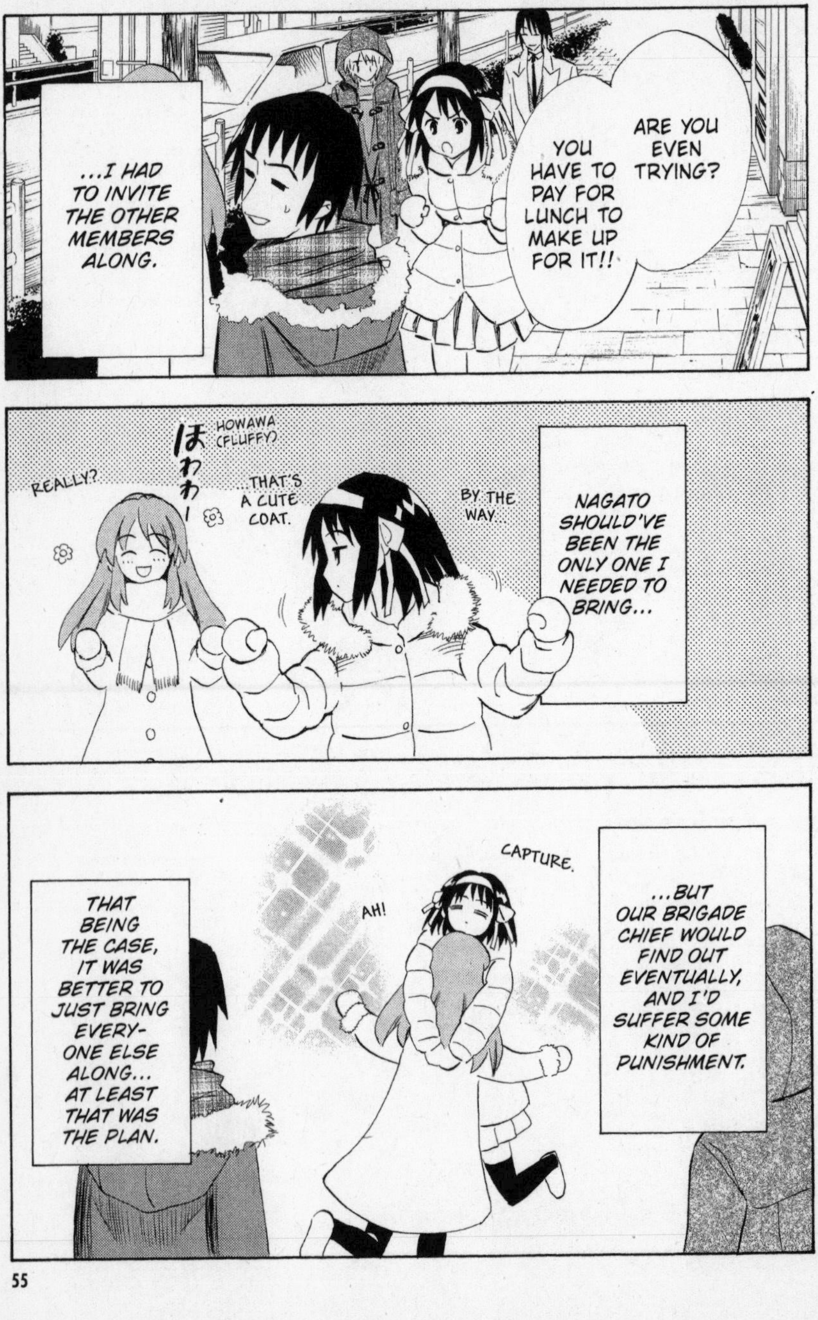
ARE YOU EVEN TRYING?
YOU HAVE TO PAY FOR LUNCH TO MAKE UP FOR IT!!
...I HAD TO INVITE THE OTHER MEMBERS ALONG.
NAGATO SHOULD'VE BEEN THE ONLY ONE I NEEDED TO BRING...
BY THE WAY...
THAT'S A CUTE COAT.
はわわ
HOWAWA (FLUFFY)
REALLY?
...BUT OUR BRIGADE CHIEF WOULD FIND OUT EVENTUALLY, AND I'D SUFFER SOME KIND OF PUNISHMENT.
CAPTURE.
AH!
THAT BEING THE CASE, IT WAS BETTER TO JUST BRING EVERY-ONE ELSE ALONG... AT LEAST THAT WAS THE PLAN.

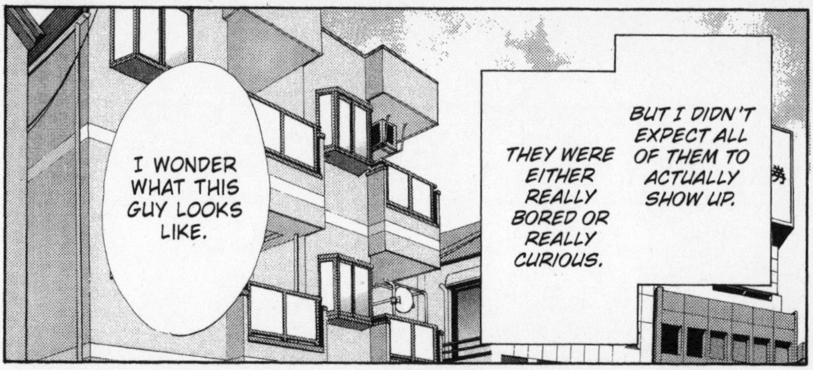
THEY WERE EITHER REALLY BORED OR REALLY CURIOUS.
BUT I DIDN'T EXPECT ALL OF THEM TO ACTUALLY SHOW UP.
I WONDER WHAT THIS GUY LOOKS LIKE.

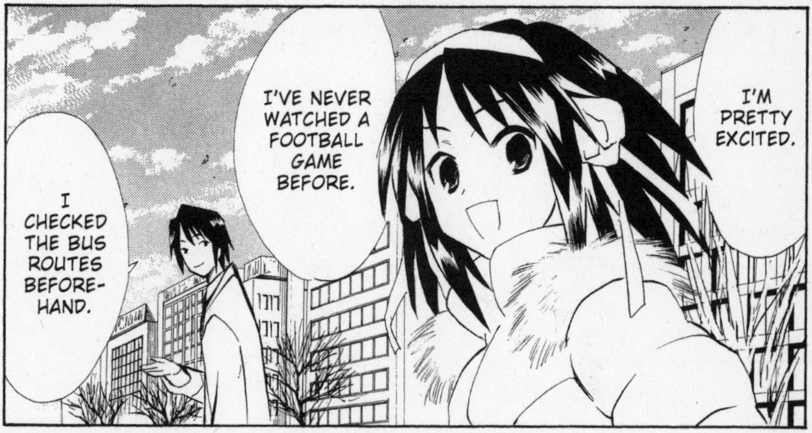
I'M PRETTY EXCITED.
I'VE NEVER WATCHED A FOOTBALL GAME BEFORE.
I CHECKED THE BUS ROUTES BEFORE-HAND.

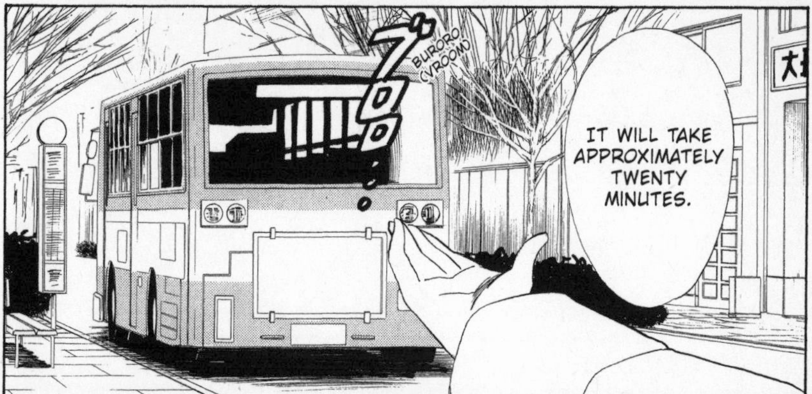
BURORO (VROOM)
IT WILL TAKE APPROXIMATELY TWENTY MINUTES.

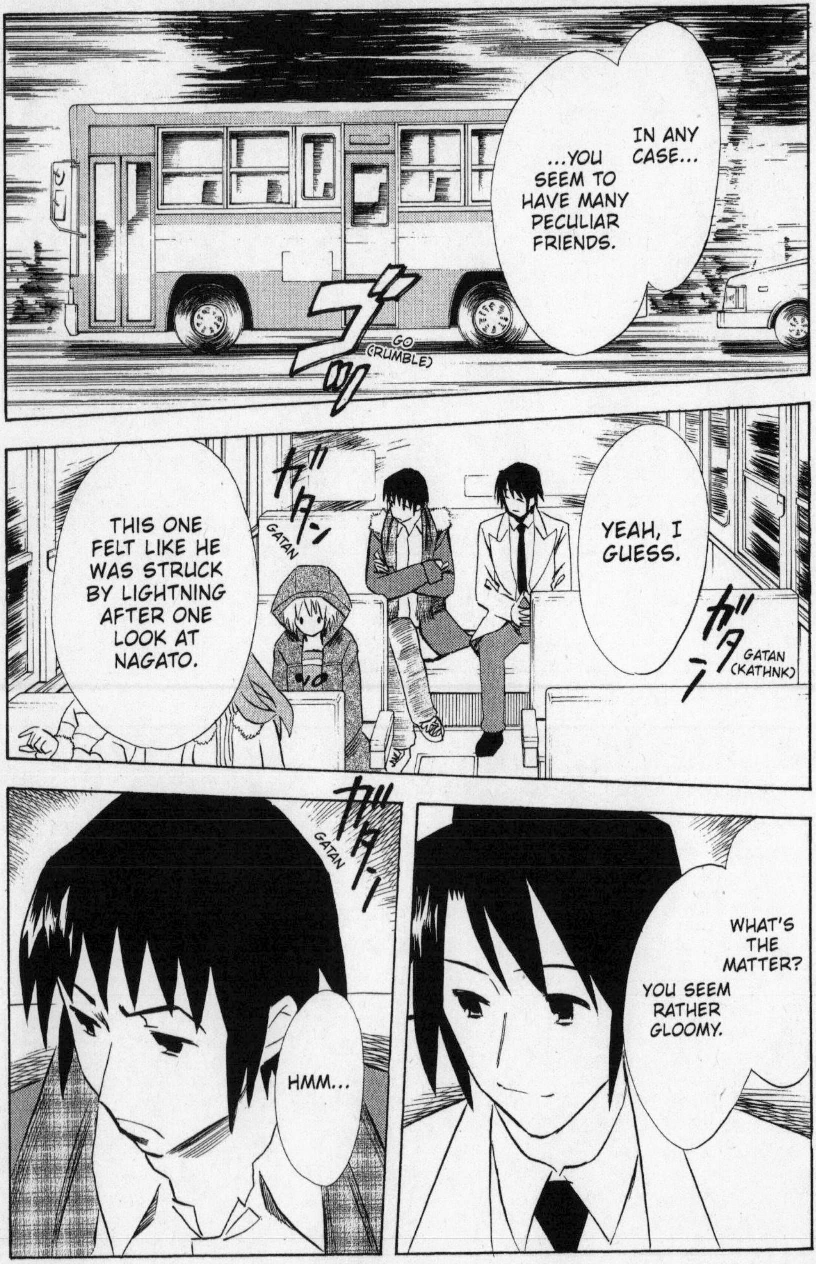

IN ANY CASE...
...YOU SEEM TO HAVE MANY PECULIAR FRIENDS.
GO (RUMBLE)
YEAH, I GUESS.
GATAN (KATHNK)
GATAN
THIS ONE FELT LIKE HE WAS STRUCK BY LIGHTNING AFTER ONE LOOK AT NAGATO.
WHAT'S THE MATTER?
YOU SEEM RATHER GLOOMY.
GATAN
HMM...

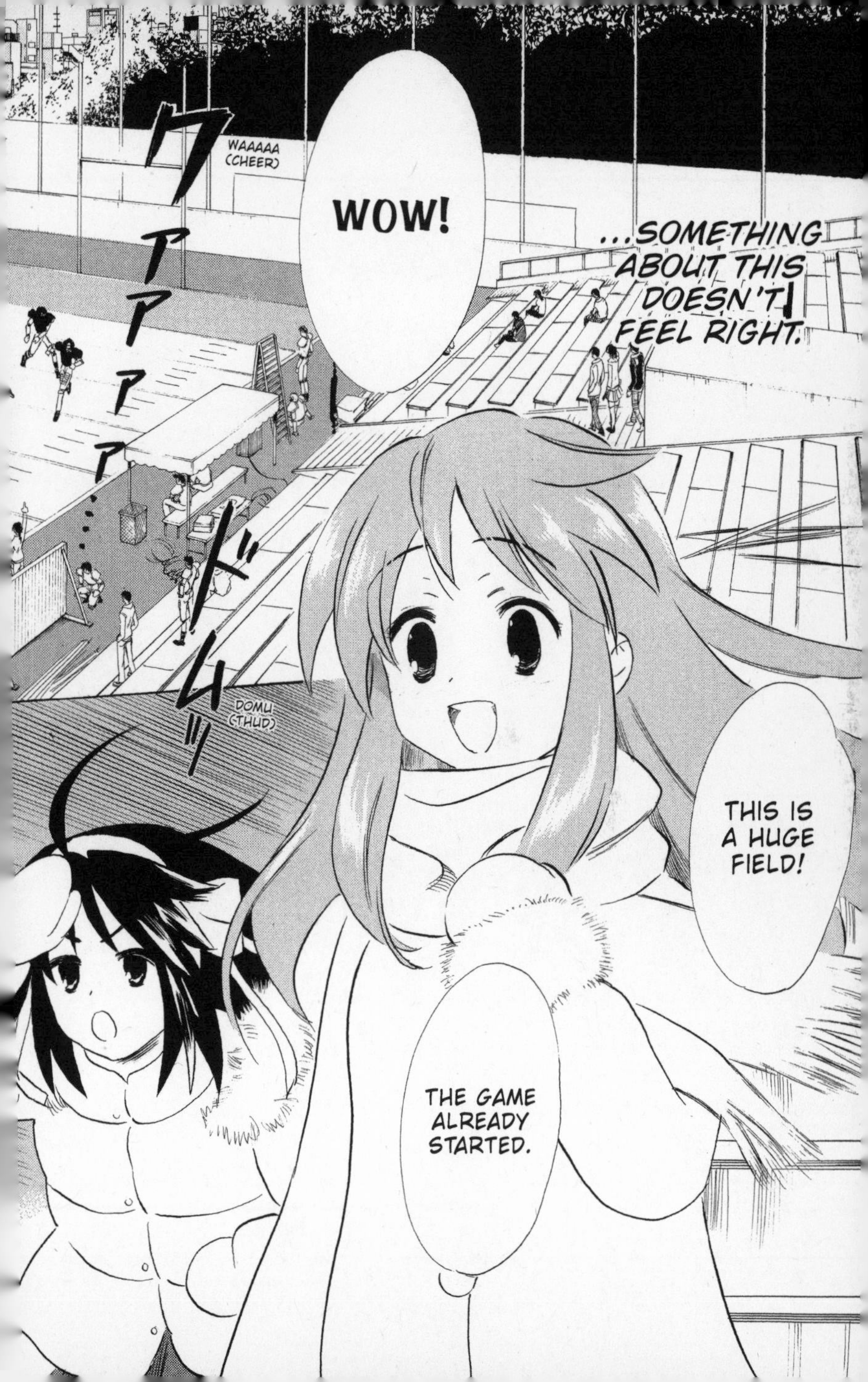
...SOMETHING ABOUT THIS DOESN'T FEEL RIGHT.
WOW!
WAAAAA (CHEER)
THIS IS A HUGE FIELD!
DOMU (THUD)
THE GAME ALREADY STARTED.

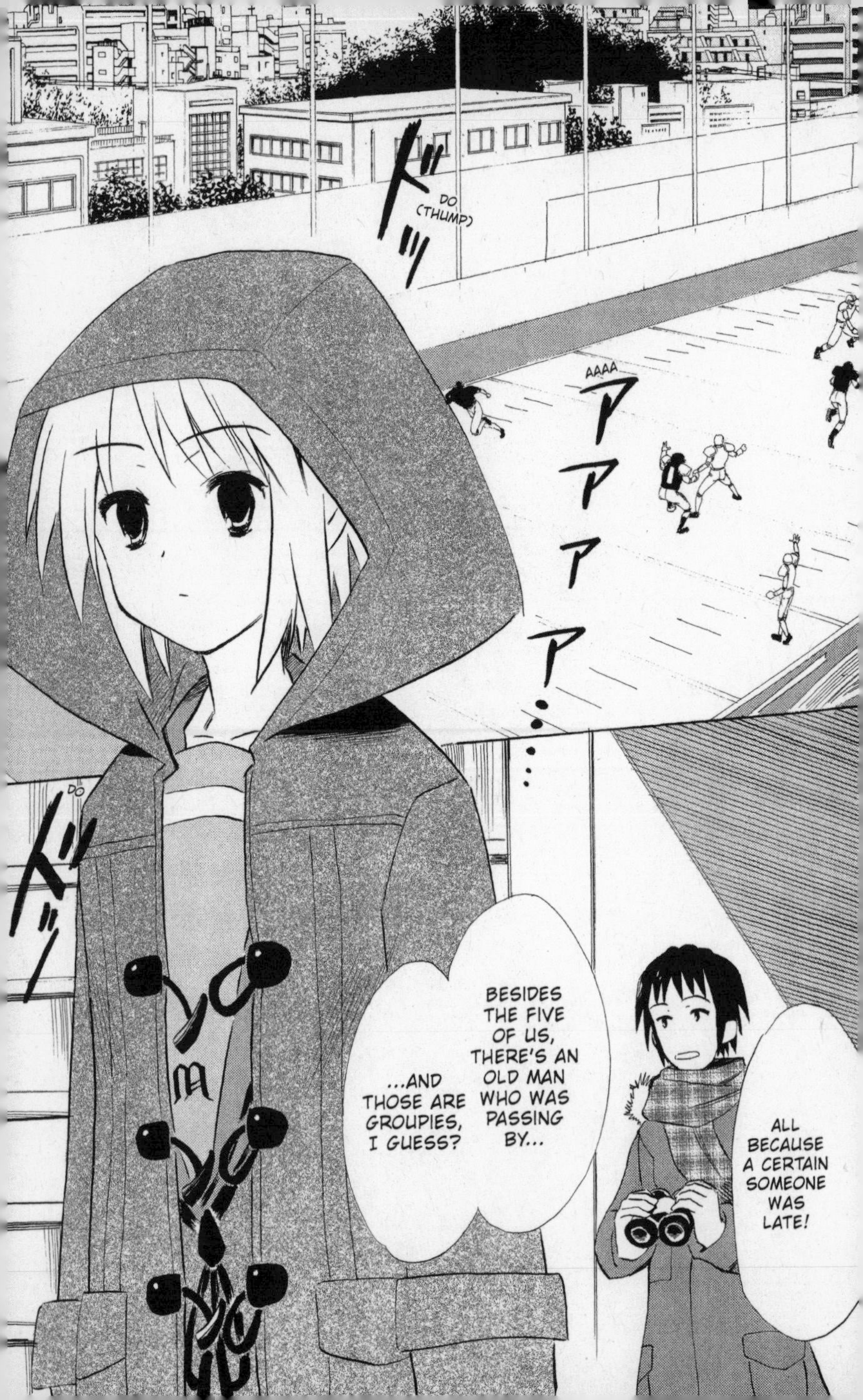ドッ
DO (THUMP)
アアアア…
AAAA
ドッ
DO
ALL BECAUSE A CERTAIN SOMEONE WAS LATE!
BESIDES THE FIVE OF US, THERE'S AN OLD MAN WHO WAS PASSING BY...
...AND THOSE ARE GROUPIES, I GUESS?

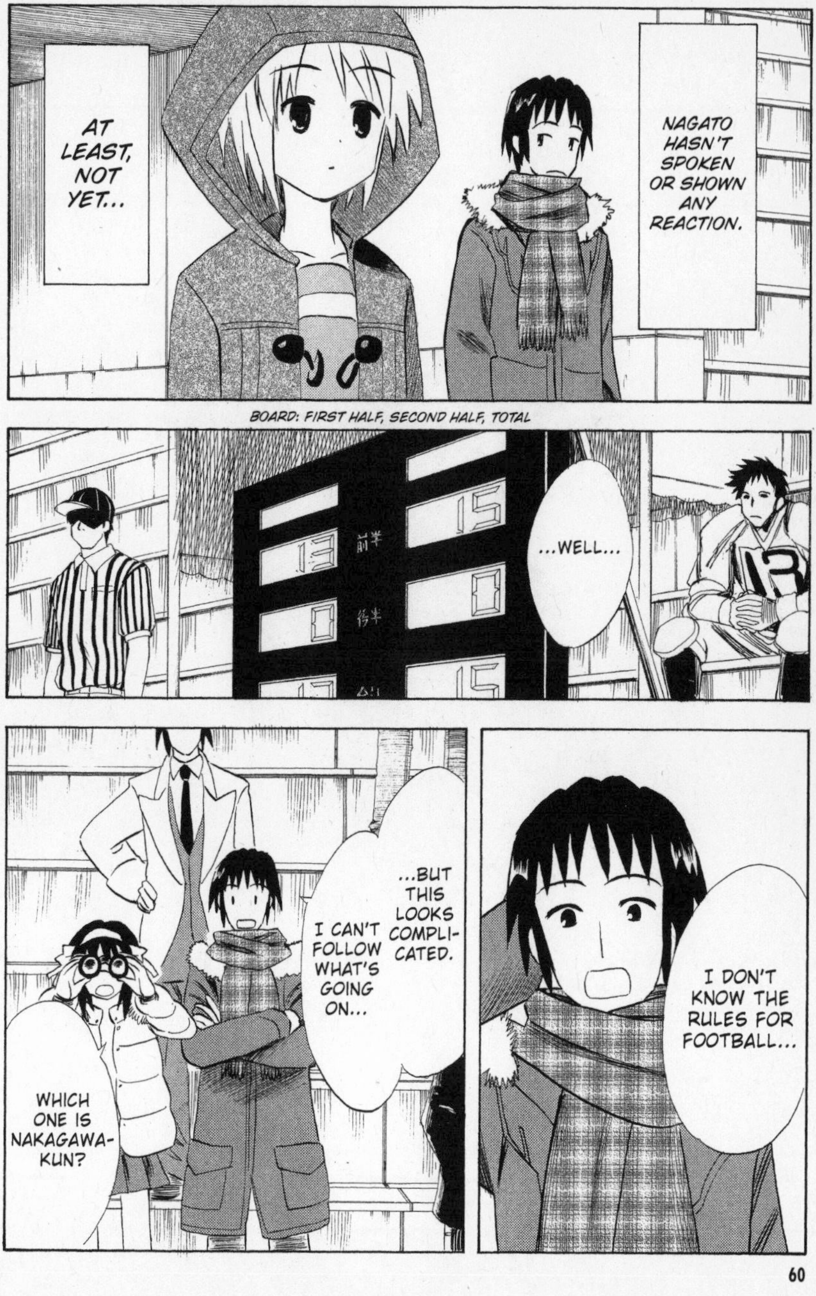
NAGATO HASN'T SPOKEN OR SHOWN ANY REACTION.
AT LEAST, NOT YET...
BOARD: FIRST HALF, SECOND HALF, TOTAL
...WELL...
I DON'T KNOW THE RULES FOR FOOTBALL...
...BUT THIS LOOKS COMPLICATED.
I CAN'T FOLLOW WHAT'S GOING ON...
WHICH ONE IS NAKAGAWA-KUN?

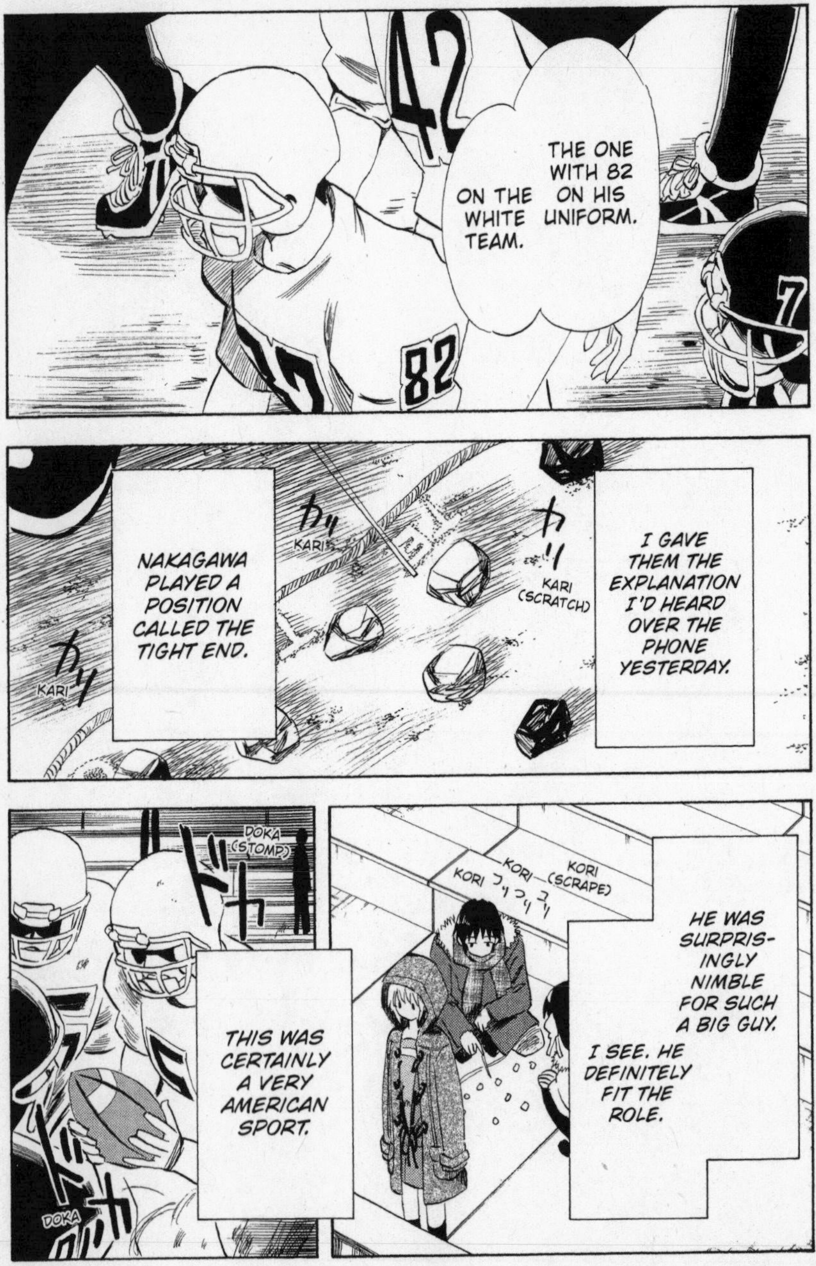
THE ONE WITH 82 ON HIS UNIFORM.
ON THE WHITE TEAM.
I GAVE THEM THE EXPLANATION I'D HEARD OVER THE PHONE YESTERDAY.
KARI (SCRATCH)
KARI
NAKAGAWA PLAYED A POSITION CALLED THE TIGHT END.
KARI
HE WAS SURPRIS-INGLY NIMBLE FOR SUCH A BIG GUY.
I SEE. HE DEFINITELY FIT THE ROLE.
KORI (SCRAPE)
KORI
KORI
DOKA (STOMP)
THIS WAS CERTAINLY A VERY AMERICAN SPORT.
DOKA

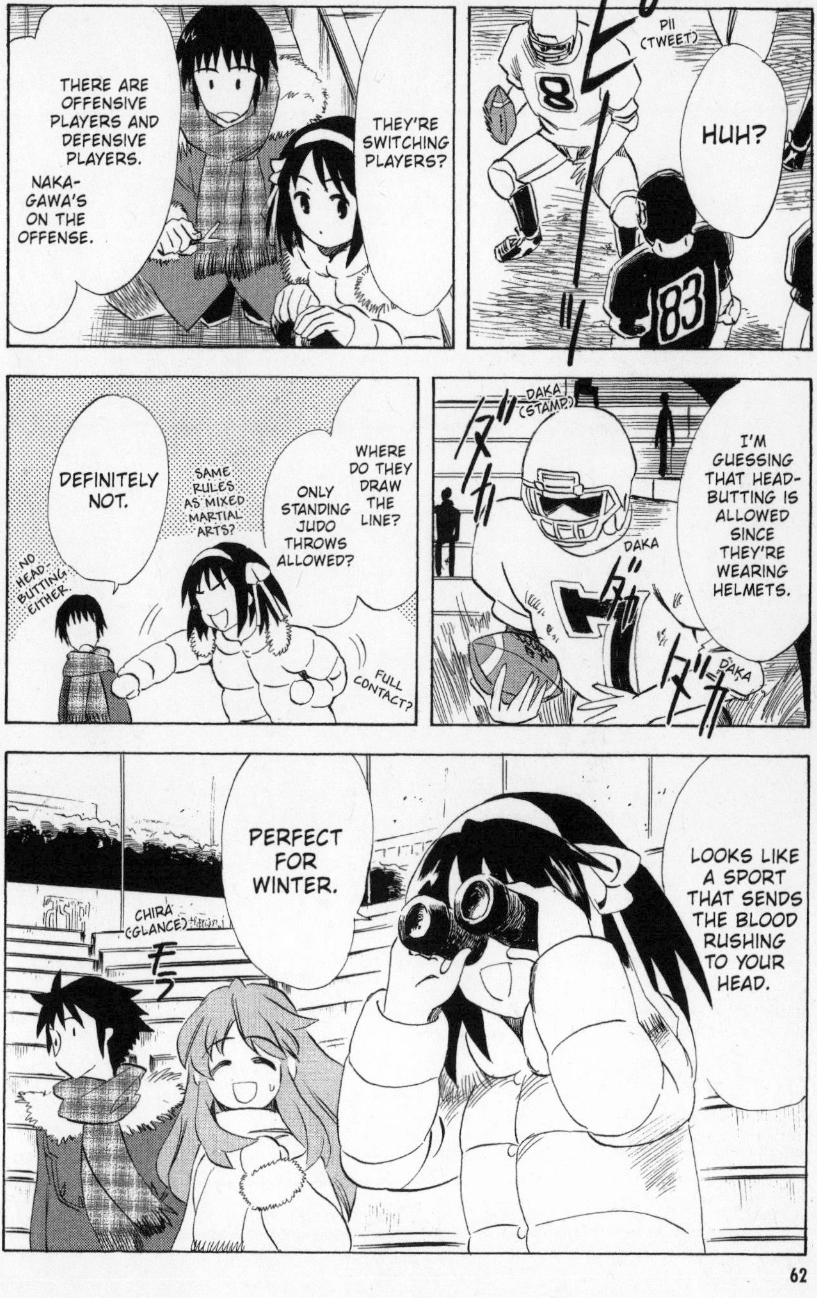
PII (TWEET)
HUH?
THEY'RE SWITCHING PLAYERS?
THERE ARE OFFENSIVE PLAYERS AND DEFENSIVE PLAYERS.
NAKA-GAWA'S ON THE OFFENSE.
DAKA (STAMP)
I'M GUESSING THAT HEAD-BUTTING IS ALLOWED SINCE THEY'RE WEARING HELMETS.
DAKA
DAKA
WHERE DO THEY DRAW THE LINE?
ONLY STANDING JUDO THROWS ALLOWED?
SAME RULES AS MIXED MARTIAL ARTS?
FULL CONTACT?
DEFINITELY NOT.
NO HEAD-BUTTING EITHER.
LOOKS LIKE A SPORT THAT SENDS THE BLOOD RUSHING TO YOUR HEAD.
PERFECT FOR WINTER.
CHIRA (GLANCE)

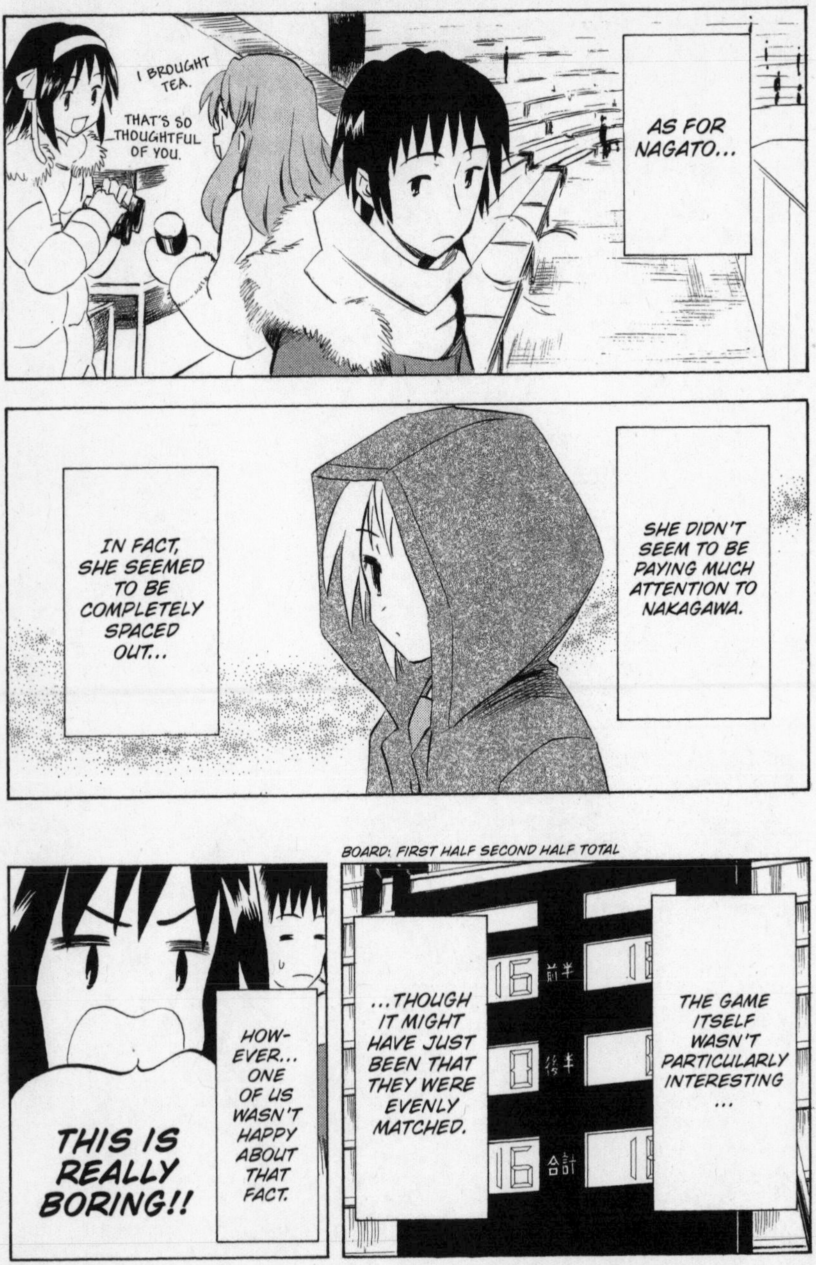
AS FOR NAGATO...
I BROUGHT TEA.
THAT'S SO THOUGHTFUL OF YOU.
SHE DIDN'T SEEM TO BE PAYING MUCH ATTENTION TO NAKAGAWA.
IN FACT, SHE SEEMED TO BE COMPLETELY SPACED OUT...
BOARD: FIRST HALF SECOND HALF TOTAL
THE GAME ITSELF WASN'T PARTICULARLY INTERESTING...
...THOUGH IT MIGHT HAVE JUST BEEN THAT THEY WERE EVENLY MATCHED.
HOW-EVER... ONE OF US WASN'T HAPPY ABOUT THAT FACT.
THIS IS REALLY BORING!!

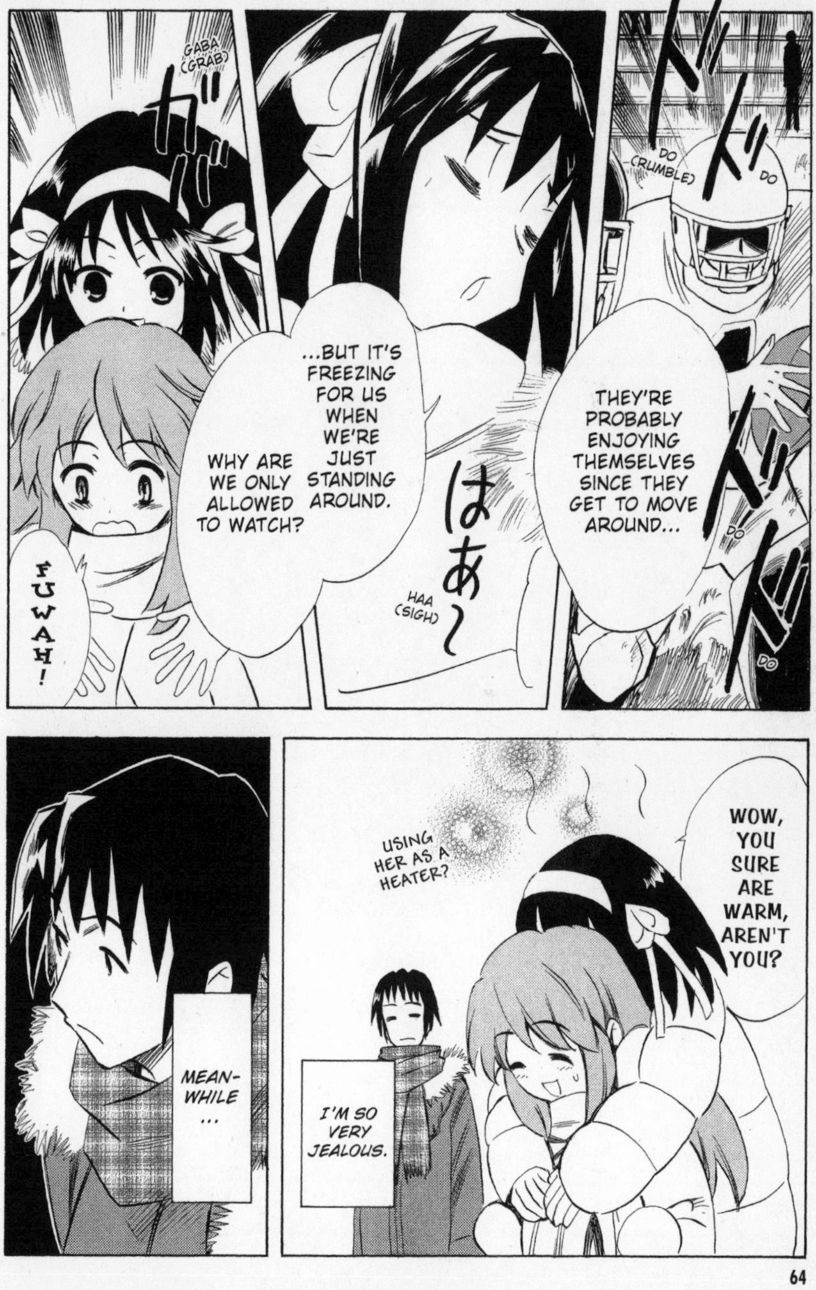
DO (RUMBLE) DO
THEY'RE PROBABLY ENJOYING THEMSELVES SINCE THEY GET TO MOVE AROUND...
DO
DO
HAA (SIGH)
...BUT IT'S FREEZING FOR US WHEN WE'RE JUST STANDING AROUND.
WHY ARE WE ONLY ALLOWED TO WATCH?
GABA (GRAB)
FUWAH!
WOW, YOU SURE ARE WARM, AREN'T YOU?
USING HER AS A HEATER?
I'M SO VERY JEALOUS.
MEAN-WHILE...

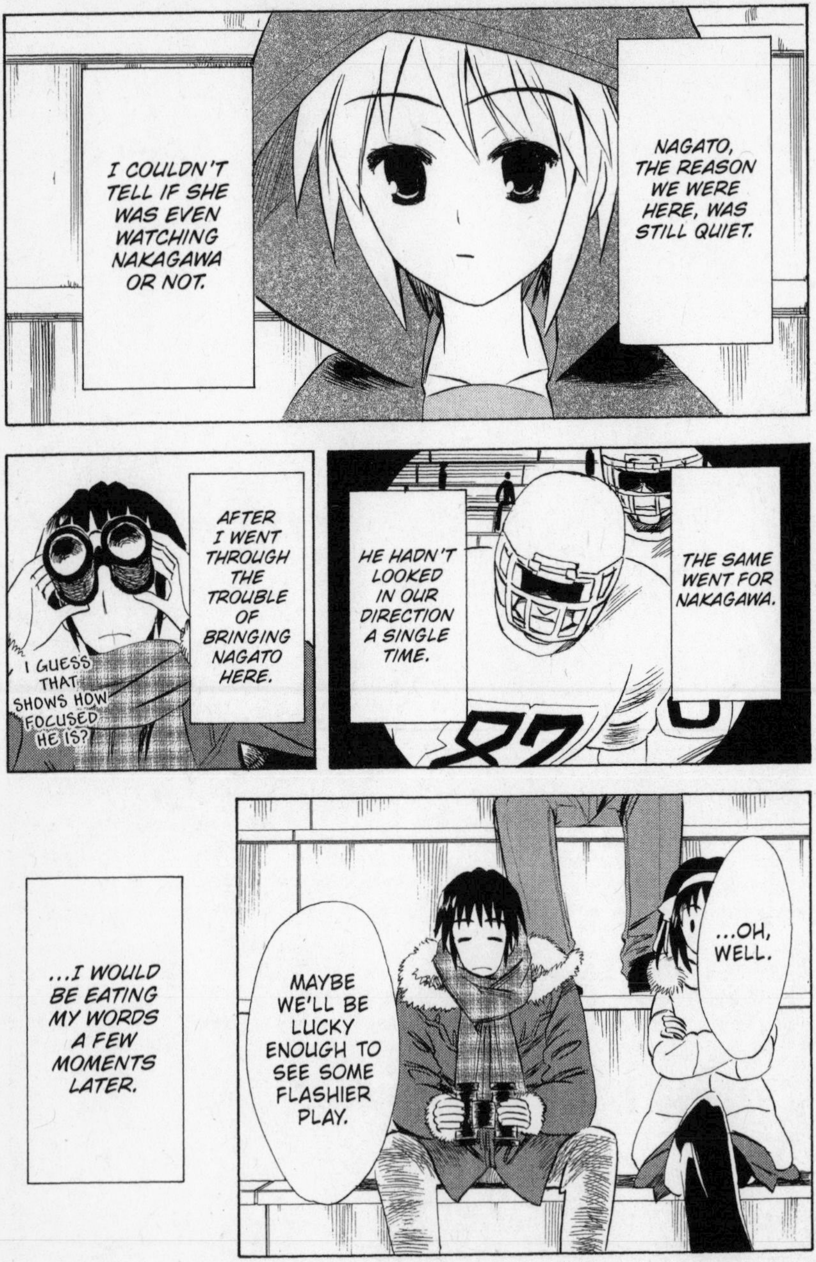
NAGATO, THE REASON WE WERE HERE, WAS STILL QUIET.
I COULDN'T TELL IF SHE WAS EVEN WATCHING NAKAGAWA OR NOT.
THE SAME WENT FOR NAKAGAWA.
HE HADN'T LOOKED IN OUR DIRECTION A SINGLE TIME.
AFTER I WENT THROUGH THE TROUBLE OF BRINGING NAGATO HERE.
I GUESS THAT SHOWS HOW FOCUSED HE IS?
...OH, WELL.
MAYBE WE'LL BE LUCKY ENOUGH TO SEE SOME FLASHIER PLAY.
...I WOULD BE EATING MY WORDS A FEW MOMENTS LATER.

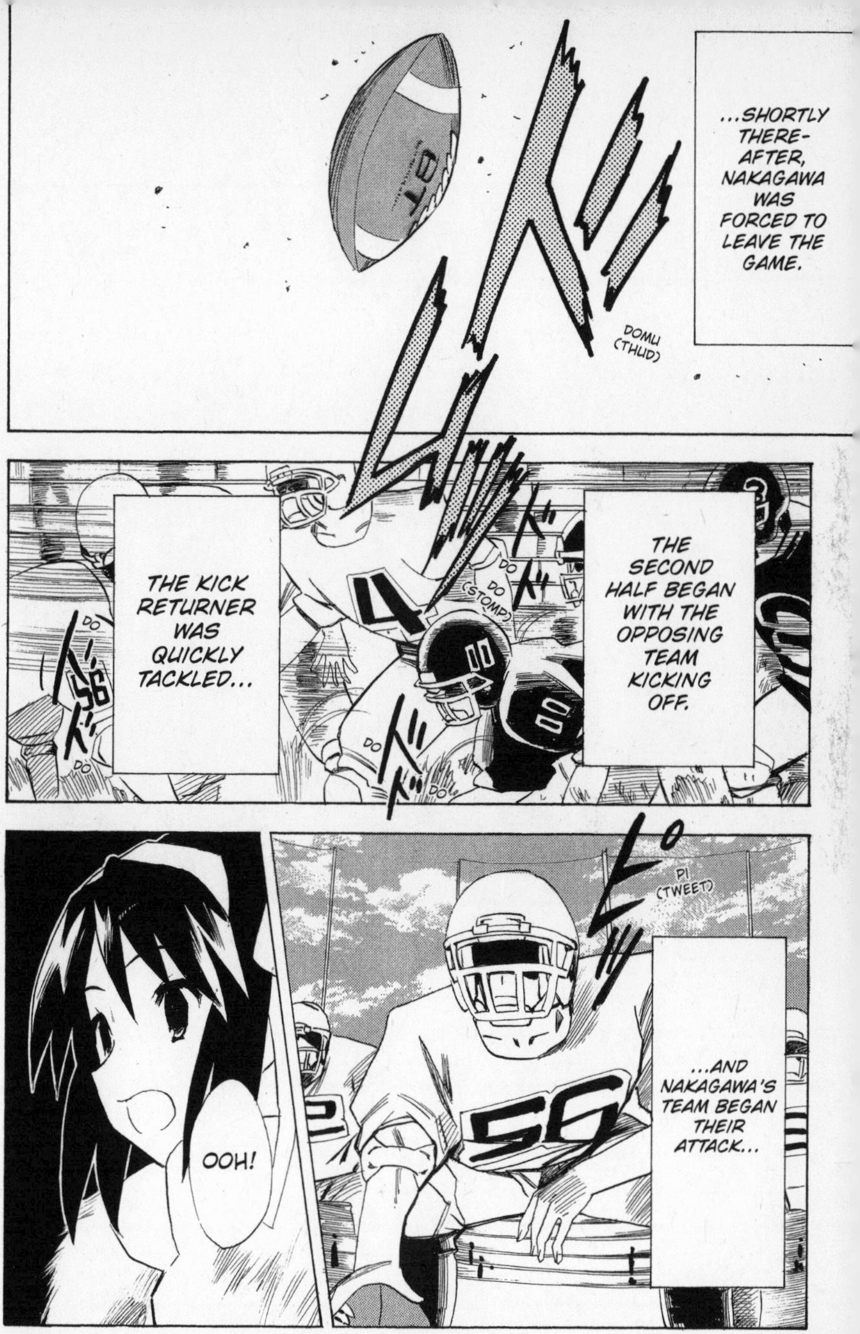
...SHORTLY THERE-AFTER, NAKAGAWA WAS FORCED TO LEAVE THE GAME.
DOMU (THUD)
THE SECOND HALF BEGAN WITH THE OPPOSING TEAM KICKING OFF.
DO DO (STOMP)
DO
DO
THE KICK RETURNER WAS QUICKLY TACKLED...
DO
DO
PI (TWEET)
...AND NAKAGAWA'S TEAM BEGAN THEIR ATTACK...
OOH!

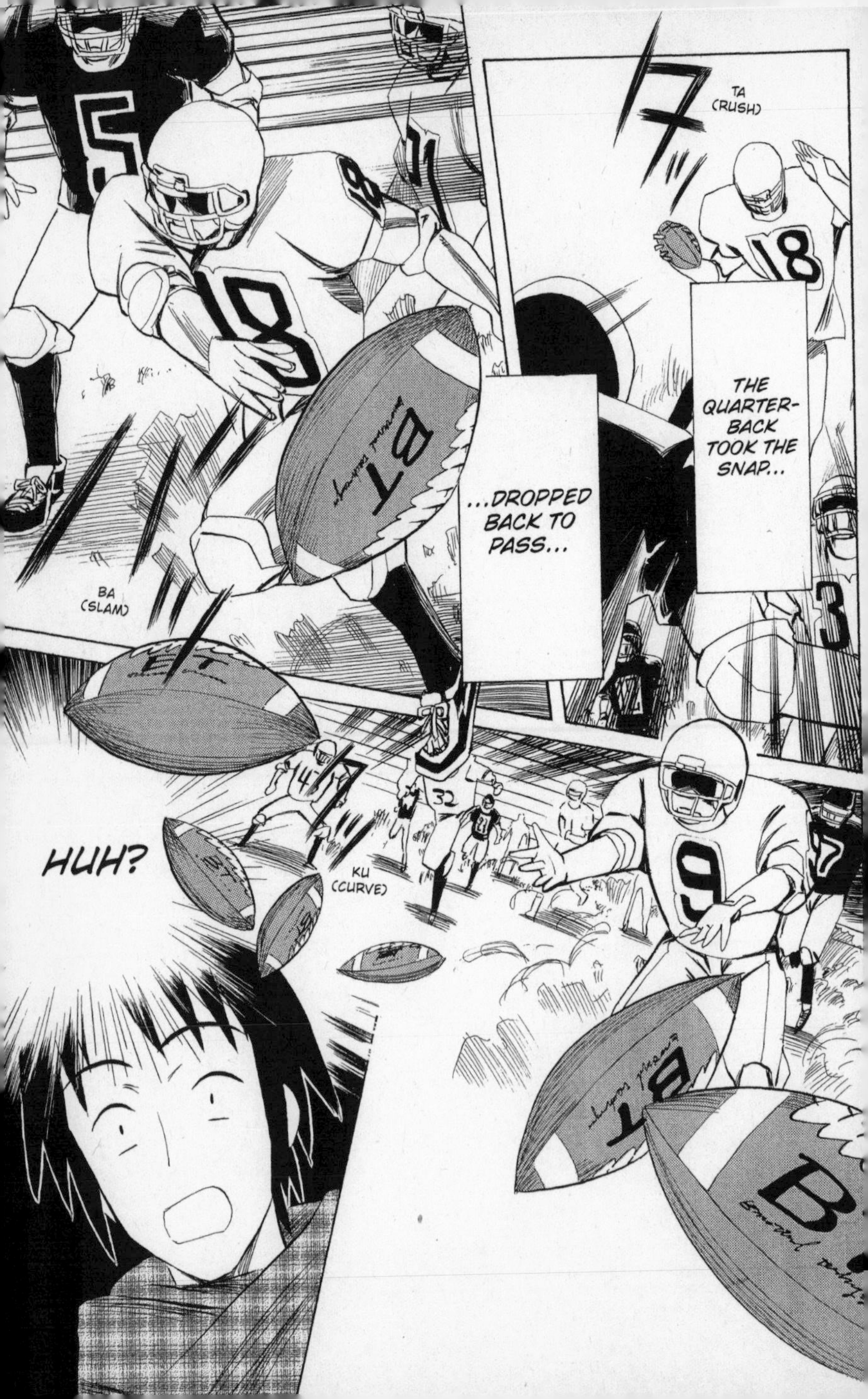
TA (RUSH)
THE QUARTER-BACK TOOK THE SNAP...
...DROPPED BACK TO PASS...
BA (SLAM)
KU (CURVE)
HUH?

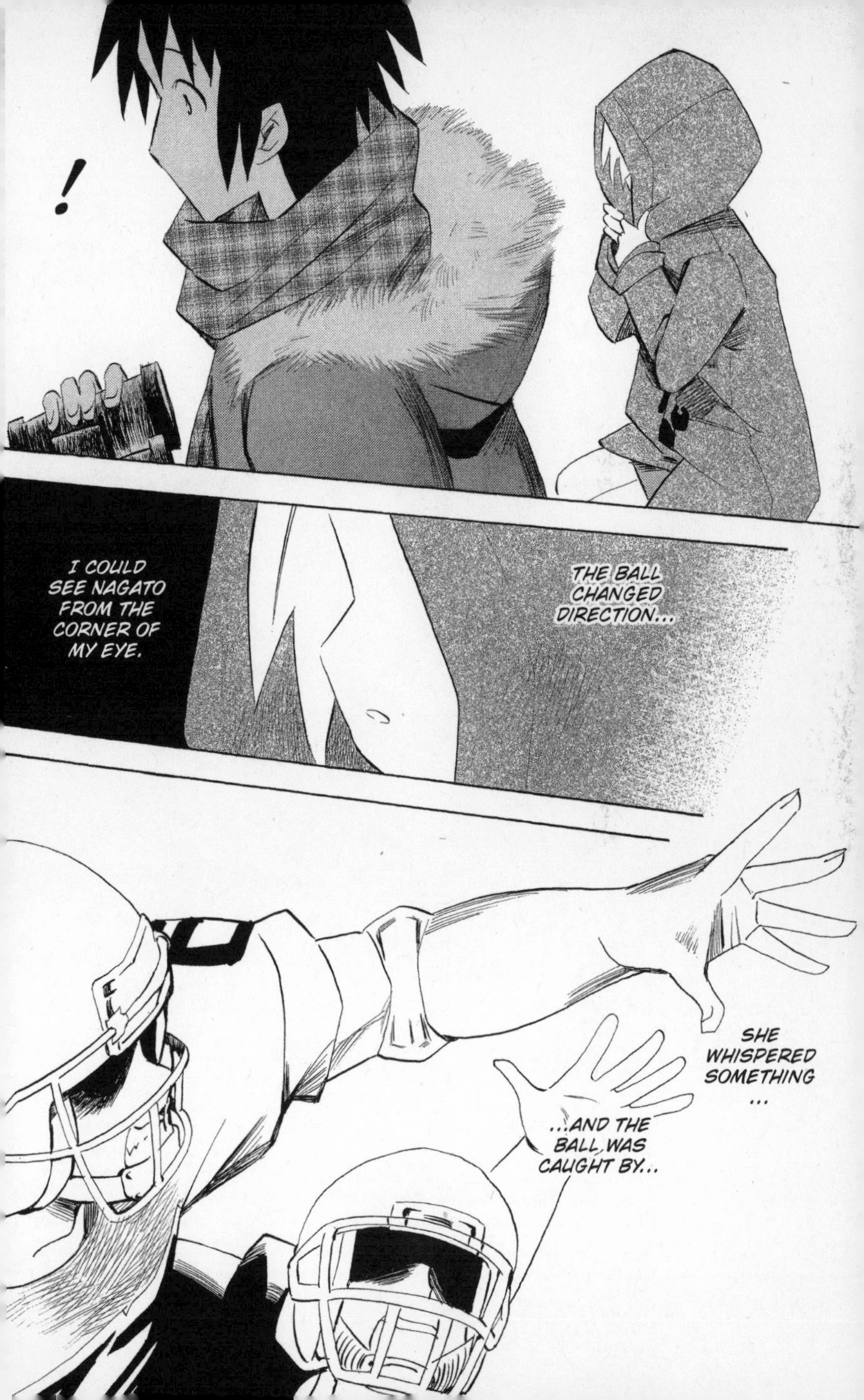
!
THE BALL CHANGED DIRECTION...
I COULD SEE NAGATO FROM THE CORNER OF MY EYE.
SHE WHISPERED SOMETHING ...
...AND THE BALL WAS CAUGHT BY...

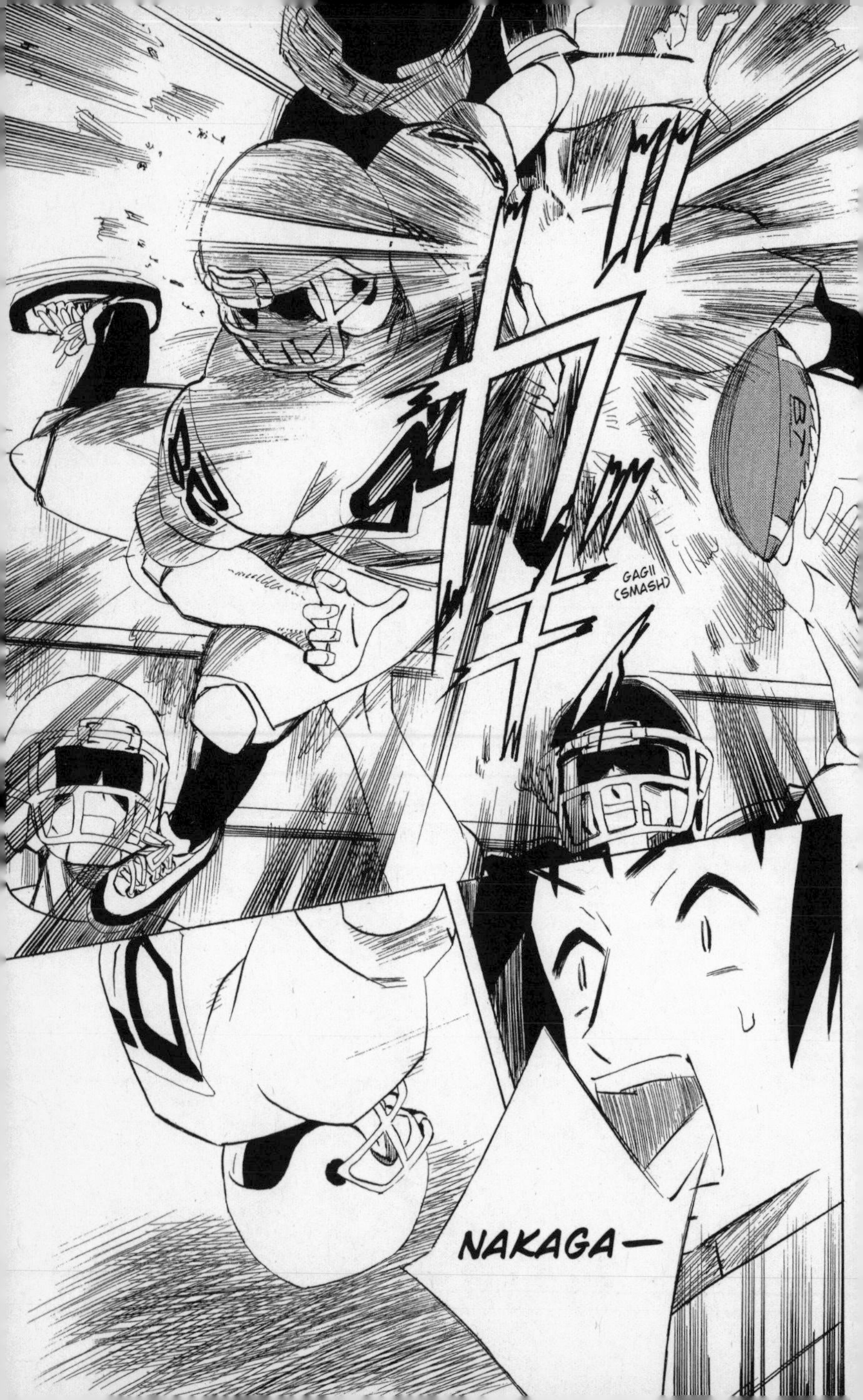
GAGII
(SMASH)
NAKAGA—

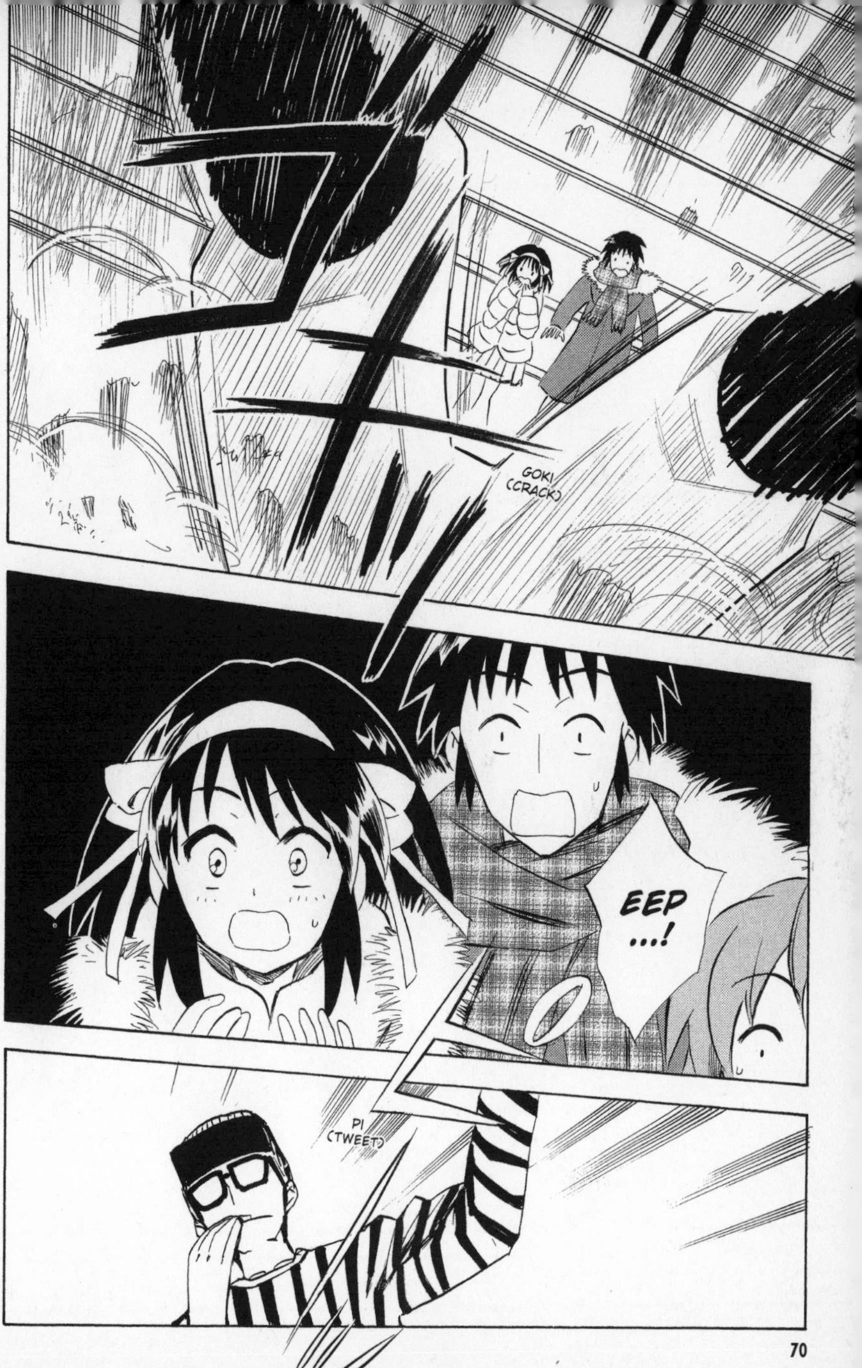
GOKI
(CRACK)
EEP
...!
PI
(TWEET)

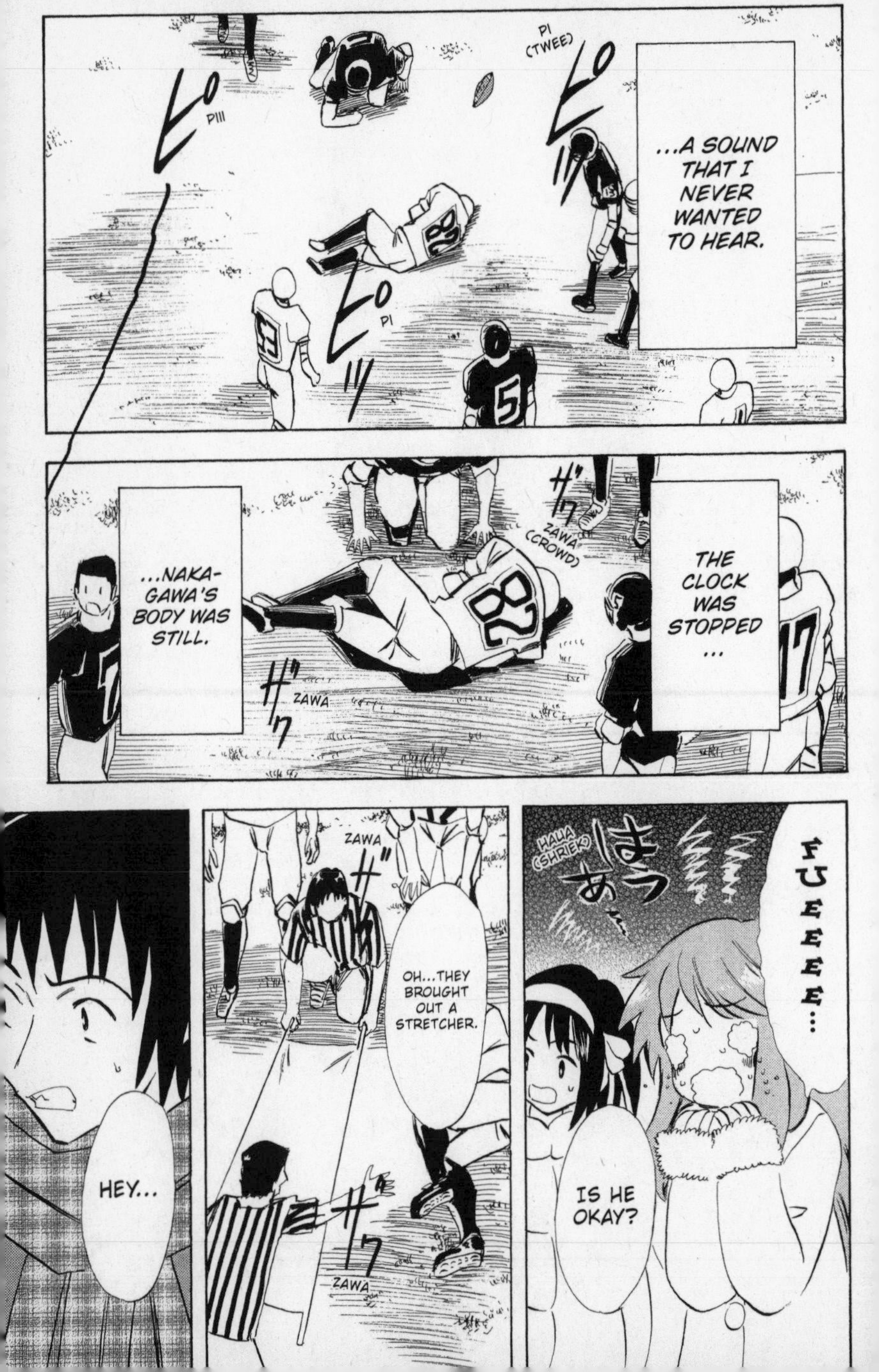
PI (TWEE)
...A SOUND THAT I NEVER WANTED TO HEAR.
PIII
PI
THE CLOCK WAS STOPPED...
ZAWA (CROWD)
...NAKA-GAWA'S BODY WAS STILL.
ZAWA
FUEEEEE...
HAUA (SHRIEK)
IS HE OKAY?
ZAWA
OH...THEY BROUGHT OUT A STRETCHER.
ZAWA
HEY...

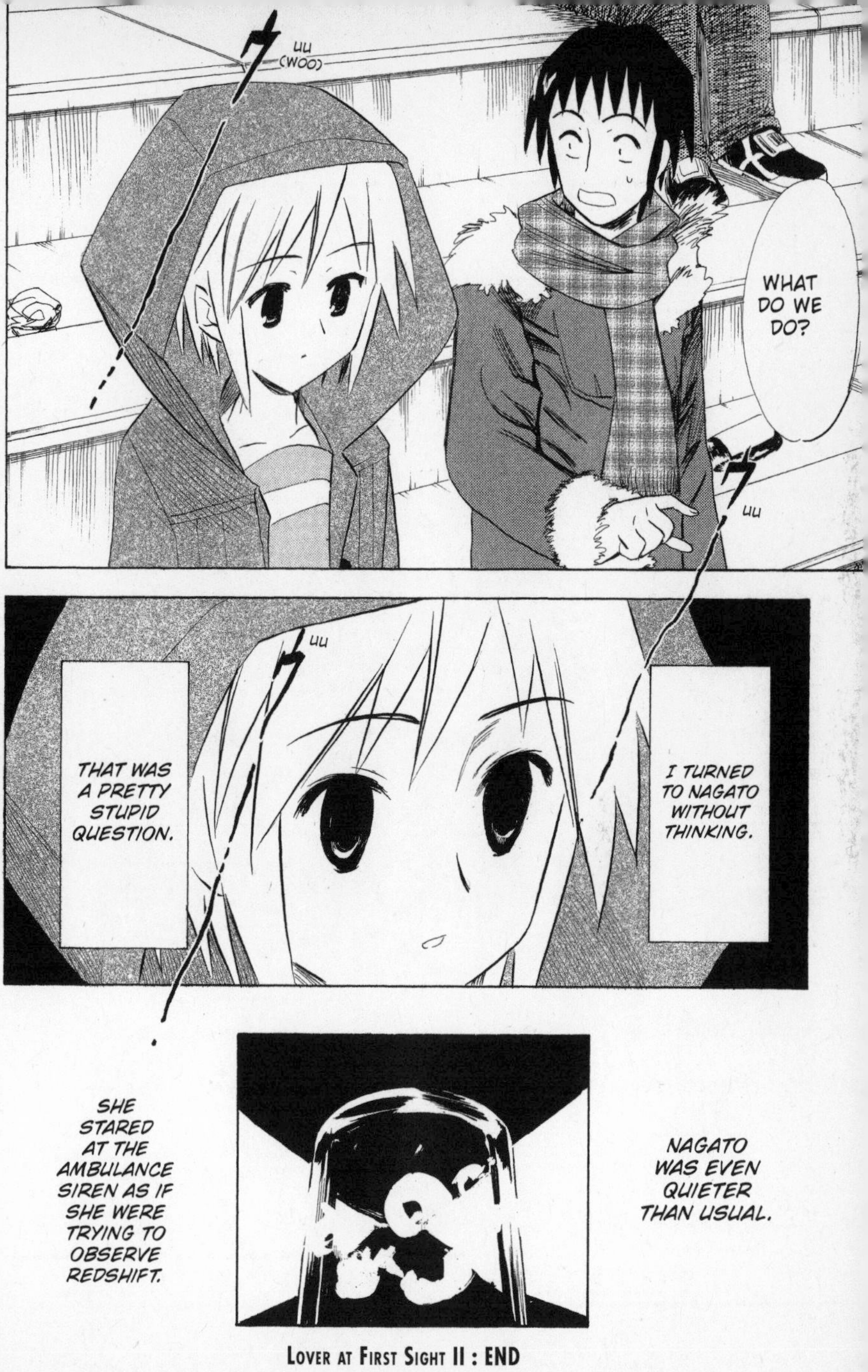
WHAT DO WE DO?
uu (WOO)
uu
I TURNED TO NAGATO WITHOUT THINKING.
uu
THAT WAS A PRETTY STUPID QUESTION.
NAGATO WAS EVEN QUIETER THAN USUAL.
SHE STARED AT THE AMBULANCE SIREN AS IF SHE WERE TRYING TO OBSERVE REDSHIFT.

Lover at First Sight II : END

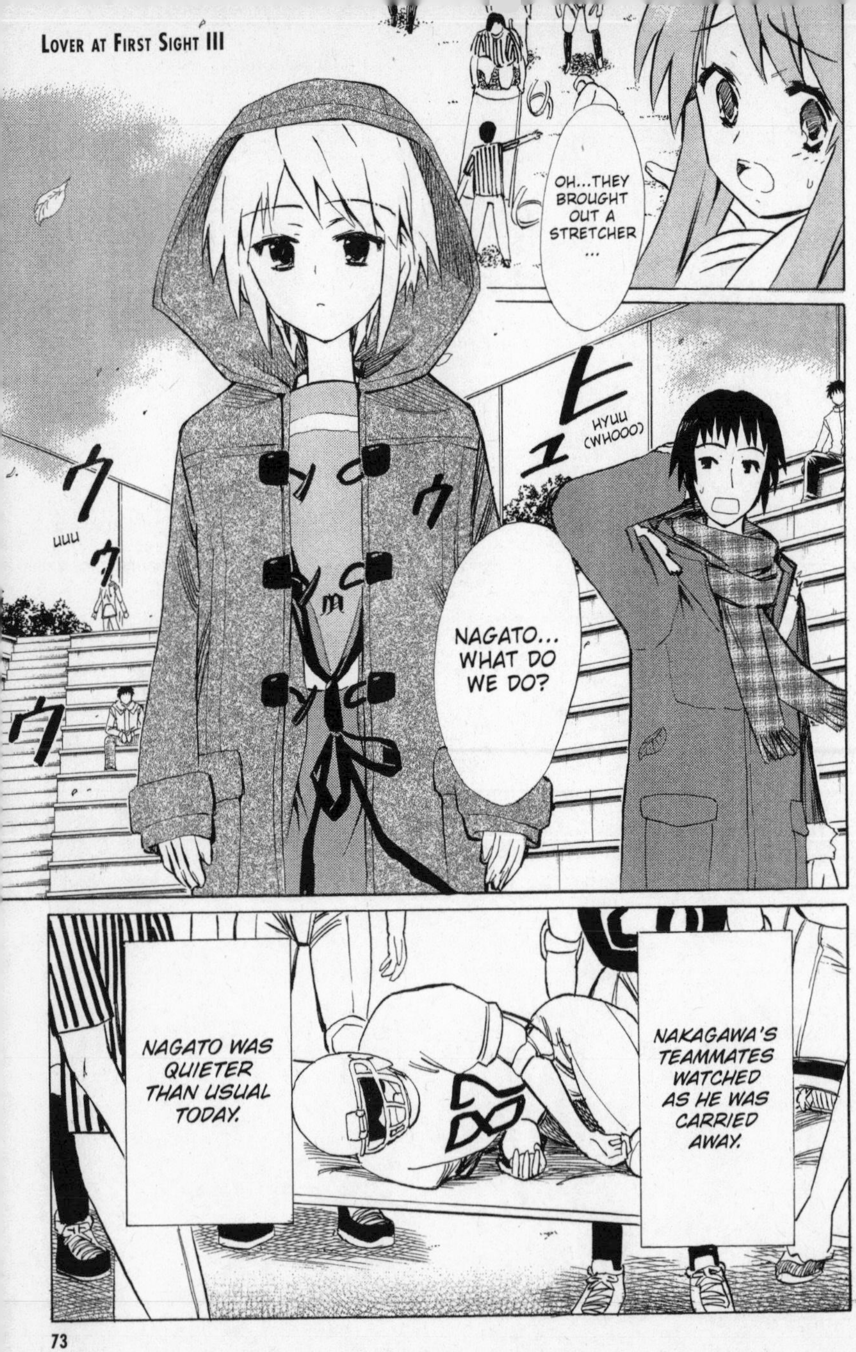
OH...THEY BROUGHT OUT A STRETCHER...
ヒュウ
HYUU (WHOOO)
ウウウ
uuu
NAGATO... WHAT DO WE DO?
NAKAGAWA'S TEAMMATES WATCHED AS HE WAS CARRIED AWAY.
NAGATO WAS QUIETER THAN USUAL TODAY.

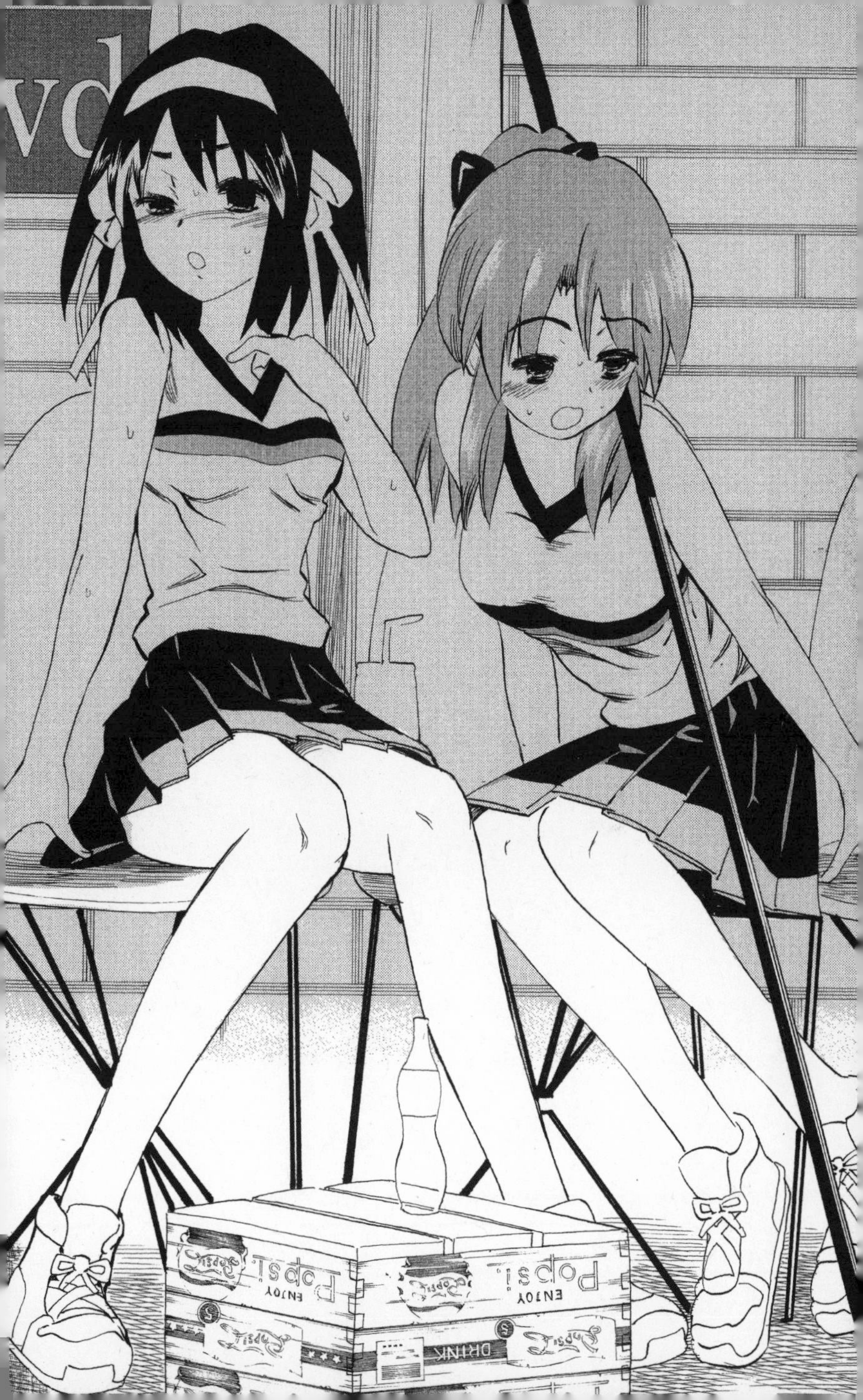
ENJOY Pepsi
ENJOY Pepsi
DRINK

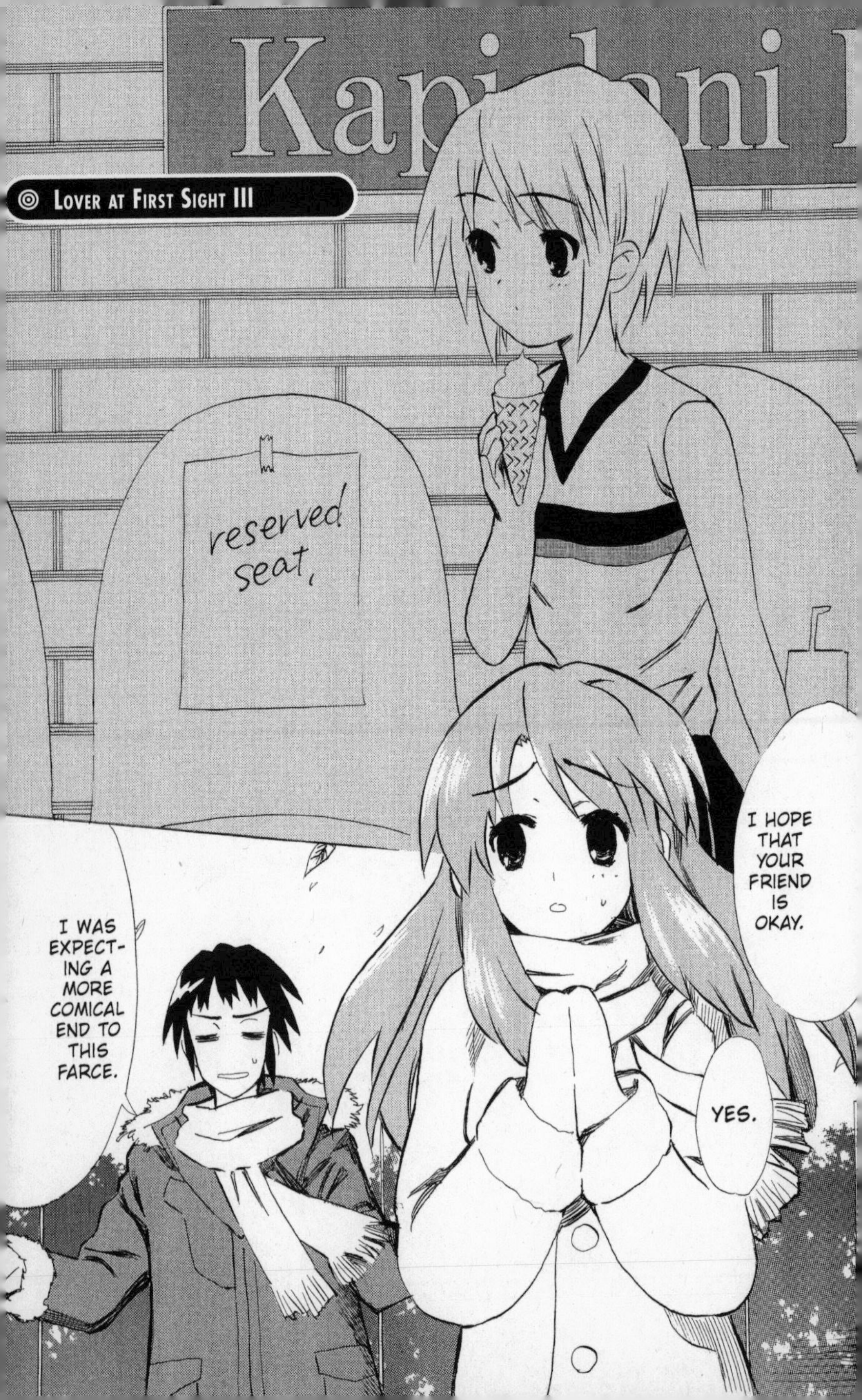
LOVER AT FIRST SIGHT III
reserved seat,
I HOPE THAT YOUR FRIEND IS OKAY.
YES.
I WAS EXPECTING A MORE COMICAL END TO THIS FARCE.

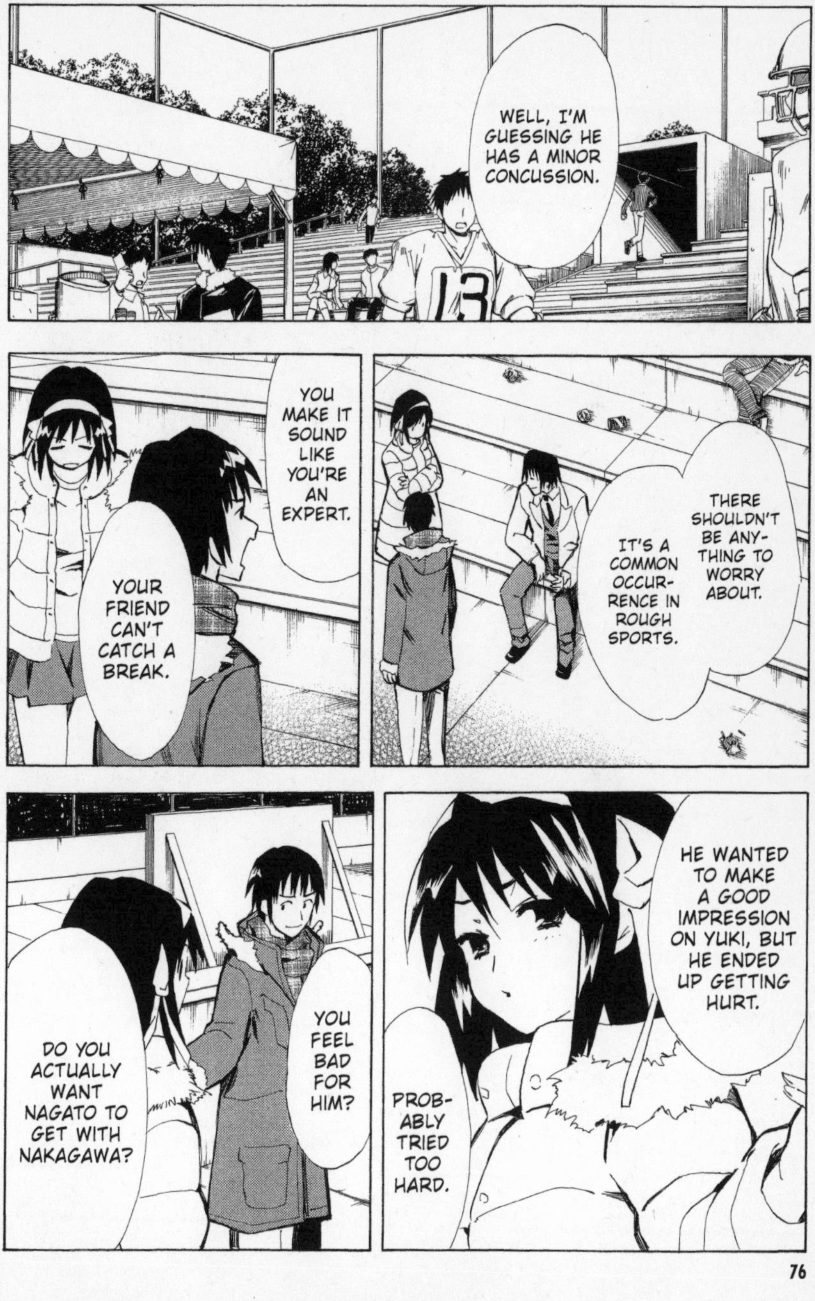
WELL, I'M GUESSING HE HAS A MINOR CONCUSSION.
THERE SHOULDN'T BE ANYTHING TO WORRY ABOUT.
IT'S A COMMON OCCURRENCE IN ROUGH SPORTS.
YOU MAKE IT SOUND LIKE YOU'RE AN EXPERT.
YOUR FRIEND CAN'T CATCH A BREAK.
HE WANTED TO MAKE A GOOD IMPRESSION ON YUKI, BUT HE ENDED UP GETTING HURT.
PROBABLY TRIED TOO HARD.
YOU FEEL BAD FOR HIM?
DO YOU ACTUALLY WANT NAGATO TO GET WITH NAKAGAWA?

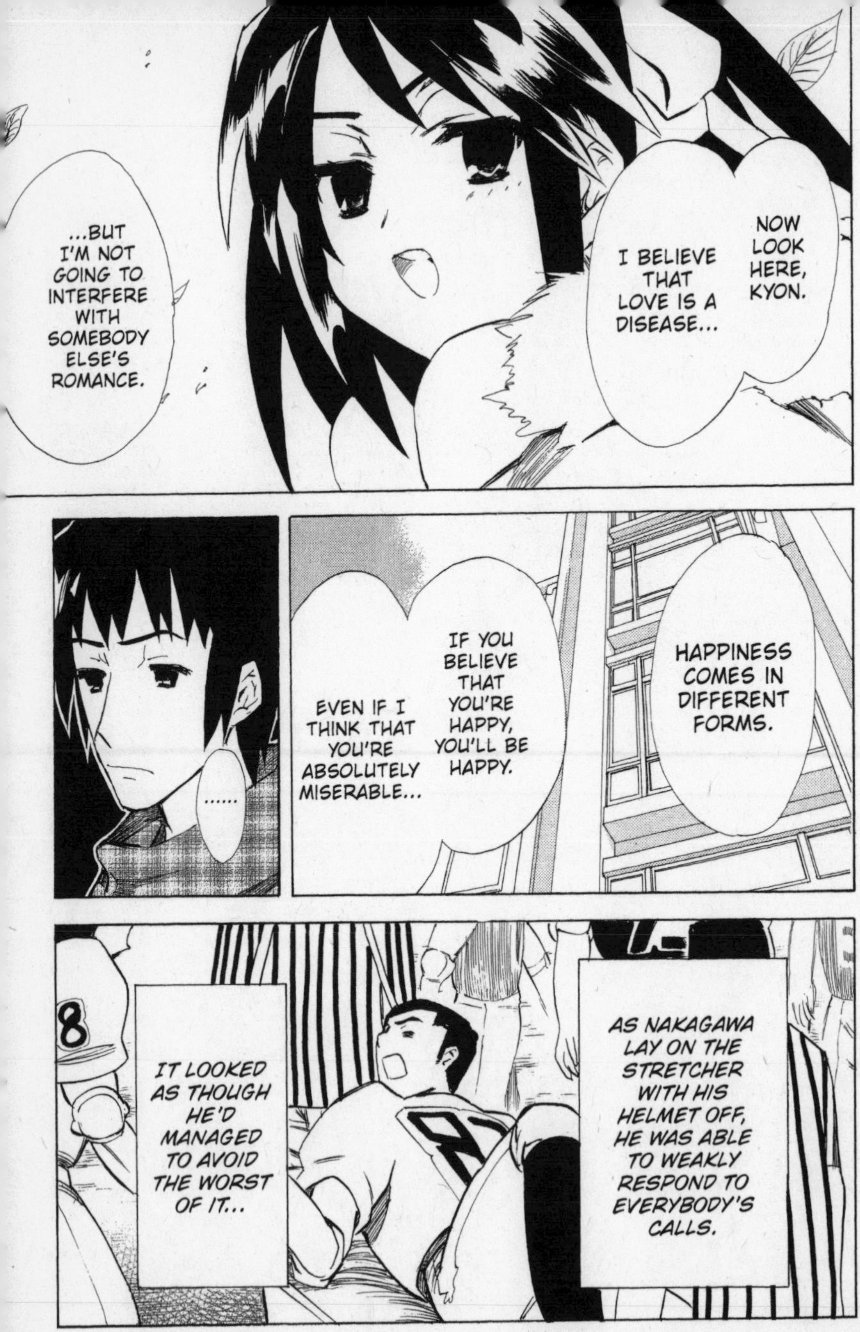
NOW LOOK HERE, KYON.
I BELIEVE THAT LOVE IS A DISEASE...
...BUT I'M NOT GOING TO INTERFERE WITH SOMEBODY ELSE'S ROMANCE.
HAPPINESS COMES IN DIFFERENT FORMS.
IF YOU BELIEVE THAT YOU'RE HAPPY, YOU'LL BE HAPPY.
EVEN IF I THINK THAT YOU'RE ABSOLUTELY MISERABLE...
......
AS NAKAGAWA LAY ON THE STRETCHER WITH HIS HELMET OFF, HE WAS ABLE TO WEAKLY RESPOND TO EVERYBODY'S CALLS.
IT LOOKED AS THOUGH HE'D MANAGED TO AVOID THE WORST OF IT...

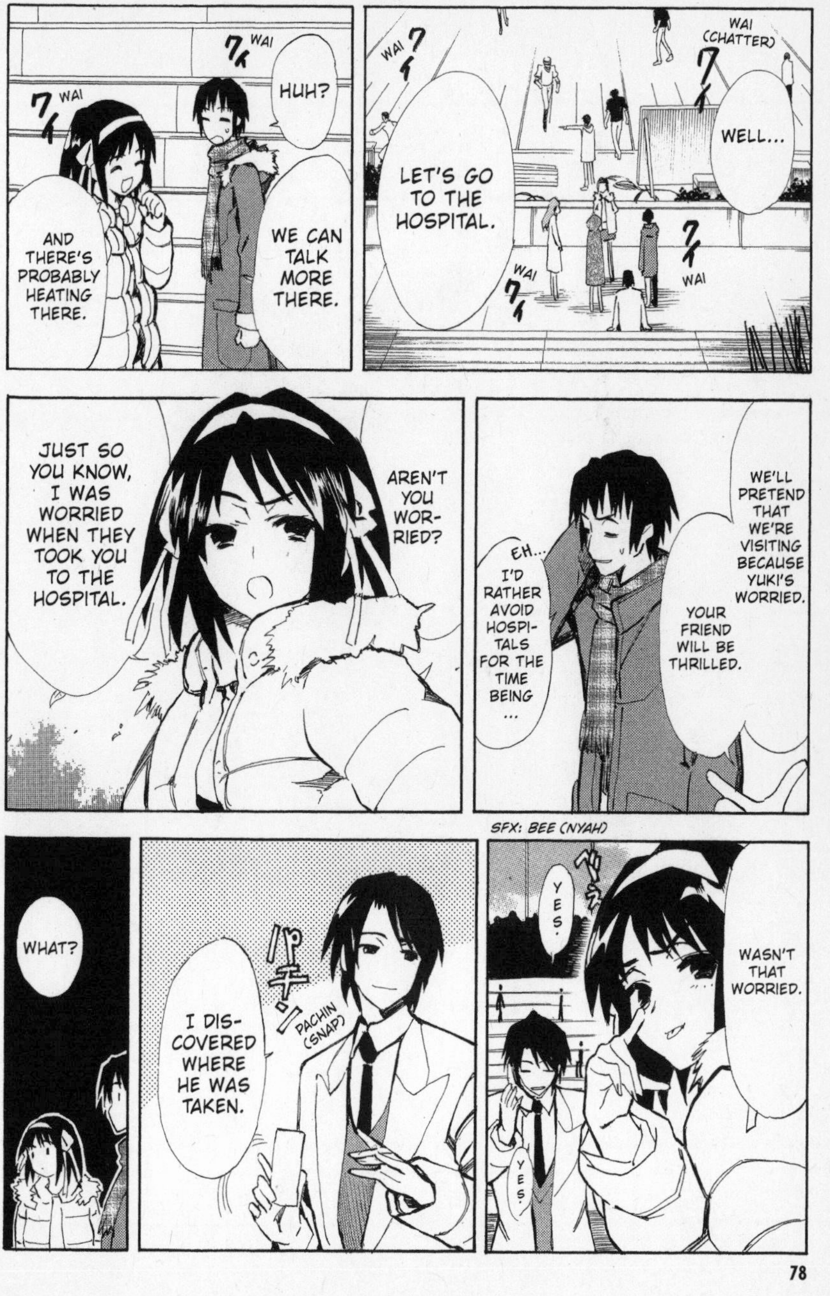
WAI (CHATTER)
WELL...
LET'S GO TO THE HOSPITAL.
WAI
WAI
WAI
WAI
HUH?
WAI
WE CAN TALK MORE THERE.
AND THERE'S PROBABLY HEATING THERE.
WE'LL PRETEND THAT WE'RE VISITING BECAUSE YUKI'S WORRIED.
YOUR FRIEND WILL BE THRILLED.
EH... I'D RATHER AVOID HOSPI-TALS FOR THE TIME BEING ...
AREN'T YOU WOR-RIED?
JUST SO YOU KNOW, I WAS WORRIED WHEN THEY TOOK YOU TO THE HOSPITAL.
SFX: BEE (NYAH)
WASN'T THAT WORRIED.
YES.
YES.
PACHIN (SNAP)
I DIS-COVERED WHERE HE WAS TAKEN.
WHAT?

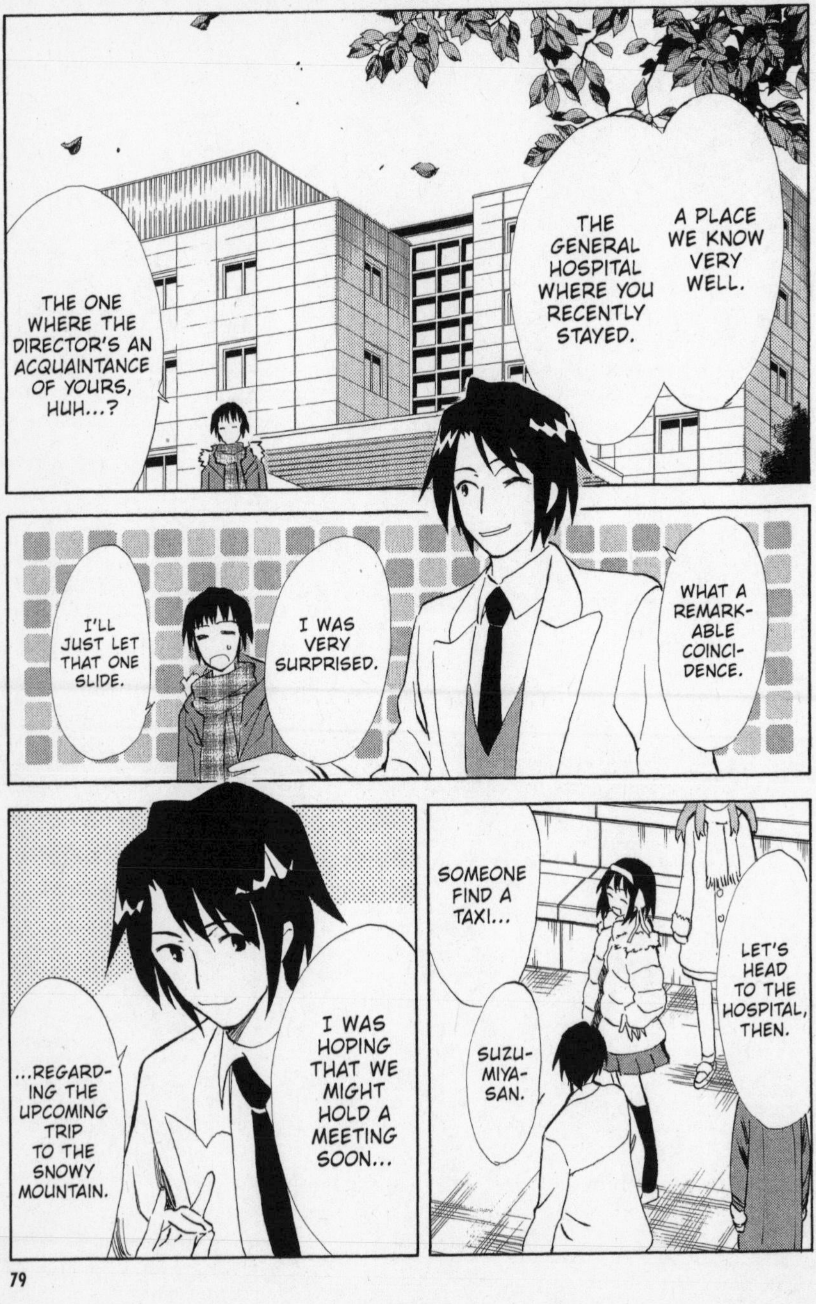
A PLACE WE KNOW VERY WELL.
THE GENERAL HOSPITAL WHERE YOU RECENTLY STAYED.
THE ONE WHERE THE DIRECTOR'S AN ACQUAINTANCE OF YOURS, HUH...?
WHAT A REMARKABLE COINCIDENCE.
I WAS VERY SURPRISED.
I'LL JUST LET THAT ONE SLIDE.
LET'S HEAD TO THE HOSPITAL, THEN.
SOMEONE FIND A TAXI...
SUZUMIYA-SAN.
I WAS HOPING THAT WE MIGHT HOLD A MEETING SOON...
...REGARDING THE UPCOMING TRIP TO THE SNOWY MOUNTAIN.

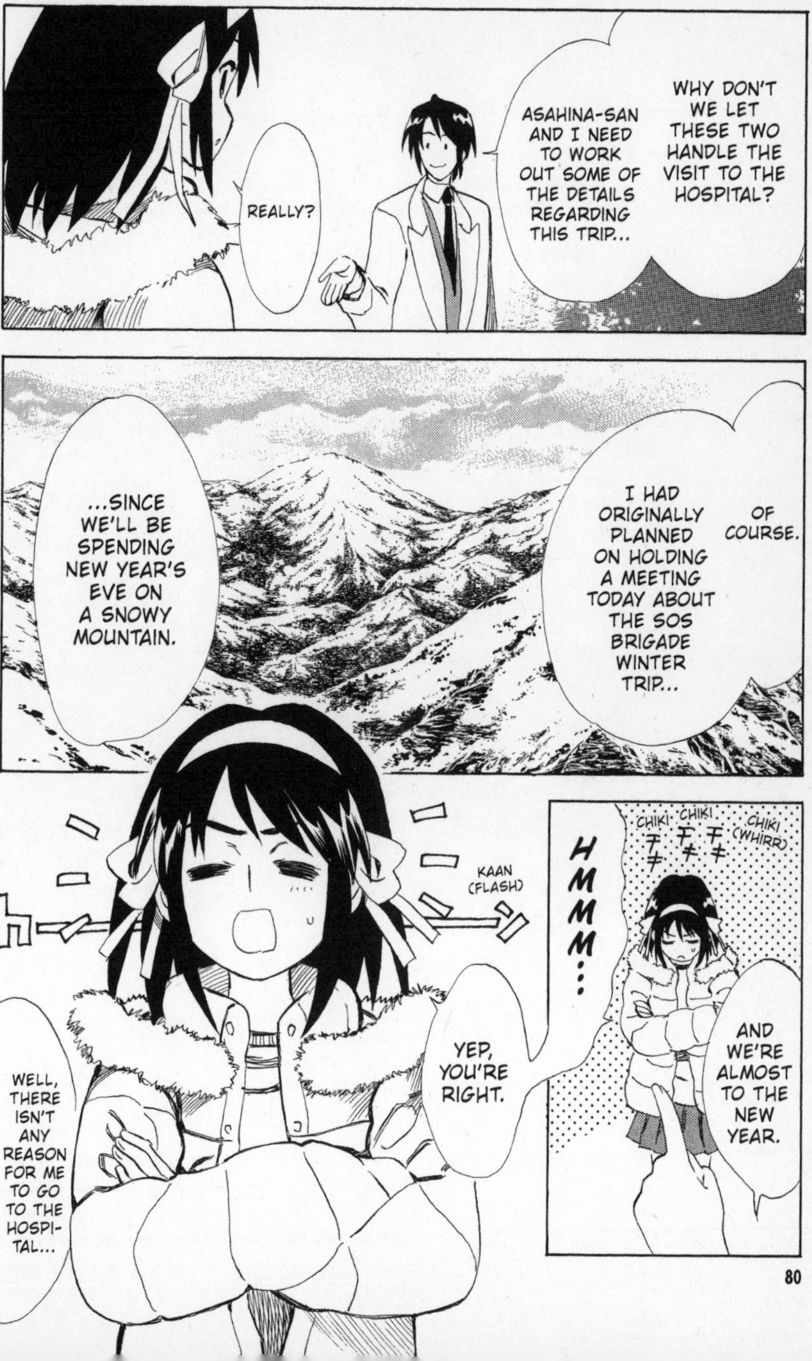
WHY DON'T WE LET THESE TWO HANDLE THE VISIT TO THE HOSPITAL?
ASAHINA-SAN AND I NEED TO WORK OUT SOME OF THE DETAILS REGARDING THIS TRIP...
REALLY?
OF COURSE.
I HAD ORIGINALLY PLANNED ON HOLDING A MEETING TODAY ABOUT THE SOS BRIGADE WINTER TRIP...
...SINCE WE'LL BE SPENDING NEW YEAR'S EVE ON A SNOWY MOUNTAIN.
CHIKI CHIKI CHIKI (WHIRR)
HMMM...
AND WE'RE ALMOST TO THE NEW YEAR.
KAAN (FLASH)
YEP, YOU'RE RIGHT.
WELL, THERE ISN'T ANY REASON FOR ME TO GO TO THE HOSPITAL...

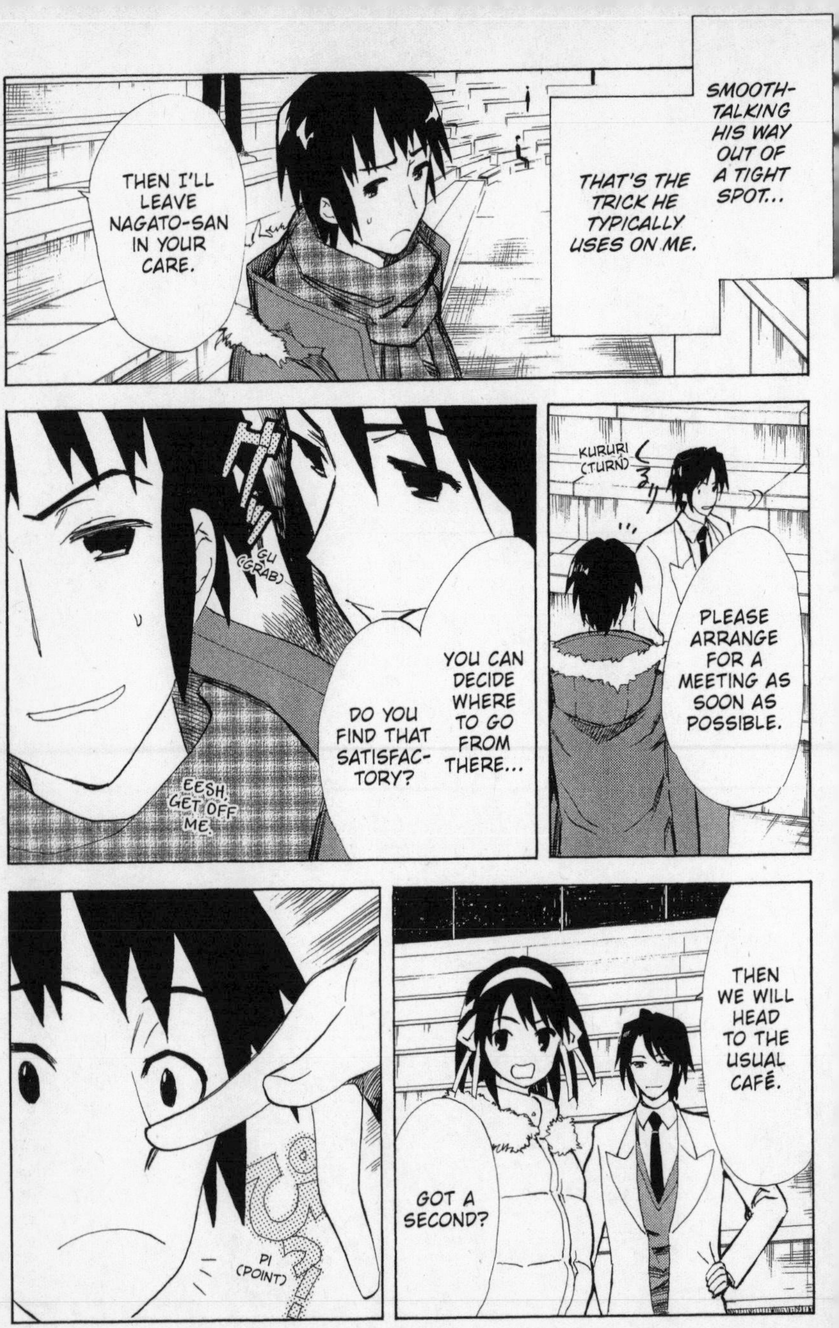
SMOOTH-TALKING HIS WAY OUT OF A TIGHT SPOT...
THAT'S THE TRICK HE TYPICALLY USES ON ME.
THEN I'LL LEAVE NAGATO-SAN IN YOUR CARE.
KURURI (TURN)
PLEASE ARRANGE FOR A MEETING AS SOON AS POSSIBLE.
GU (GRAB)
YOU CAN DECIDE WHERE TO GO FROM THERE...
DO YOU FIND THAT SATISFACTORY?
EESH, GET OFF ME.
THEN WE WILL HEAD TO THE USUAL CAFÉ.
GOT A SECOND?
PI (POINT)

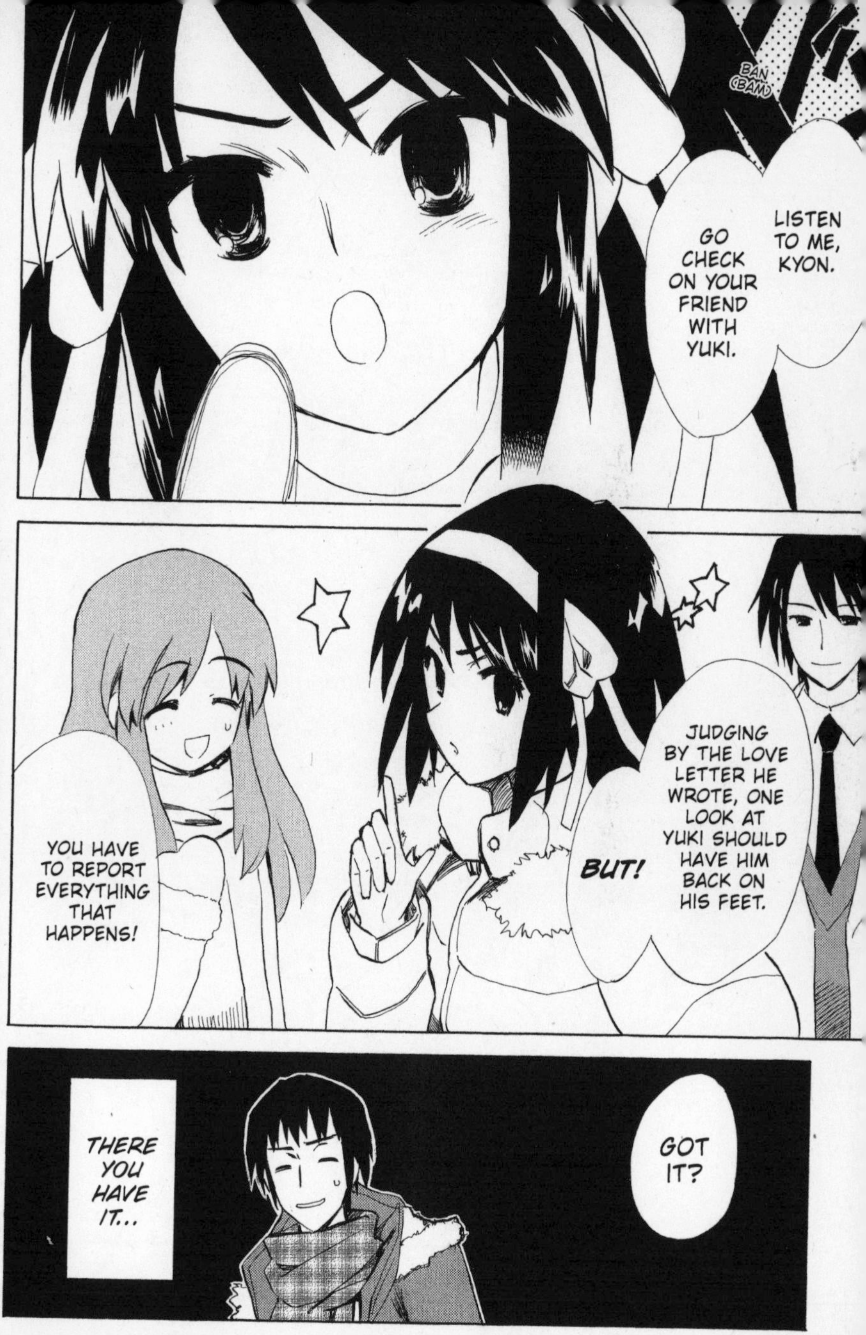
BAN (BAM)
LISTEN TO ME, KYON.
GO CHECK ON YOUR FRIEND WITH YUKI.
JUDGING BY THE LOVE LETTER HE WROTE, ONE LOOK AT YUKI SHOULD HAVE HIM BACK ON HIS FEET.
BUT!
YOU HAVE TO REPORT EVERYTHING THAT HAPPENS!
GOT IT?
THERE YOU HAVE IT...

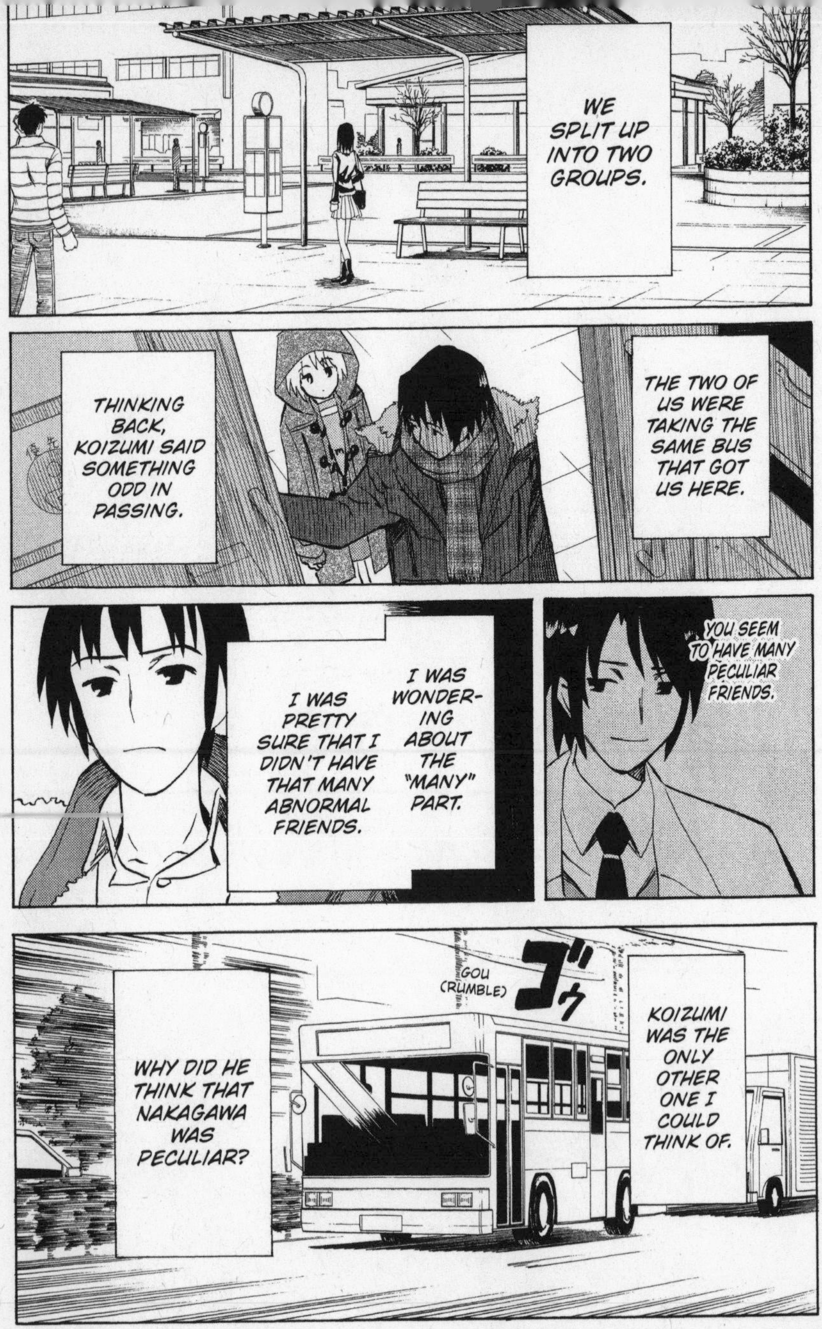
WE SPLIT UP INTO TWO GROUPS.
THE TWO OF US WERE TAKING THE SAME BUS THAT GOT US HERE.
THINKING BACK, KOIZUMI SAID SOMETHING ODD IN PASSING.
YOU SEEM TO HAVE MANY PECULIAR FRIENDS.
I WAS WONDERING ABOUT THE "MANY" PART.
I WAS PRETTY SURE THAT I DIDN'T HAVE THAT MANY ABNORMAL FRIENDS.
KOIZUMI WAS THE ONLY OTHER ONE I COULD THINK OF.
ゴウ
GOU (RUMBLE)
WHY DID HE THINK THAT NAKAGAWA WAS PECULIAR?

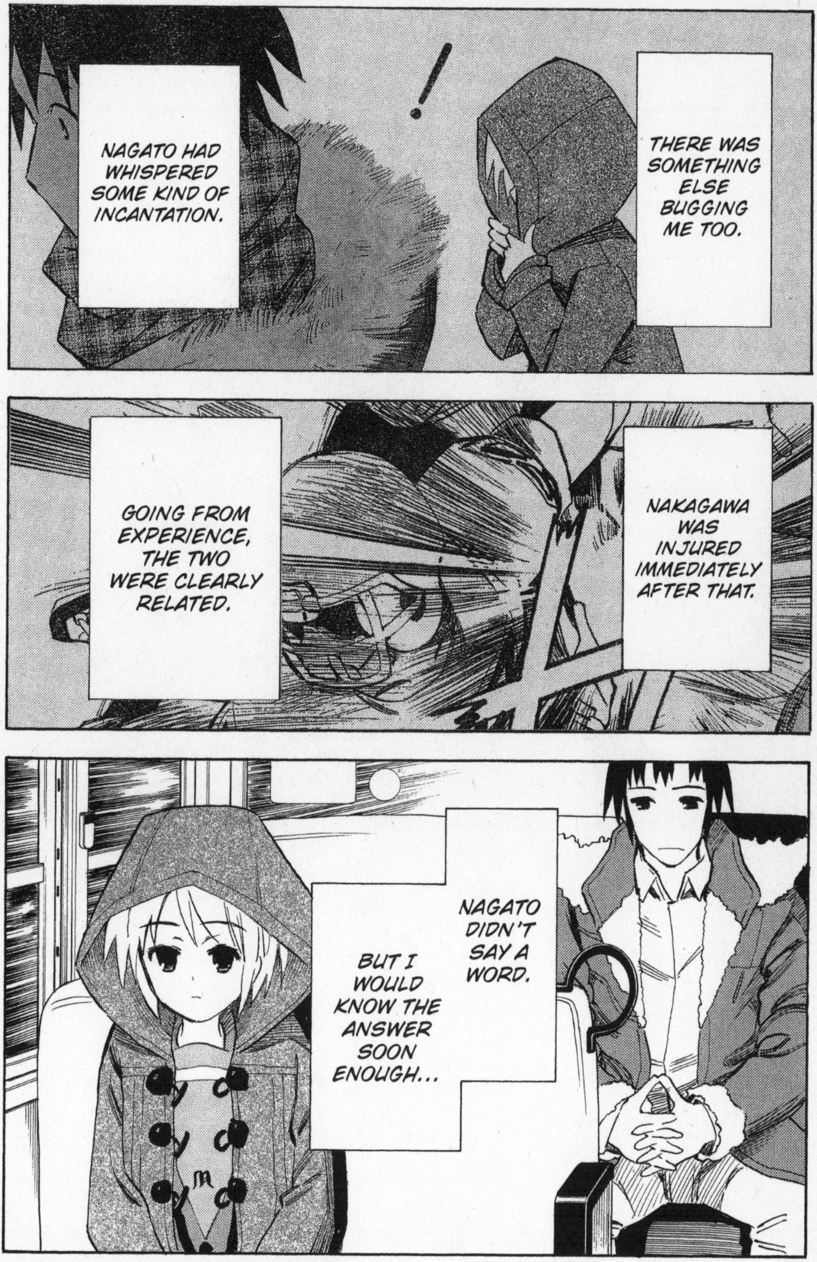
THERE WAS SOMETHING ELSE BUGGING ME TOO.
!
NAGATO HAD WHISPERED SOME KIND OF INCANTATION.
NAKAGAWA WAS INJURED IMMEDIATELY AFTER THAT.
GOING FROM EXPERIENCE, THE TWO WERE CLEARLY RELATED.
NAGATO DIDN'T SAY A WORD.
BUT I WOULD KNOW THE ANSWER SOON ENOUGH...

SIGN: ORTHOPEDICS DESK

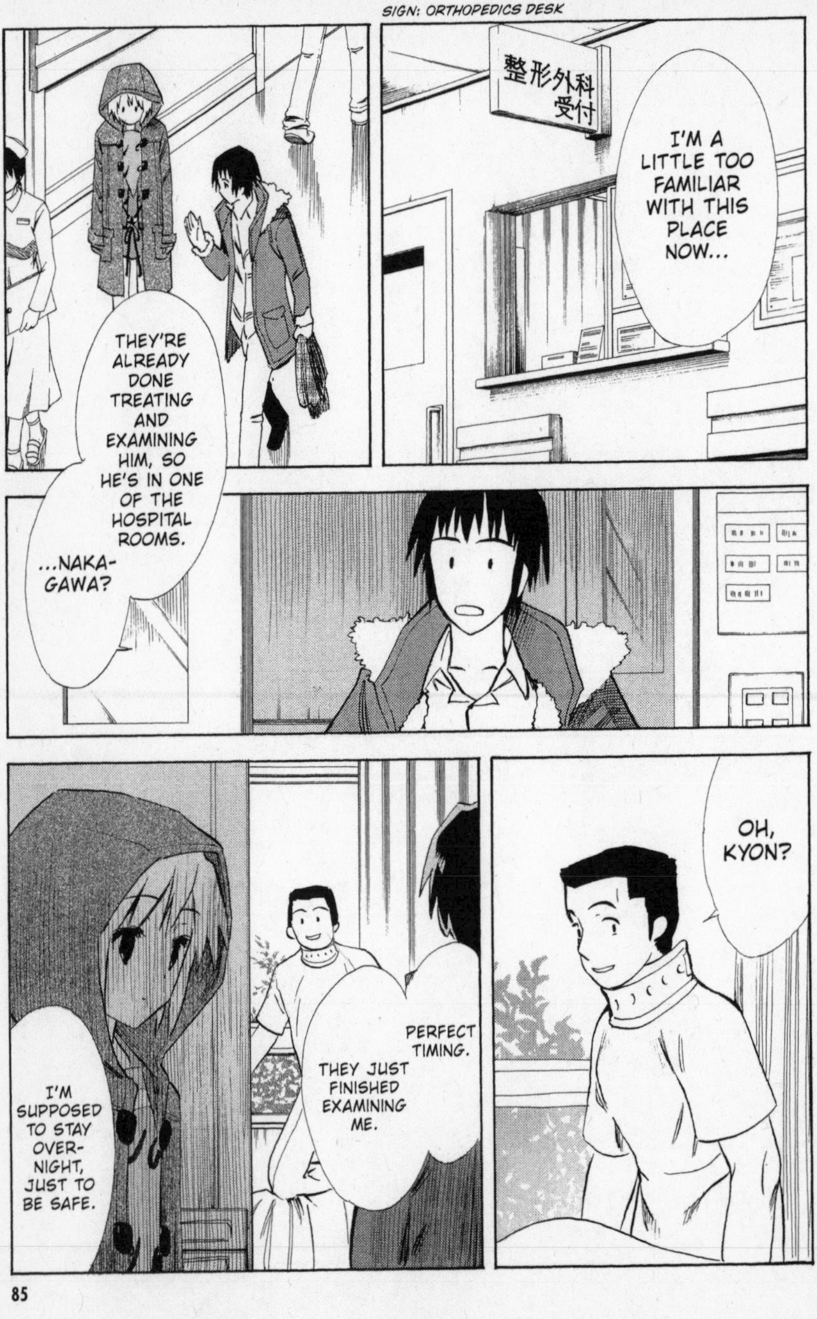

整形外科受付
I'M A LITTLE TOO FAMILIAR WITH THIS PLACE NOW...
THEY'RE ALREADY DONE TREATING AND EXAMINING HIM, SO HE'S IN ONE OF THE HOSPITAL ROOMS.
...NAKA-GAWA?
OH, KYON?
PERFECT TIMING.
THEY JUST FINISHED EXAMINING ME.
I'M SUPPOSED TO STAY OVER-NIGHT, JUST TO BE SAFE.

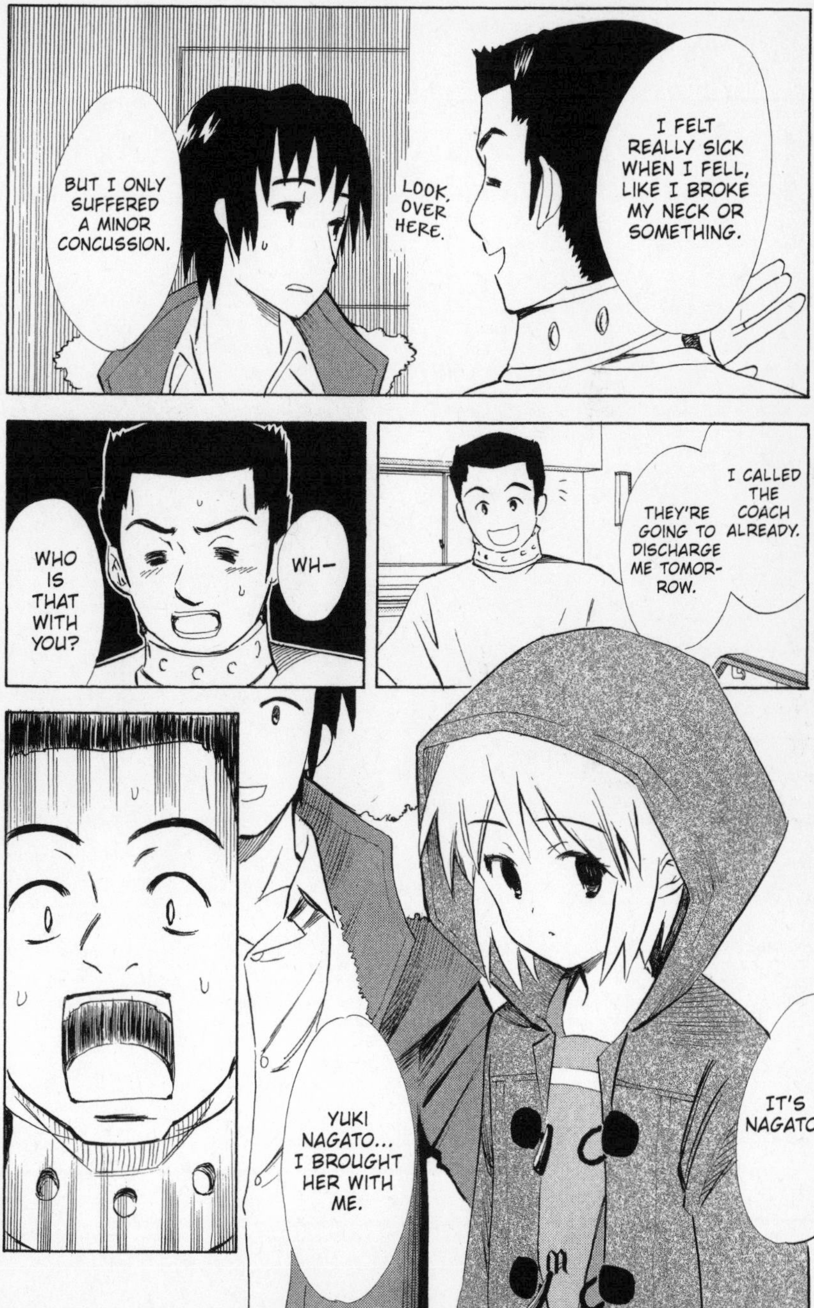

I FELT REALLY SICK WHEN I FELL, LIKE I BROKE MY NECK OR SOMETHING.
LOOK, OVER HERE.
BUT I ONLY SUFFERED A MINOR CONCUSSION.
I CALLED THE COACH ALREADY.
THEY'RE GOING TO DISCHARGE ME TOMORROW.
WH-
WHO IS THAT WITH YOU?
IT'S NAGATO.
YUKI NAGATO... I BROUGHT HER WITH ME.

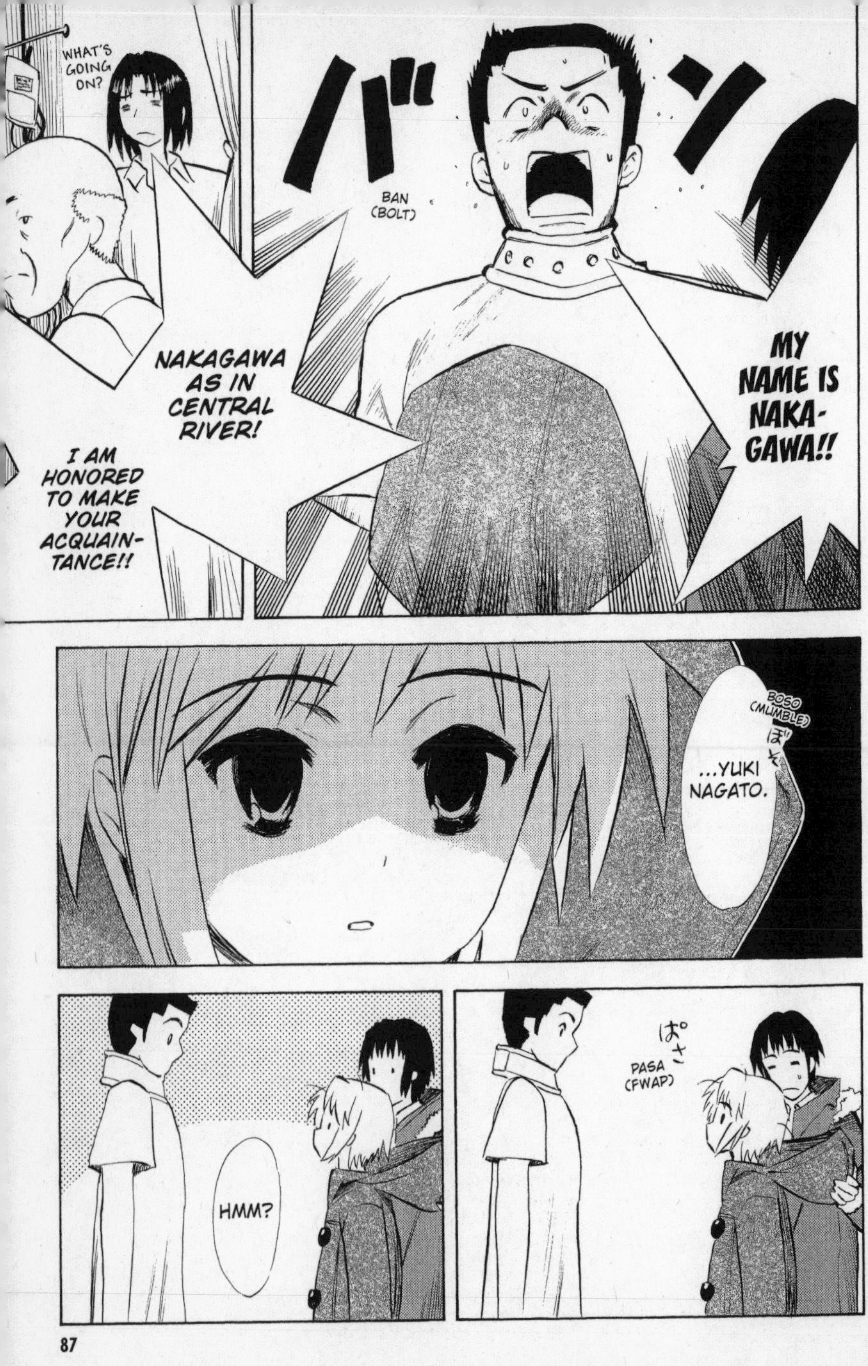
BAN (BOLT)
MY NAME IS NAKA-GAWA!!
NAKAGAWA AS IN CENTRAL RIVER!
I AM HONORED TO MAKE YOUR ACQUAIN-TANCE!!
WHAT'S GOING ON?
ぼそ
BOSO (MUMBLE)
...YUKI NAGATO.
ぱさ
PASA (FWAP)
HMM?

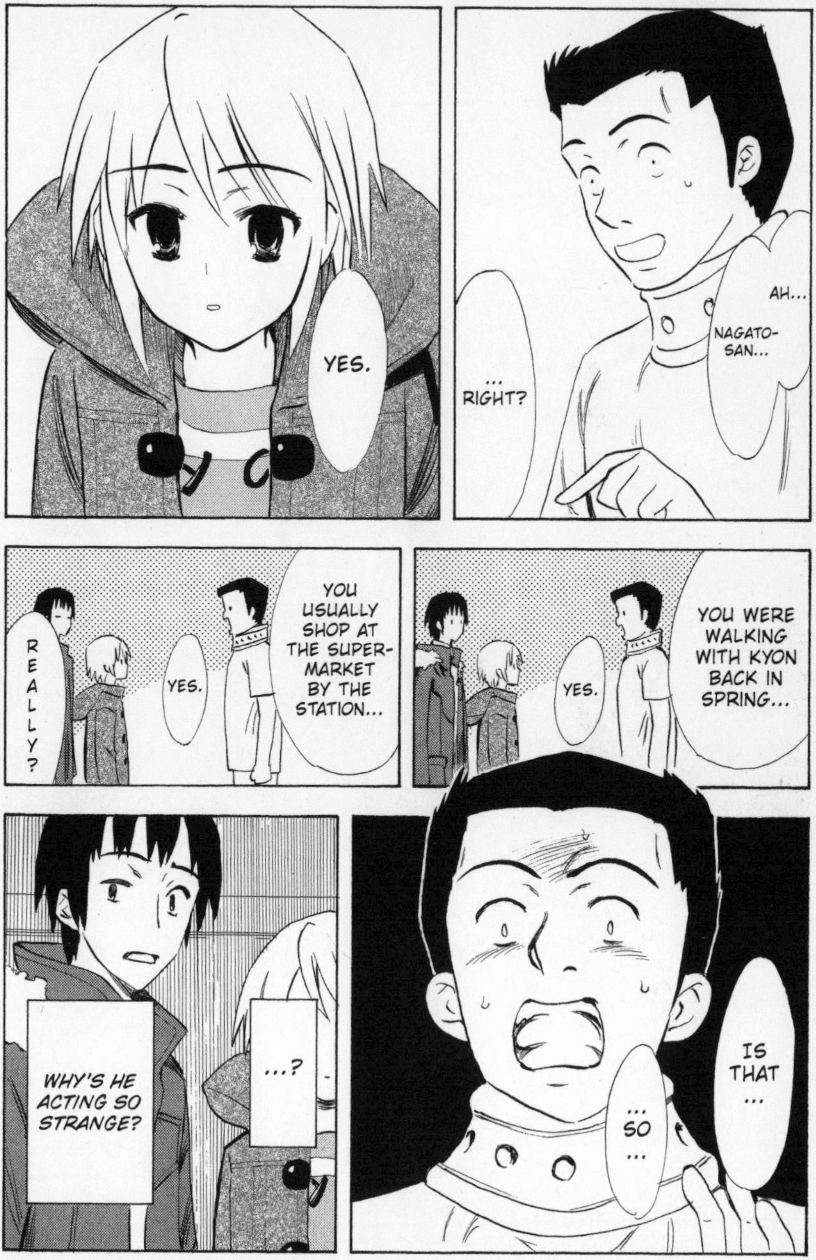
AH...
NAGATO-SAN...
... RIGHT?
YES.
YOU WERE WALKING WITH KYON BACK IN SPRING...
YES.
YOU USUALLY SHOP AT THE SUPER-MARKET BY THE STATION...
YES.
REALLY?
IS THAT ...
... SO ...
...?
WHY'S HE ACTING SO STRANGE?

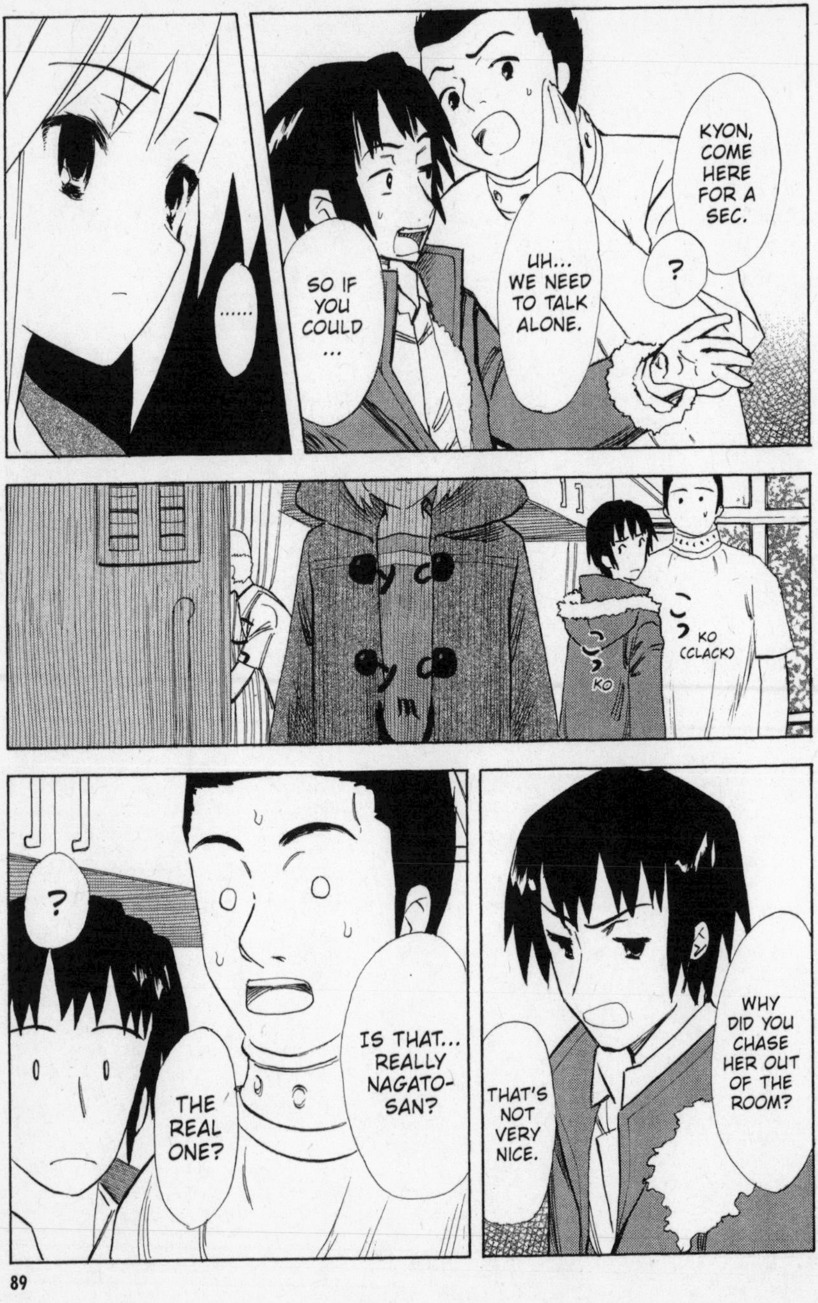
KYON, COME HERE FOR A SEC.
?
UH... WE NEED TO TALK ALONE.
SO IF YOU COULD ...
......
KO (CLACK)
KO
WHY DID YOU CHASE HER OUT OF THE ROOM?
THAT'S NOT VERY NICE.
IS THAT... REALLY NAGATO-SAN?
THE REAL ONE?
?

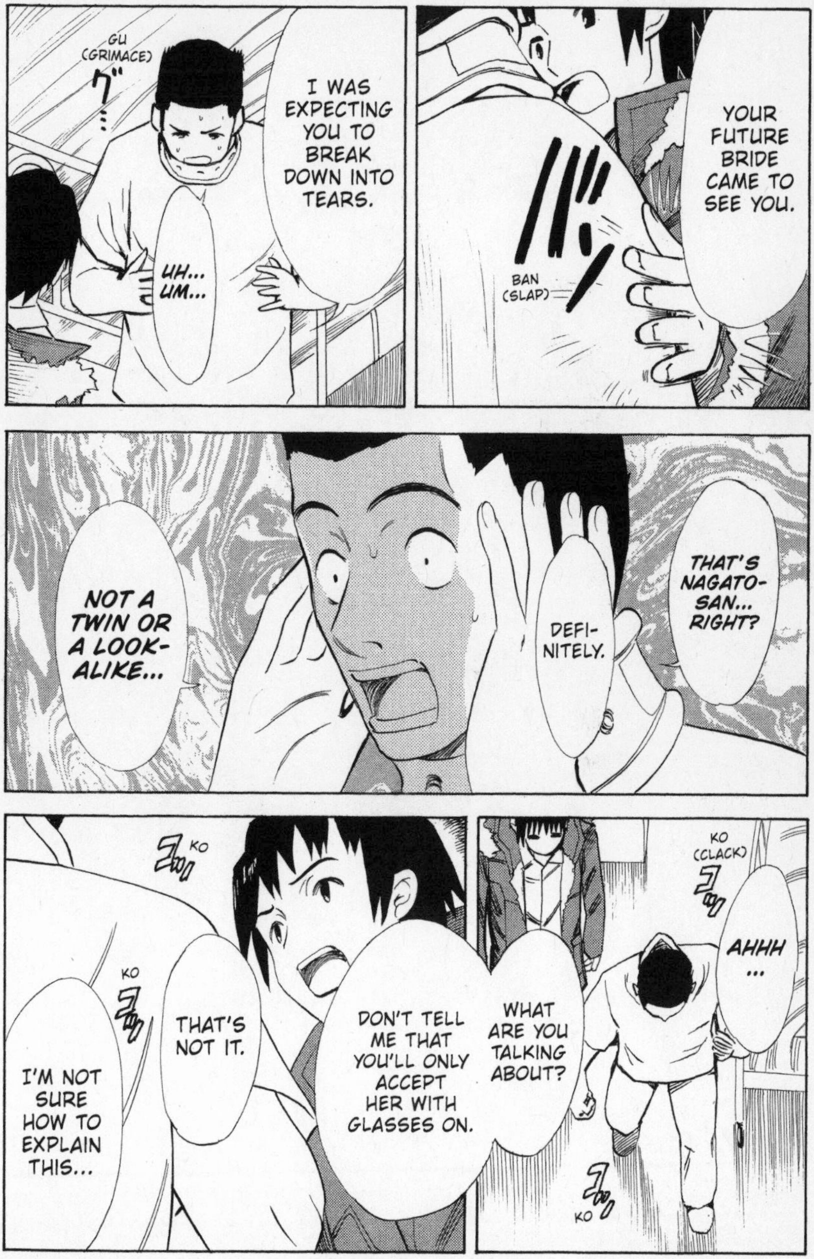
YOUR FUTURE BRIDE CAME TO SEE YOU.
BAN (SLAP)
I WAS EXPECTING YOU TO BREAK DOWN INTO TEARS.
GU (GRIMACE)
UH... UM...
THAT'S NAGATO-SAN... RIGHT?
DEFI-NITELY.
NOT A TWIN OR A LOOK-ALIKE...
KO (CLACK)
AHHH...
KO
WHAT ARE YOU TALKING ABOUT?
DON'T TELL ME THAT YOU'LL ONLY ACCEPT HER WITH GLASSES ON.
KO
THAT'S NOT IT.
KO
I'M NOT SURE HOW TO EXPLAIN THIS...

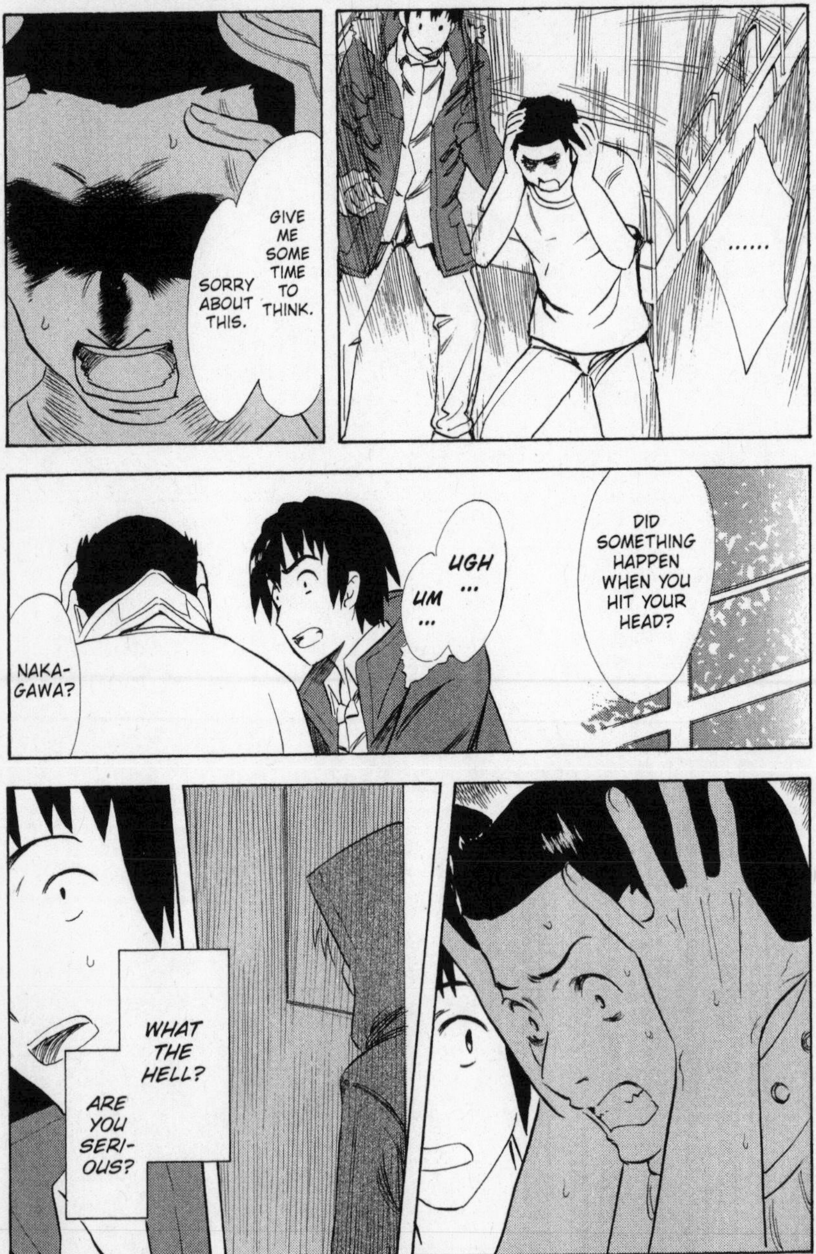
......
GIVE ME SOME TIME TO THINK.
SORRY ABOUT THIS.
DID SOMETHING HAPPEN WHEN YOU HIT YOUR HEAD?
UGH ...
UM ...
NAKA-GAWA?
WHAT THE HELL?
ARE YOU SERI-OUS?

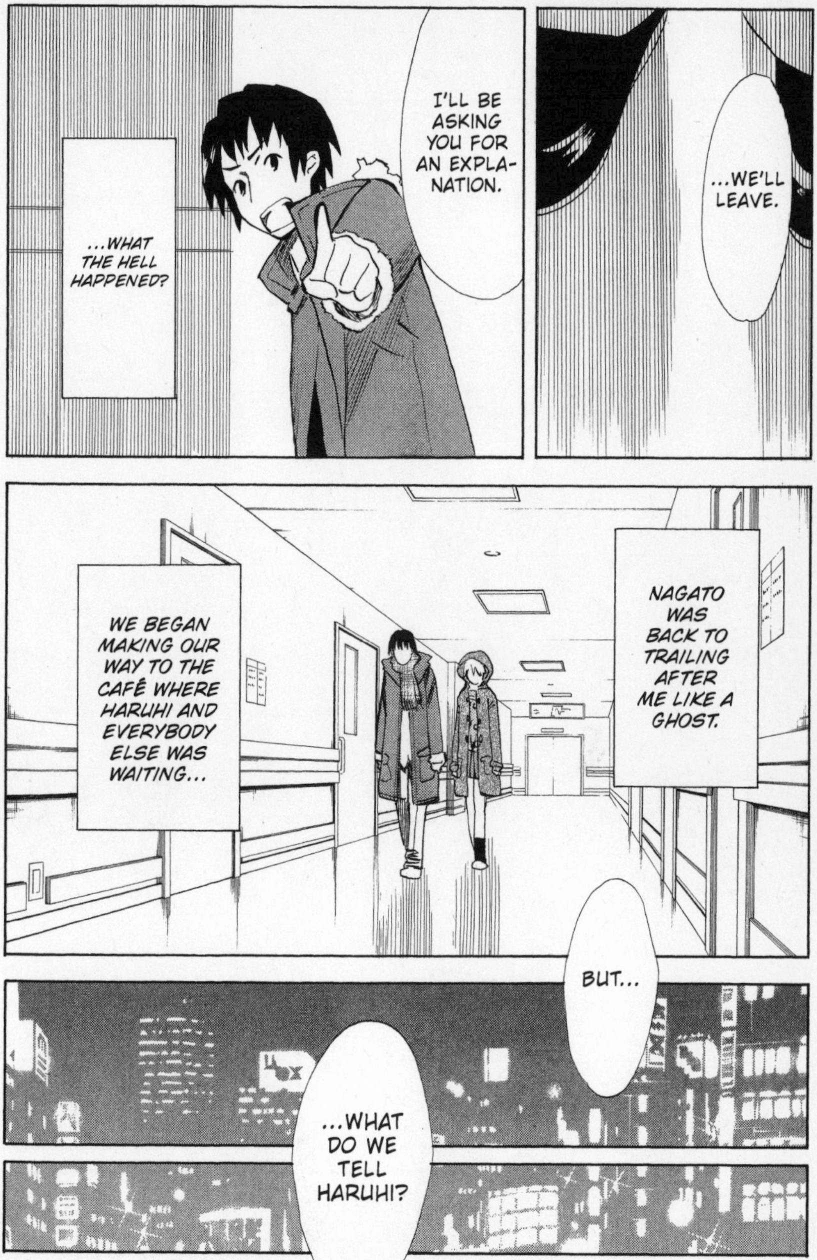
...WE'LL LEAVE.
I'LL BE ASKING YOU FOR AN EXPLANATION.
...WHAT THE HELL HAPPENED?
NAGATO WAS BACK TO TRAILING AFTER ME LIKE A GHOST.
WE BEGAN MAKING OUR WAY TO THE CAFÉ WHERE HARUHI AND EVERYBODY ELSE WAS WAITING...
BUT...
...WHAT DO WE TELL HARUHI?

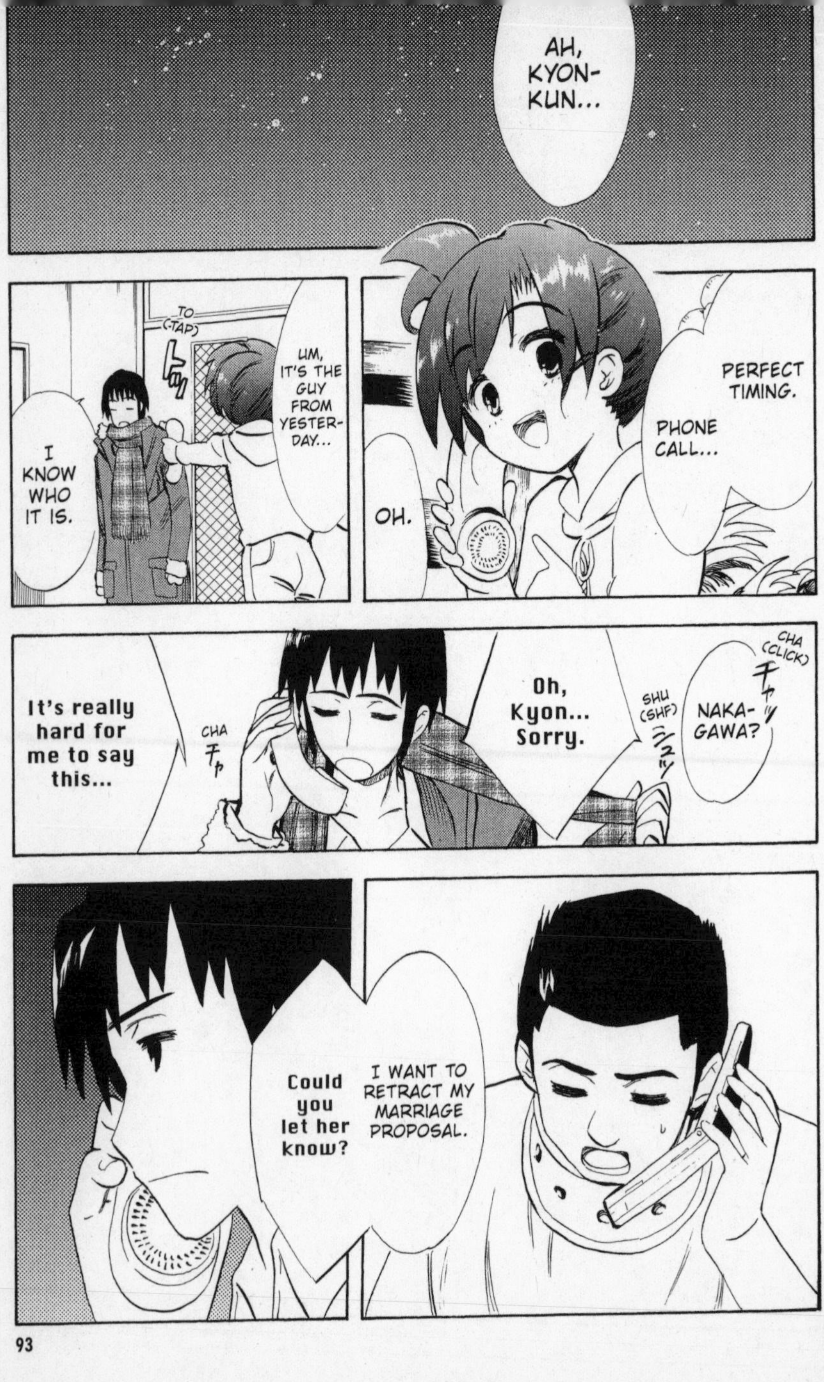
AH, KYON-KUN...
PERFECT TIMING.
PHONE CALL...
OH.
UM, IT'S THE GUY FROM YESTER-DAY...
TO (-TAP)
I KNOW WHO IT IS.
CHA (CLICK)
NAKA-GAWA?
SHU (SHF)
Oh, Kyon... Sorry.
CHA
It's really hard for me to say this...
I WANT TO RETRACT MY MARRIAGE PROPOSAL.
Could you let her know?

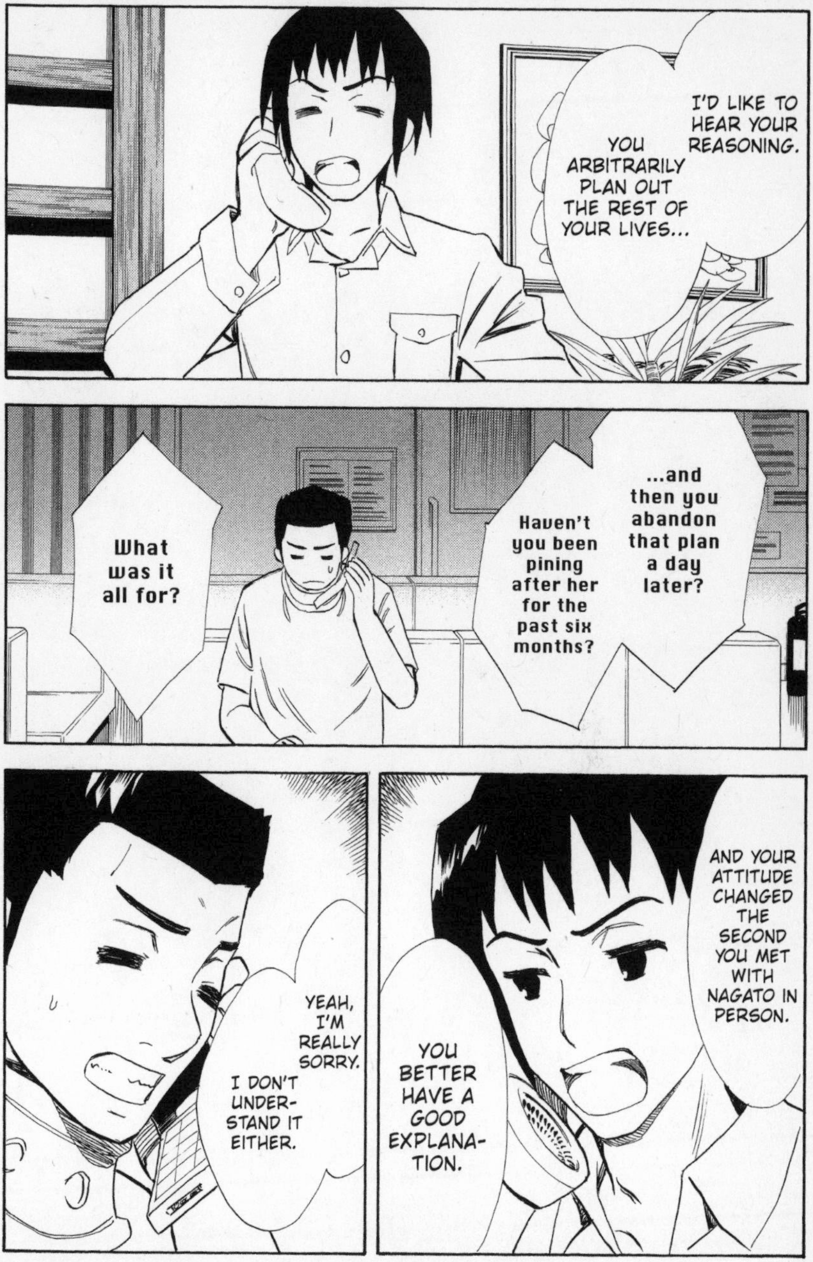
I'D LIKE TO HEAR YOUR REASONING.
YOU ARBITRARILY PLAN OUT THE REST OF YOUR LIVES...
...and then you abandon that plan a day later?
Haven't you been pining after her for the past six months?
What was it all for?
AND YOUR ATTITUDE CHANGED THE SECOND YOU MET WITH NAGATO IN PERSON.
YOU BETTER HAVE A GOOD EXPLANATION.
YEAH, I'M REALLY SORRY.
I DON'T UNDERSTAND IT EITHER.

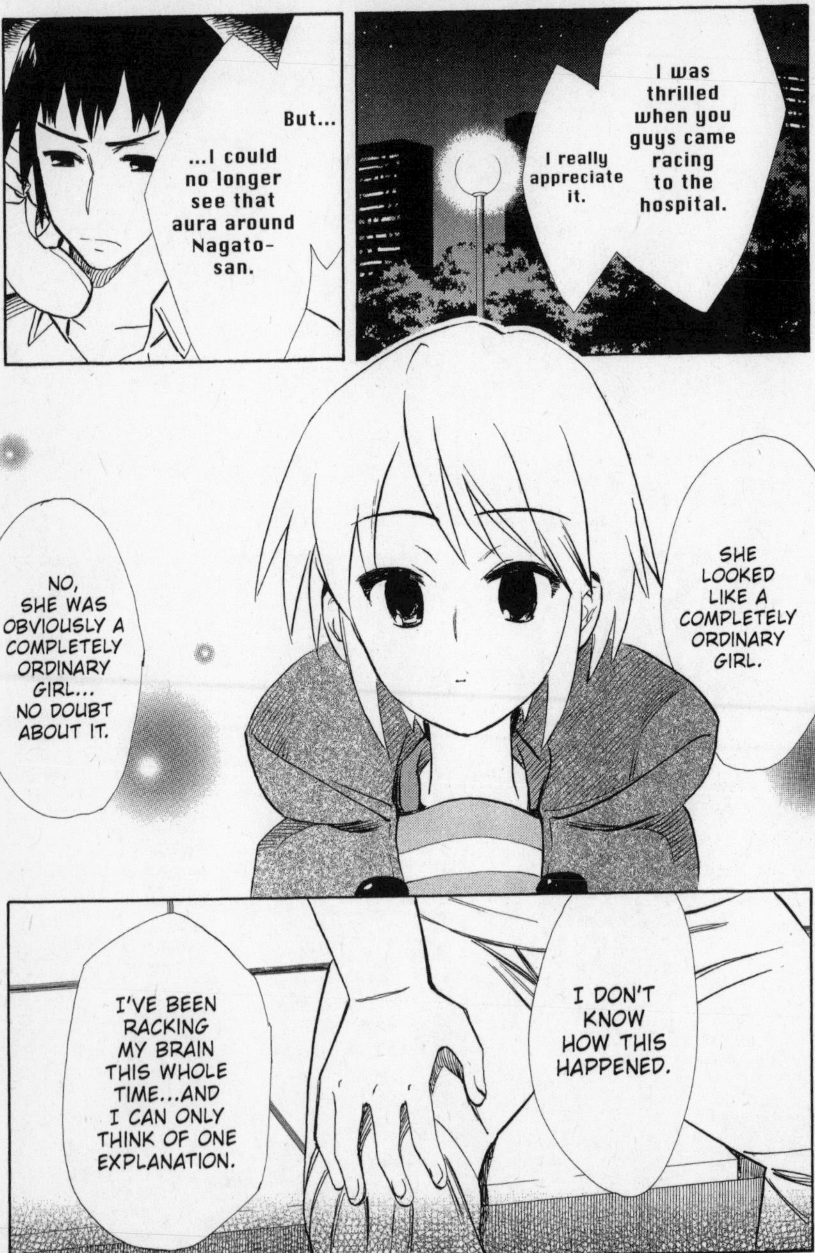
I was thrilled when you guys came racing to the hospital.
I really appreciate it.
But...
...I could no longer see that aura around Nagato-san.
SHE LOOKED LIKE A COMPLETELY ORDINARY GIRL.
NO, SHE WAS OBVIOUSLY A COMPLETELY ORDINARY GIRL... NO DOUBT ABOUT IT.
I DON'T KNOW HOW THIS HAPPENED.
I'VE BEEN RACKING MY BRAIN THIS WHOLE TIME...AND I CAN ONLY THINK OF ONE EXPLANATION.

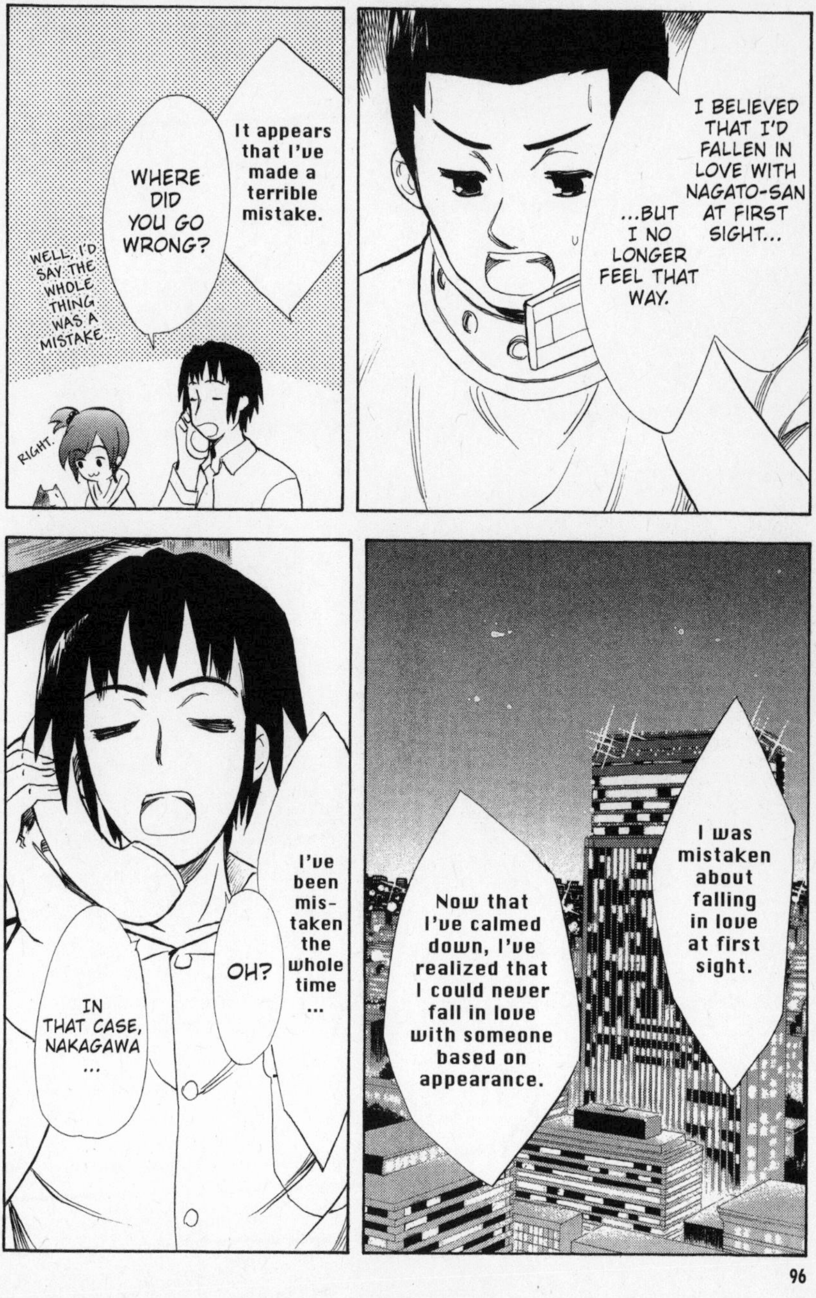
I BELIEVED THAT I'D FALLEN IN LOVE WITH NAGATO-SAN AT FIRST SIGHT...
...BUT I NO LONGER FEEL THAT WAY.
It appears that I've made a terrible mistake.
WHERE DID YOU GO WRONG?
WELL, I'D SAY THE WHOLE THING WAS A MISTAKE.
RIGHT.
I was mistaken about falling in love at first sight.
Now that I've calmed down, I've realized that I could never fall in love with someone based on appearance.
I've been mis-taken the whole time...
OH?
IN THAT CASE, NAKAGAWA...

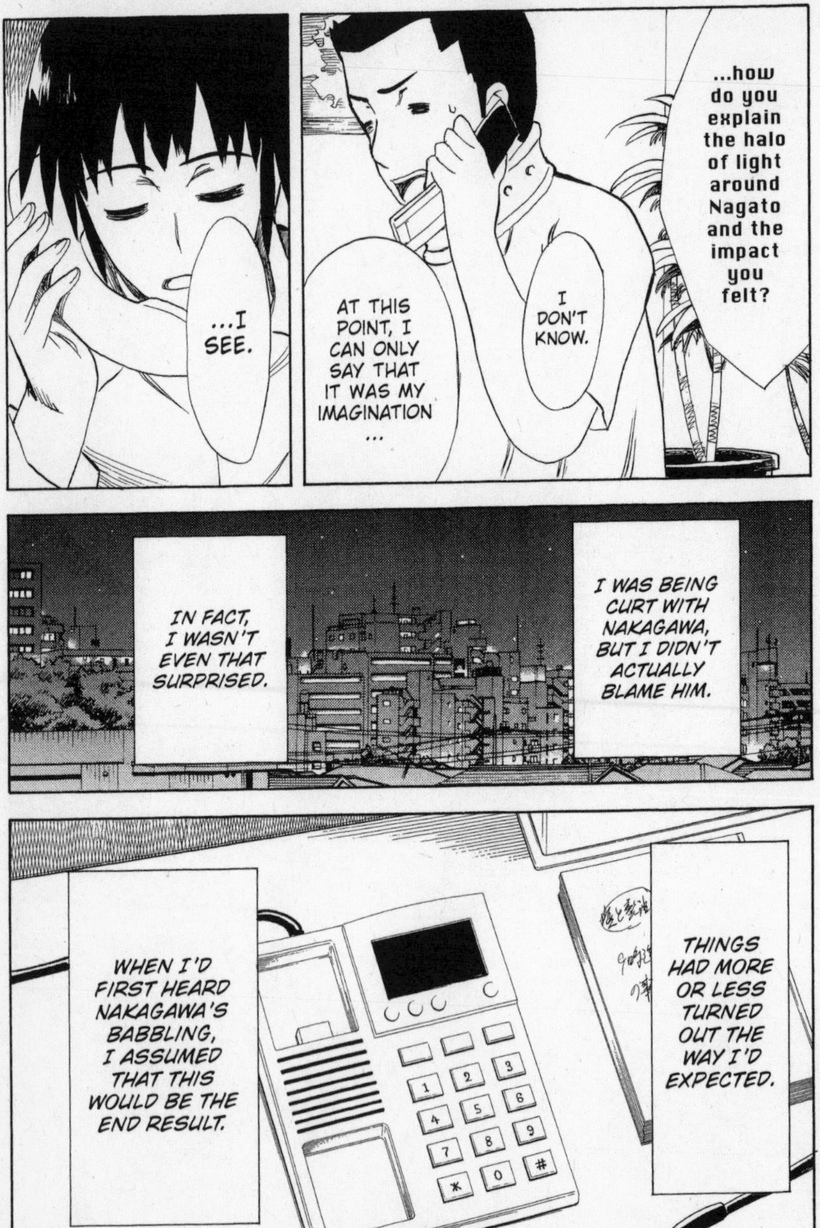
...how do you explain the halo of light around Nagato and the impact you felt?
I DON'T KNOW.
AT THIS POINT, I CAN ONLY SAY THAT IT WAS MY IMAGINATION ...
...I SEE.
I WAS BEING CURT WITH NAKAGAWA, BUT I DIDN'T ACTUALLY BLAME HIM.
IN FACT, I WASN'T EVEN THAT SURPRISED.
THINGS HAD MORE OR LESS TURNED OUT THE WAY I'D EXPECTED.
WHEN I'D FIRST HEARD NAKAGAWA'S BABBLING, I ASSUMED THAT THIS WOULD BE THE END RESULT.

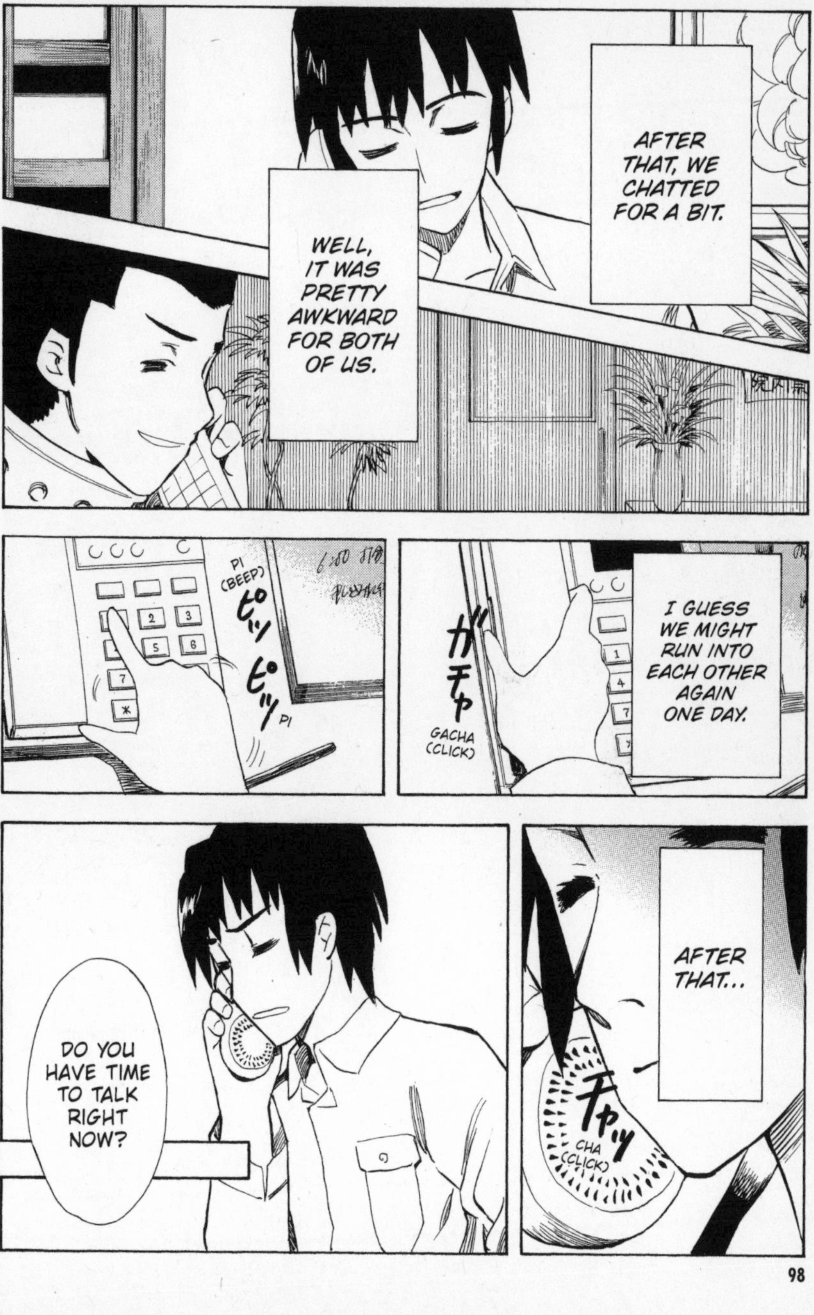
AFTER THAT, WE CHATTED FOR A BIT.
WELL, IT WAS PRETTY AWKWARD FOR BOTH OF US.
I GUESS WE MIGHT RUN INTO EACH OTHER AGAIN ONE DAY.
ガチャ
GACHA (CLICK)
PI (BEEP)
ピッ
ピッ
PI
AFTER THAT...
チャッ
CHA (CLICK)
DO YOU HAVE TIME TO TALK RIGHT NOW?

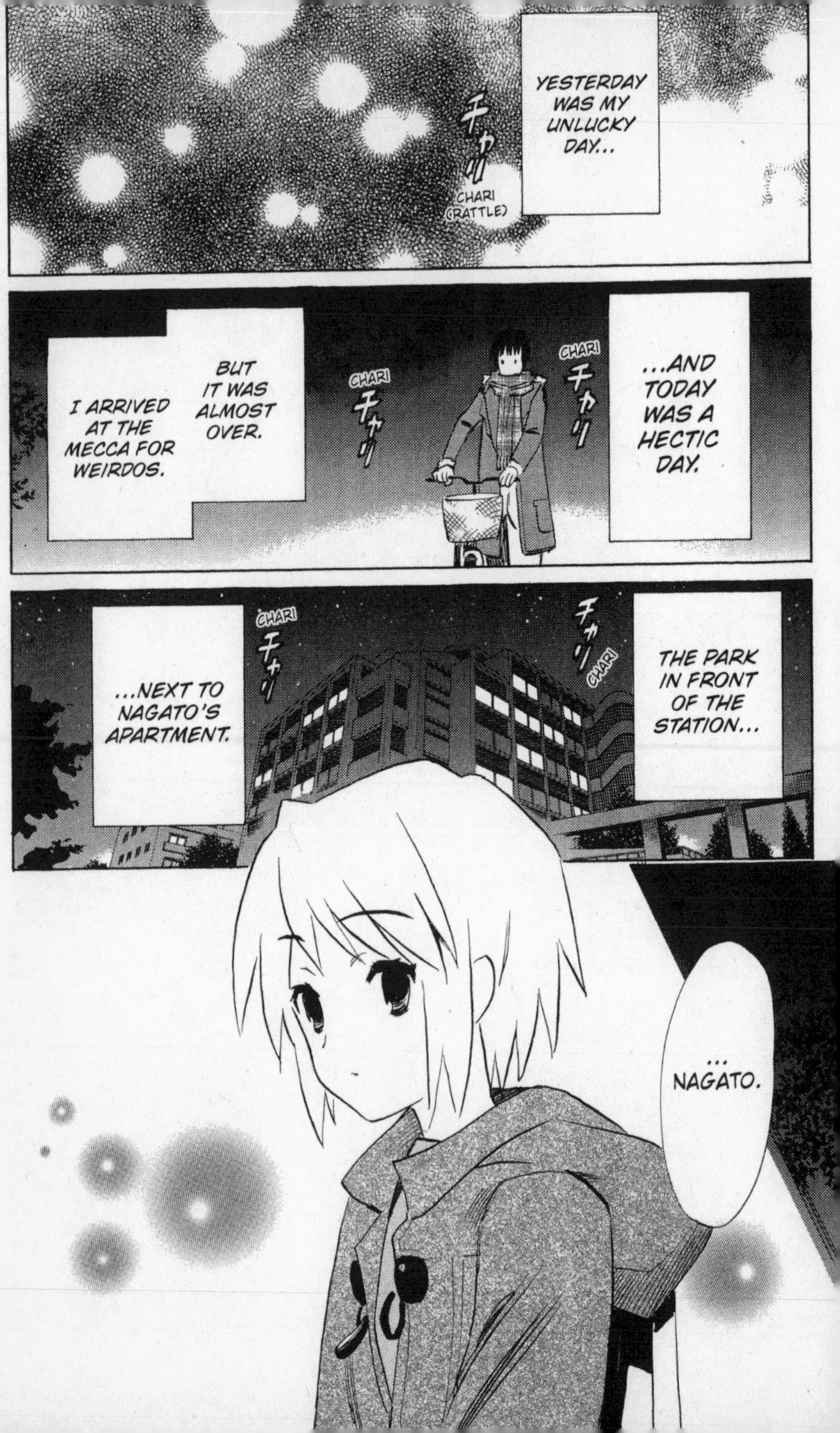
YESTERDAY WAS MY UNLUCKY DAY...
チャリ
CHARI (RATTLE)
...AND TODAY WAS A HECTIC DAY.
CHARI
チャリ
CHARI
チャリ
BUT IT WAS ALMOST OVER.
I ARRIVED AT THE MECCA FOR WEIRDOS.
THE PARK IN FRONT OF THE STATION...
チャリ
CHARI
CHARI
チャリ
...NEXT TO NAGATO'S APARTMENT.
... NAGATO.

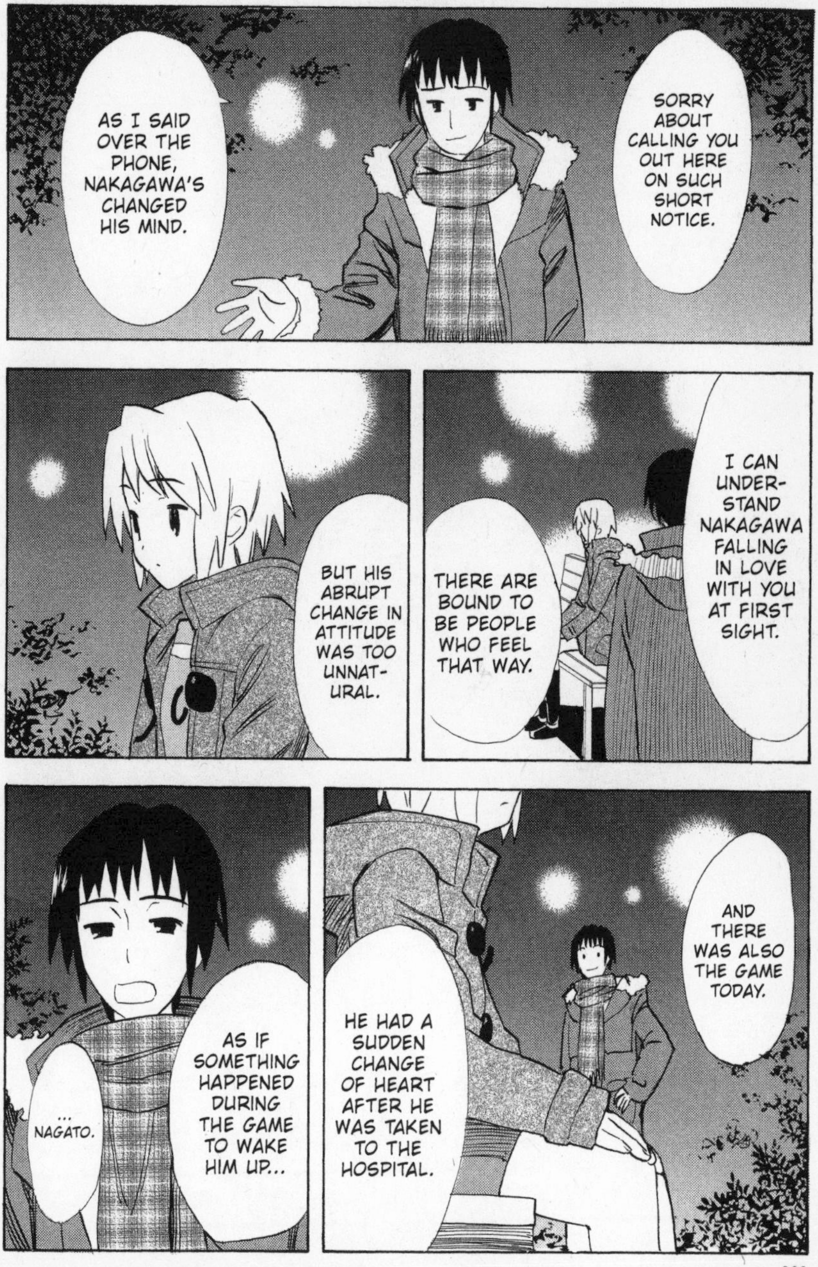
SORRY ABOUT CALLING YOU OUT HERE ON SUCH SHORT NOTICE.
AS I SAID OVER THE PHONE, NAKAGAWA'S CHANGED HIS MIND.
I CAN UNDER-STAND NAKAGAWA FALLING IN LOVE WITH YOU AT FIRST SIGHT.
THERE ARE BOUND TO BE PEOPLE WHO FEEL THAT WAY.
BUT HIS ABRUPT CHANGE IN ATTITUDE WAS TOO UNNAT-URAL.
AND THERE WAS ALSO THE GAME TODAY.
HE HAD A SUDDEN CHANGE OF HEART AFTER HE WAS TAKEN TO THE HOSPITAL.
AS IF SOMETHING HAPPENED DURING THE GAME TO WAKE HIM UP...
... NAGATO.

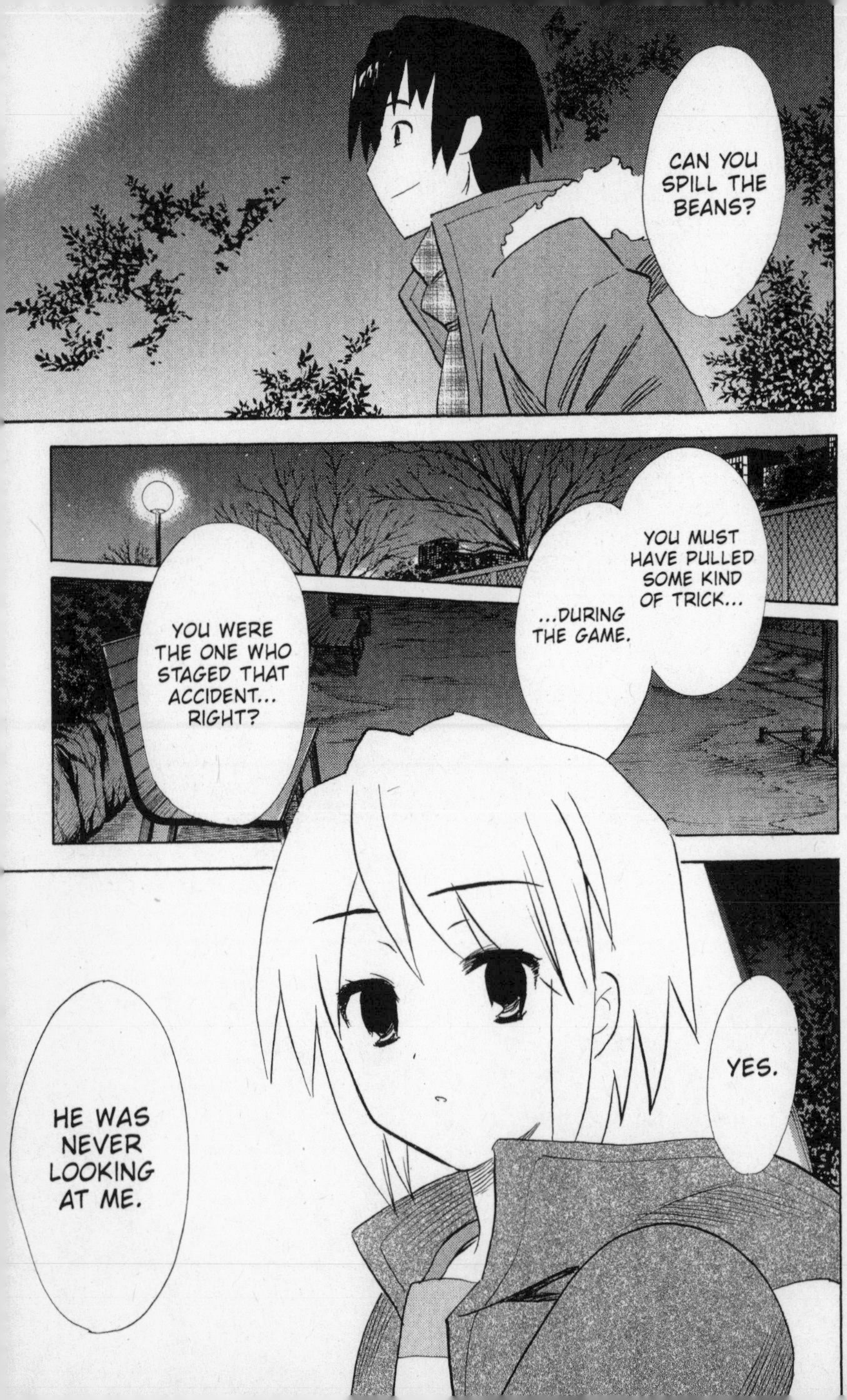
CAN YOU SPILL THE BEANS?
YOU MUST HAVE PULLED SOME KIND OF TRICK...
...DURING THE GAME.
YOU WERE THE ONE WHO STAGED THAT ACCIDENT... RIGHT?
YES.
HE WAS NEVER LOOKING AT ME.

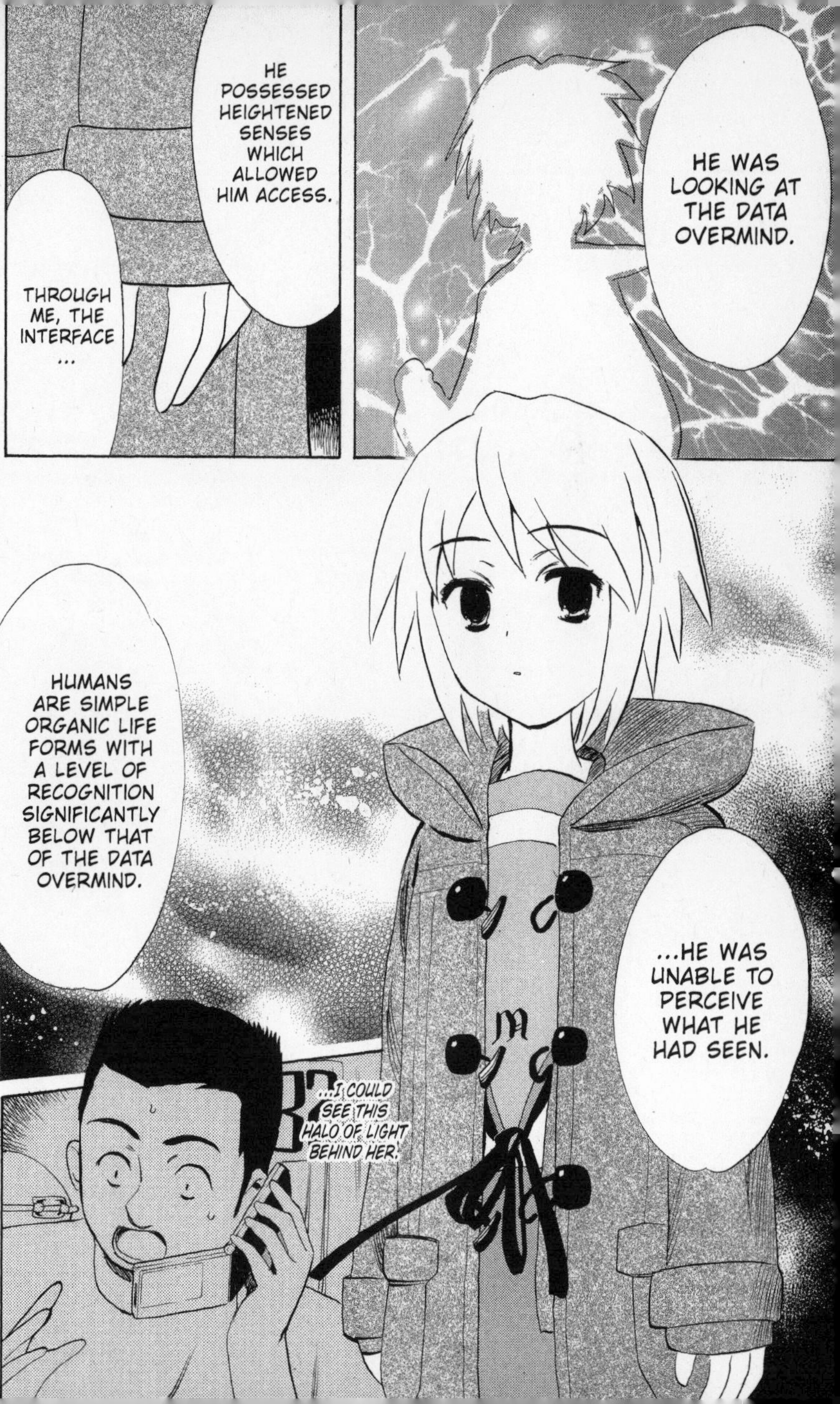
HE WAS LOOKING AT THE DATA OVERMIND.
HE POSSESSED HEIGHTENED SENSES WHICH ALLOWED HIM ACCESS.
THROUGH ME, THE INTERFACE ...
HUMANS ARE SIMPLE ORGANIC LIFE FORMS WITH A LEVEL OF RECOGNITION SIGNIFICANTLY BELOW THAT OF THE DATA OVERMIND.
...HE WAS UNABLE TO PERCEIVE WHAT HE HAD SEEN.
...I COULD SEE THIS HALO OF LIGHT BEHIND HER.

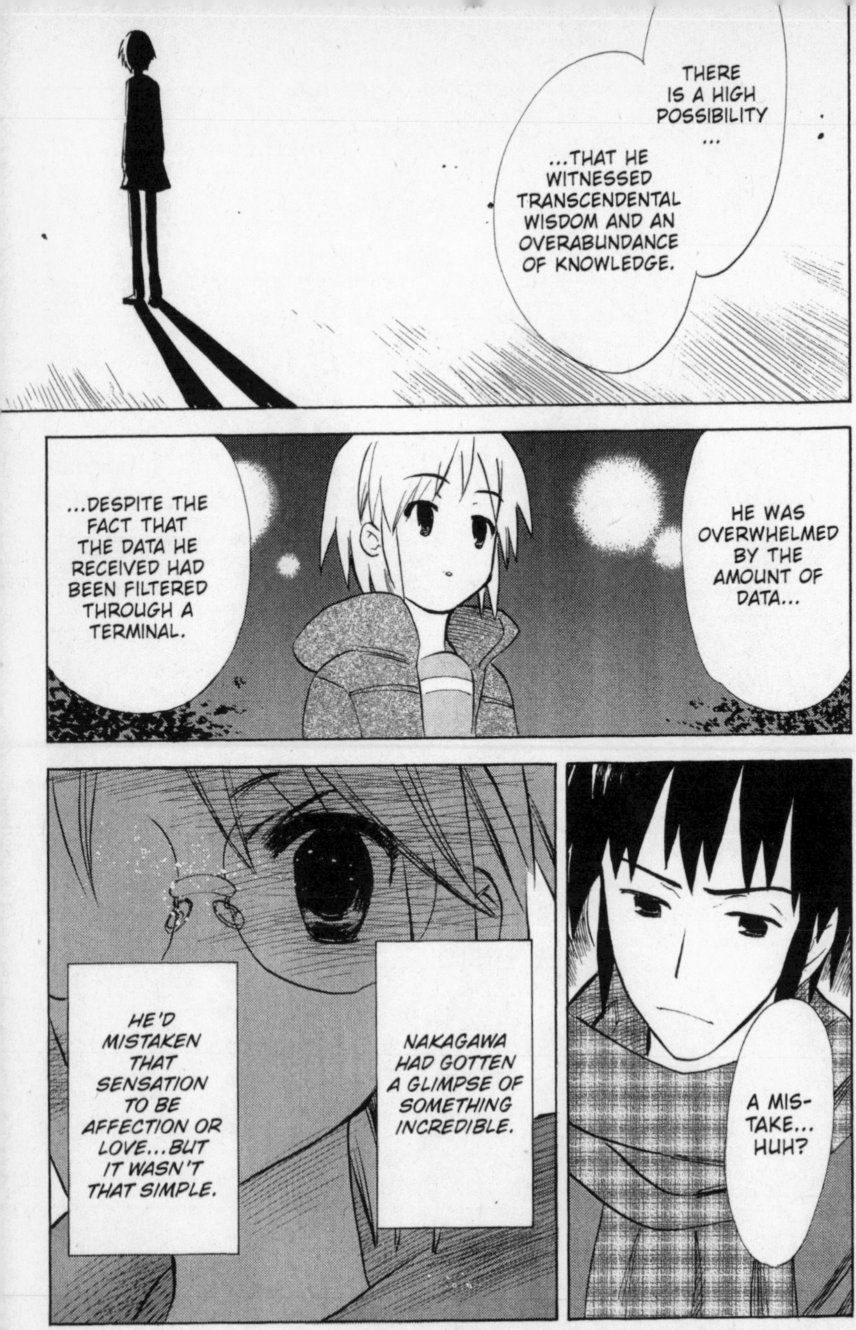
THERE IS A HIGH POSSIBILITY ...
...THAT HE WITNESSED TRANSCENDENTAL WISDOM AND AN OVERABUNDANCE OF KNOWLEDGE.
HE WAS OVERWHELMED BY THE AMOUNT OF DATA...
...DESPITE THE FACT THAT THE DATA HE RECEIVED HAD BEEN FILTERED THROUGH A TERMINAL.
A MIS-TAKE... HUH?
NAKAGAWA HAD GOTTEN A GLIMPSE OF SOMETHING INCREDIBLE.
HE'D MISTAKEN THAT SENSATION TO BE AFFECTION OR LOVE...BUT IT WASN'T THAT SIMPLE.

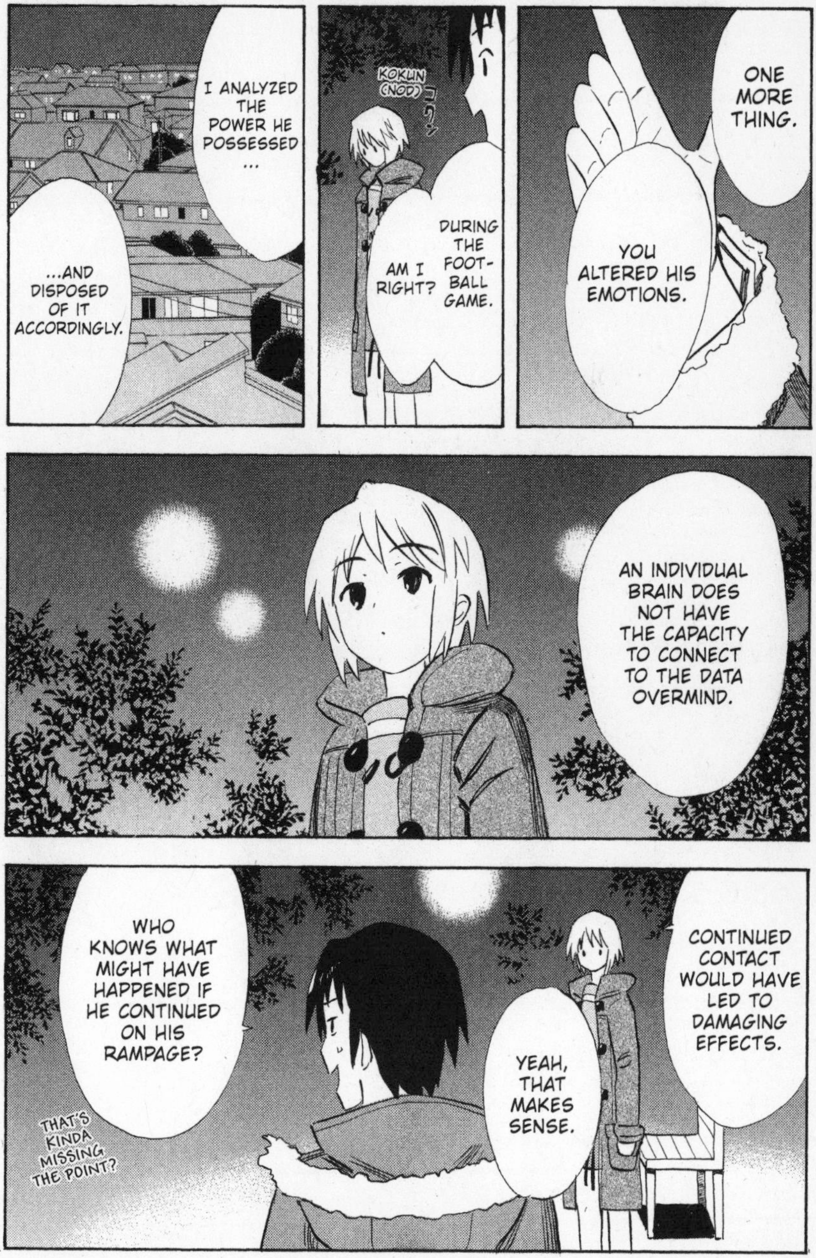
ONE MORE THING.
YOU ALTERED HIS EMOTIONS.
KOKUN (NOD)
DURING THE FOOT-BALL GAME.
AM I RIGHT?
I ANALYZED THE POWER HE POSSESSED ...
...AND DISPOSED OF IT ACCORDINGLY.
AN INDIVIDUAL BRAIN DOES NOT HAVE THE CAPACITY TO CONNECT TO THE DATA OVERMIND.
CONTINUED CONTACT WOULD HAVE LED TO DAMAGING EFFECTS.
YEAH, THAT MAKES SENSE.
WHO KNOWS WHAT MIGHT HAVE HAPPENED IF HE CONTINUED ON HIS RAMPAGE?
THAT'S KINDA MISSING THE POINT?

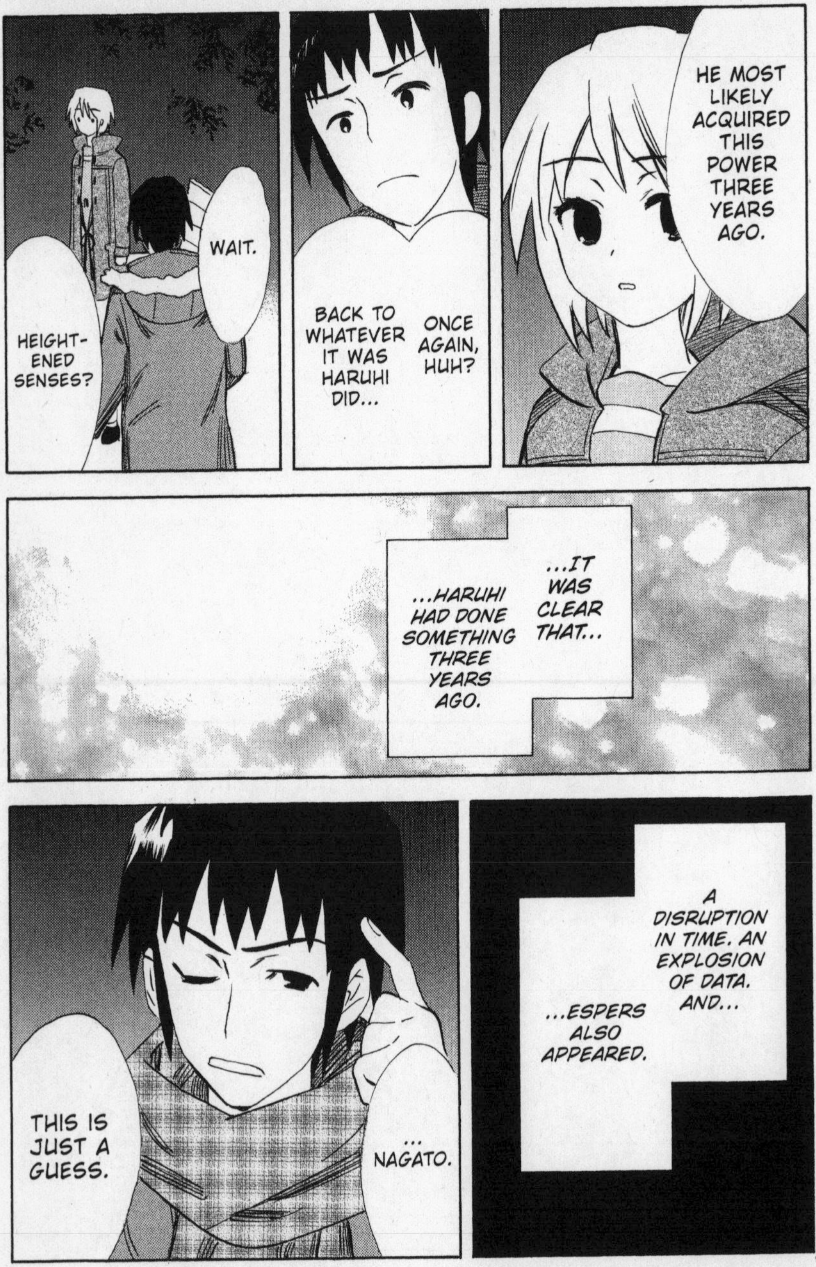
HE MOST LIKELY ACQUIRED THIS POWER THREE YEARS AGO.
ONCE AGAIN, HUH?
BACK TO WHATEVER IT WAS HARUHI DID...
WAIT.
HEIGHT-ENED SENSES?
...IT WAS CLEAR THAT...
...HARUHI HAD DONE SOMETHING THREE YEARS AGO.
A DISRUPTION IN TIME. AN EXPLOSION OF DATA. AND...
...ESPERS ALSO APPEARED.
... NAGATO.
THIS IS JUST A GUESS.

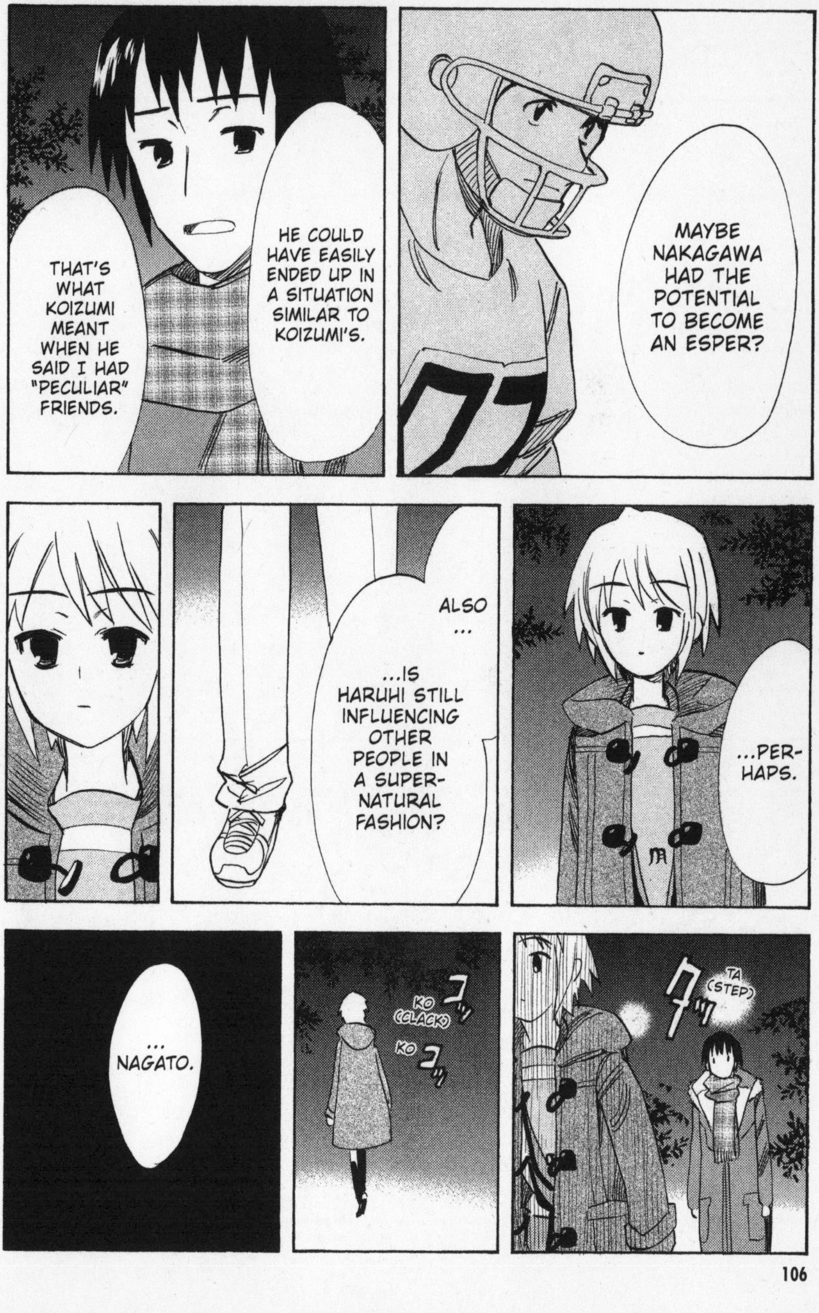
MAYBE NAKAGAWA HAD THE POTENTIAL TO BECOME AN ESPER?
HE COULD HAVE EASILY ENDED UP IN A SITUATION SIMILAR TO KOIZUMI'S.
THAT'S WHAT KOIZUMI MEANT WHEN HE SAID I HAD "PECULIAR" FRIENDS.
...PER-HAPS.
ALSO ...
...IS HARUHI STILL INFLUENCING OTHER PEOPLE IN A SUPER-NATURAL FASHION?
TA (STEP)
KO (CLACK)
KO
... NAGATO.

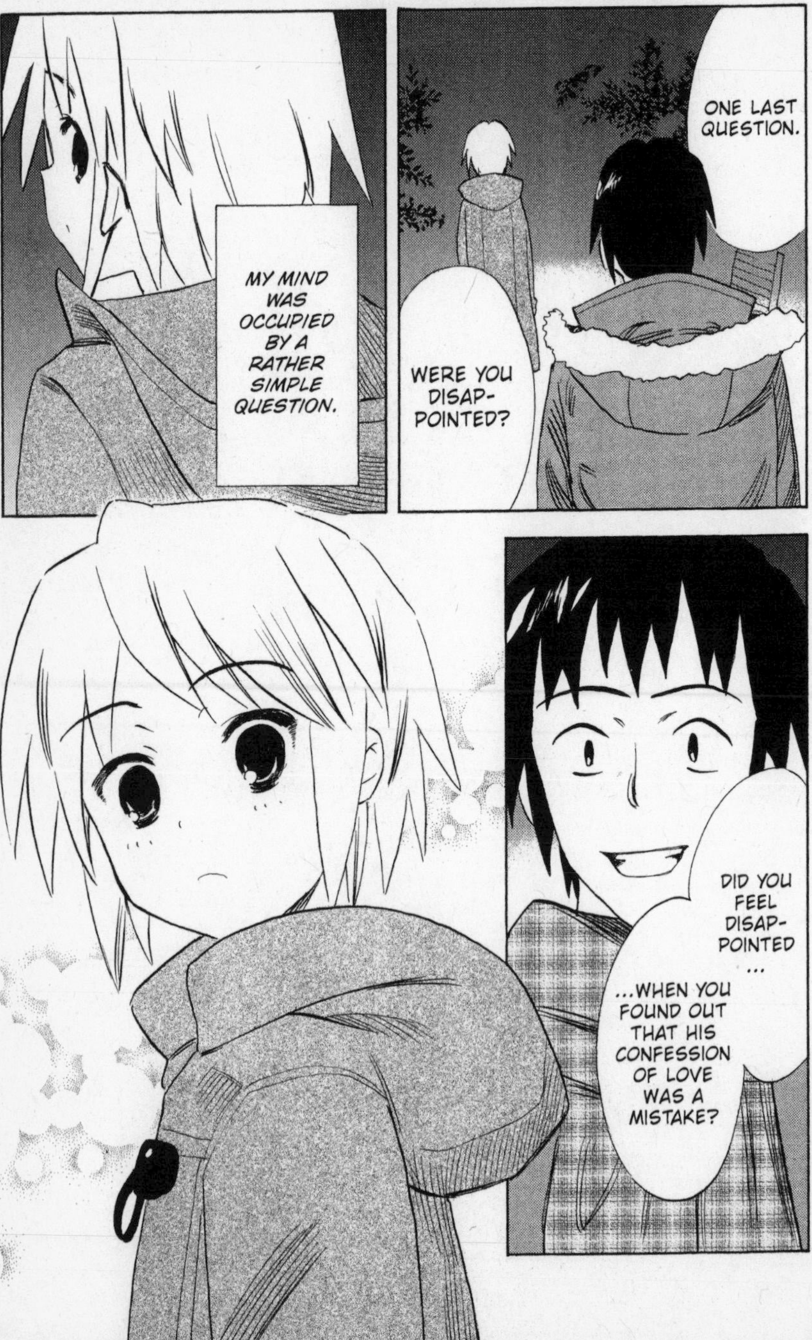
ONE LAST QUESTION.
WERE YOU DISAP-POINTED?
MY MIND WAS OCCUPIED BY A RATHER SIMPLE QUESTION.
DID YOU FEEL DISAP-POINTED ...
...WHEN YOU FOUND OUT THAT HIS CONFESSION OF LOVE WAS A MISTAKE?

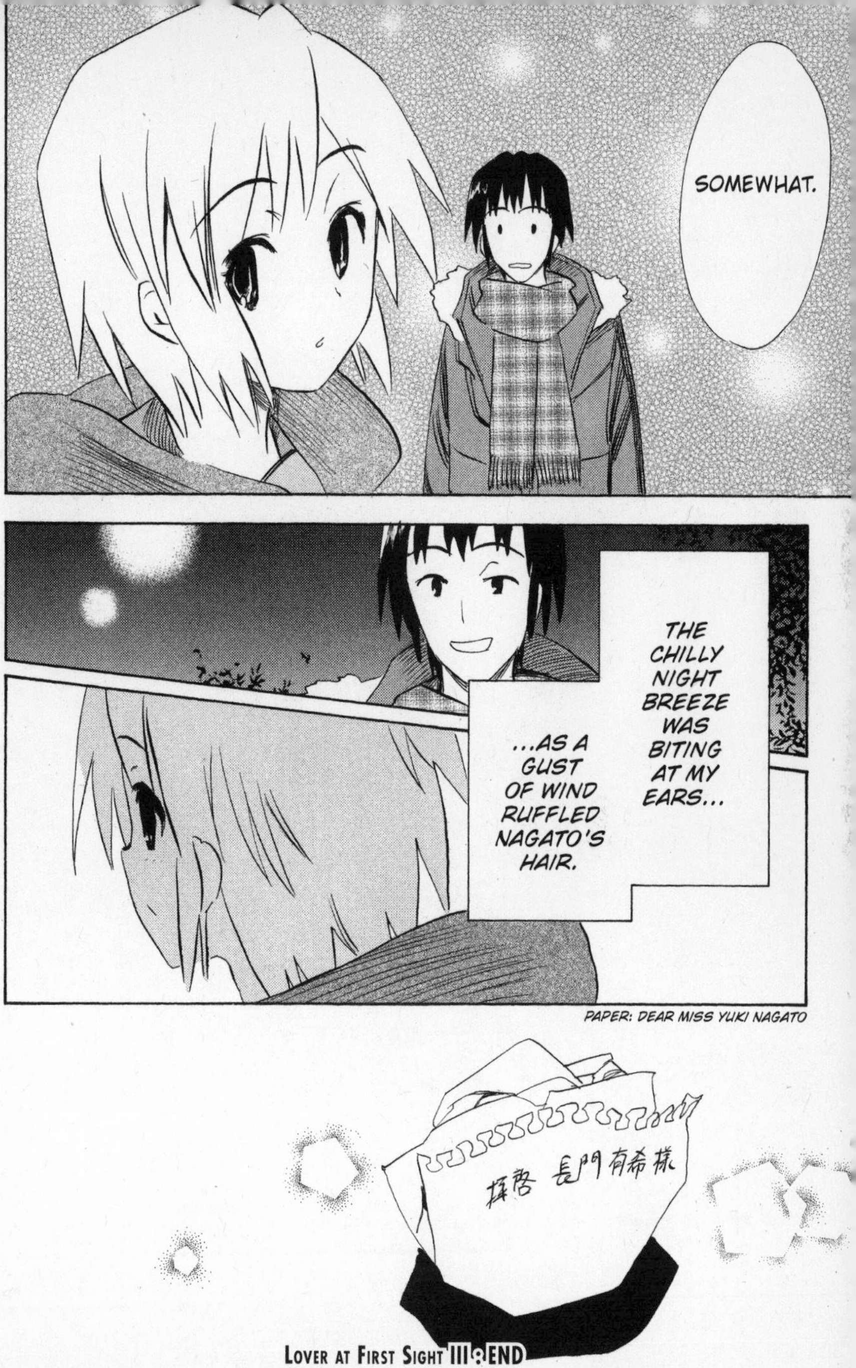
SOMEWHAT.
THE CHILLY NIGHT BREEZE WAS BITING AT MY EARS...
...AS A GUST OF WIND RUFFLED NAGATO'S HAIR.
PAPER: DEAR MISS YUKI NAGATO
拝啓 長門有希様

LOVER AT FIRST SIGHT III: END

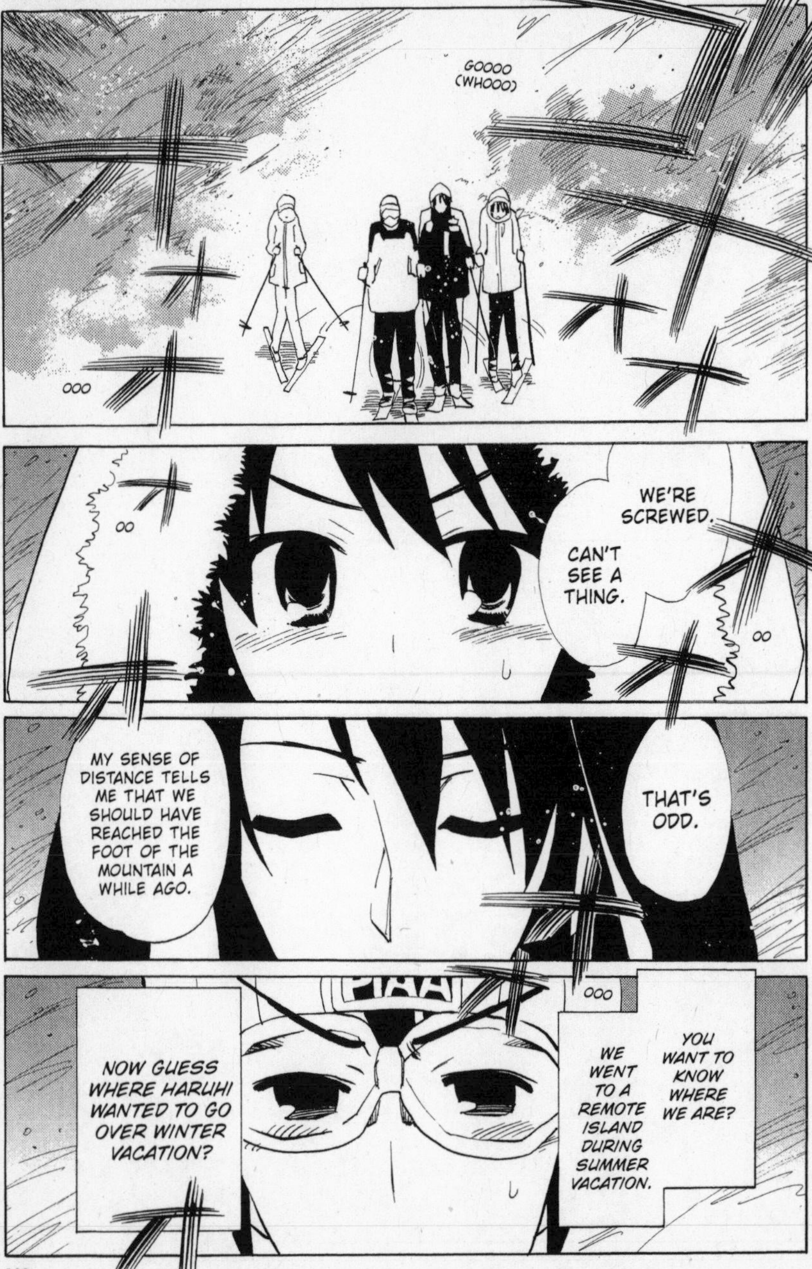
GOOOO
(WHOOO)
OOO
WE'RE SCREWED.
CAN'T SEE A THING.
OO
OO
THAT'S ODD.
MY SENSE OF DISTANCE TELLS ME THAT WE SHOULD HAVE REACHED THE FOOT OF THE MOUNTAIN A WHILE AGO.
OOO
YOU WANT TO KNOW WHERE WE ARE?
WE WENT TO A REMOTE ISLAND DURING SUMMER VACATION.
NOW GUESS WHERE HARUHI WANTED TO GO OVER WINTER VACATION?

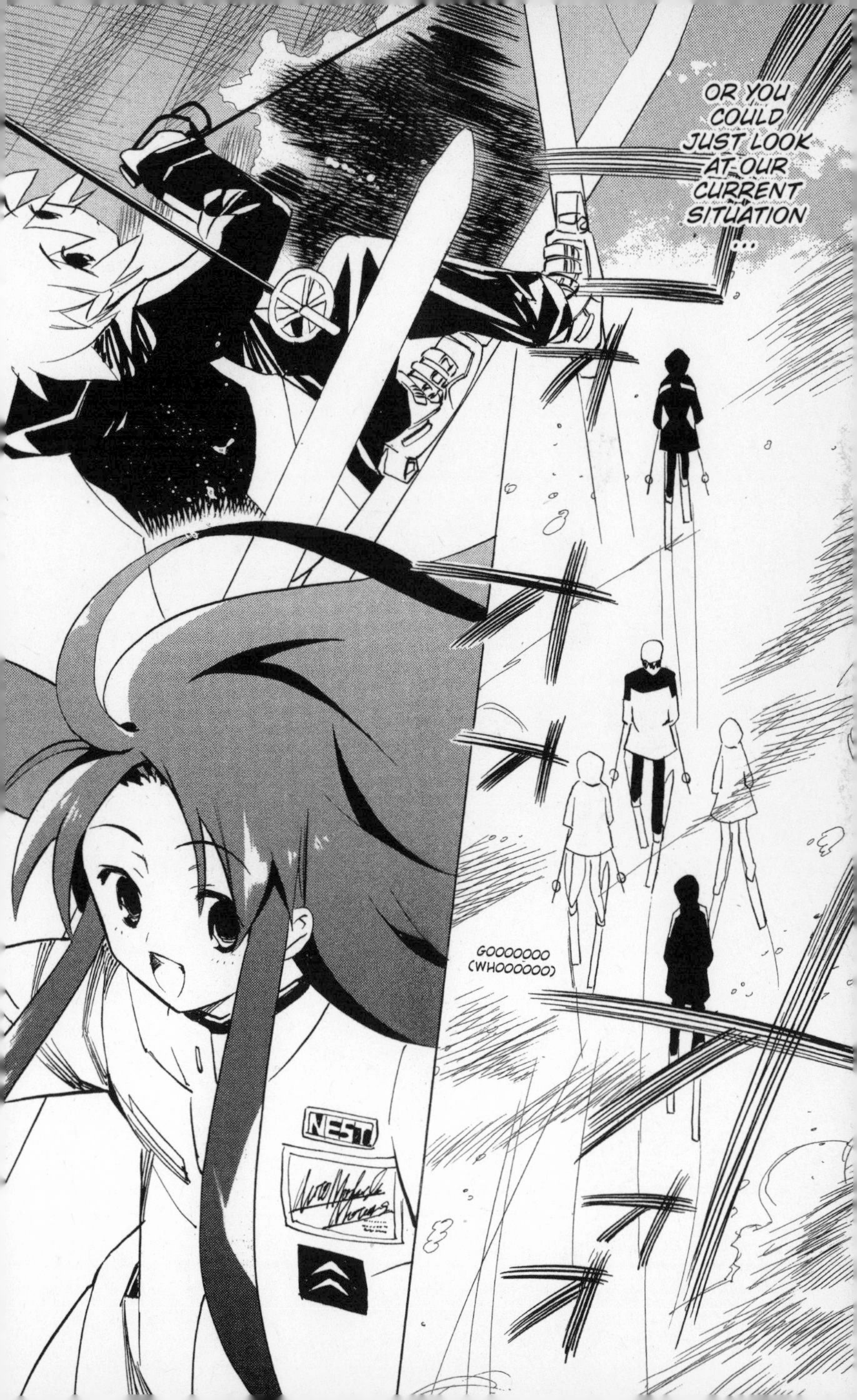
OR YOU COULD JUST LOOK AT OUR CURRENT SITUATION ...
GOOOOOOO (WHOOOOOO)
NEST

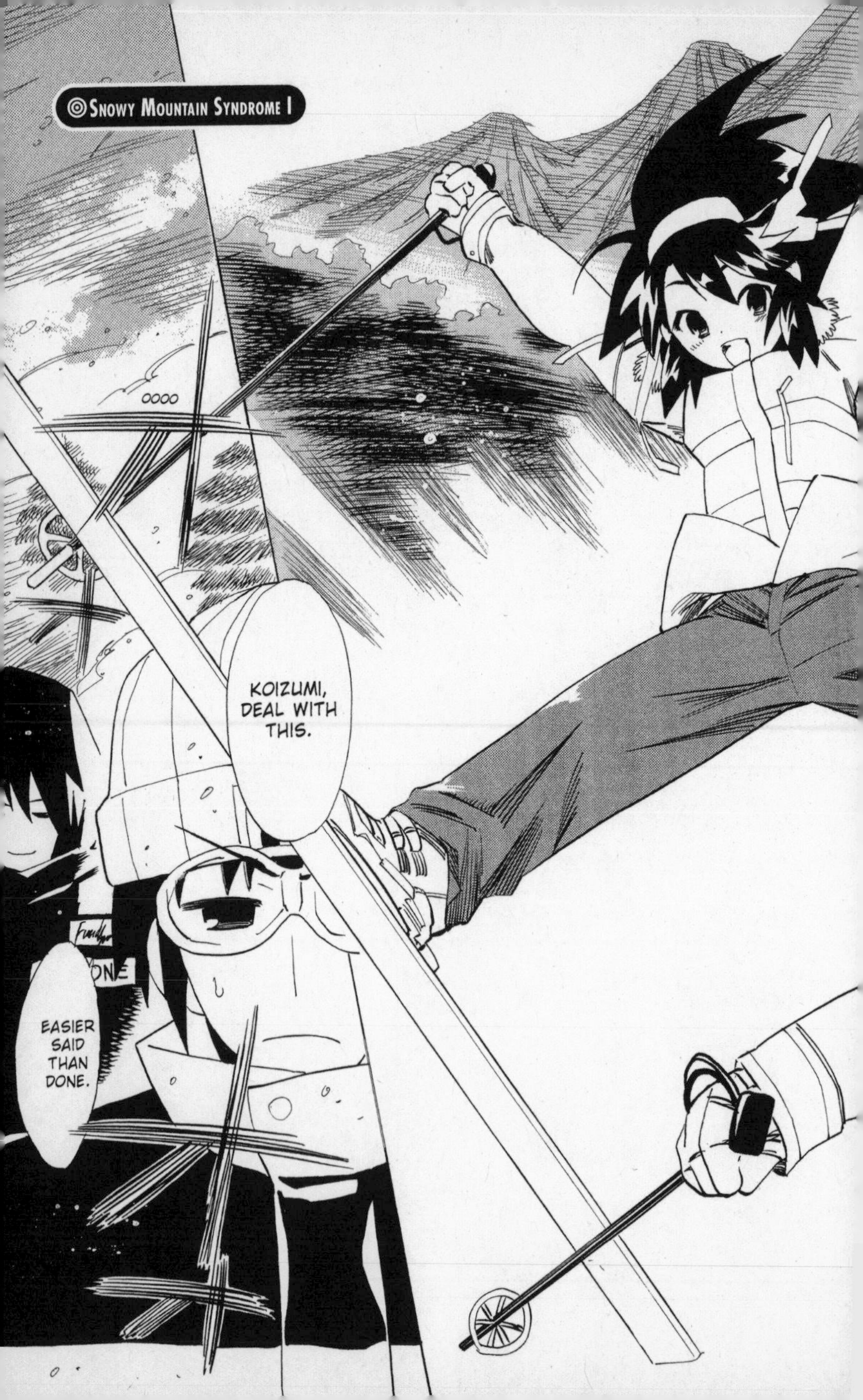
SNOWY MOUNTAIN SYNDROME I
OOOO
KOIZUMI, DEAL WITH THIS.
EASIER SAID THAN DONE.

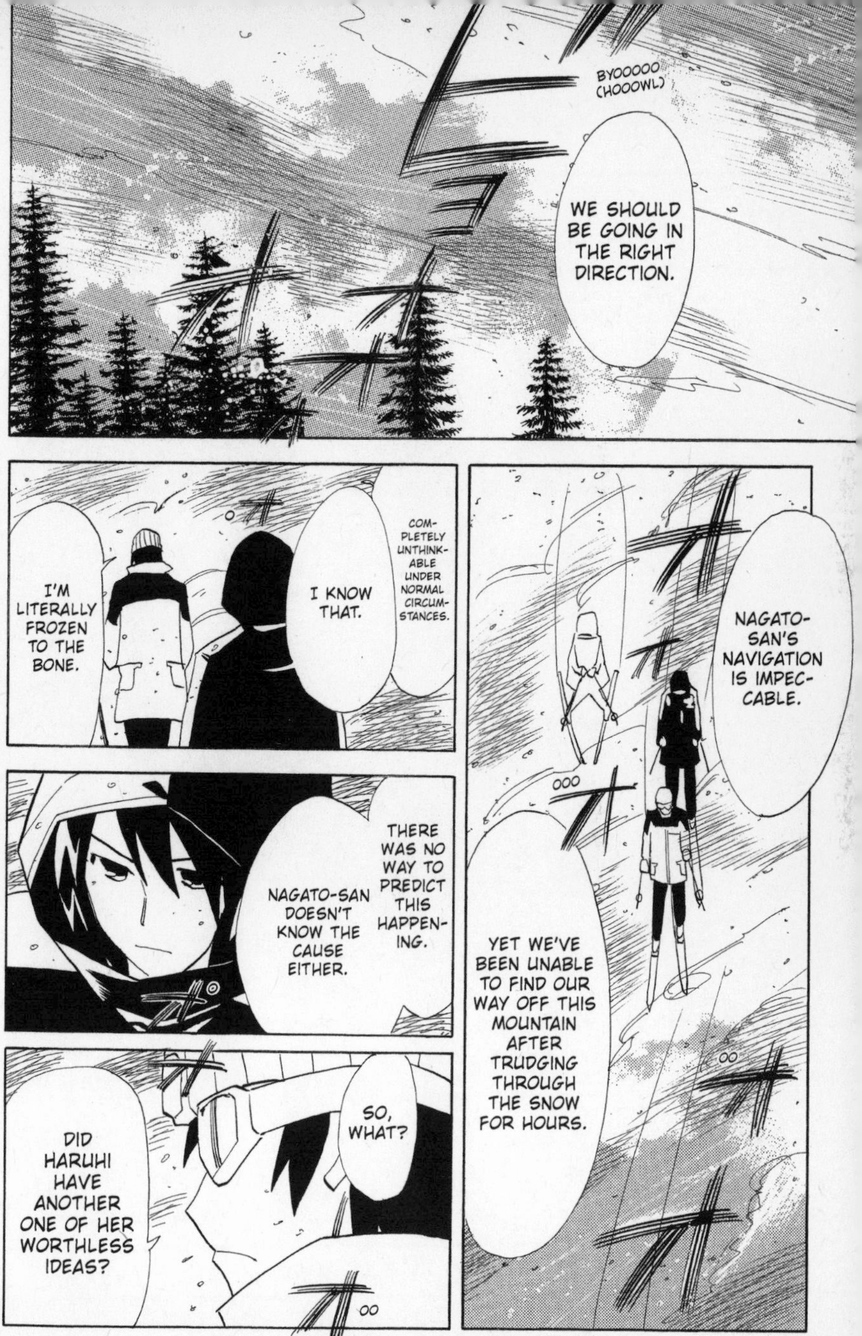
BYOOOOO (HOOOWL)
WE SHOULD BE GOING IN THE RIGHT DIRECTION.
NAGATO-SAN'S NAVIGATION IS IMPECCABLE.
OOO
YET WE'VE BEEN UNABLE TO FIND OUR WAY OFF THIS MOUNTAIN AFTER TRUDGING THROUGH THE SNOW FOR HOURS.
OO
COMPLETELY UNTHINKABLE UNDER NORMAL CIRCUMSTANCES.
I KNOW THAT.
I'M LITERALLY FROZEN TO THE BONE.
THERE WAS NO WAY TO PREDICT THIS HAPPENING.
NAGATO-SAN DOESN'T KNOW THE CAUSE EITHER.
SO, WHAT?
DID HARUHI HAVE ANOTHER ONE OF HER WORTHLESS IDEAS?
OO

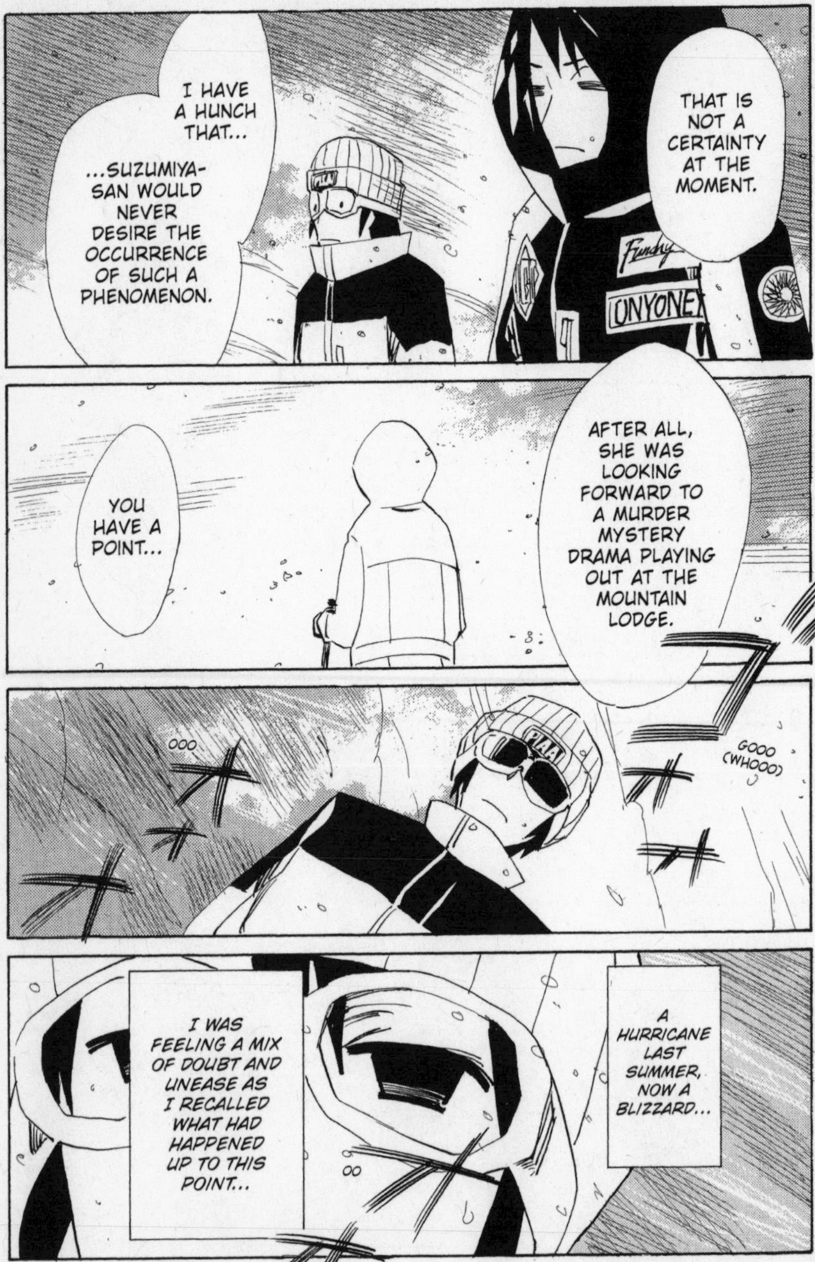

THAT IS NOT A CERTAINTY AT THE MOMENT.
I HAVE A HUNCH THAT...
...SUZUMIYA-SAN WOULD NEVER DESIRE THE OCCURRENCE OF SUCH A PHENOMENON.
AFTER ALL, SHE WAS LOOKING FORWARD TO A MURDER MYSTERY DRAMA PLAYING OUT AT THE MOUNTAIN LODGE.
YOU HAVE A POINT...
GOOO (WHOOO)
OOO
A HURRICANE LAST SUMMER, NOW A BLIZZARD...
I WAS FEELING A MIX OF DOUBT AND UNEASE AS I RECALLED WHAT HAD HAPPENED UP TO THIS POINT...
OO

PAPER: COUNTING DOWN TO THE NEW YEAR IN A BLIZZARD

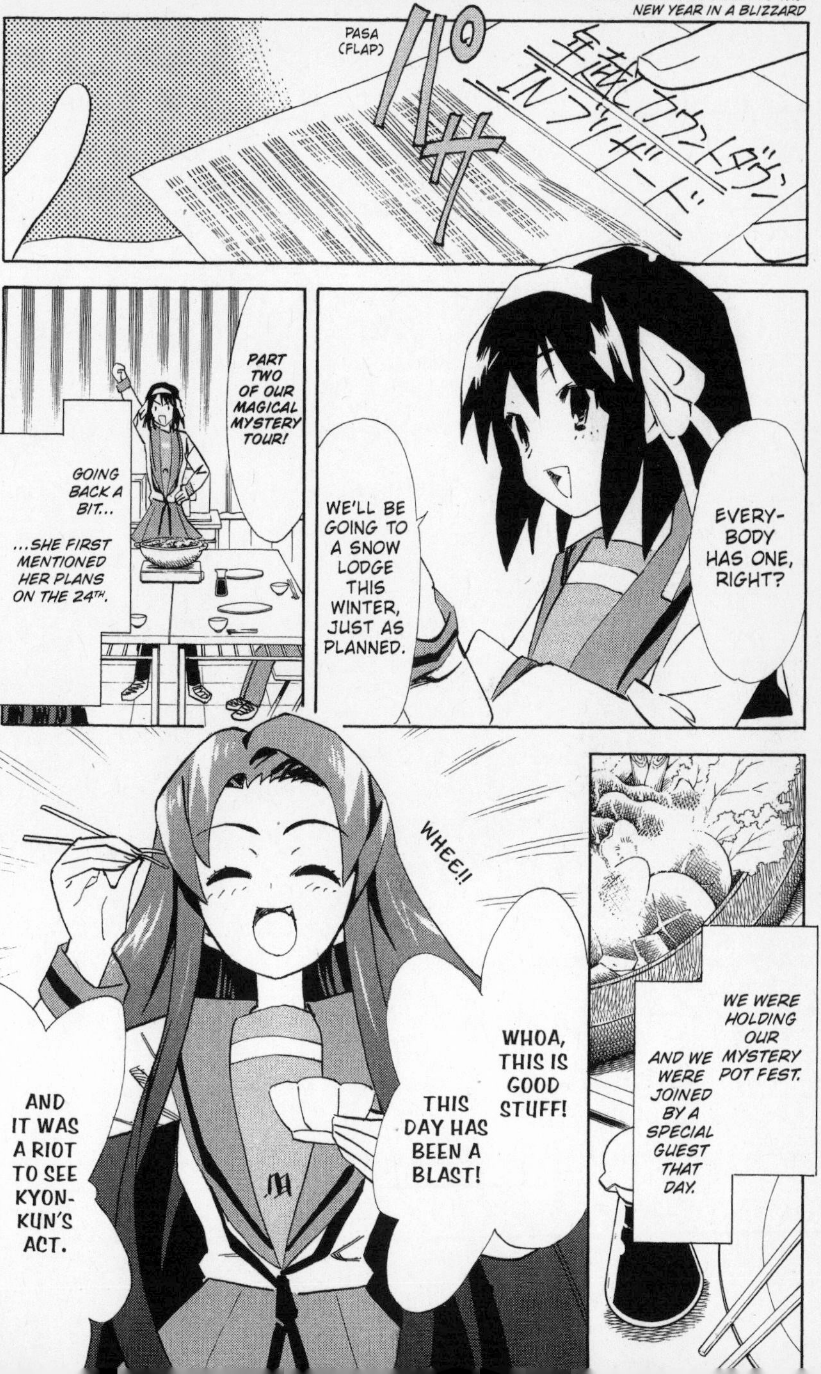
PASA (FLAP)
年越しカウントダウン INブリザード
EVERY-BODY HAS ONE, RIGHT?
WE'LL BE GOING TO A SNOW LODGE THIS WINTER, JUST AS PLANNED.
PART TWO OF OUR MAGICAL MYSTERY TOUR!
GOING BACK A BIT...
...SHE FIRST MENTIONED HER PLANS ON THE 24TH.
WE WERE HOLDING OUR MYSTERY POT FEST.
AND WE WERE JOINED BY A SPECIAL GUEST THAT DAY.
WHEE!!
WHOA, THIS IS GOOD STUFF!
THIS DAY HAS BEEN A BLAST!
AND IT WAS A RIOT TO SEE KYON-KUN'S ACT.

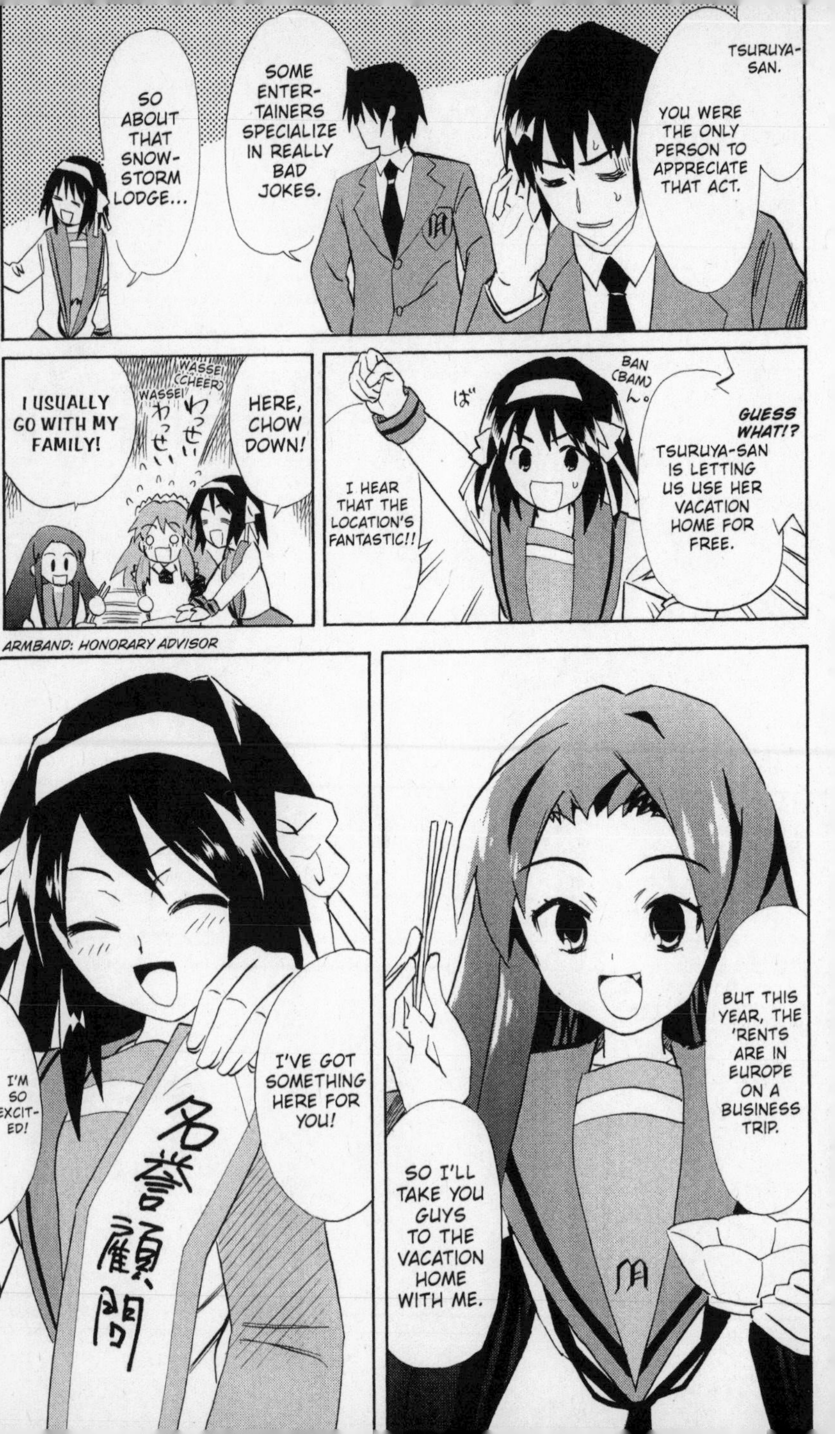

TSURUYA-SAN.
YOU WERE THE ONLY PERSON TO APPRECIATE THAT ACT.
SOME ENTERTAINERS SPECIALIZE IN REALLY BAD JOKES.
SO ABOUT THAT SNOWSTORM LODGE...
BAN (BAM) ばん。
GUESS WHAT!? TSURUYA-SAN IS LETTING US USE HER VACATION HOME FOR FREE.
I HEAR THAT THE LOCATION'S FANTASTIC!!
HERE, CHOW DOWN!
WASSEI (CHEER) わっせい
WASSEI わっせい
I USUALLY GO WITH MY FAMILY!
ARMBAND: HONORARY ADVISOR
BUT THIS YEAR, THE 'RENTS ARE IN EUROPE ON A BUSINESS TRIP.
SO I'LL TAKE YOU GUYS TO THE VACATION HOME WITH ME.
I'VE GOT SOMETHING HERE FOR YOU!
I'M SO EXCITED!
名誉顧問

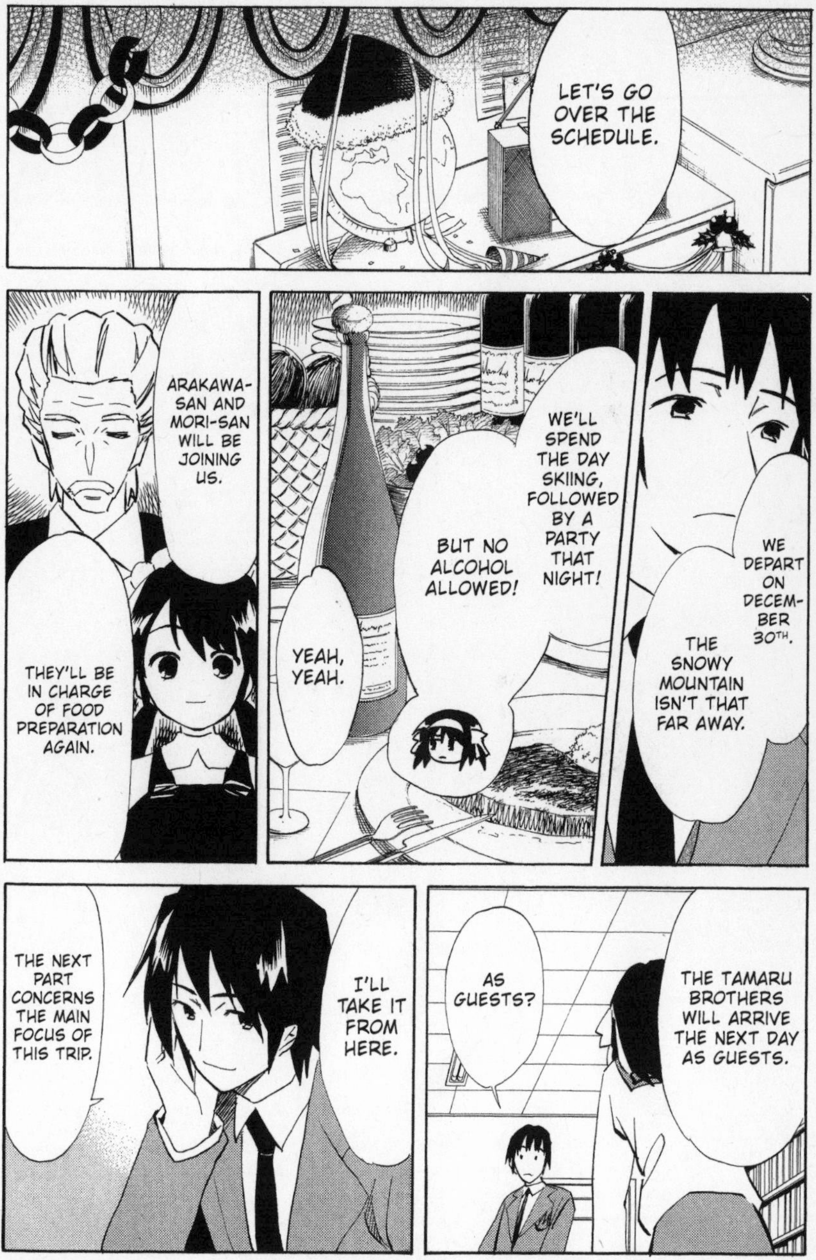
LET'S GO OVER THE SCHEDULE.
WE DEPART ON DECEMBER 30TH.
THE SNOWY MOUNTAIN ISN'T THAT FAR AWAY.
WE'LL SPEND THE DAY SKIING, FOLLOWED BY A PARTY THAT NIGHT!
BUT NO ALCOHOL ALLOWED!
YEAH, YEAH.
ARAKAWA-SAN AND MORI-SAN WILL BE JOINING US.
THEY'LL BE IN CHARGE OF FOOD PREPARATION AGAIN.
THE TAMARU BROTHERS WILL ARRIVE THE NEXT DAY AS GUESTS.
AS GUESTS?
I'LL TAKE IT FROM HERE.
THE NEXT PART CONCERNS THE MAIN FOCUS OF THIS TRIP.

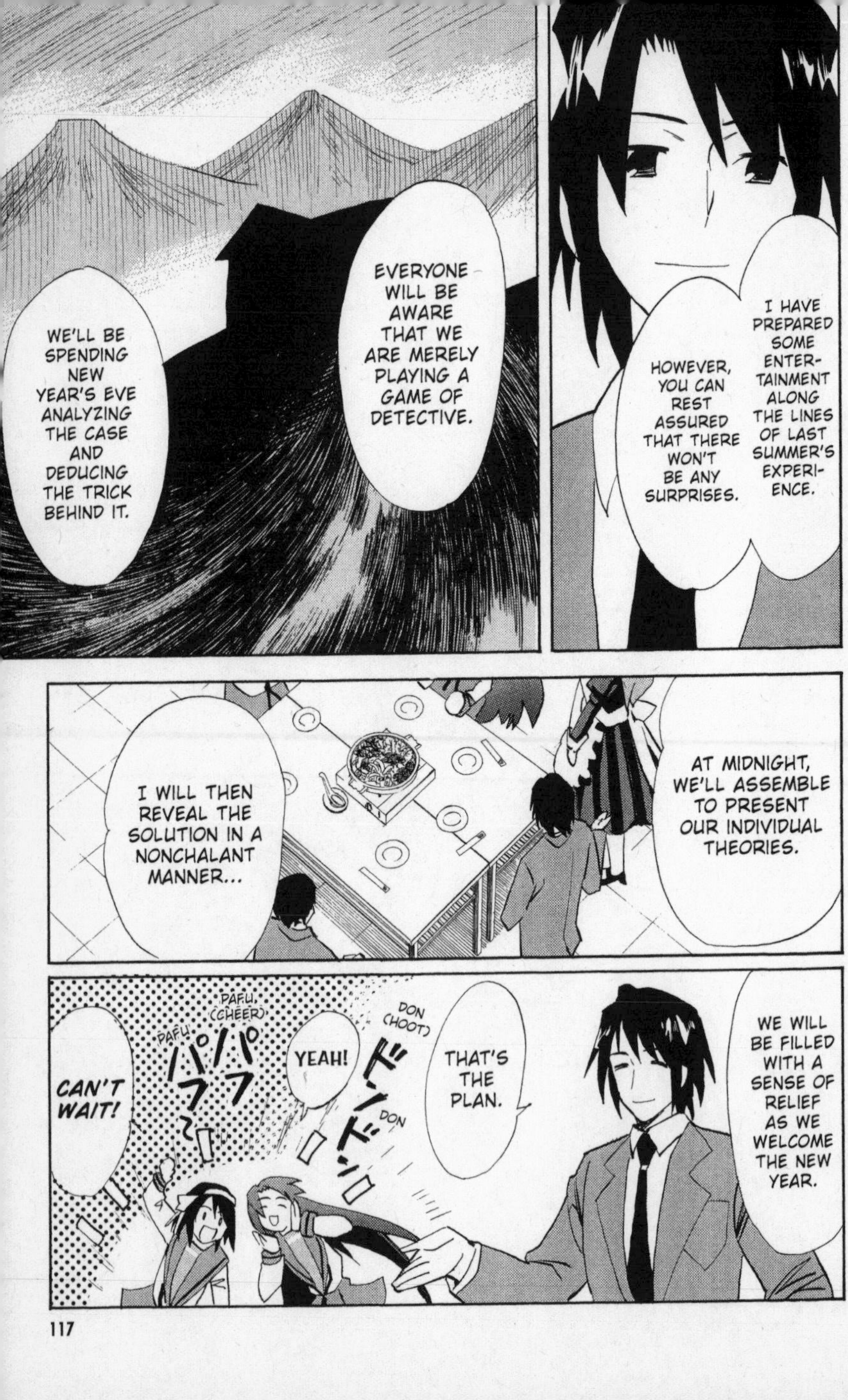
I HAVE PREPARED SOME ENTERTAINMENT ALONG THE LINES OF LAST SUMMER'S EXPERIENCE.
HOWEVER, YOU CAN REST ASSURED THAT THERE WON'T BE ANY SURPRISES.
EVERYONE WILL BE AWARE THAT WE ARE MERELY PLAYING A GAME OF DETECTIVE.
WE'LL BE SPENDING NEW YEAR'S EVE ANALYZING THE CASE AND DEDUCING THE TRICK BEHIND IT.
AT MIDNIGHT, WE'LL ASSEMBLE TO PRESENT OUR INDIVIDUAL THEORIES.
I WILL THEN REVEAL THE SOLUTION IN A NONCHALANT MANNER...
WE WILL BE FILLED WITH A SENSE OF RELIEF AS WE WELCOME THE NEW YEAR.
THAT'S THE PLAN.
DON (HOOT)
DON
YEAH!
PAFU (CHEER)
PAFU
CAN'T WAIT!

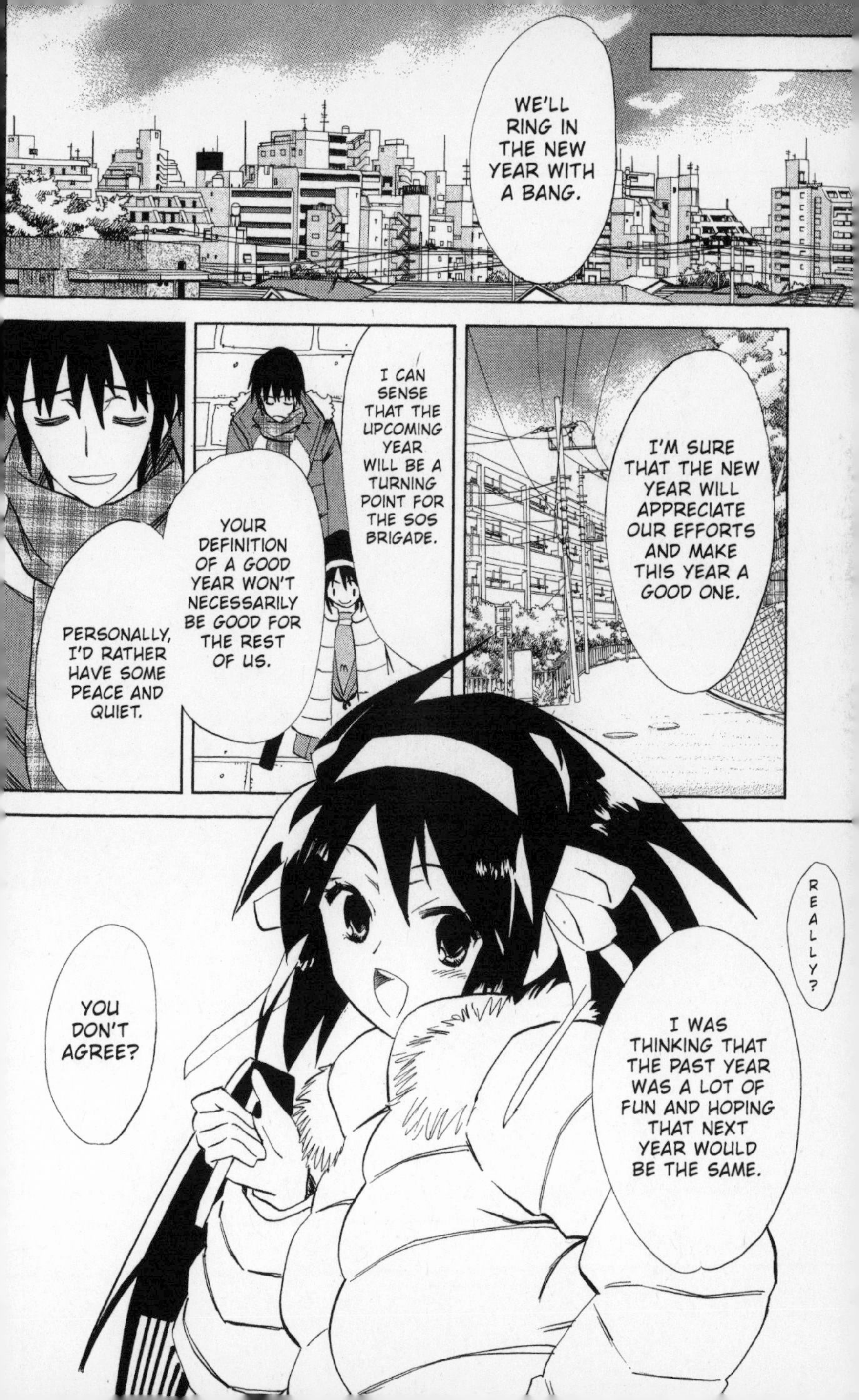
WE'LL RING IN THE NEW YEAR WITH A BANG.
I'M SURE THAT THE NEW YEAR WILL APPRECIATE OUR EFFORTS AND MAKE THIS YEAR A GOOD ONE.
I CAN SENSE THAT THE UPCOMING YEAR WILL BE A TURNING POINT FOR THE SOS BRIGADE.
YOUR DEFINITION OF A GOOD YEAR WON'T NECESSARILY BE GOOD FOR THE REST OF US.
PERSONALLY, I'D RATHER HAVE SOME PEACE AND QUIET.
REALLY?
I WAS THINKING THAT THE PAST YEAR WAS A LOT OF FUN AND HOPING THAT NEXT YEAR WOULD BE THE SAME.
YOU DON'T AGREE?

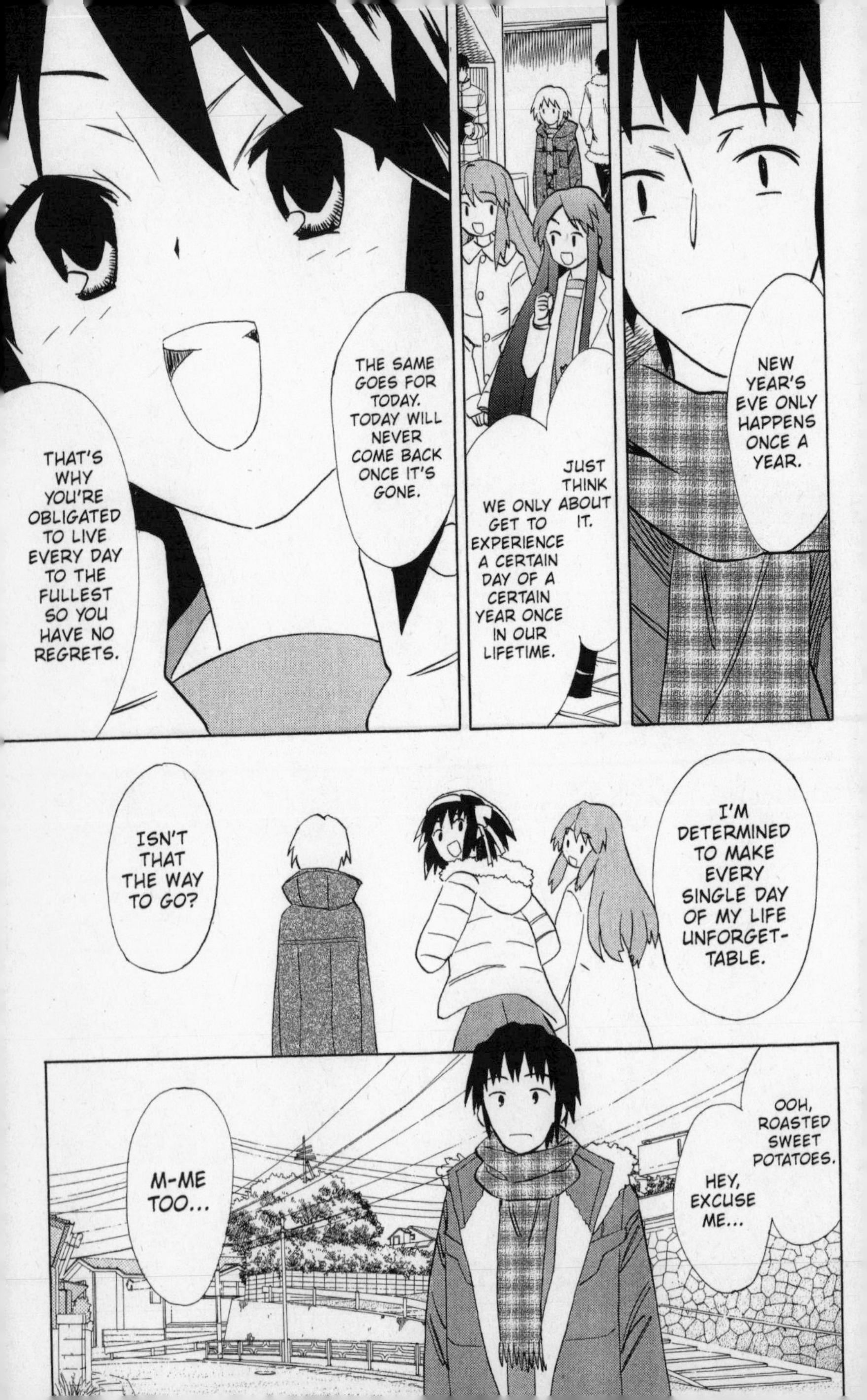
NEW YEAR'S EVE ONLY HAPPENS ONCE A YEAR.
JUST THINK ABOUT IT.
WE ONLY GET TO EXPERIENCE A CERTAIN DAY OF A CERTAIN YEAR ONCE IN OUR LIFETIME.
THE SAME GOES FOR TODAY. TODAY WILL NEVER COME BACK ONCE IT'S GONE.
THAT'S WHY YOU'RE OBLIGATED TO LIVE EVERY DAY TO THE FULLEST SO YOU HAVE NO REGRETS.
I'M DETERMINED TO MAKE EVERY SINGLE DAY OF MY LIFE UNFORGET-TABLE.
ISN'T THAT THE WAY TO GO?
OOH, ROASTED SWEET POTATOES.
HEY, EXCUSE ME...
M-ME TOO...

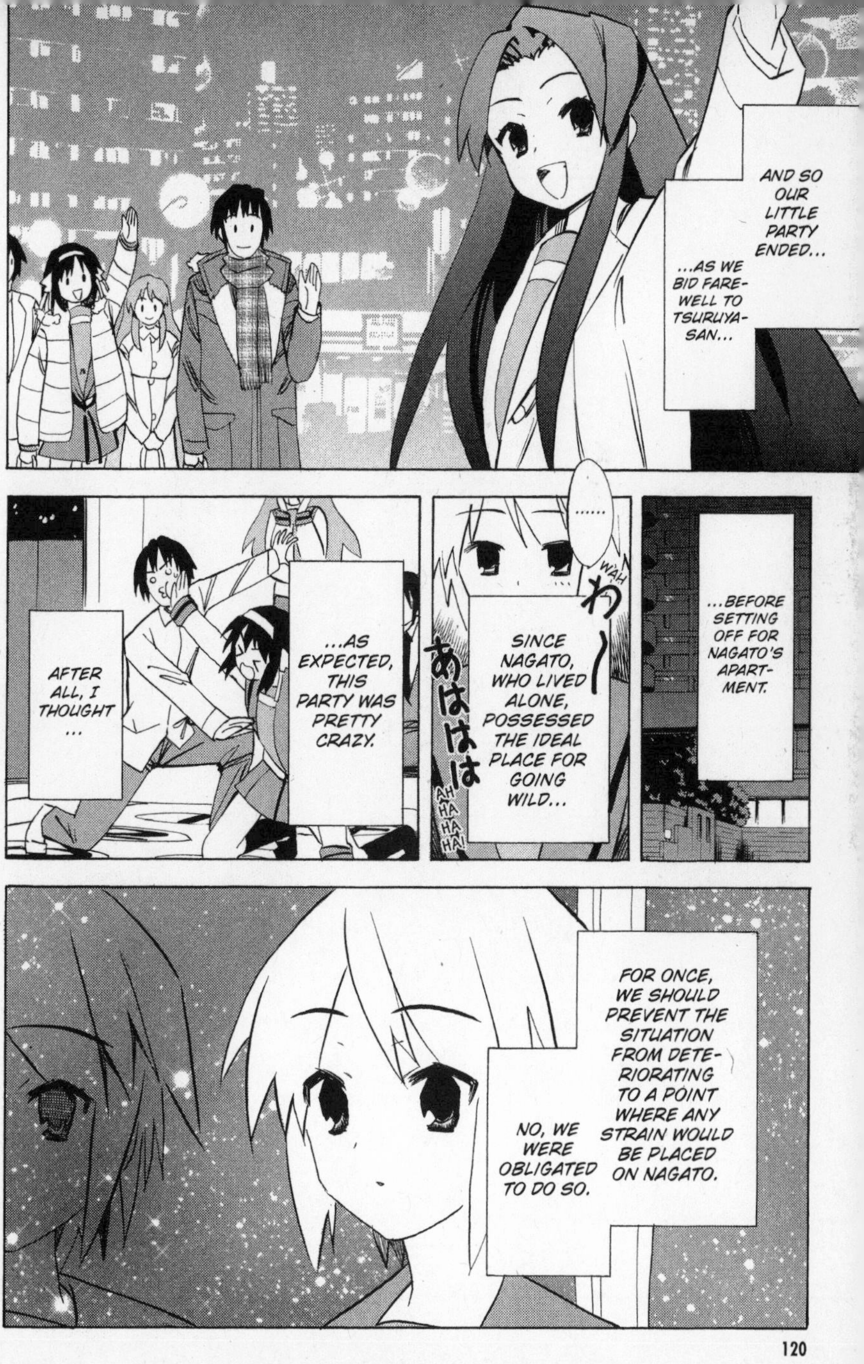
AND SO OUR LITTLE PARTY ENDED...
...AS WE BID FARE-WELL TO TSURUYA-SAN...
...BEFORE SETTING OFF FOR NAGATO'S APART-MENT.
......
わー
WAH
SINCE NAGATO, WHO LIVED ALONE, POSSESSED THE IDEAL PLACE FOR GOING WILD...
あははは
AH HA HA HA!
...AS EXPECTED, THIS PARTY WAS PRETTY CRAZY.
AFTER ALL, I THOUGHT ...
FOR ONCE, WE SHOULD PREVENT THE SITUATION FROM DETE-RIORATING TO A POINT WHERE ANY STRAIN WOULD BE PLACED ON NAGATO.
NO, WE WERE OBLIGATED TO DO SO.

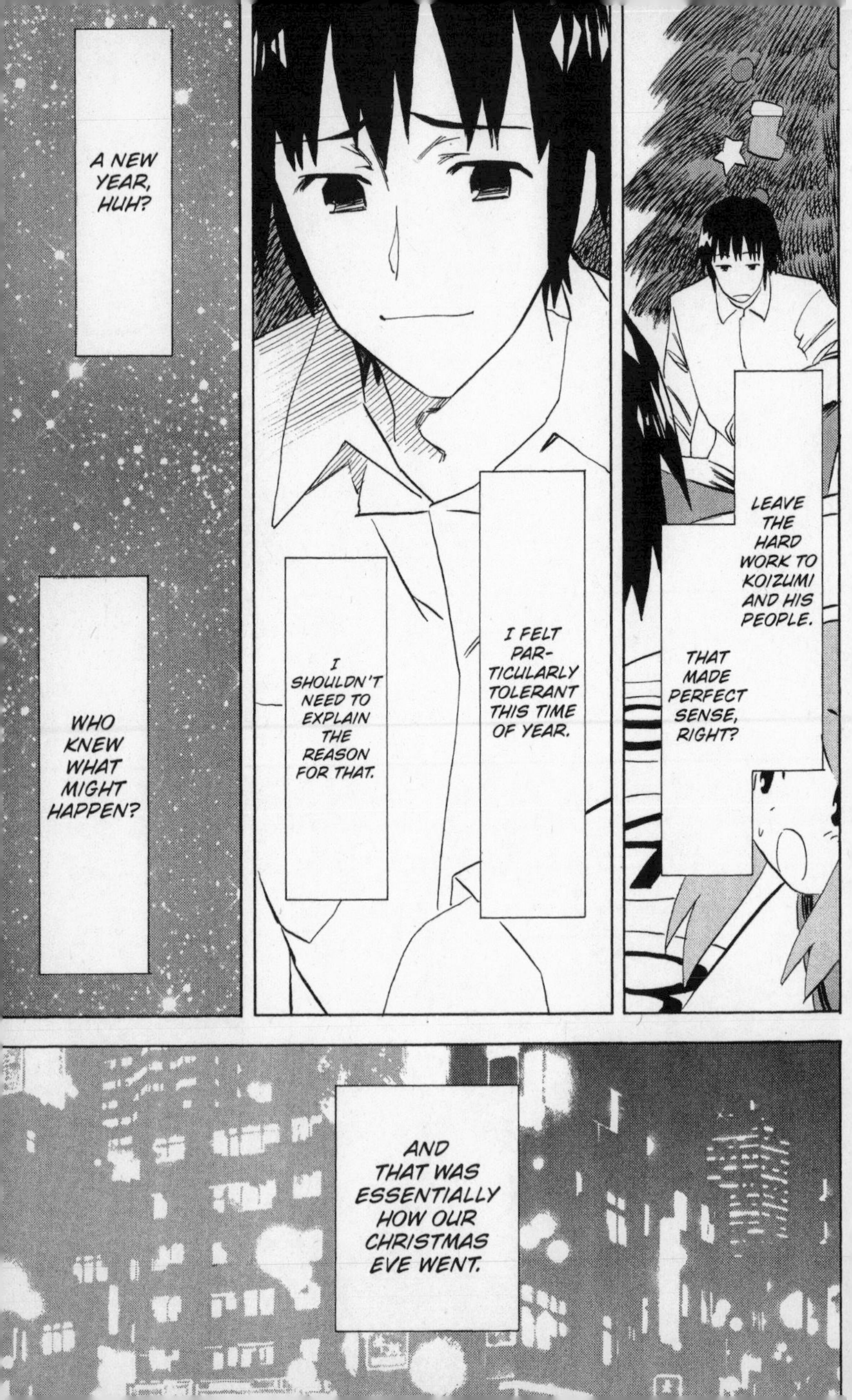
LEAVE THE HARD WORK TO KOIZUMI AND HIS PEOPLE.
THAT MADE PERFECT SENSE, RIGHT?
I FELT PARTICULARLY TOLERANT THIS TIME OF YEAR.
I SHOULDN'T NEED TO EXPLAIN THE REASON FOR THAT.
A NEW YEAR, HUH?
WHO KNEW WHAT MIGHT HAPPEN?
AND THAT WAS ESSENTIALLY HOW OUR CHRISTMAS EVE WENT.

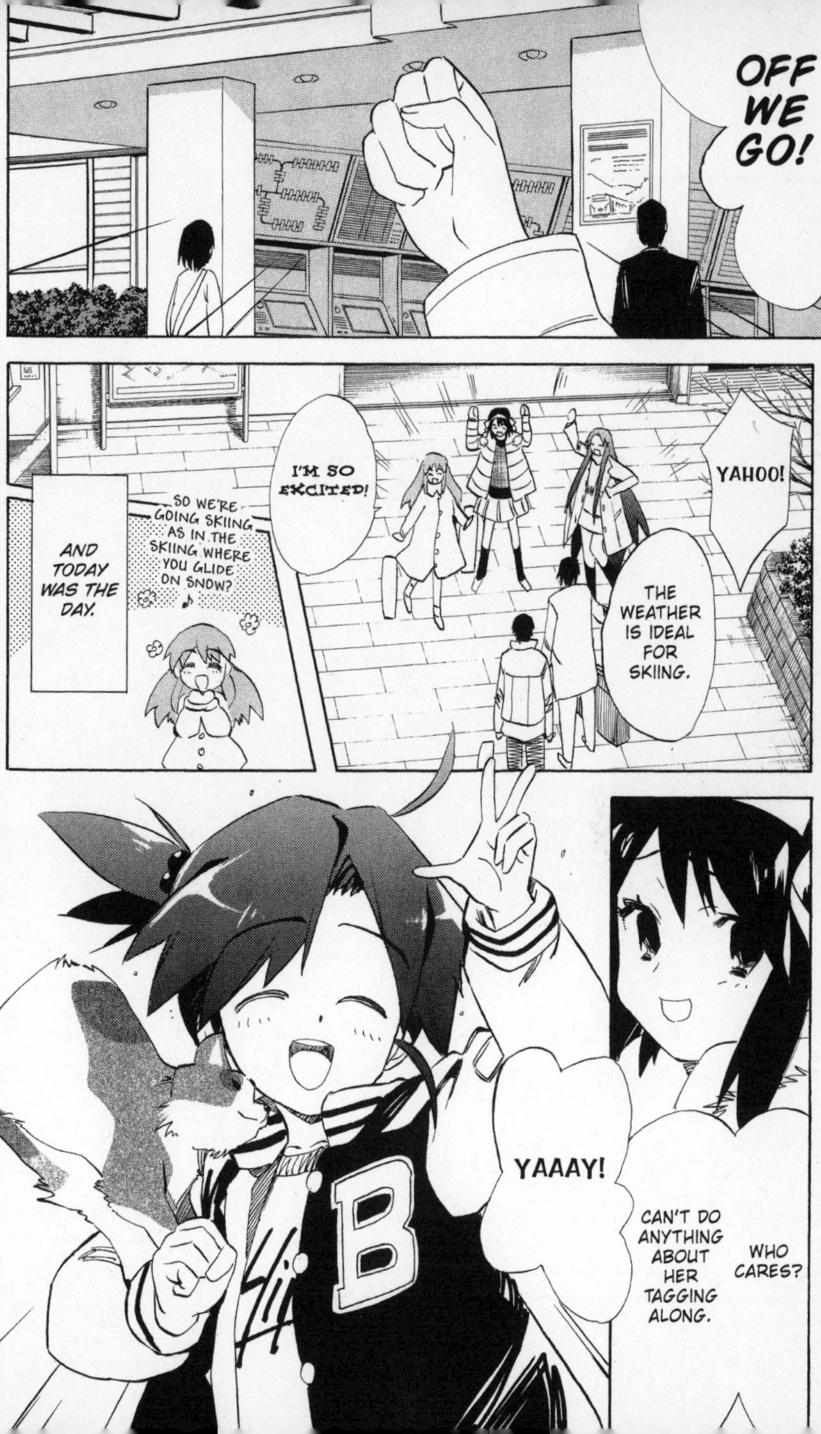
OFF WE GO!
YAHOO!
THE WEATHER IS IDEAL FOR SKIING.
I'M SO EXCITED!
AND TODAY WAS THE DAY.
SO WE'RE GOING SKIING AS IN THE SKIING WHERE YOU GLIDE ON SNOW?
WHO CARES?
CAN'T DO ANYTHING ABOUT HER TAGGING ALONG.
YAAAY!

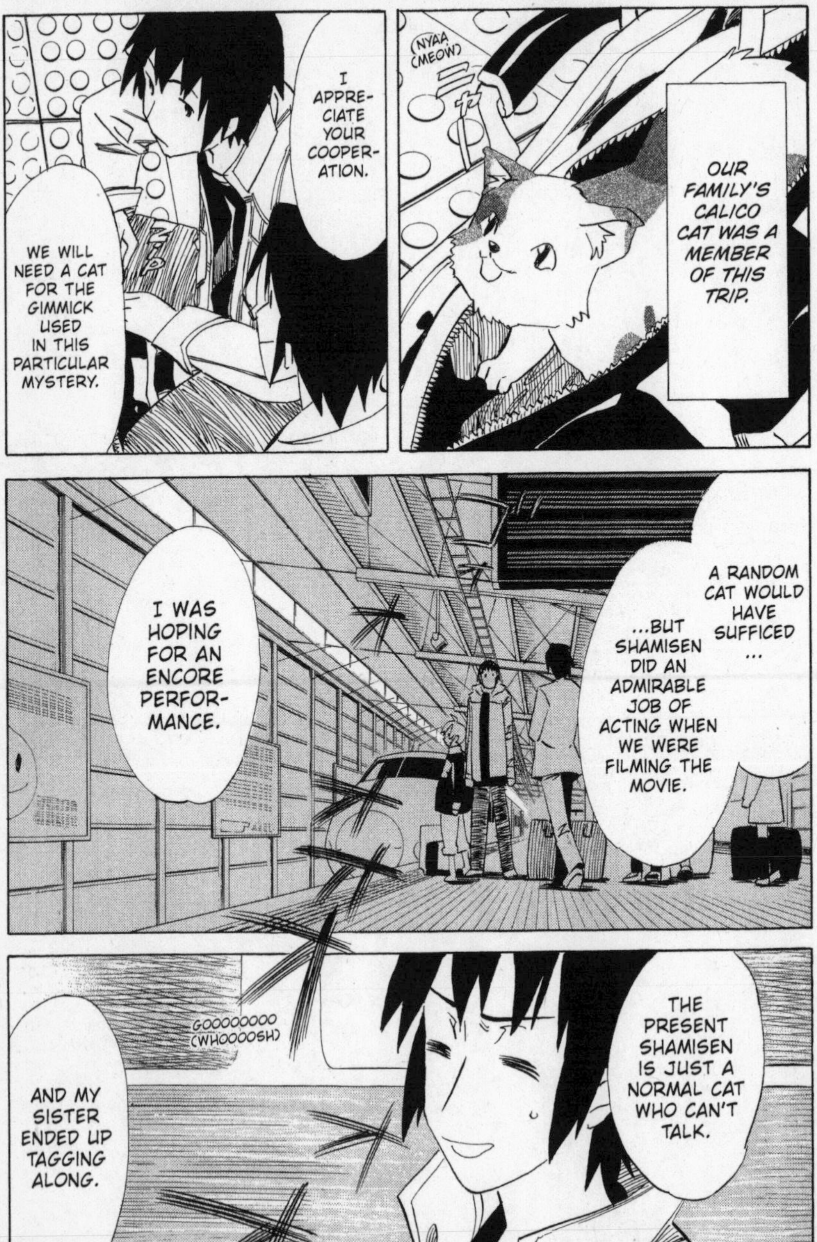
OUR FAMILY'S CALICO CAT WAS A MEMBER OF THIS TRIP.
NYAA (MEOW)
I APPRECIATE YOUR COOPERATION.
WE WILL NEED A CAT FOR THE GIMMICK USED IN THIS PARTICULAR MYSTERY.
A RANDOM CAT WOULD HAVE SUFFICED...
...BUT SHAMISEN DID AN ADMIRABLE JOB OF ACTING WHEN WE WERE FILMING THE MOVIE.
I WAS HOPING FOR AN ENCORE PERFORMANCE.
THE PRESENT SHAMISEN IS JUST A NORMAL CAT WHO CAN'T TALK.
GOOOOOOOO (WHOOOOSH)
AND MY SISTER ENDED UP TAGGING ALONG.

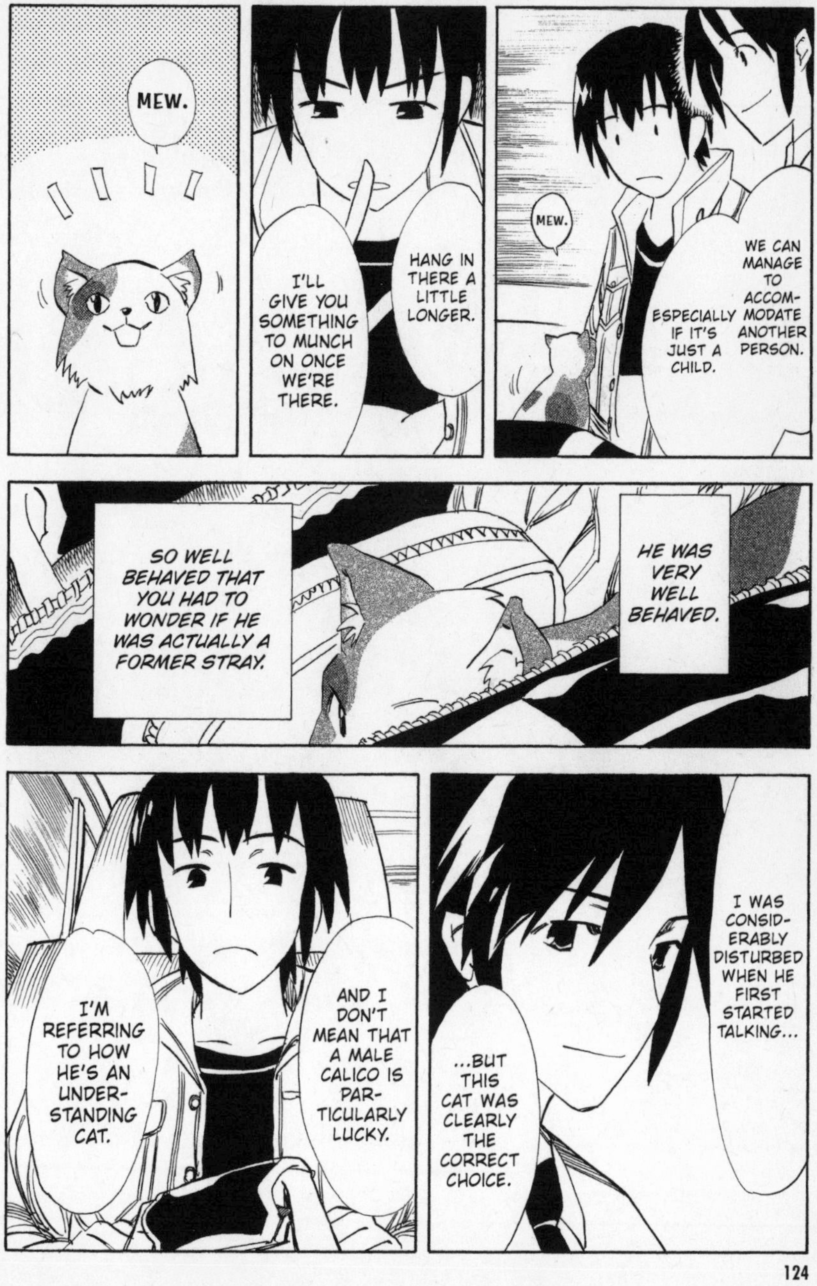
WE CAN MANAGE TO ACCOMMODATE ANOTHER PERSON.
ESPECIALLY IF IT'S JUST A CHILD.
MEW.
HANG IN THERE A LITTLE LONGER.
I'LL GIVE YOU SOMETHING TO MUNCH ON ONCE WE'RE THERE.
MEW.
HE WAS VERY WELL BEHAVED.
SO WELL BEHAVED THAT YOU HAD TO WONDER IF HE WAS ACTUALLY A FORMER STRAY.
I WAS CONSIDERABLY DISTURBED WHEN HE FIRST STARTED TALKING...
...BUT THIS CAT WAS CLEARLY THE CORRECT CHOICE.
AND I DON'T MEAN THAT A MALE CALICO IS PARTICULARLY LUCKY.
I'M REFERRING TO HOW HE'S AN UNDERSTANDING CAT.

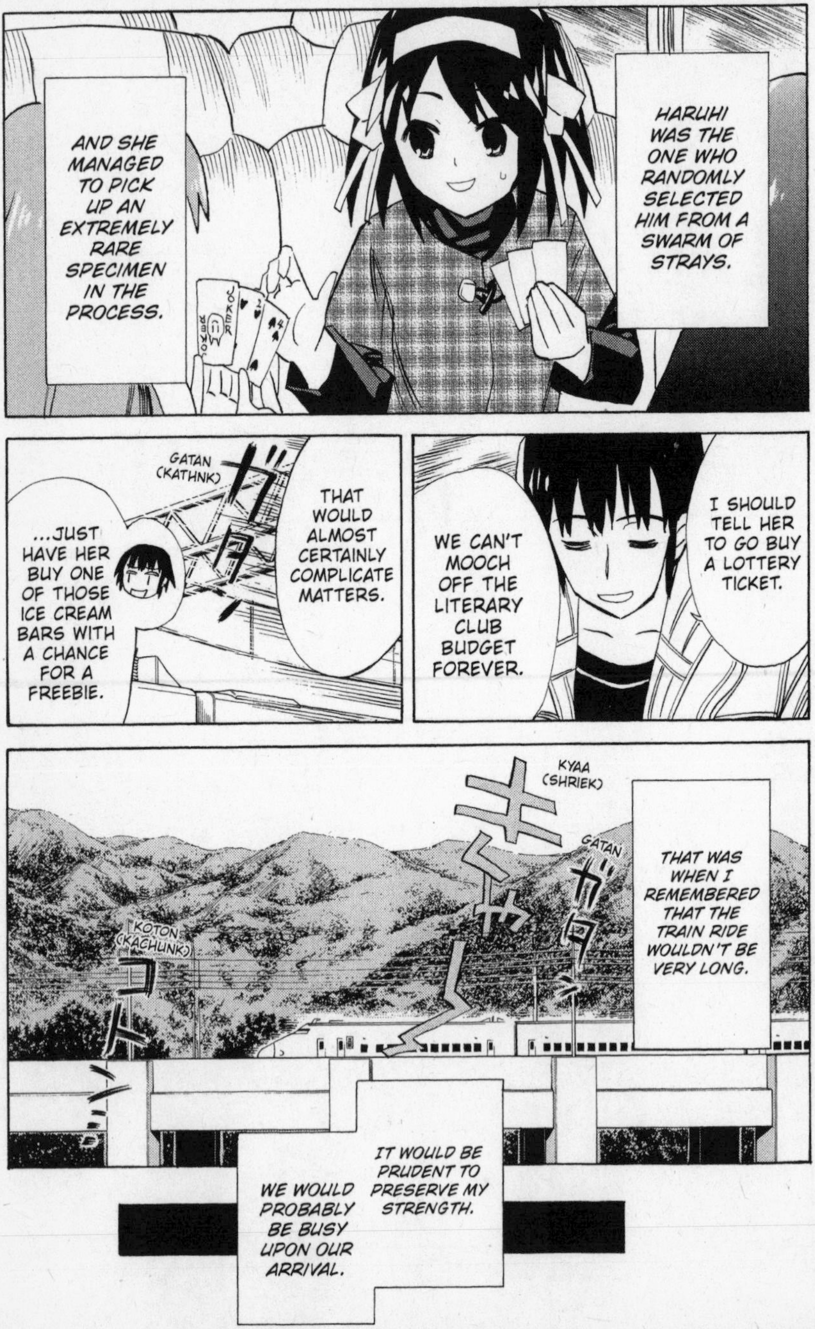
HARUHI WAS THE ONE WHO RANDOMLY SELECTED HIM FROM A SWARM OF STRAYS.
AND SHE MANAGED TO PICK UP AN EXTREMELY RARE SPECIMEN IN THE PROCESS.
JOKER
I SHOULD TELL HER TO GO BUY A LOTTERY TICKET.
WE CAN'T MOOCH OFF THE LITERARY CLUB BUDGET FOREVER.
GATAN (KATHNK)
THAT WOULD ALMOST CERTAINLY COMPLICATE MATTERS.
...JUST HAVE HER BUY ONE OF THOSE ICE CREAM BARS WITH A CHANCE FOR A FREEBIE.
THAT WAS WHEN I REMEMBERED THAT THE TRAIN RIDE WOULDN'T BE VERY LONG.
KYAA (SHRIEK)
GATAN
KOTON (KACHUNK)
IT WOULD BE PRUDENT TO PRESERVE MY STRENGTH.
WE WOULD PROBABLY BE BUSY UPON OUR ARRIVAL.

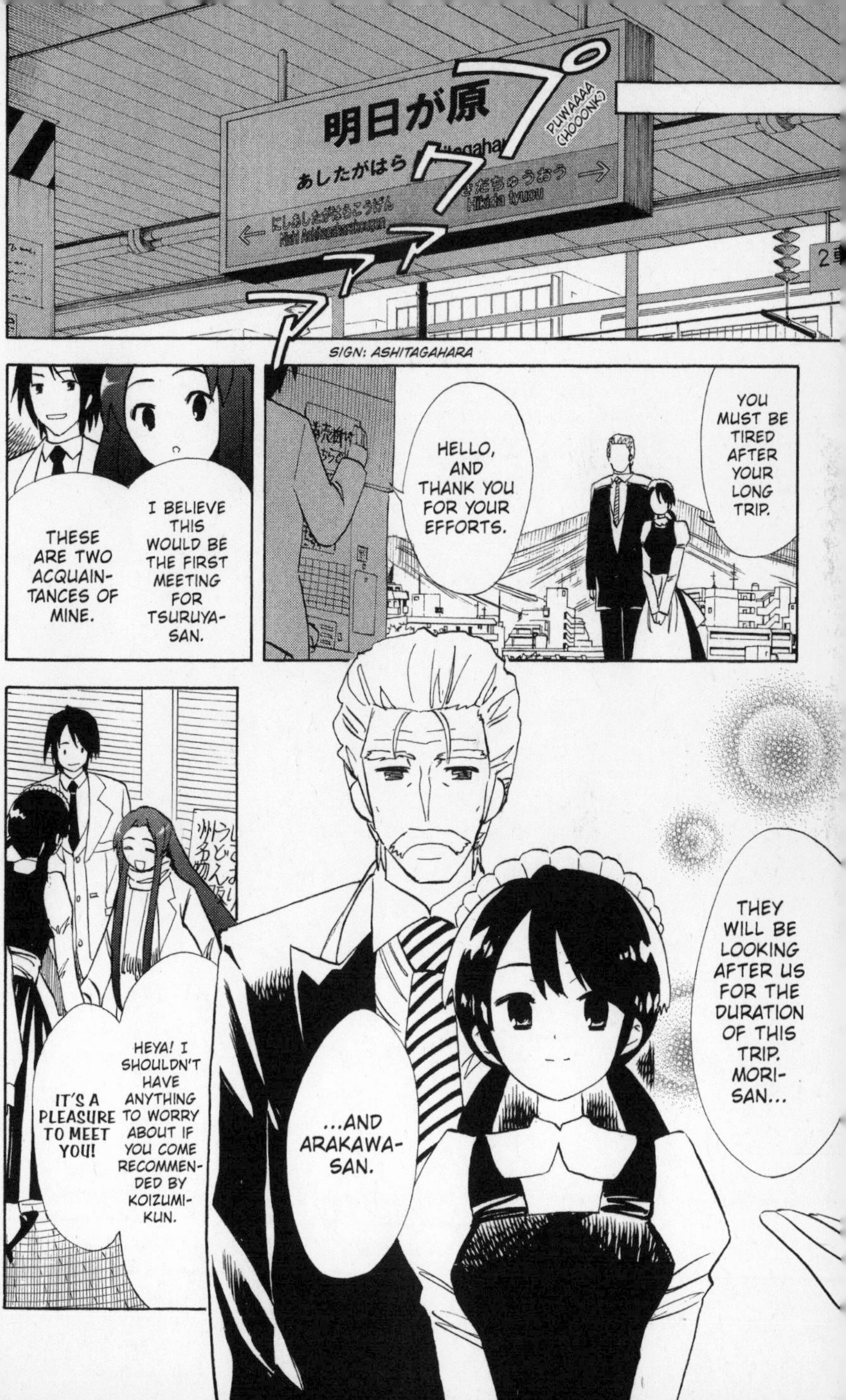
明日が原
あしたがはら
にしあしたがはらこうげん
Hikida tyuou
プワァァァ
PUWAAAA (HOOONK)
SIGN: ASHITAGAHARA
YOU MUST BE TIRED AFTER YOUR LONG TRIP.
HELLO, AND THANK YOU FOR YOUR EFFORTS.
I BELIEVE THIS WOULD BE THE FIRST MEETING FOR TSURUYA-SAN.
THESE ARE TWO ACQUAINTANCES OF MINE.
THEY WILL BE LOOKING AFTER US FOR THE DURATION OF THIS TRIP. MORI-SAN...
...AND ARAKAWA-SAN.
HEYA! I SHOULDN'T HAVE ANYTHING TO WORRY ABOUT IF YOU COME RECOMMENDED BY KOIZUMI-KUN.
IT'S A PLEASURE TO MEET YOU!

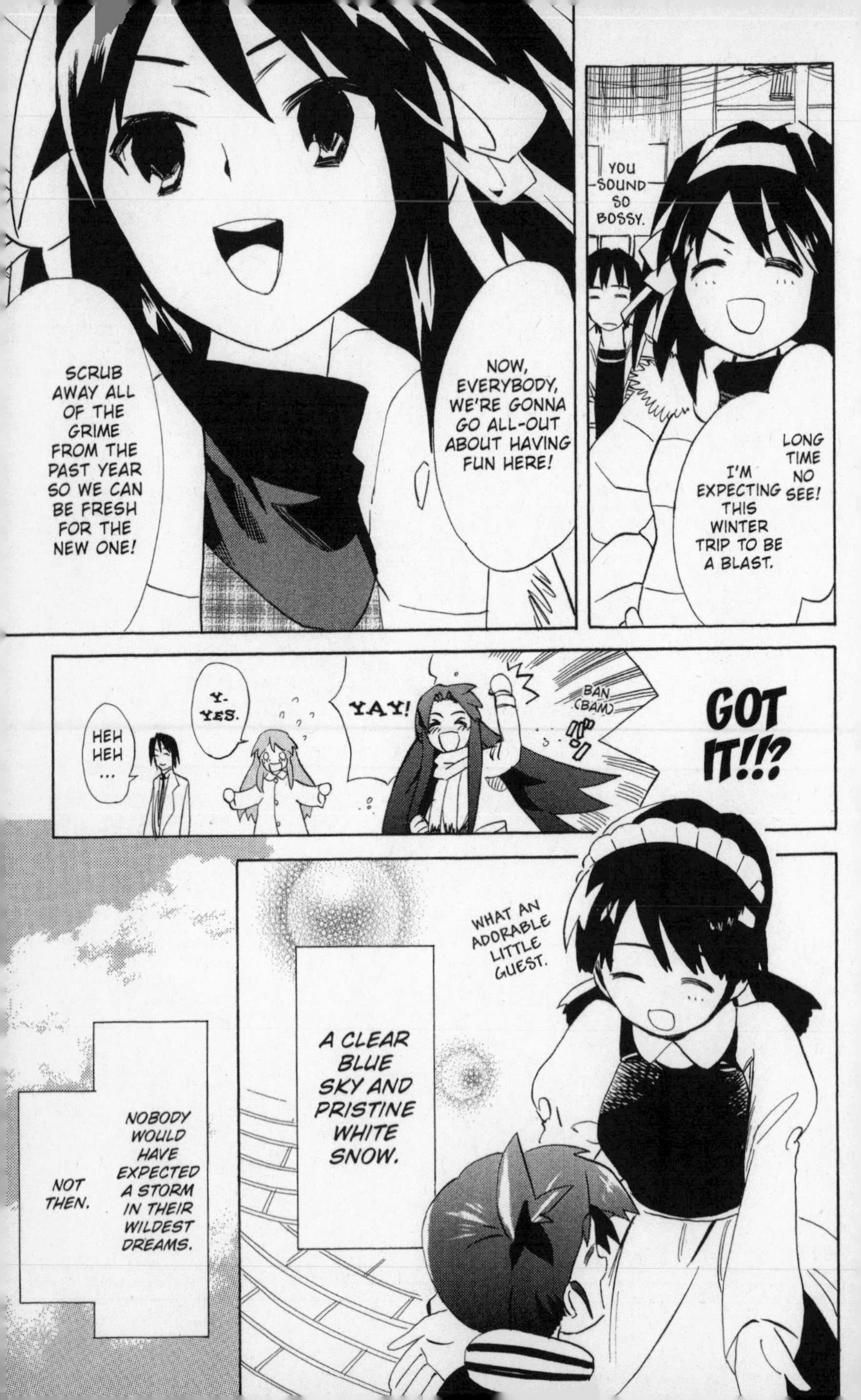

YOU SOUND SO BOSSY.
LONG TIME NO SEE!
I'M EXPECTING THIS WINTER TRIP TO BE A BLAST.
NOW, EVERYBODY, WE'RE GONNA GO ALL-OUT ABOUT HAVING FUN HERE!
SCRUB AWAY ALL OF THE GRIME FROM THE PAST YEAR SO WE CAN BE FRESH FOR THE NEW ONE!
GOT IT!!?
BAN (BAM)
YAY!
Y-YES.
HEH HEH ...
WHAT AN ADORABLE LITTLE GUEST.
A CLEAR BLUE SKY AND PRISTINE WHITE SNOW.
NOBODY WOULD HAVE EXPECTED A STORM IN THEIR WILDEST DREAMS.
NOT THEN.

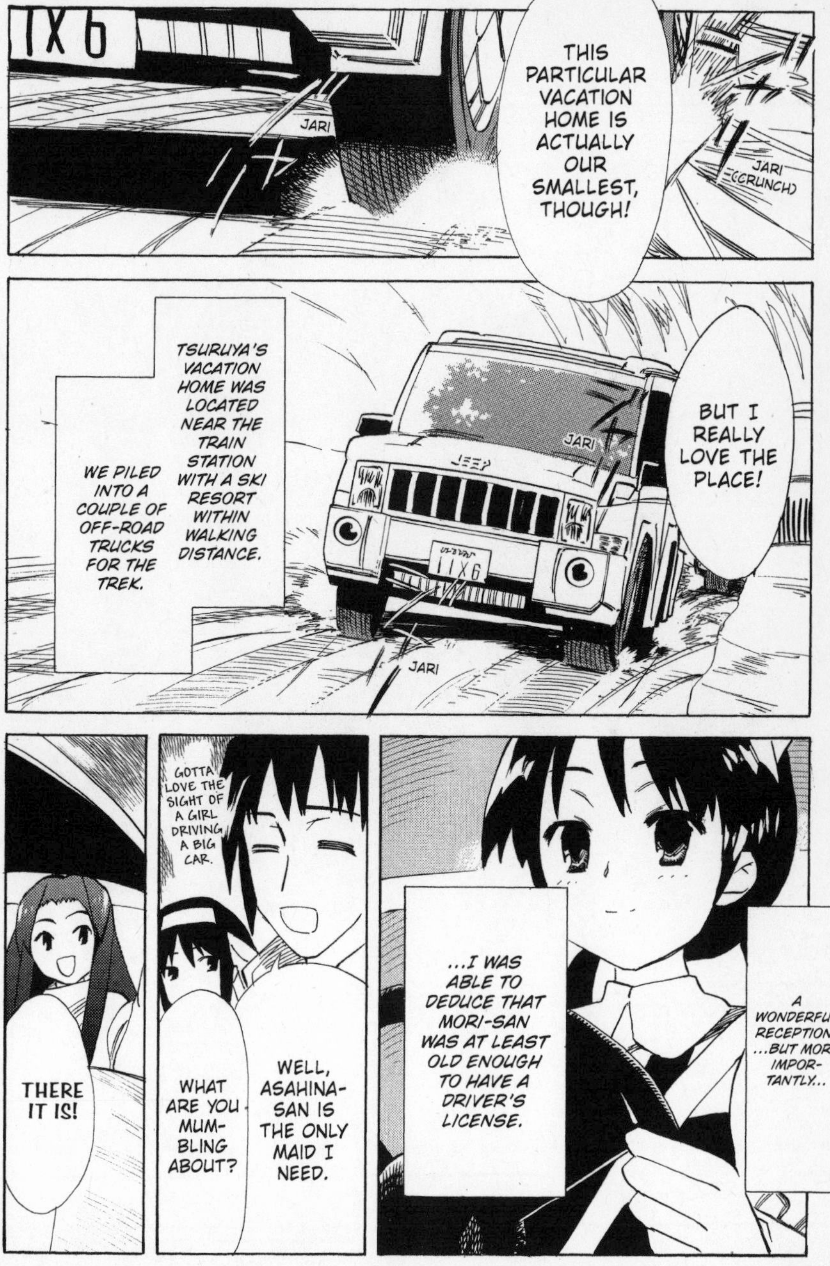
THIS PARTICULAR VACATION HOME IS ACTUALLY OUR SMALLEST, THOUGH!
JARI (CRUNCH)
JARI
BUT I REALLY LOVE THE PLACE!
JARI
TSURUYA'S VACATION HOME WAS LOCATED NEAR THE TRAIN STATION WITH A SKI RESORT WITHIN WALKING DISTANCE.
WE PILED INTO A COUPLE OF OFF-ROAD TRUCKS FOR THE TREK.
JARI
A WONDERFUL RECEPTION. ...BUT MORE IMPOR-TANTLY...
...I WAS ABLE TO DEDUCE THAT MORI-SAN WAS AT LEAST OLD ENOUGH TO HAVE A DRIVER'S LICENSE.
GOTTA LOVE THE SIGHT OF A GIRL DRIVING A BIG CAR.
WELL, ASAHINA-SAN IS THE ONLY MAID I NEED.
WHAT ARE YOU MUM-BLING ABOUT?
THERE IT IS!

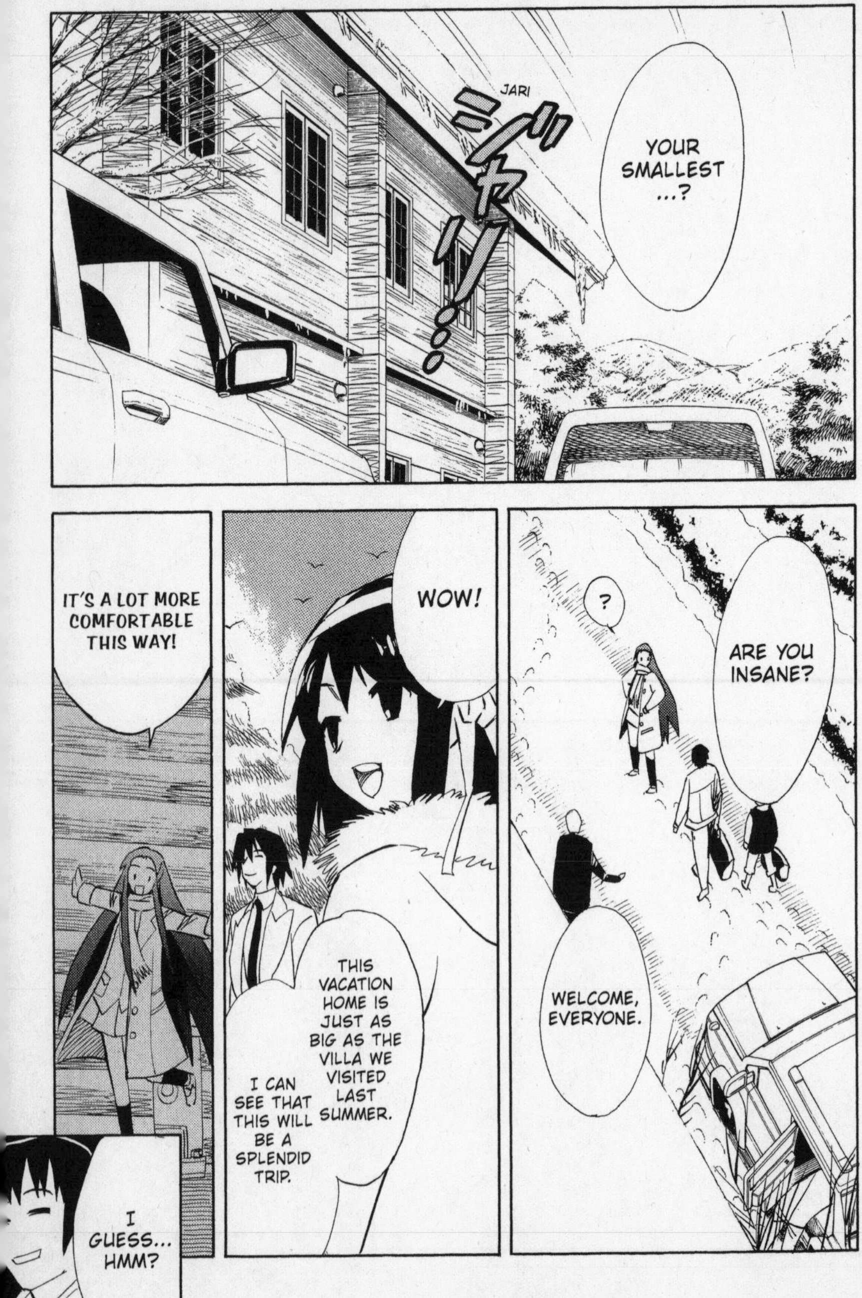
YOUR SMALLEST ...?
JARI
ARE YOU INSANE?
?
WELCOME, EVERYONE.
WOW!
THIS VACATION HOME IS JUST AS BIG AS THE VILLA WE VISITED LAST SUMMER.
I CAN SEE THAT THIS WILL BE A SPLENDID TRIP.
IT'S A LOT MORE COMFORTABLE THIS WAY!
I GUESS... HMM?

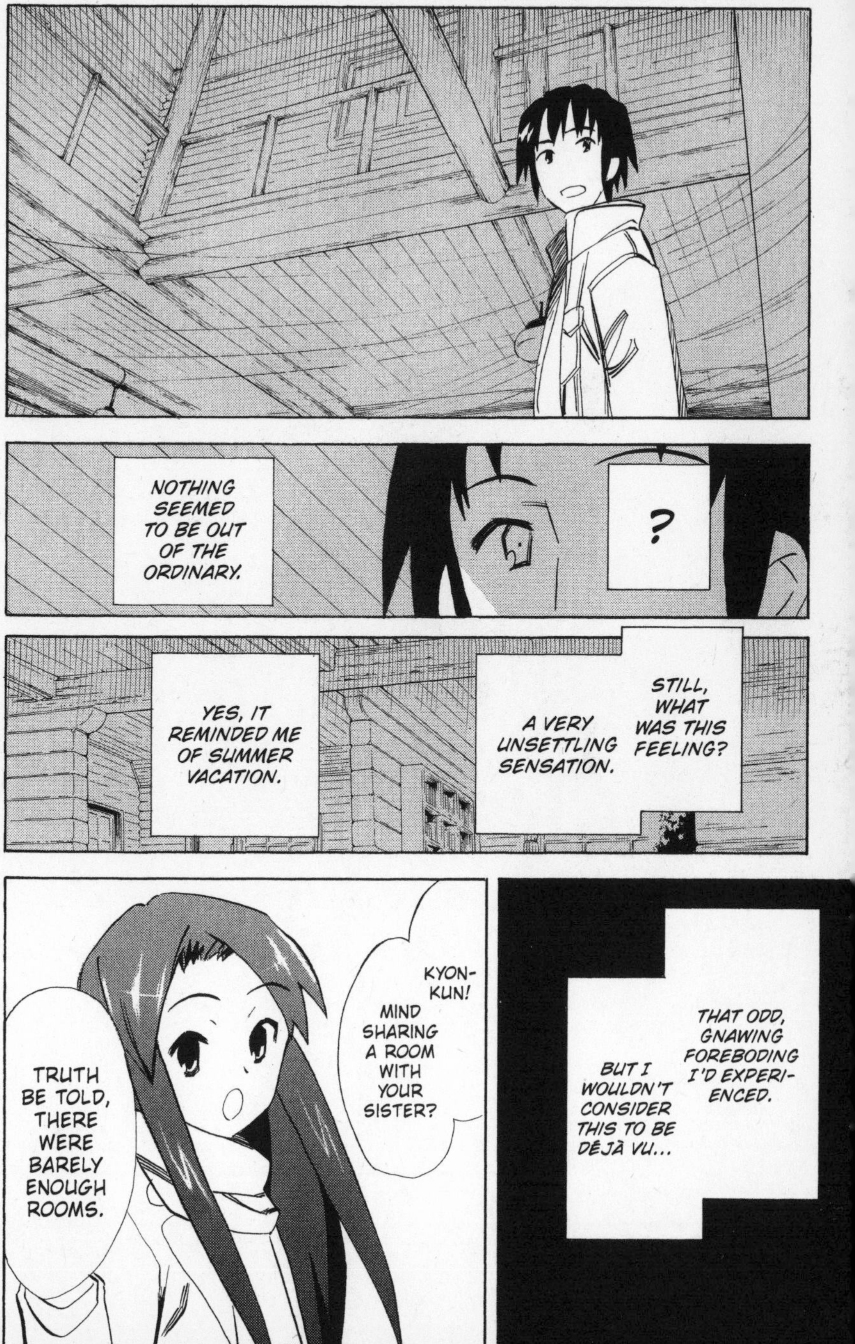
?
NOTHING SEEMED TO BE OUT OF THE ORDINARY.
STILL, WHAT WAS THIS FEELING?
A VERY UNSETTLING SENSATION.
YES, IT REMINDED ME OF SUMMER VACATION.
THAT ODD, GNAWING FOREBODING I'D EXPERIENCED.
BUT I WOULDN'T CONSIDER THIS TO BE DÉJÀ VU...
KYON-KUN! MIND SHARING A ROOM WITH YOUR SISTER?
TRUTH BE TOLD, THERE WERE BARELY ENOUGH ROOMS.

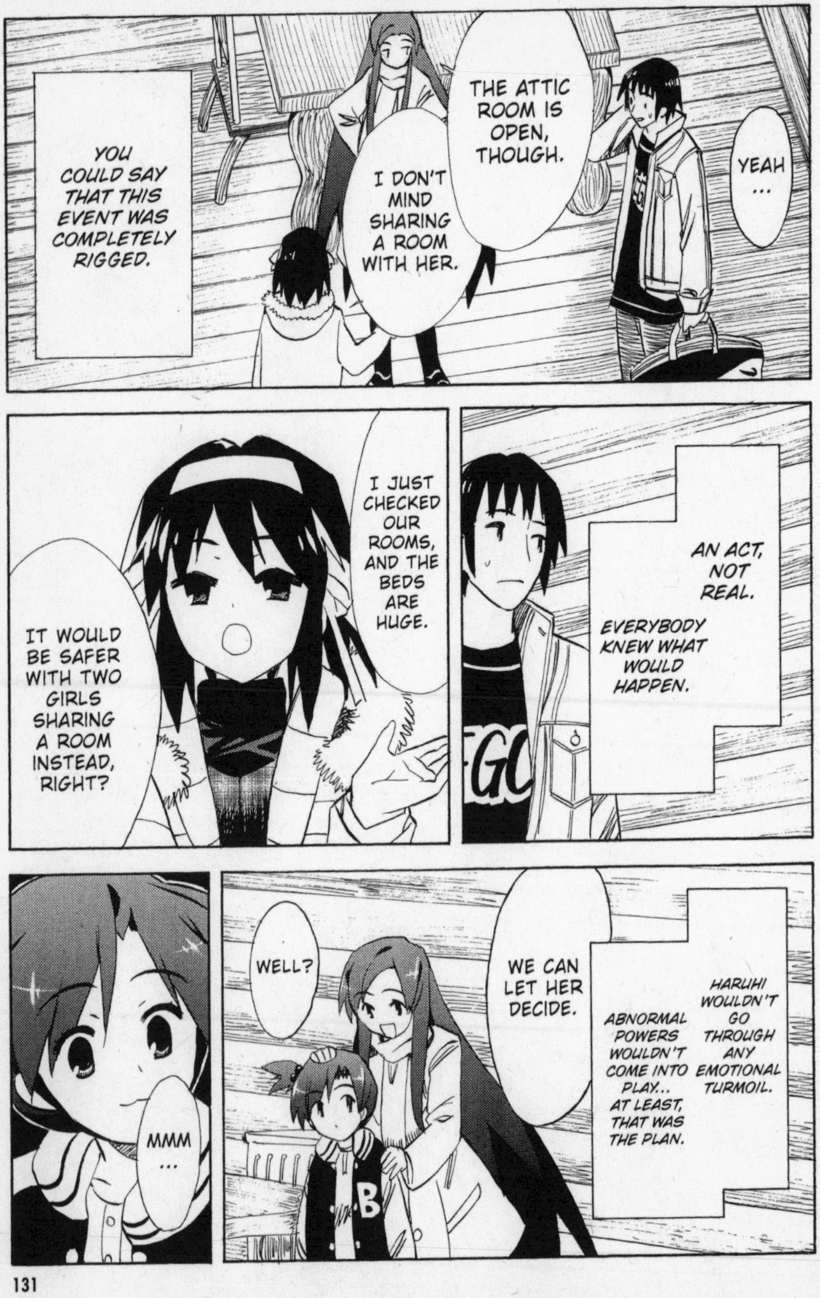
YEAH ...
THE ATTIC ROOM IS OPEN, THOUGH.
I DON'T MIND SHARING A ROOM WITH HER.
YOU COULD SAY THAT THIS EVENT WAS COMPLETELY RIGGED.
AN ACT, NOT REAL.
EVERYBODY KNEW WHAT WOULD HAPPEN.
I JUST CHECKED OUR ROOMS, AND THE BEDS ARE HUGE.
IT WOULD BE SAFER WITH TWO GIRLS SHARING A ROOM INSTEAD, RIGHT?
HARUHI WOULDN'T GO THROUGH ANY EMOTIONAL TURMOIL.
ABNORMAL POWERS WOULDN'T COME INTO PLAY... AT LEAST, THAT WAS THE PLAN.
WE CAN LET HER DECIDE.
WELL?
MMM ...

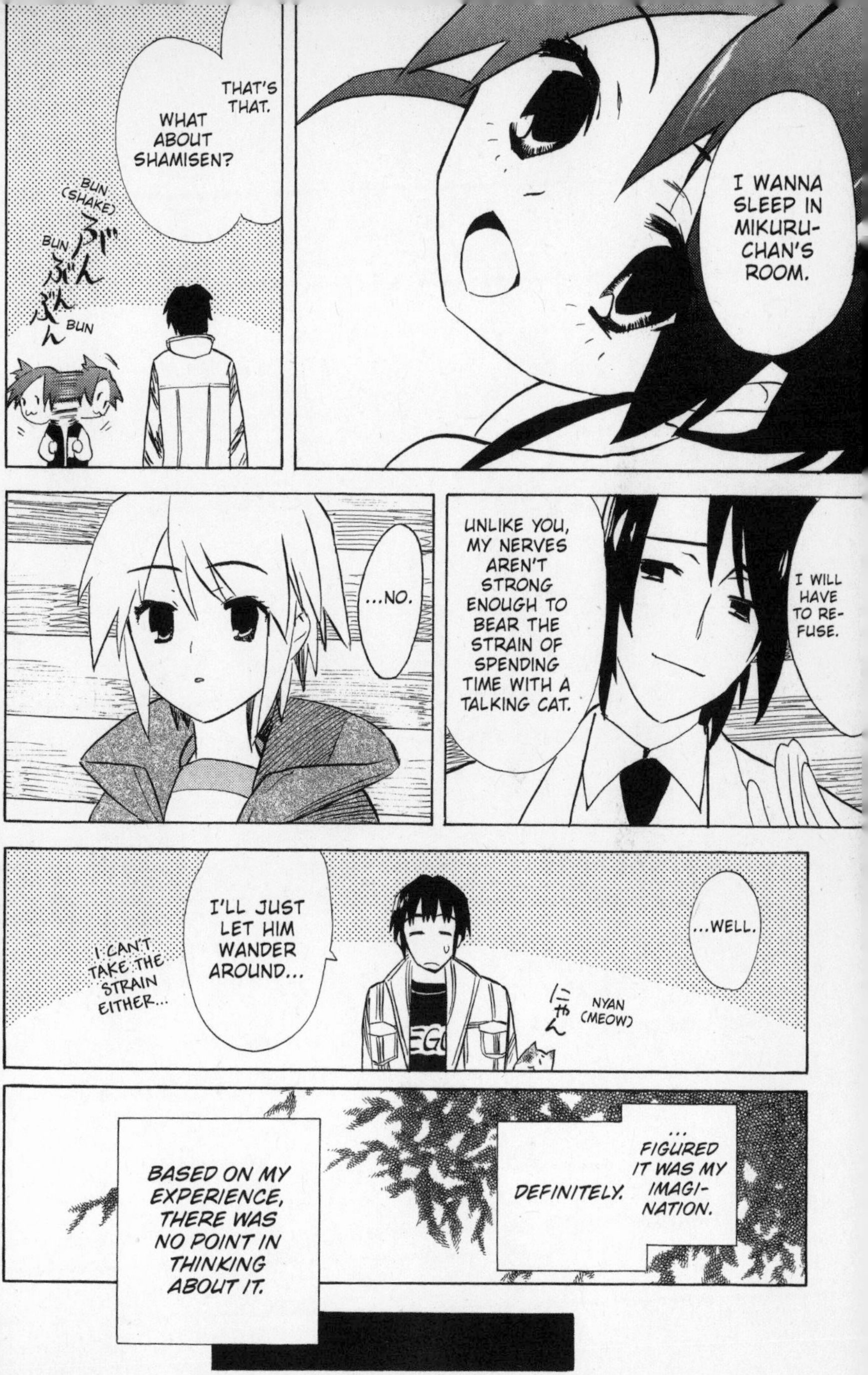
I WANNA SLEEP IN MIKURU-CHAN'S ROOM.
THAT'S THAT.
WHAT ABOUT SHAMISEN?
BUN (SHAKE)
ぶん
BUN
ぶん
BUN
ぶん
I WILL HAVE TO RE-FUSE.
UNLIKE YOU, MY NERVES AREN'T STRONG ENOUGH TO BEAR THE STRAIN OF SPENDING TIME WITH A TALKING CAT.
...NO.
...WELL.
にゃん
NYAN (MEOW)
I'LL JUST LET HIM WANDER AROUND...
I CAN'T TAKE THE STRAIN EITHER...
...FIGURED IT WAS MY IMAGINATION.
DEFINITELY.
BASED ON MY EXPERIENCE, THERE WAS NO POINT IN THINKING ABOUT IT.

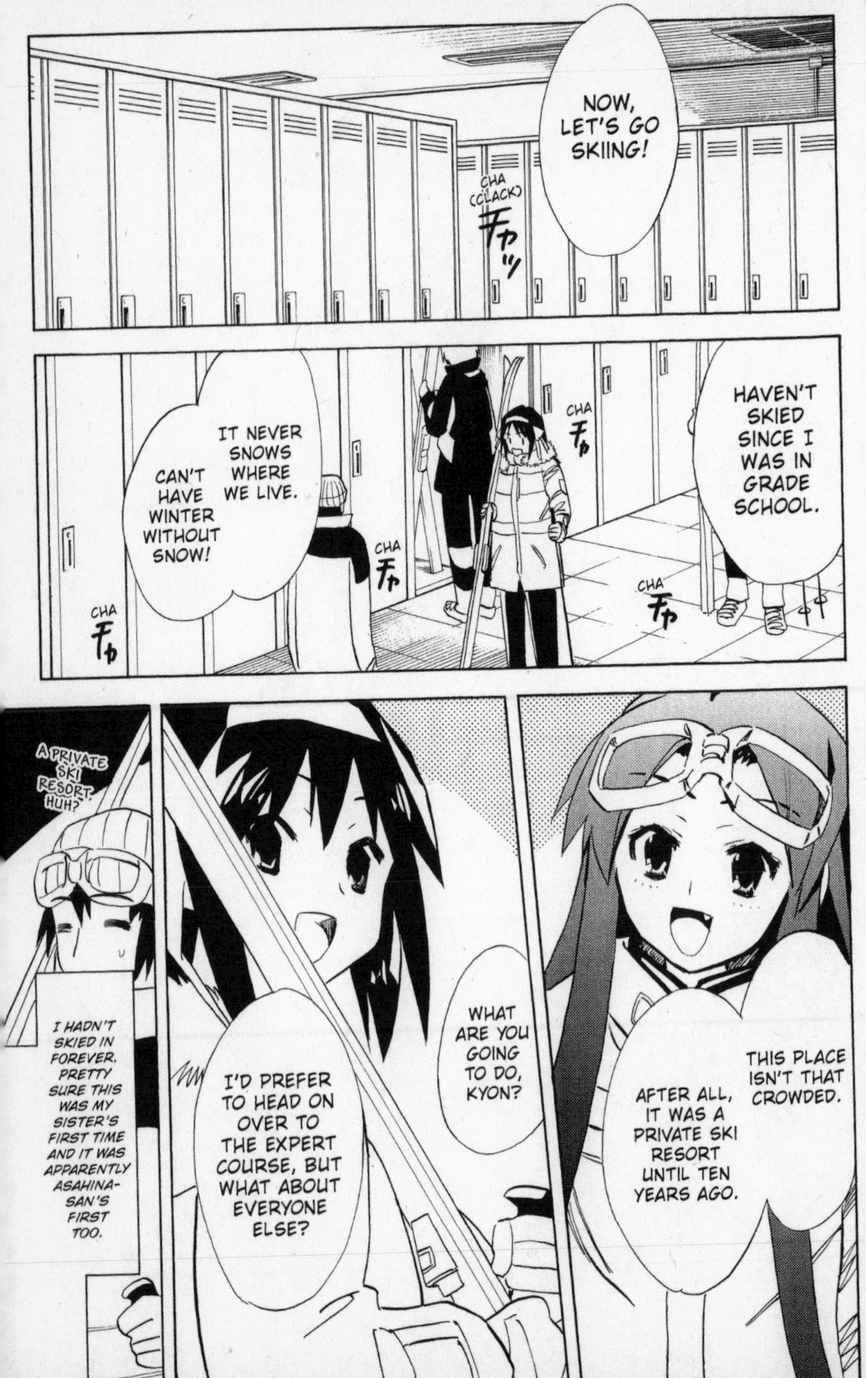
NOW, LET'S GO SKIING!
CHA (CLACK)
HAVEN'T SKIED SINCE I WAS IN GRADE SCHOOL.
CHA
CHA
IT NEVER SNOWS WHERE WE LIVE.
CAN'T HAVE WINTER WITHOUT SNOW!
CHA
CHA
THIS PLACE ISN'T THAT CROWDED.
AFTER ALL, IT WAS A PRIVATE SKI RESORT UNTIL TEN YEARS AGO.
WHAT ARE YOU GOING TO DO, KYON?
I'D PREFER TO HEAD ON OVER TO THE EXPERT COURSE, BUT WHAT ABOUT EVERYONE ELSE?
A PRIVATE SKI RESORT, HUH?
I HADN'T SKIED IN FOREVER. PRETTY SURE THIS WAS MY SISTER'S FIRST TIME AND IT WAS APPARENTLY ASAHINA-SAN'S FIRST TOO.

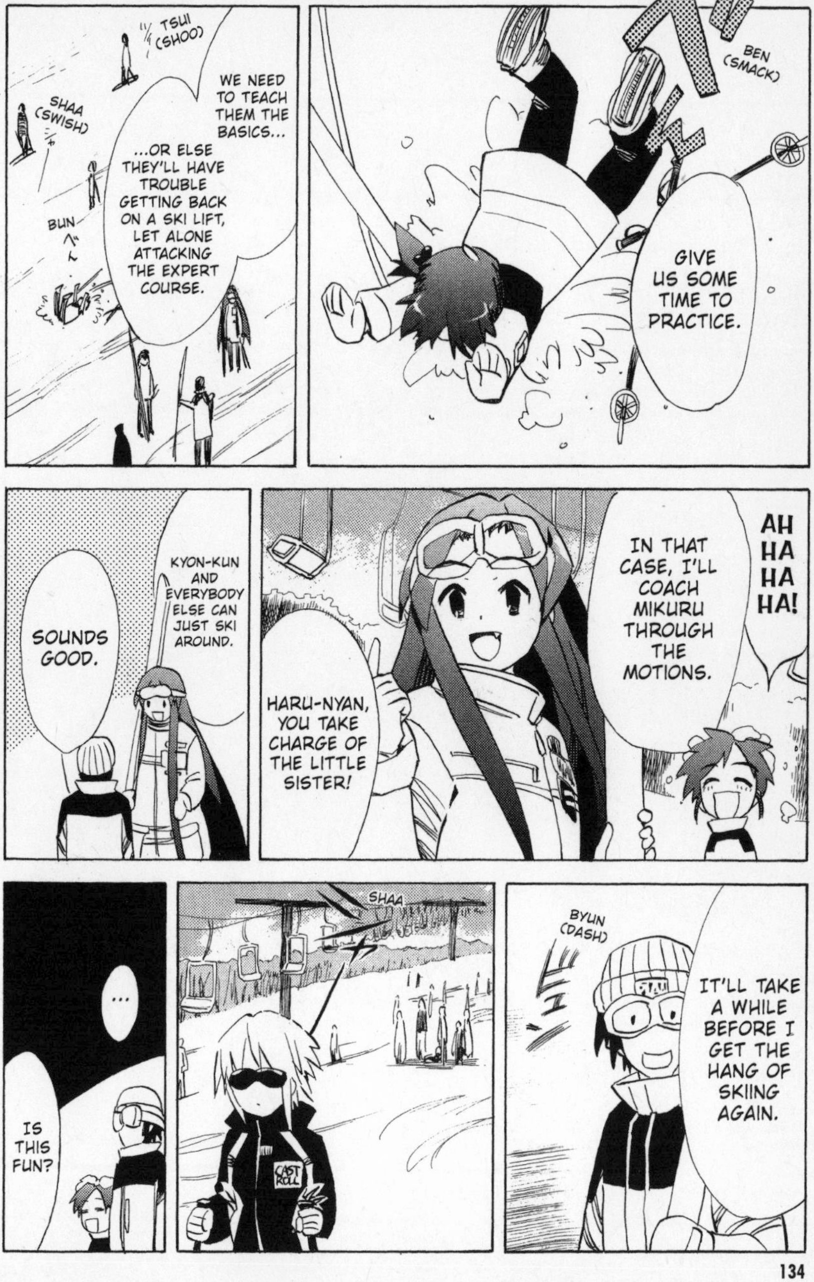
BEN (SMACK)
GIVE US SOME TIME TO PRACTICE.
WE NEED TO TEACH THEM THE BASICS...
TSUI (SHOO)
...OR ELSE THEY'LL HAVE TROUBLE GETTING BACK ON A SKI LIFT, LET ALONE ATTACKING THE EXPERT COURSE.
SHAA (SWISH)
BUN
AH HA HA HA!
IN THAT CASE, I'LL COACH MIKURU THROUGH THE MOTIONS.
HARU-NYAN, YOU TAKE CHARGE OF THE LITTLE SISTER!
KYON-KUN AND EVERYBODY ELSE CAN JUST SKI AROUND.
SOUNDS GOOD.
BYUN (DASH)
IT'LL TAKE A WHILE BEFORE I GET THE HANG OF SKIING AGAIN.
SHAA
CAST ROLL
...
IS THIS FUN?

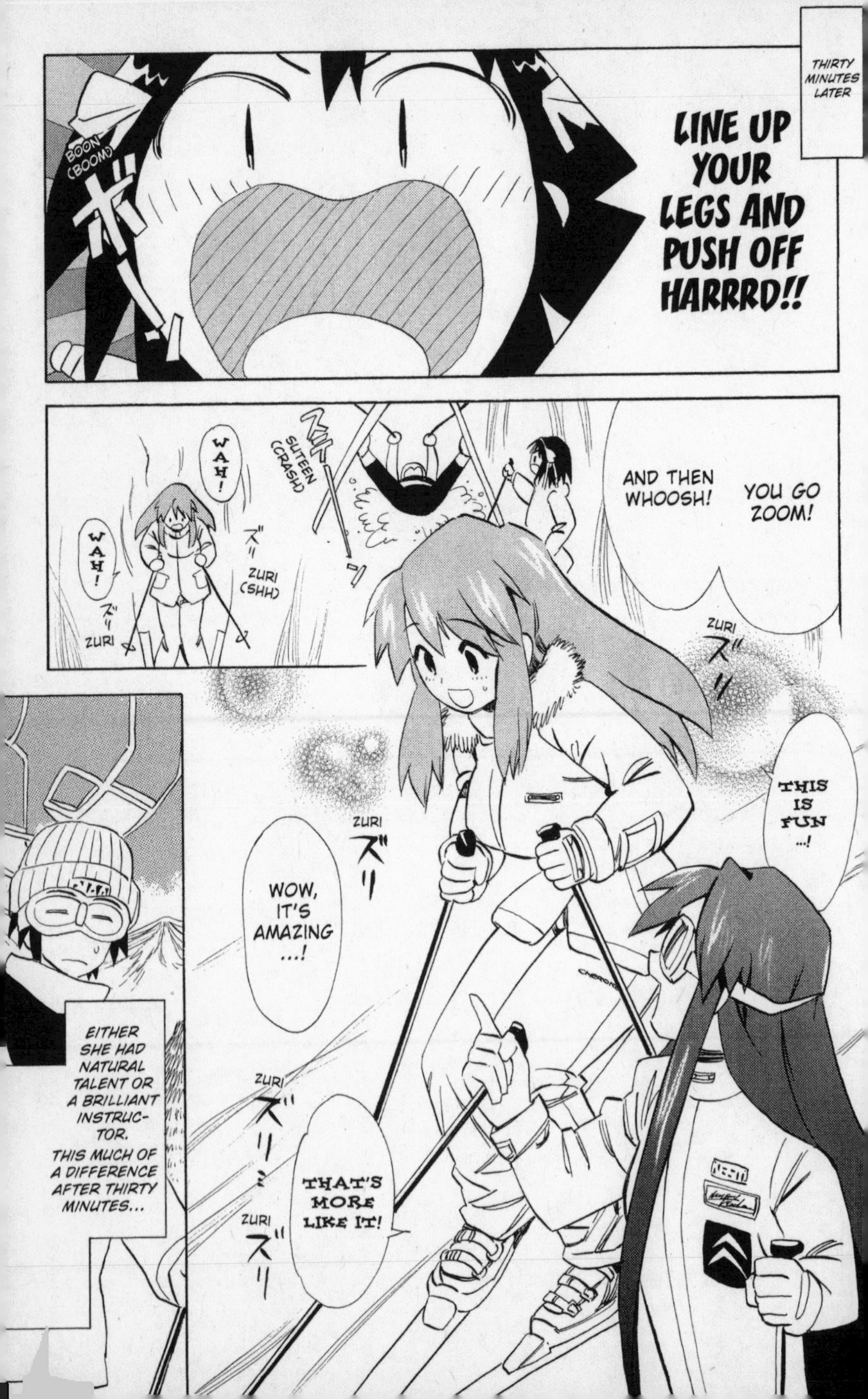
THIRTY MINUTES LATER
LINE UP YOUR LEGS AND PUSH OFF HARRRD!!
BOON (BOOM)
AND THEN WHOOSH!
YOU GO ZOOM!
SUTEEN (CRASH)
WAH!
WAH!
ZURI (SHH)
ZURI
ZURI
THIS IS FUN ...!
ZURI
WOW, IT'S AMAZING ...!
EITHER SHE HAD NATURAL TALENT OR A BRILLIANT INSTRUCTOR. THIS MUCH OF A DIFFERENCE AFTER THIRTY MINUTES...
THAT'S MORE LIKE IT!
ZURI
ZURI

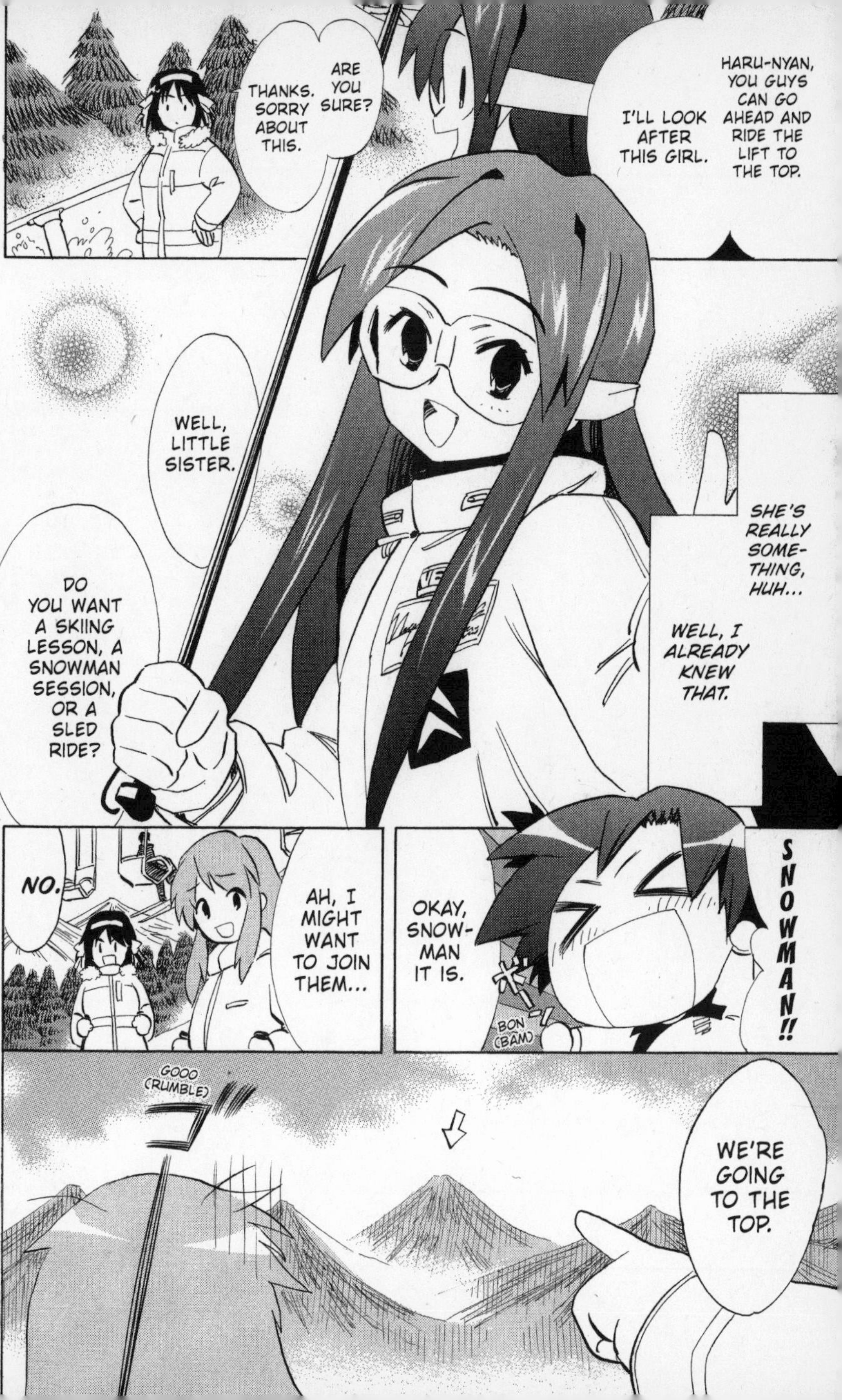
HARU-NYAN, YOU GUYS CAN GO AHEAD AND RIDE THE LIFT TO THE TOP.
I'LL LOOK AFTER THIS GIRL.
ARE YOU SURE?
THANKS. SORRY ABOUT THIS.
SHE'S REALLY SOME-THING, HUH...
WELL, I ALREADY KNEW THAT.
WELL, LITTLE SISTER.
DO YOU WANT A SKIING LESSON, A SNOWMAN SESSION, OR A SLED RIDE?
SNOWMAN!!
OKAY, SNOWMAN IT IS.
BON (BAM)
AH, I MIGHT WANT TO JOIN THEM...
NO.
WE'RE GOING TO THE TOP.
GOOO (RUMBLE)

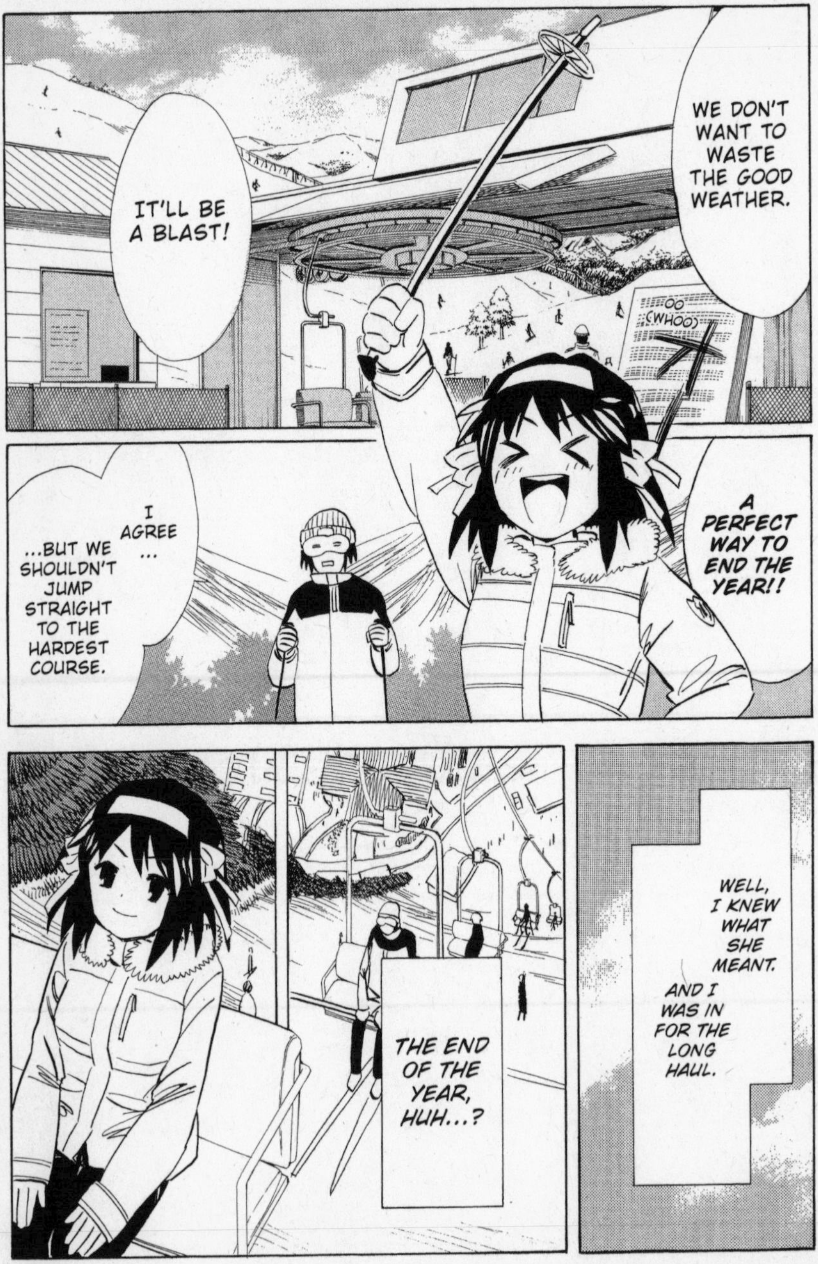
WE DON'T WANT TO WASTE THE GOOD WEATHER.
IT'LL BE A BLAST!
OO (WHOO)
A PERFECT WAY TO END THE YEAR!!
I AGREE ...
...BUT WE SHOULDN'T JUMP STRAIGHT TO THE HARDEST COURSE.
WELL, I KNEW WHAT SHE MEANT.
AND I WAS IN FOR THE LONG HAUL.
THE END OF THE YEAR, HUH...?

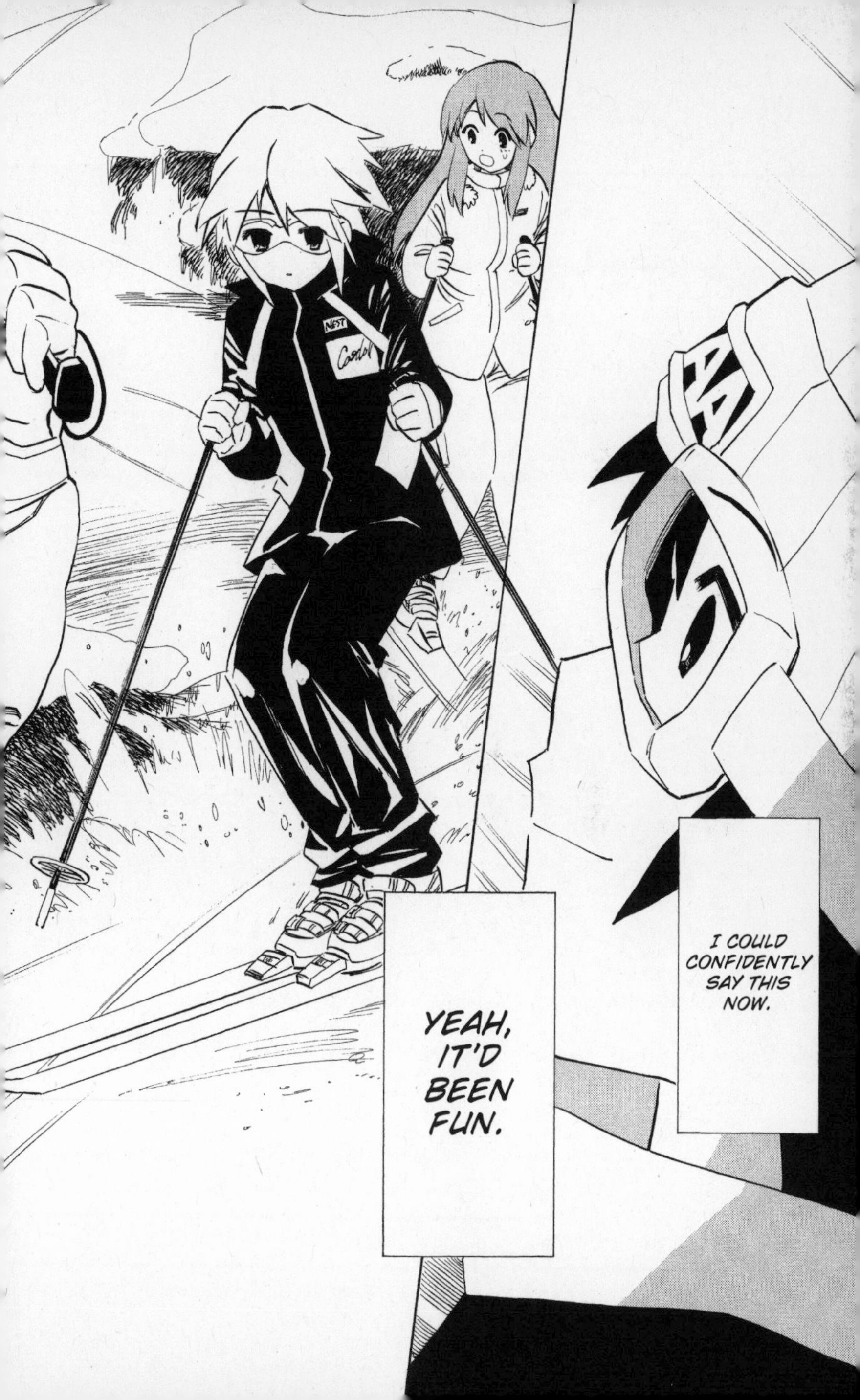
I COULD CONFIDENTLY SAY THIS NOW.
YEAH, IT'D BEEN FUN.

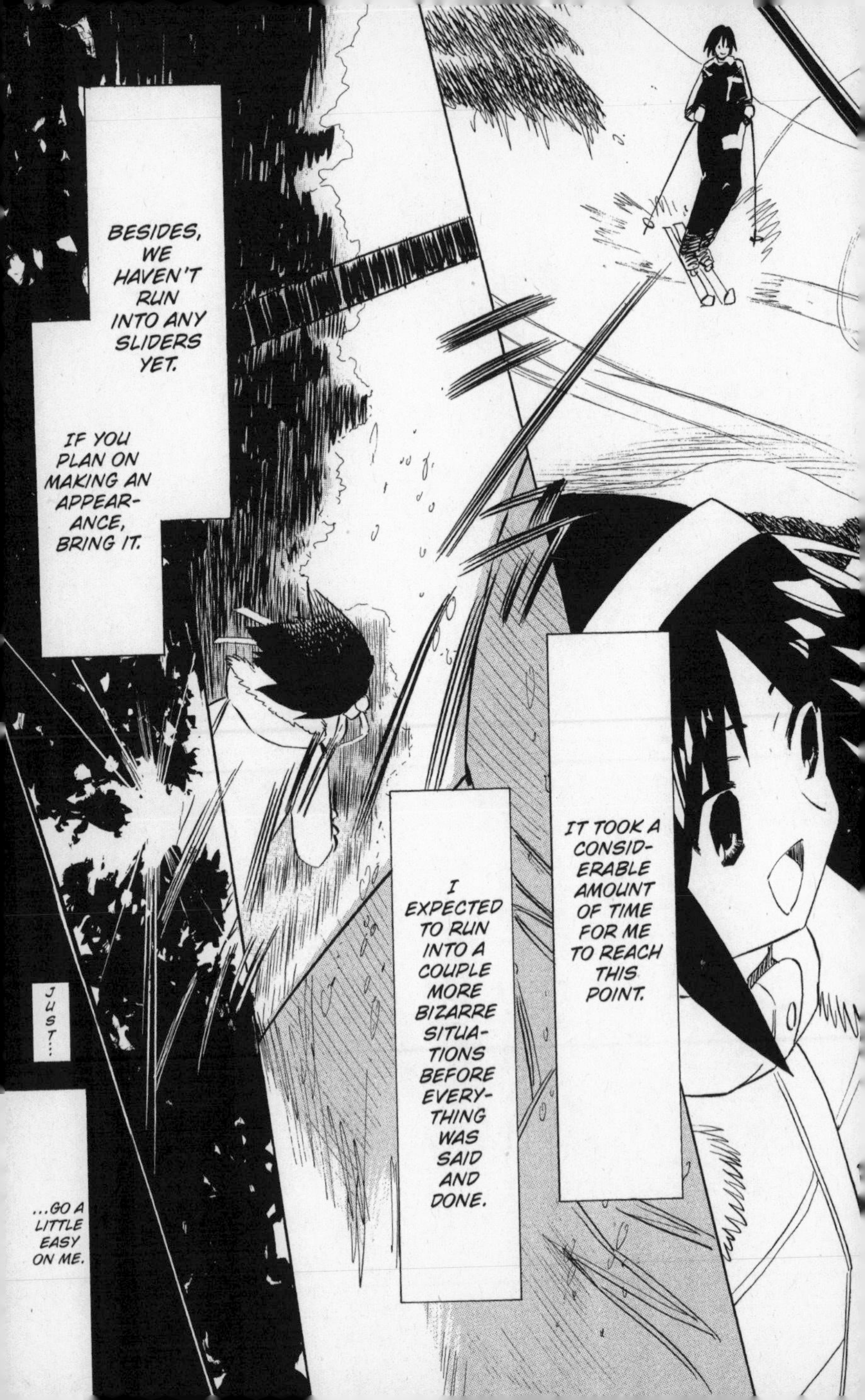
IT TOOK A CONSID-ERABLE AMOUNT OF TIME FOR ME TO REACH THIS POINT.
I EXPECTED TO RUN INTO A COUPLE MORE BIZARRE SITUA-TIONS BEFORE EVERY-THING WAS SAID AND DONE.
BESIDES, WE HAVEN'T RUN INTO ANY SLIDERS YET.
IF YOU PLAN ON MAKING AN APPEAR-ANCE, BRING IT.
JUST...
...GO A LITTLE EASY ON ME.

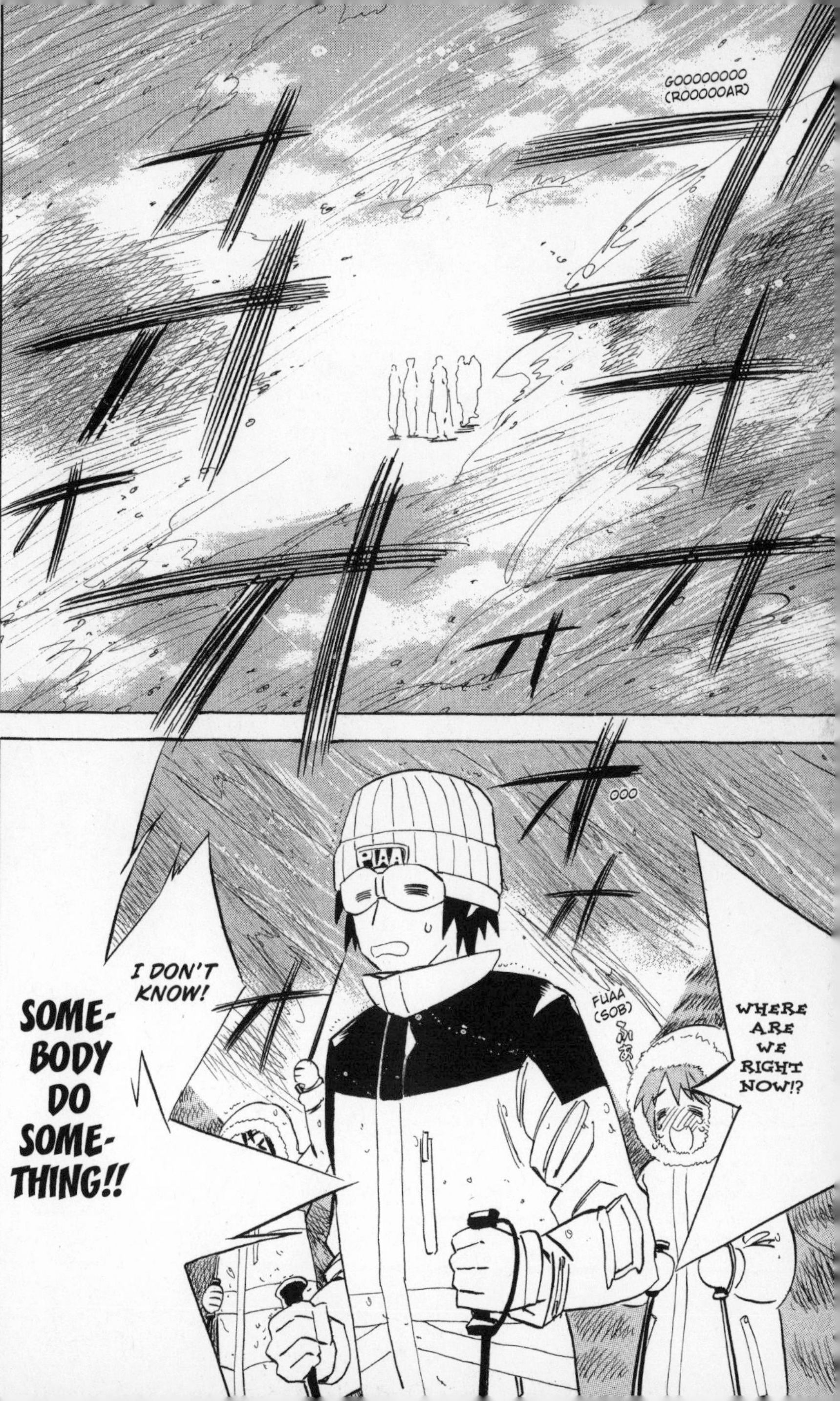
GOOOOOOOO
(ROOOOOAR)
OOO
WHERE ARE WE RIGHT NOW!?
FUAA (SOB)
I DON'T KNOW!
SOME-BODY DO SOME-THING!!

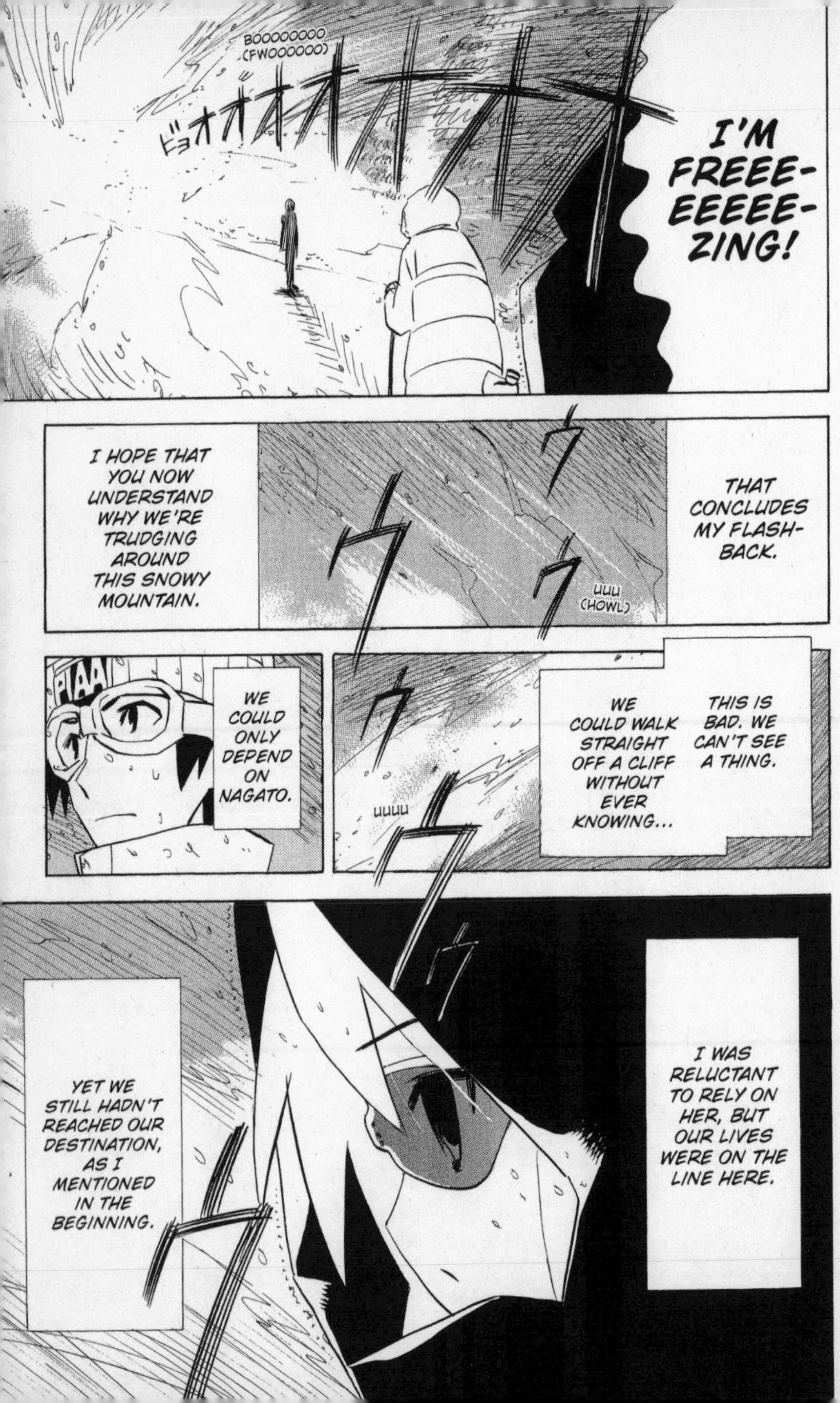
I'M FREEEE-EEEEE-ZING!
BOOOOOOOO (FWOOOOOO)
THAT CONCLUDES MY FLASH-BACK.
uuu (HOWL)
I HOPE THAT YOU NOW UNDERSTAND WHY WE'RE TRUDGING AROUND THIS SNOWY MOUNTAIN.
THIS IS BAD. WE CAN'T SEE A THING.
WE COULD WALK STRAIGHT OFF A CLIFF WITHOUT EVER KNOWING...
uuuu
WE COULD ONLY DEPEND ON NAGATO.
PIAA
I WAS RELUCTANT TO RELY ON HER, BUT OUR LIVES WERE ON THE LINE HERE.
YET WE STILL HADN'T REACHED OUR DESTINATION, AS I MENTIONED IN THE BEGINNING.

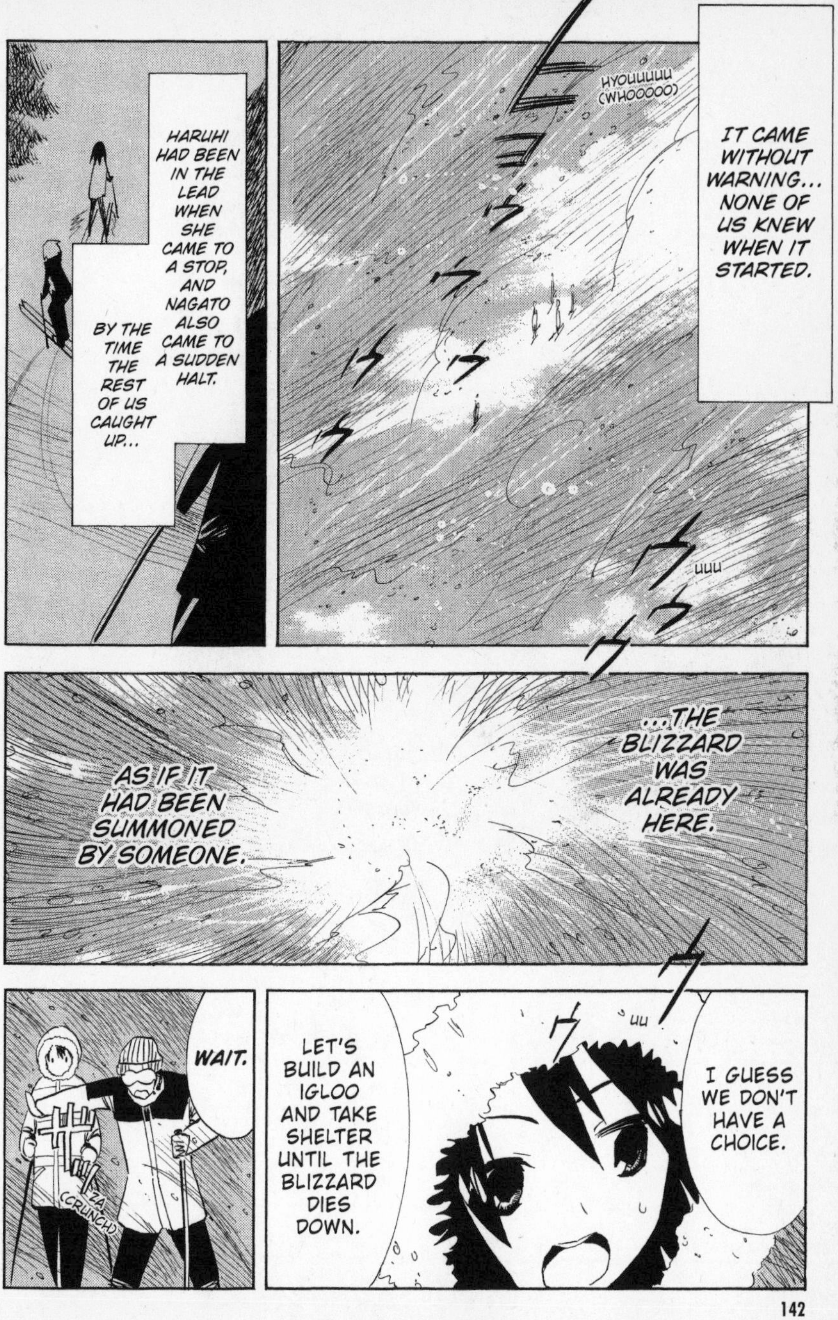
IT CAME WITHOUT WARNING... NONE OF US KNEW WHEN IT STARTED.
HYOUUUUU (WHOOOOO)
UUU
HARUHI HAD BEEN IN THE LEAD WHEN SHE CAME TO A STOP, AND NAGATO ALSO CAME TO A SUDDEN HALT.
BY THE TIME THE REST OF US CAUGHT UP...
...THE BLIZZARD WAS ALREADY HERE.
AS IF IT HAD BEEN SUMMONED BY SOMEONE.
UU
I GUESS WE DON'T HAVE A CHOICE.
LET'S BUILD AN IGLOO AND TAKE SHELTER UNTIL THE BLIZZARD DIES DOWN.
WAIT.
ZA (CRUNCH)

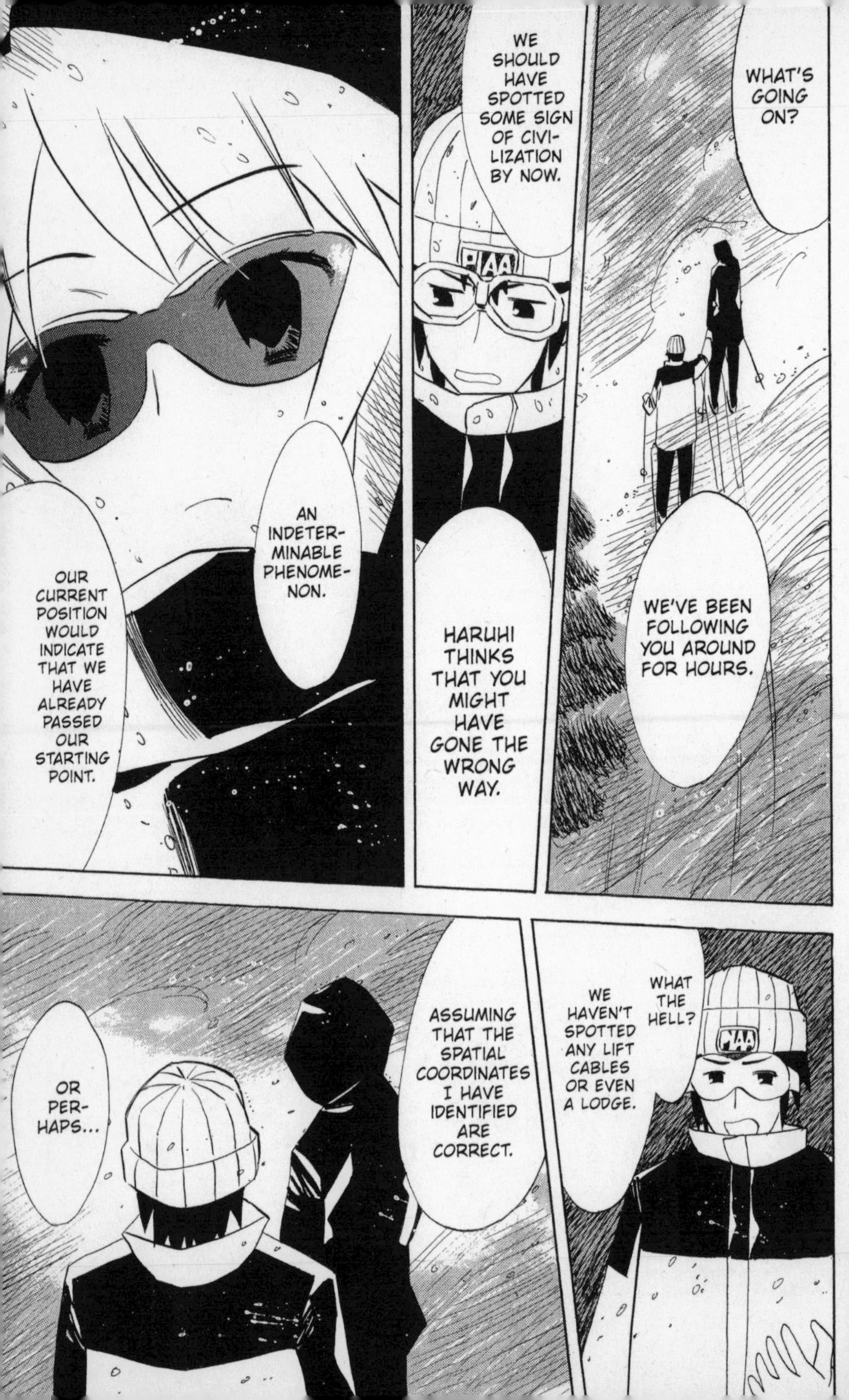
WHAT'S GOING ON?
WE'VE BEEN FOLLOWING YOU AROUND FOR HOURS.
WE SHOULD HAVE SPOTTED SOME SIGN OF CIVILIZATION BY NOW.
HARUHI THINKS THAT YOU MIGHT HAVE GONE THE WRONG WAY.
AN INDETERMINABLE PHENOMENON.
OUR CURRENT POSITION WOULD INDICATE THAT WE HAVE ALREADY PASSED OUR STARTING POINT.
WHAT THE HELL?
WE HAVEN'T SPOTTED ANY LIFT CABLES OR EVEN A LODGE.
ASSUMING THAT THE SPATIAL COORDINATES I HAVE IDENTIFIED ARE CORRECT.
OR PERHAPS...

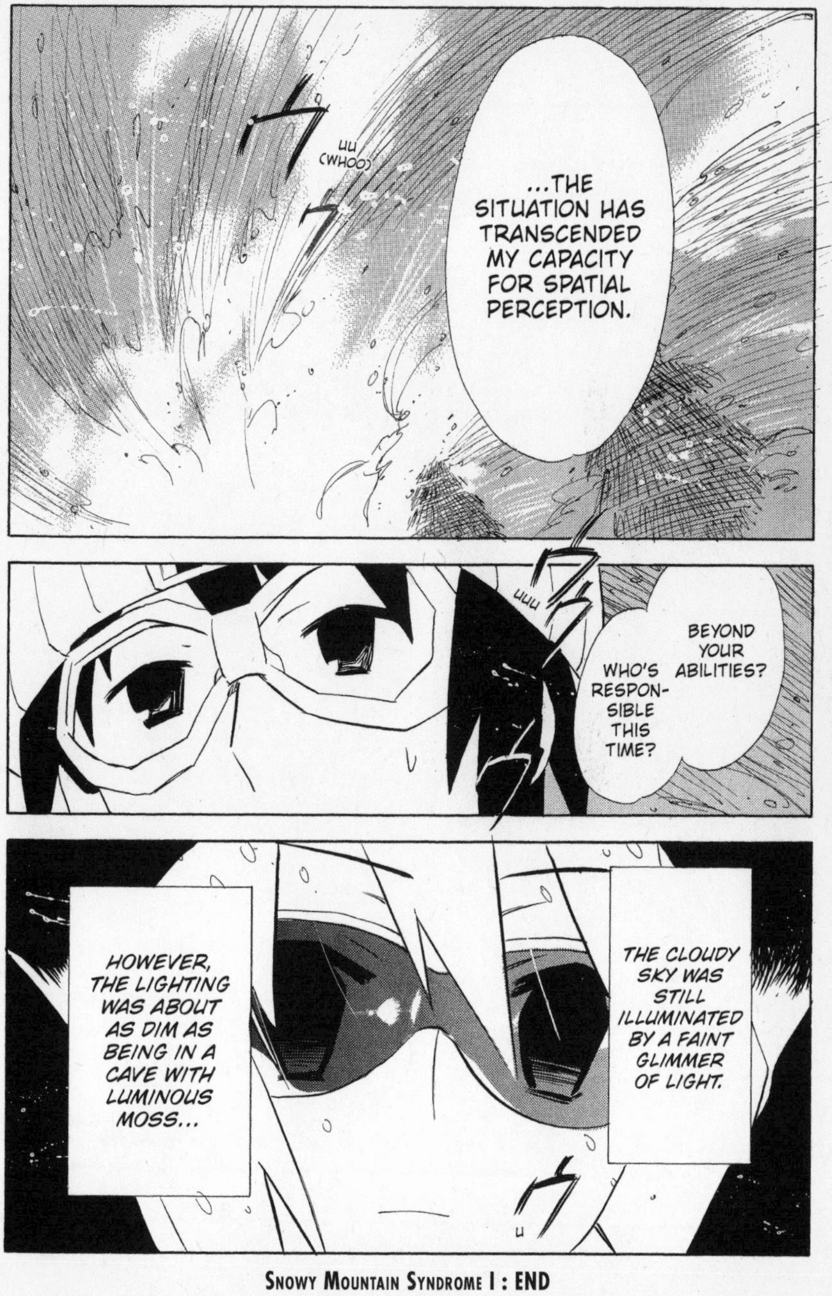
...THE SITUATION HAS TRANSCENDED MY CAPACITY FOR SPATIAL PERCEPTION.
UU (WHOO)
UUU
BEYOND YOUR ABILITIES? WHO'S RESPONSIBLE THIS TIME?
THE CLOUDY SKY WAS STILL ILLUMINATED BY A FAINT GLIMMER OF LIGHT.
HOWEVER, THE LIGHTING WAS ABOUT AS DIM AS BEING IN A CAVE WITH LUMINOUS MOSS...
U

Snowy Mountain Syndrome I : END

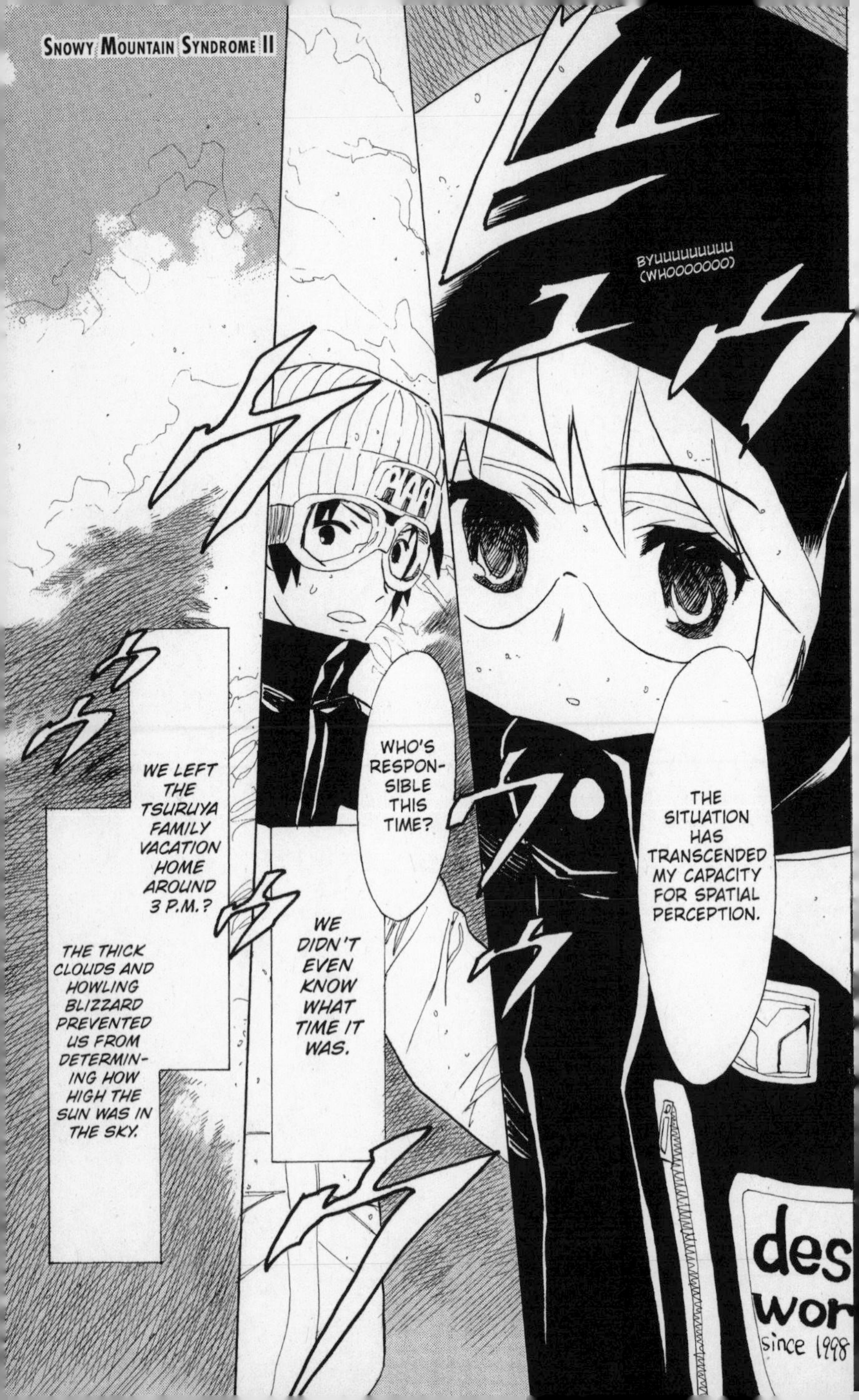
BYUUUUUUUUU
(WHOOOOOOO)
THE SITUATION HAS TRANSCENDED MY CAPACITY FOR SPATIAL PERCEPTION.
WHO'S RESPON-SIBLE THIS TIME?
WE DIDN'T EVEN KNOW WHAT TIME IT WAS.
WE LEFT THE TSURUYA FAMILY VACATION HOME AROUND 3 P.M.?
THE THICK CLOUDS AND HOWLING BLIZZARD PREVENTED US FROM DETERMIN-ING HOW HIGH THE SUN WAS IN THE SKY.

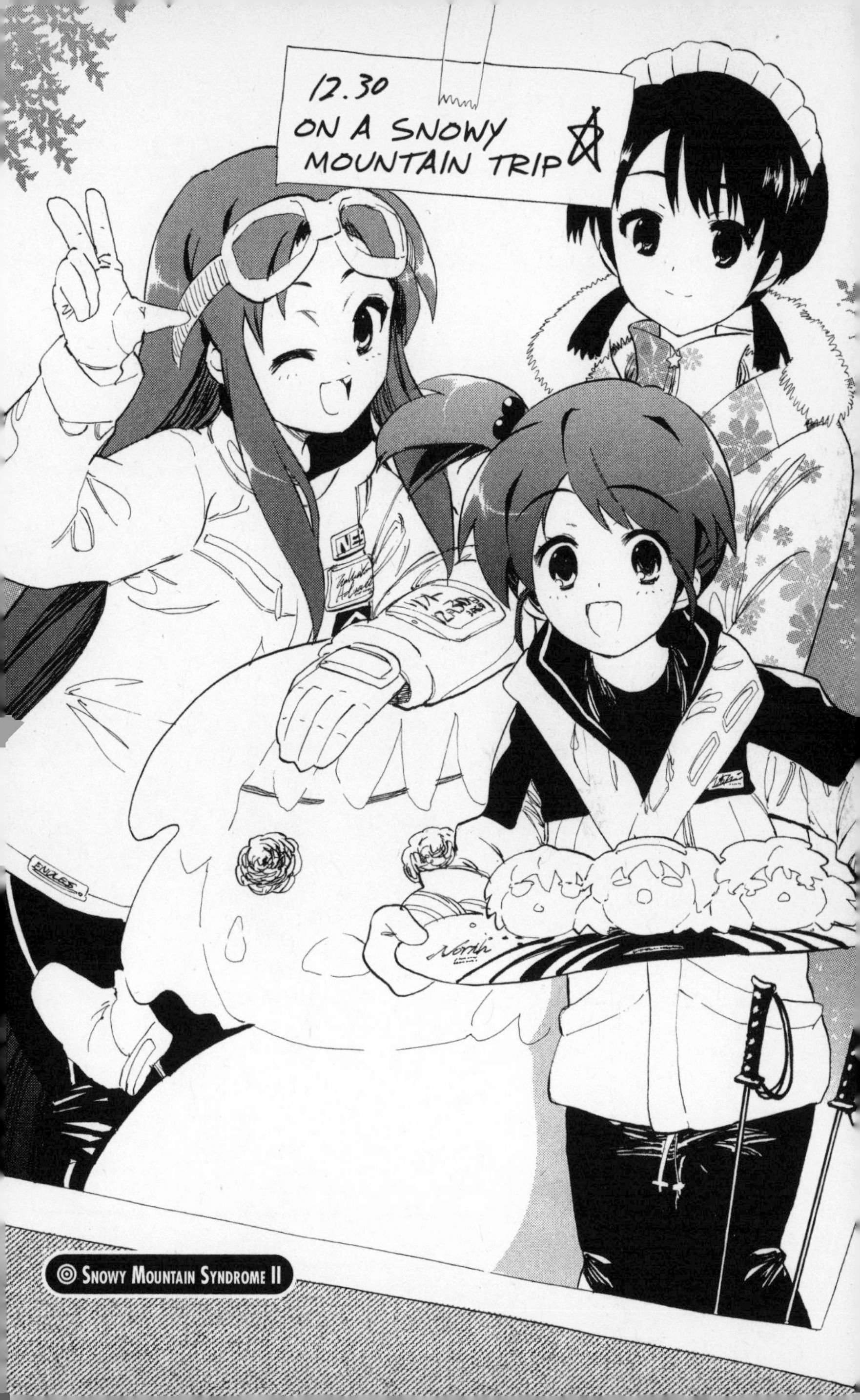

12.30
ON A SNOWY MOUNTAIN TRIP
◎ SNOWY MOUNTAIN SYNDROME II

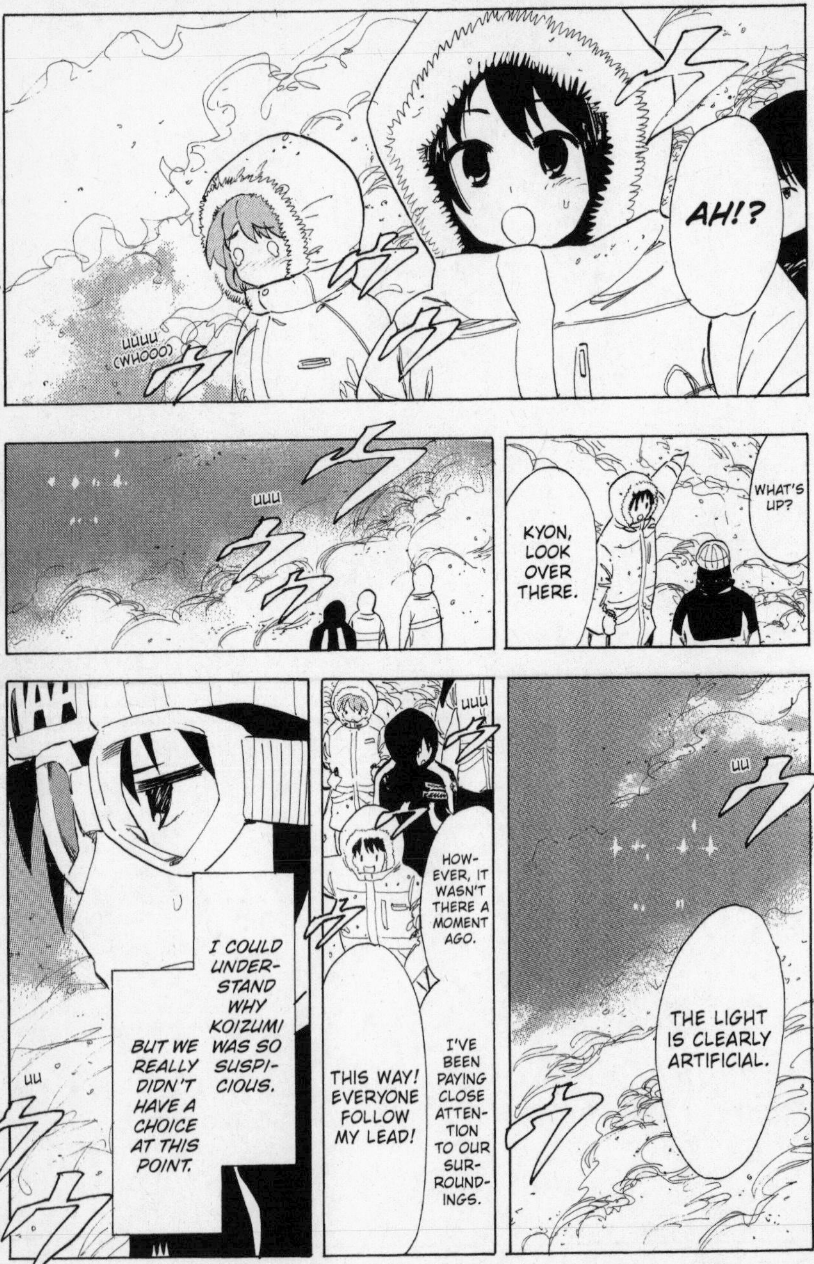
AH!?
uuuu (WHOOO)
WHAT'S UP?
KYON, LOOK OVER THERE.
uuu
uu
THE LIGHT IS CLEARLY ARTIFICIAL.
uuu
HOWEVER, IT WASN'T THERE A MOMENT AGO.
I'VE BEEN PAYING CLOSE ATTENTION TO OUR SURROUNDINGS.
THIS WAY! EVERYONE FOLLOW MY LEAD!
I COULD UNDERSTAND WHY KOIZUMI WAS SO SUSPICIOUS.
BUT WE REALLY DIDN'T HAVE A CHOICE AT THIS POINT.
uu

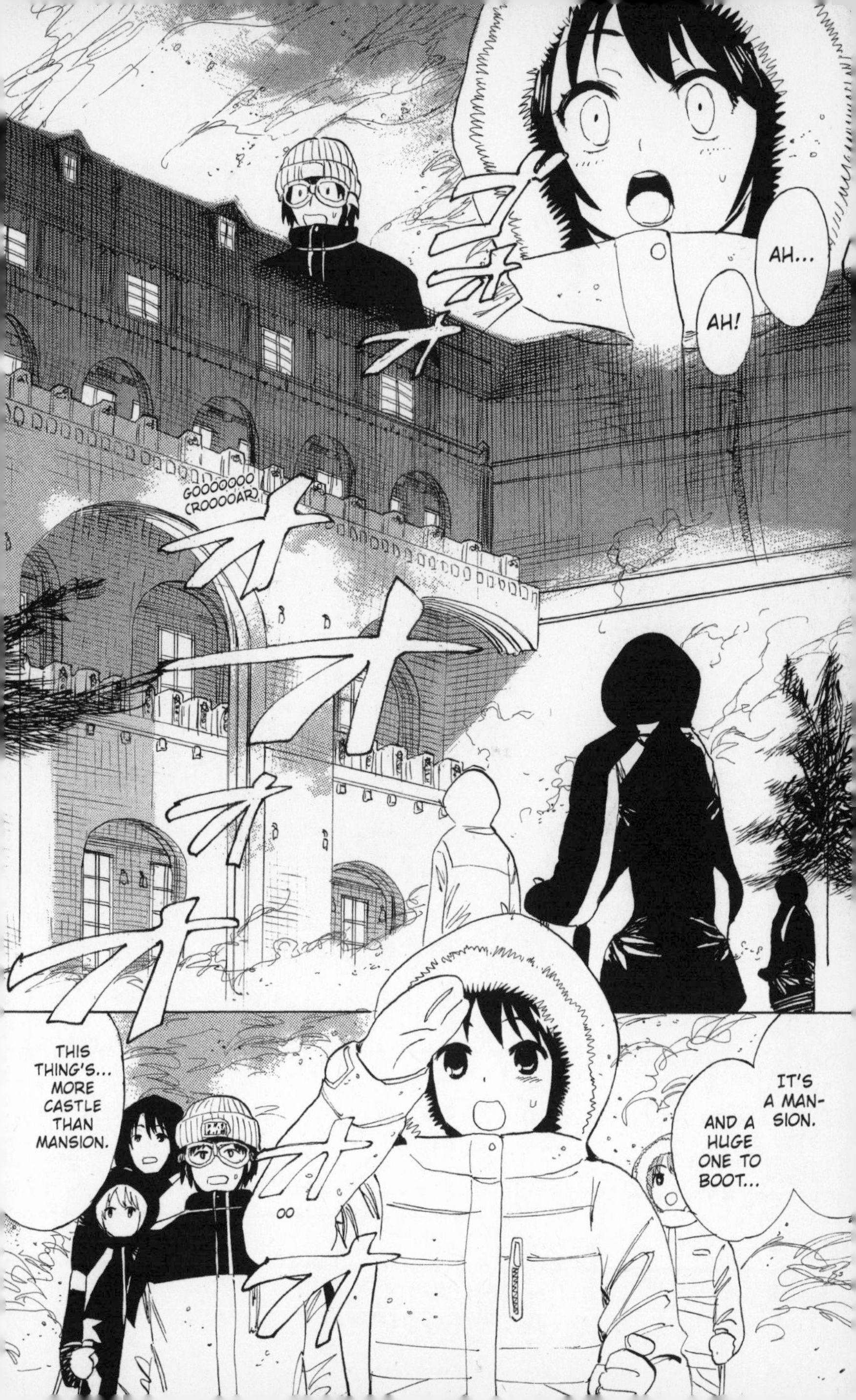
AH...
AH!
GOOOOOOO (ROOOOAR)
IT'S A MAN-SION.
AND A HUGE ONE TO BOOT...
THIS THING'S... MORE CASTLE THAN MANSION.

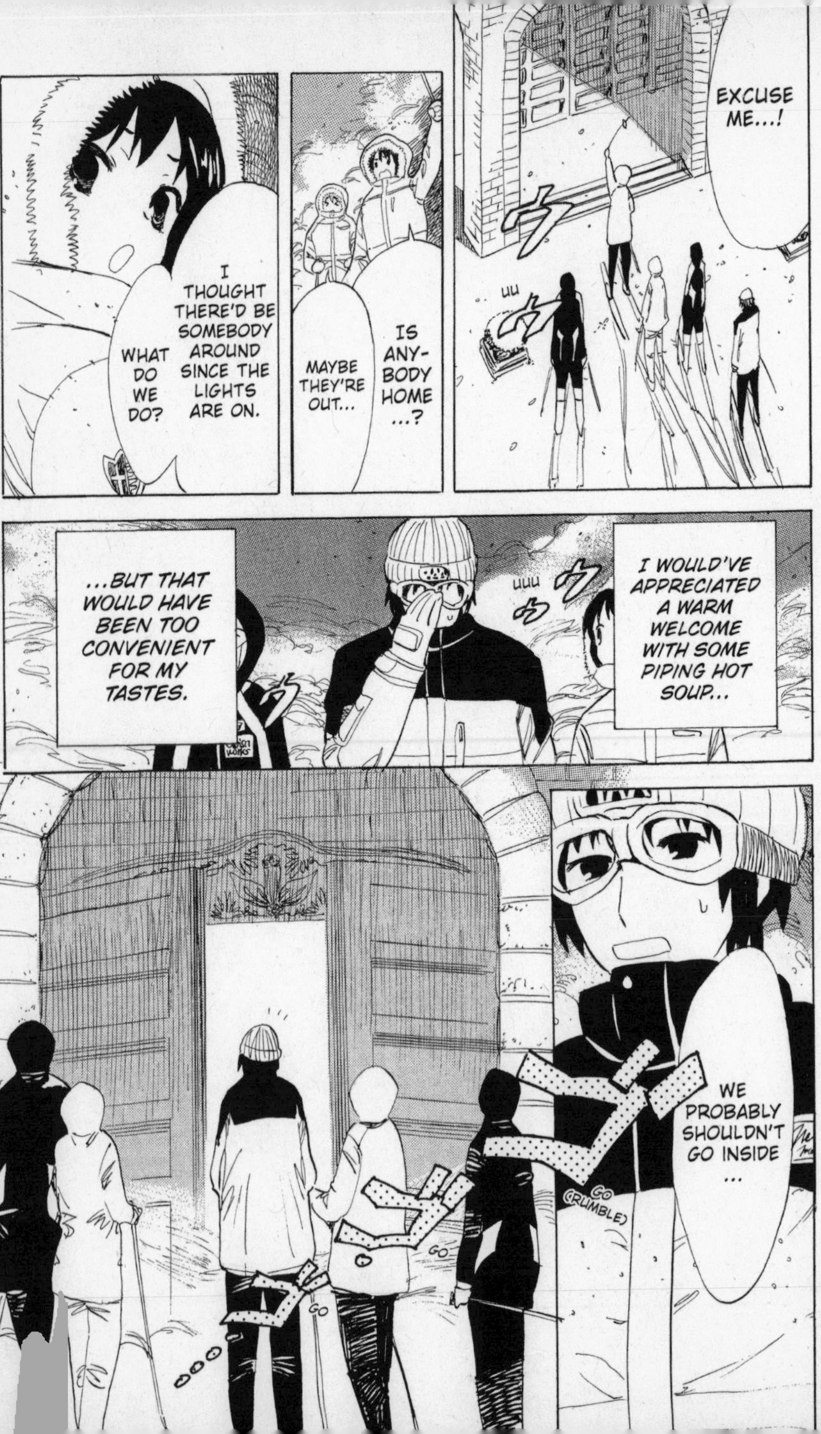
EXCUSE ME...!
UU
IS ANY-BODY HOME ...?
MAYBE THEY'RE OUT...
I THOUGHT THERE'D BE SOMEBODY AROUND SINCE THE LIGHTS ARE ON.
WHAT DO WE DO?
I WOULD'VE APPRECIATED A WARM WELCOME WITH SOME PIPING HOT SOUP...
UUU
...BUT THAT WOULD HAVE BEEN TOO CONVENIENT FOR MY TASTES.
WE PROBABLY SHOULDN'T GO INSIDE ...
GO (RUMBLE)
GO
GO

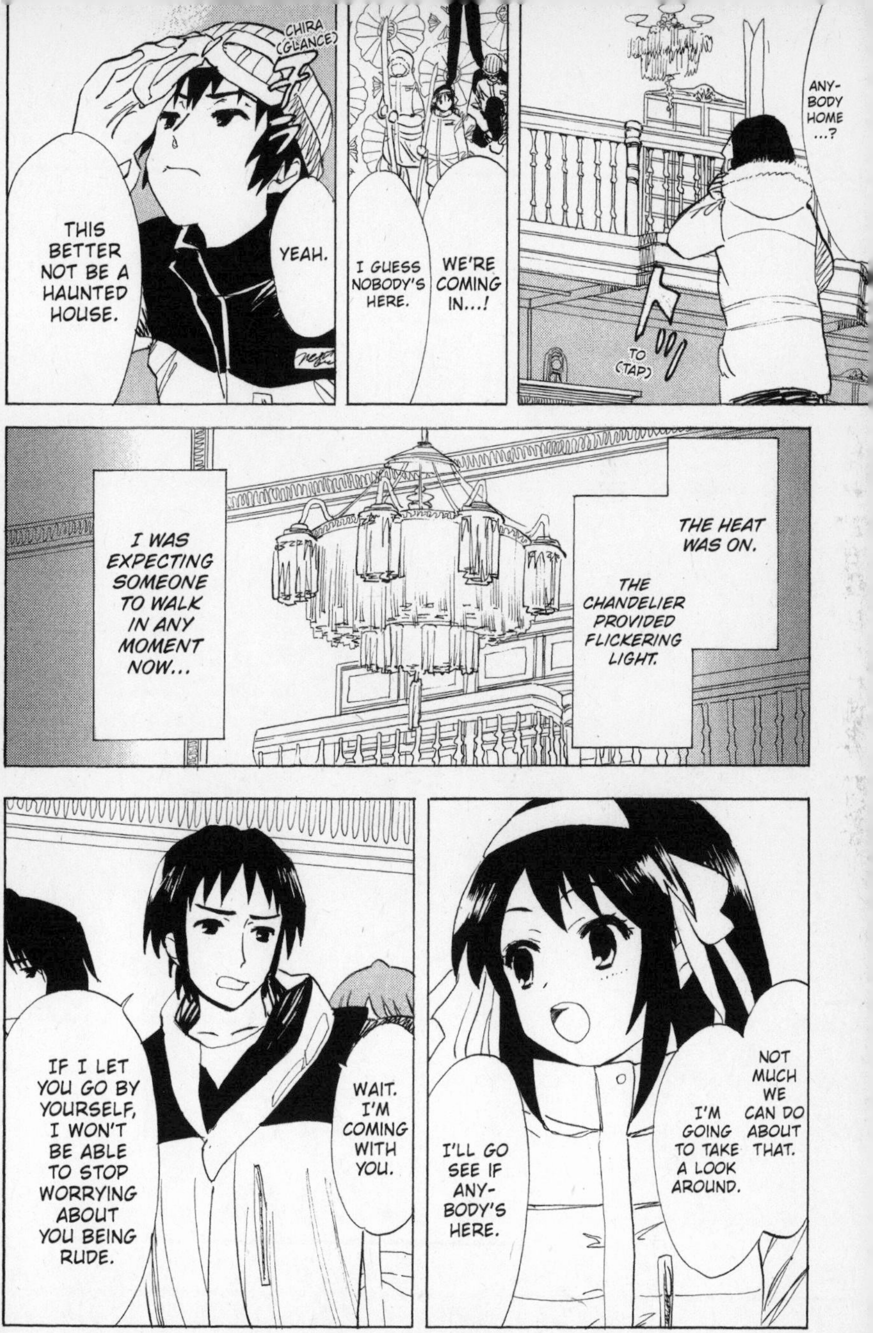
ANY-BODY HOME ...?
TO (TAP)
WE'RE COMING IN...!
I GUESS NOBODY'S HERE.
CHIRA (GLANCE)
YEAH.
THIS BETTER NOT BE A HAUNTED HOUSE.
THE HEAT WAS ON.
THE CHANDELIER PROVIDED FLICKERING LIGHT.
I WAS EXPECTING SOMEONE TO WALK IN ANY MOMENT NOW...
NOT MUCH WE CAN DO ABOUT THAT.
I'M GOING TO TAKE A LOOK AROUND.
I'LL GO SEE IF ANY-BODY'S HERE.
WAIT. I'M COMING WITH YOU.
IF I LET YOU GO BY YOURSELF, I WON'T BE ABLE TO STOP WORRYING ABOUT YOU BEING RUDE.

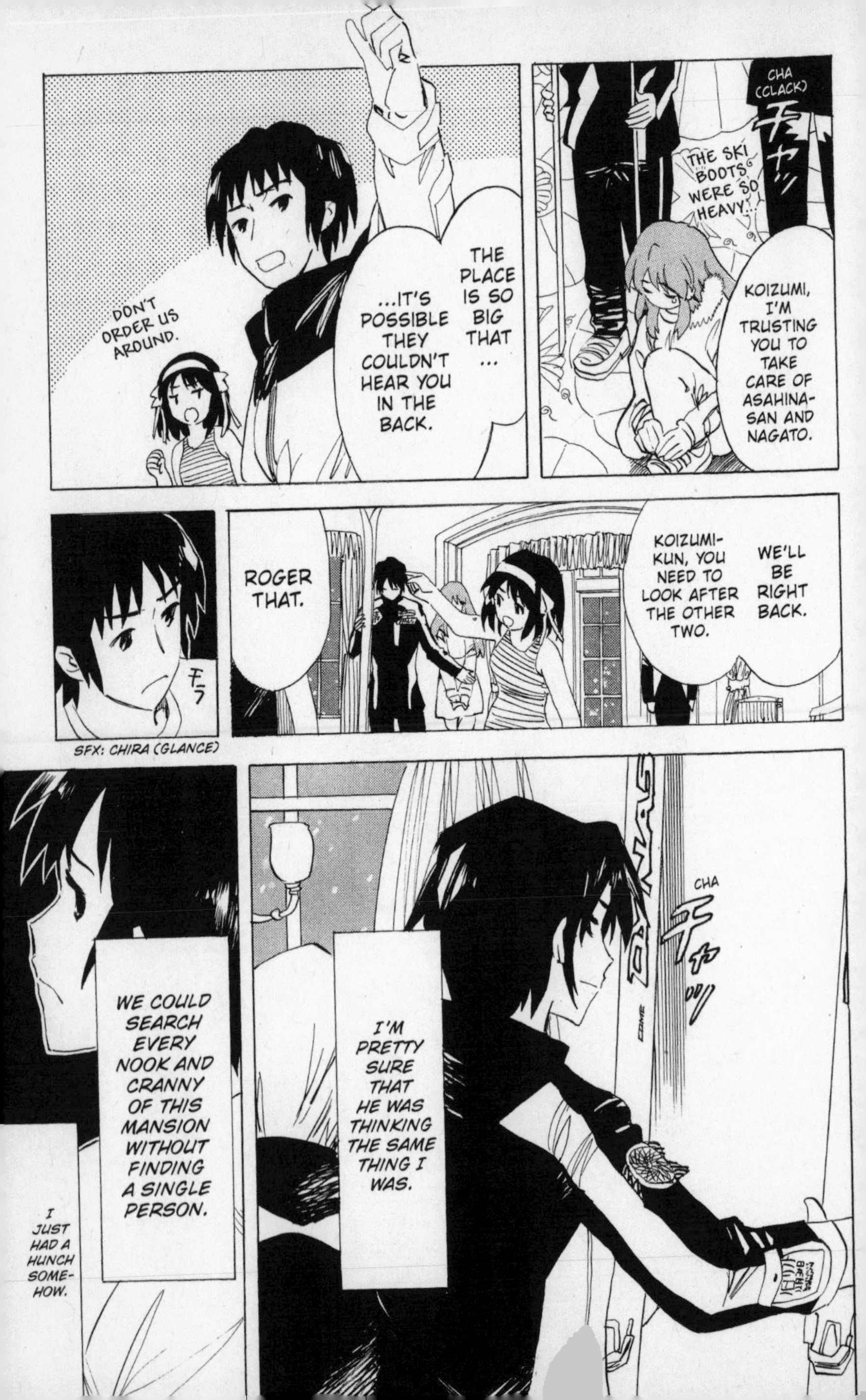
CHA (CLACK)
THE SKI BOOTS WERE SO HEAVY...
KOIZUMI, I'M TRUSTING YOU TO TAKE CARE OF ASAHINA-SAN AND NAGATO.
THE PLACE IS SO BIG THAT ...
...IT'S POSSIBLE THEY COULDN'T HEAR YOU IN THE BACK.
DON'T ORDER US AROUND.
WE'LL BE RIGHT BACK.
KOIZUMI-KUN, YOU NEED TO LOOK AFTER THE OTHER TWO.
ROGER THAT.
SFX: CHIRA (GLANCE)
CHA
I'M PRETTY SURE THAT HE WAS THINKING THE SAME THING I WAS.
WE COULD SEARCH EVERY NOOK AND CRANNY OF THIS MANSION WITHOUT FINDING A SINGLE PERSON.
I JUST HAD A HUNCH SOME-HOW.

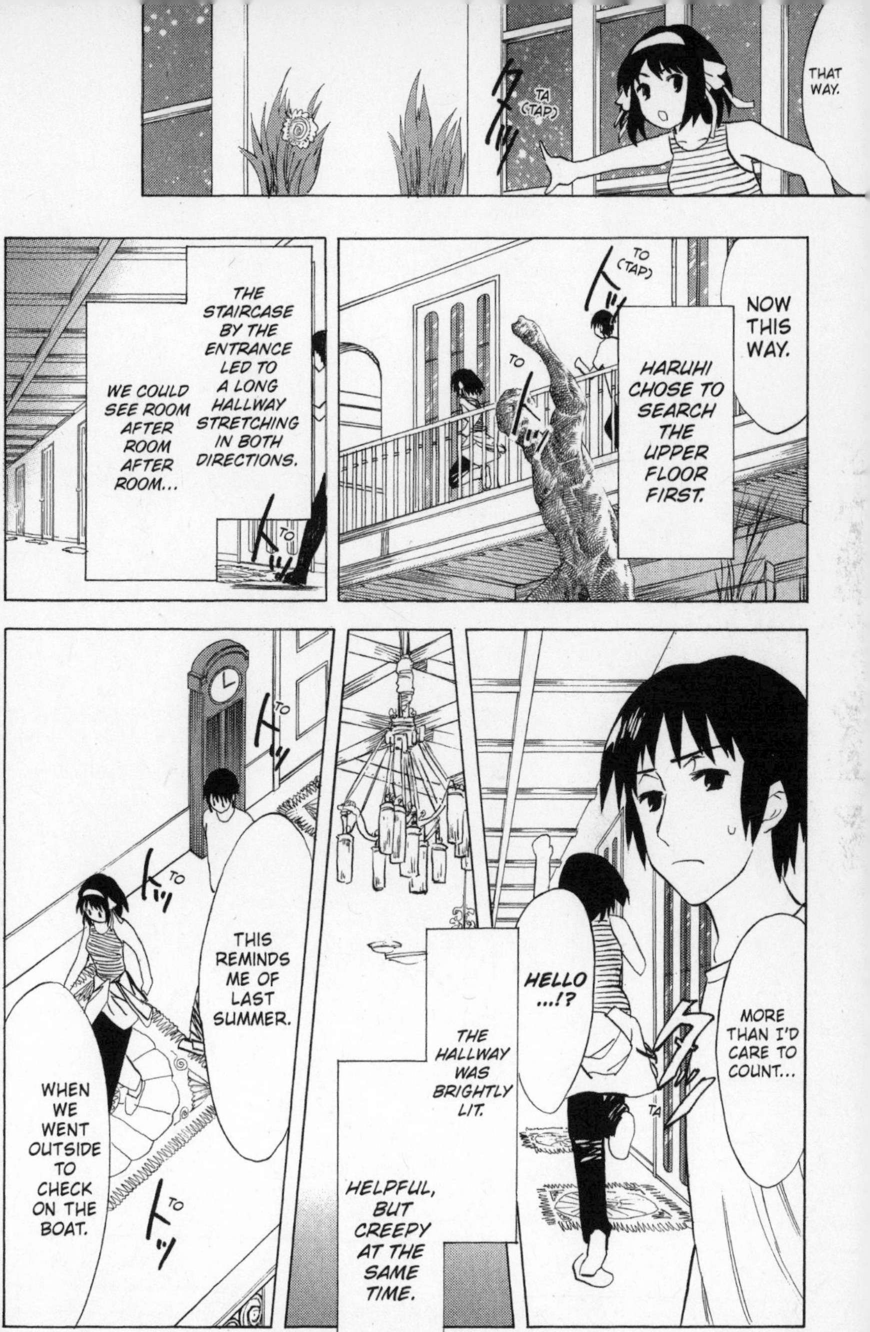
THAT WAY.
TA (TAP)
NOW THIS WAY.
TO (TAP)
HARUHI CHOSE TO SEARCH THE UPPER FLOOR FIRST.
TO
THE STAIRCASE BY THE ENTRANCE LED TO A LONG HALLWAY STRETCHING IN BOTH DIRECTIONS.
WE COULD SEE ROOM AFTER ROOM AFTER ROOM...
TO
MORE THAN I'D CARE TO COUNT...
HELLO ...!?
TA
THE HALLWAY WAS BRIGHTLY LIT.
HELPFUL, BUT CREEPY AT THE SAME TIME.
TO
THIS REMINDS ME OF LAST SUMMER.
TO
WHEN WE WENT OUTSIDE TO CHECK ON THE BOAT.
TO

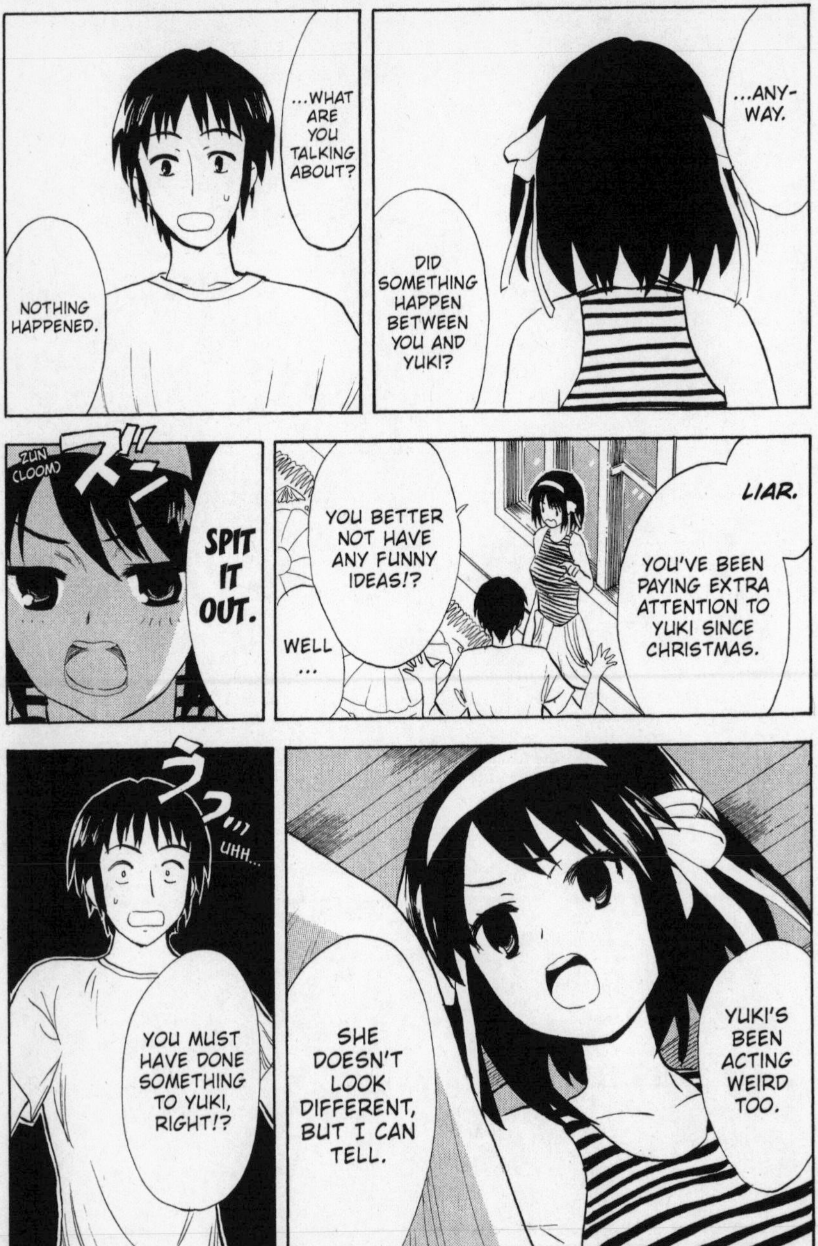
...ANY-WAY.
DID SOMETHING HAPPEN BETWEEN YOU AND YUKI?
...WHAT ARE YOU TALKING ABOUT?
NOTHING HAPPENED.
LIAR.
YOU'VE BEEN PAYING EXTRA ATTENTION TO YUKI SINCE CHRISTMAS.
YOU BETTER NOT HAVE ANY FUNNY IDEAS!?
WELL ...
ZUN (LOOM)
SPIT IT OUT.
YUKI'S BEEN ACTING WEIRD TOO.
SHE DOESN'T LOOK DIFFERENT, BUT I CAN TELL.
UHH...
YOU MUST HAVE DONE SOMETHING TO YUKI, RIGHT!?

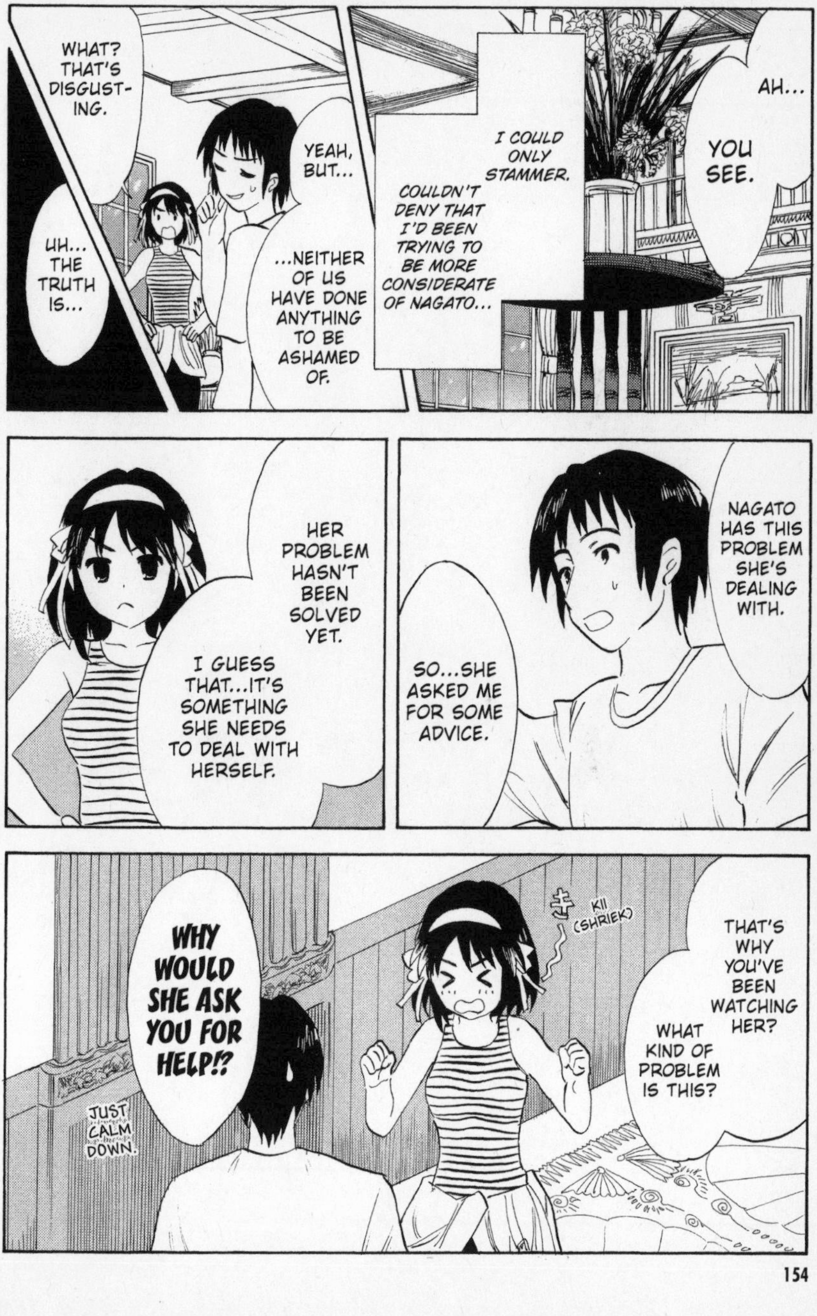
AH...
YOU SEE.
I COULD ONLY STAMMER.
COULDN'T DENY THAT I'D BEEN TRYING TO BE MORE CONSIDERATE OF NAGATO...
YEAH, BUT...
...NEITHER OF US HAVE DONE ANYTHING TO BE ASHAMED OF.
WHAT? THAT'S DISGUST-ING.
UH... THE TRUTH IS...
NAGATO HAS THIS PROBLEM SHE'S DEALING WITH.
SO...SHE ASKED ME FOR SOME ADVICE.
HER PROBLEM HASN'T BEEN SOLVED YET.
I GUESS THAT...IT'S SOMETHING SHE NEEDS TO DEAL WITH HERSELF.
THAT'S WHY YOU'VE BEEN WATCHING HER?
WHAT KIND OF PROBLEM IS THIS?
き
KII (SHRIEK)
WHY WOULD SHE ASK YOU FOR HELP!?
JUST CALM DOWN.

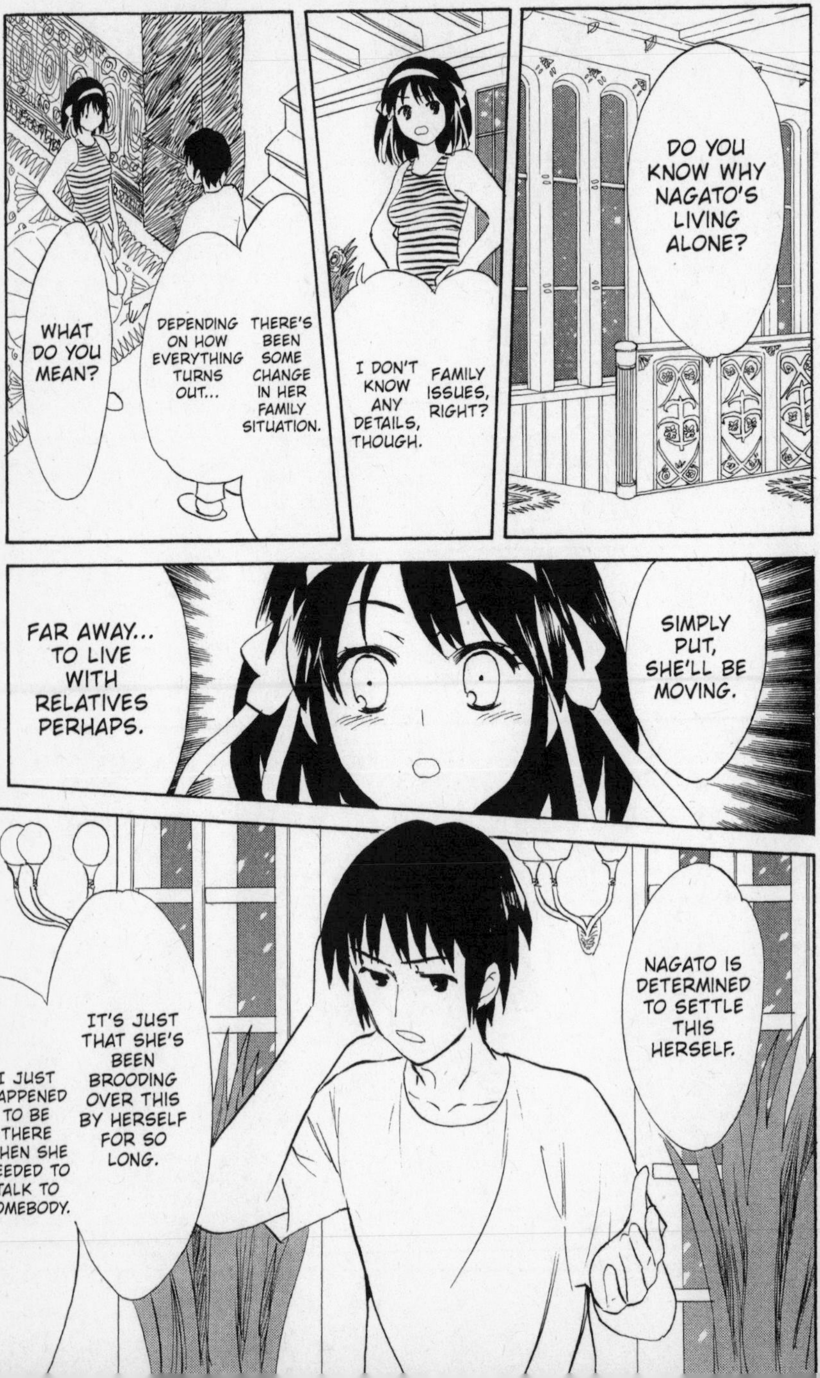
DO YOU KNOW WHY NAGATO'S LIVING ALONE?
FAMILY ISSUES, RIGHT?
I DON'T KNOW ANY DETAILS, THOUGH.
THERE'S BEEN SOME CHANGE IN HER FAMILY SITUATION.
DEPENDING ON HOW EVERYTHING TURNS OUT...
WHAT DO YOU MEAN?
SIMPLY PUT, SHE'LL BE MOVING.
FAR AWAY... TO LIVE WITH RELATIVES PERHAPS.
NAGATO IS DETERMINED TO SETTLE THIS HERSELF.
IT'S JUST THAT SHE'S BEEN BROODING OVER THIS BY HERSELF FOR SO LONG.
I JUST HAPPENED TO BE THERE WHEN SHE NEEDED TO TALK TO SOMEBODY.

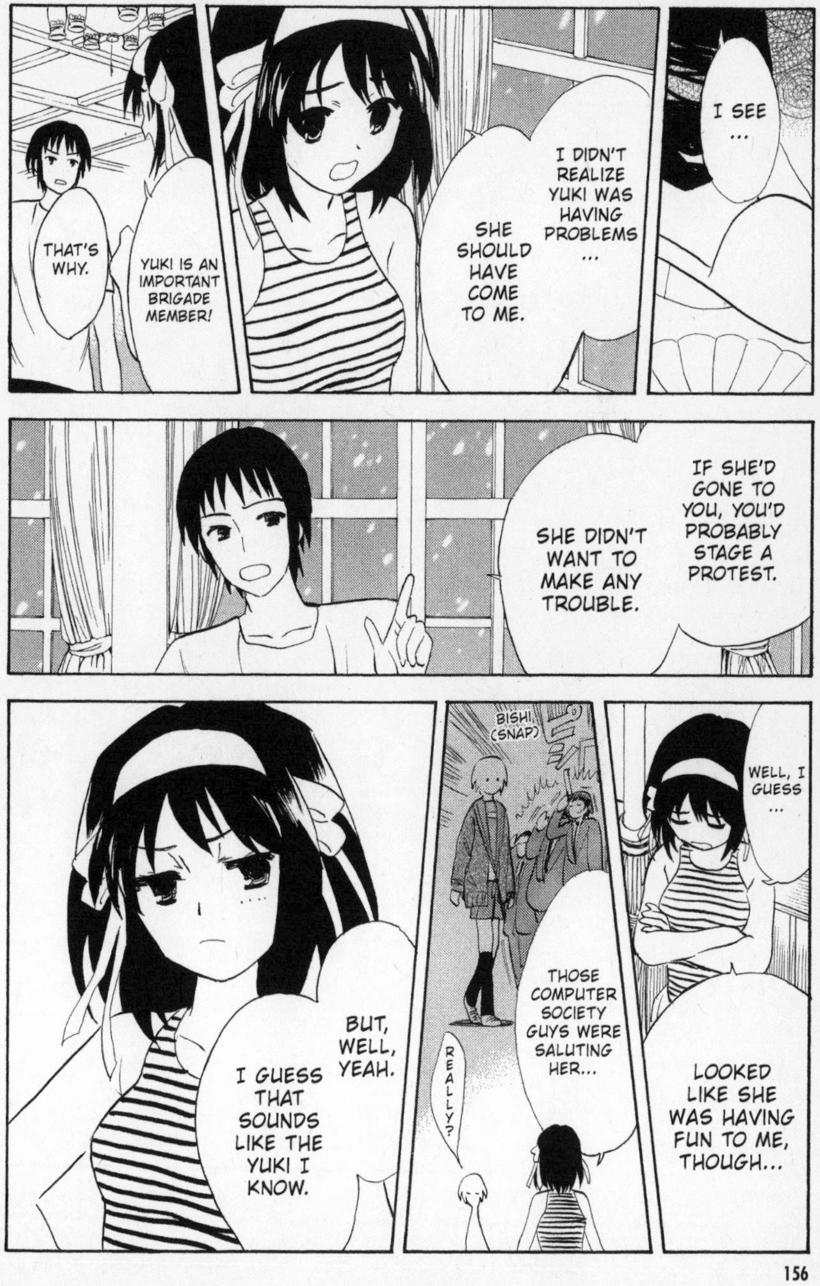
I SEE ...
I DIDN'T REALIZE YUKI WAS HAVING PROBLEMS ...
SHE SHOULD HAVE COME TO ME.
YUKI IS AN IMPORTANT BRIGADE MEMBER!
THAT'S WHY.
IF SHE'D GONE TO YOU, YOU'D PROBABLY STAGE A PROTEST.
SHE DIDN'T WANT TO MAKE ANY TROUBLE.
WELL, I GUESS ...
LOOKED LIKE SHE WAS HAVING FUN TO ME, THOUGH...
BISHI (SNAP)
THOSE COMPUTER SOCIETY GUYS WERE SALUTING HER...
REALLY?
BUT, WELL, YEAH.
I GUESS THAT SOUNDS LIKE THE YUKI I KNOW.

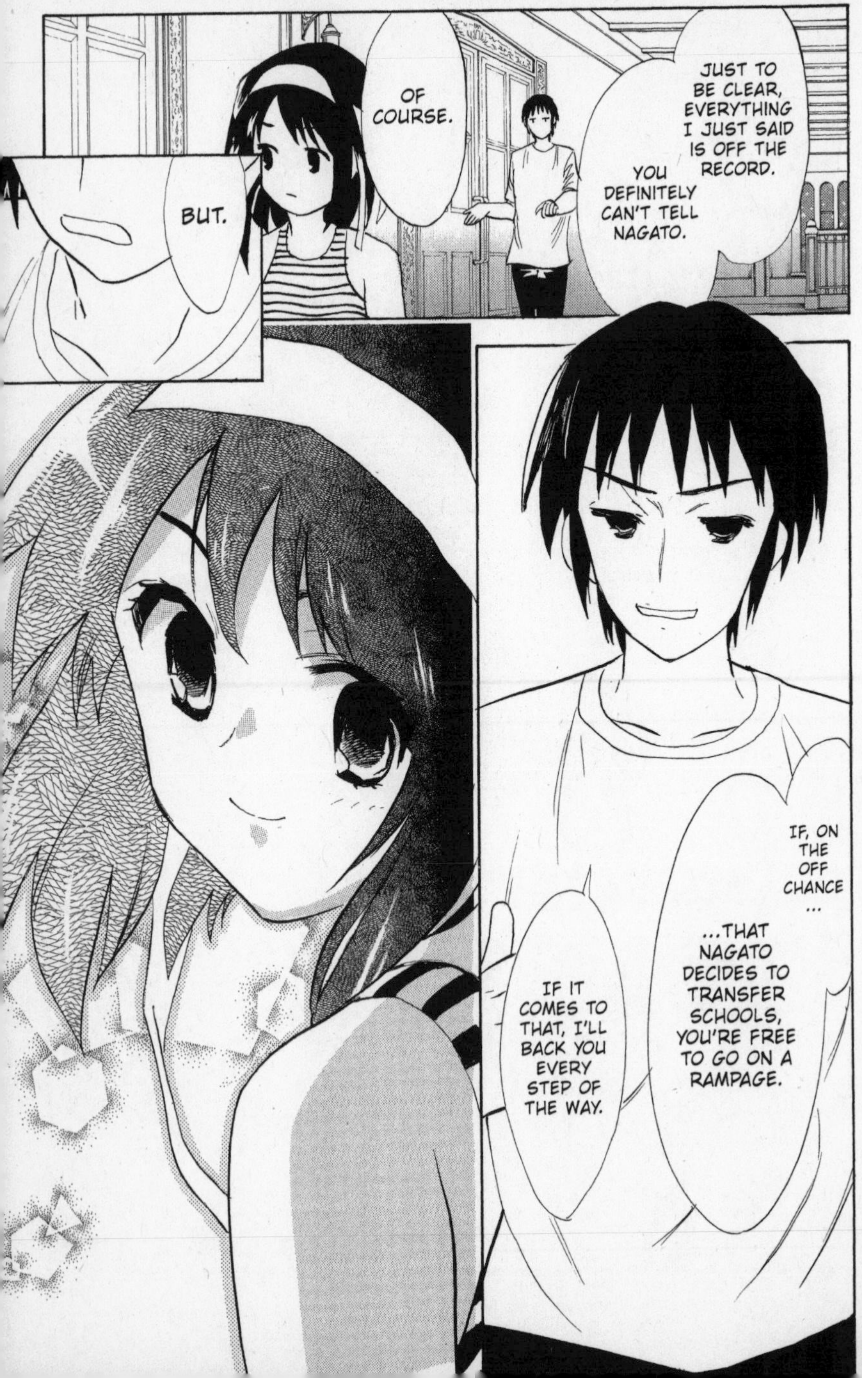
JUST TO BE CLEAR, EVERYTHING I JUST SAID IS OFF THE RECORD.
YOU DEFINITELY CAN'T TELL NAGATO.
OF COURSE.
BUT.
IF, ON THE OFF CHANCE...
...THAT NAGATO DECIDES TO TRANSFER SCHOOLS, YOU'RE FREE TO GO ON A RAMPAGE.
IF IT COMES TO THAT, I'LL BACK YOU EVERY STEP OF THE WAY.

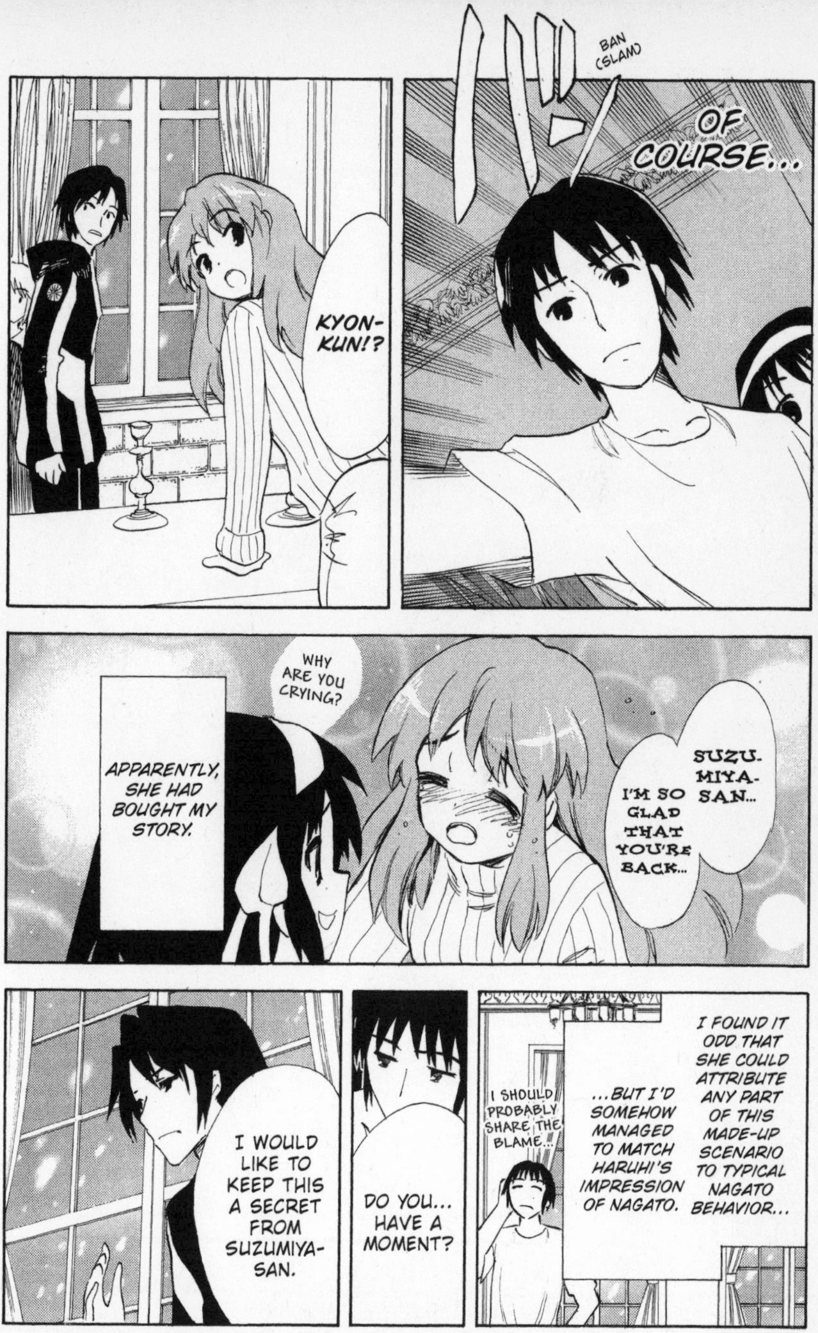
BAN (SLAM)
OF COURSE...
KYON-KUN!?
SUZUMIYA-SAN...
I'M SO GLAD THAT YOU'RE BACK...
WHY ARE YOU CRYING?
APPARENTLY, SHE HAD BOUGHT MY STORY.
I FOUND IT ODD THAT SHE COULD ATTRIBUTE ANY PART OF THIS MADE-UP SCENARIO TO TYPICAL NAGATO BEHAVIOR...
...BUT I'D SOMEHOW MANAGED TO MATCH HARUHI'S IMPRESSION OF NAGATO.
I SHOULD PROBABLY SHARE THE BLAME...
DO YOU... HAVE A MOMENT?
I WOULD LIKE TO KEEP THIS A SECRET FROM SUZUMIYA-SAN.

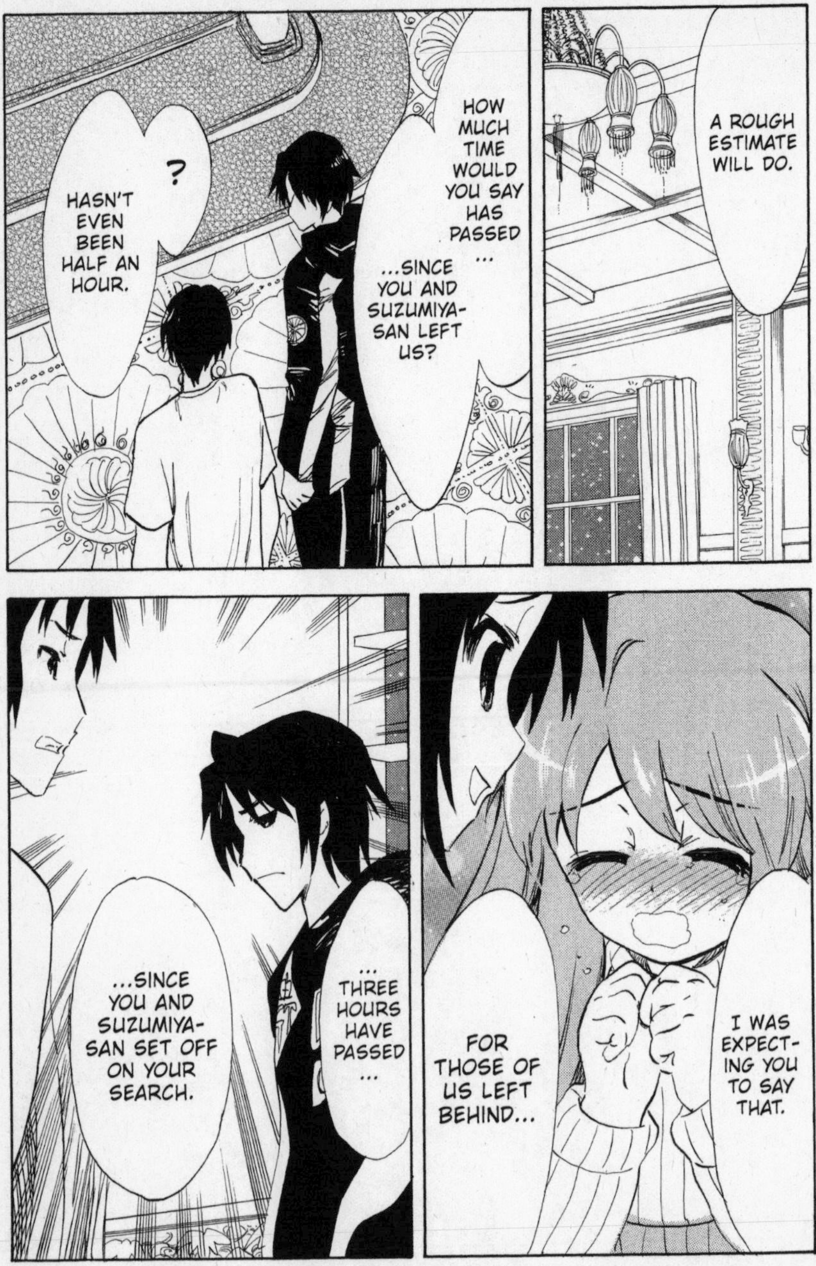
A ROUGH ESTIMATE WILL DO.
HOW MUCH TIME WOULD YOU SAY HAS PASSED ...
...SINCE YOU AND SUZUMIYA-SAN LEFT US?
?
HASN'T EVEN BEEN HALF AN HOUR.
I WAS EXPECT-ING YOU TO SAY THAT.
FOR THOSE OF US LEFT BEHIND...
... THREE HOURS HAVE PASSED ...
...SINCE YOU AND SUZUMIYA-SAN SET OFF ON YOUR SEARCH.

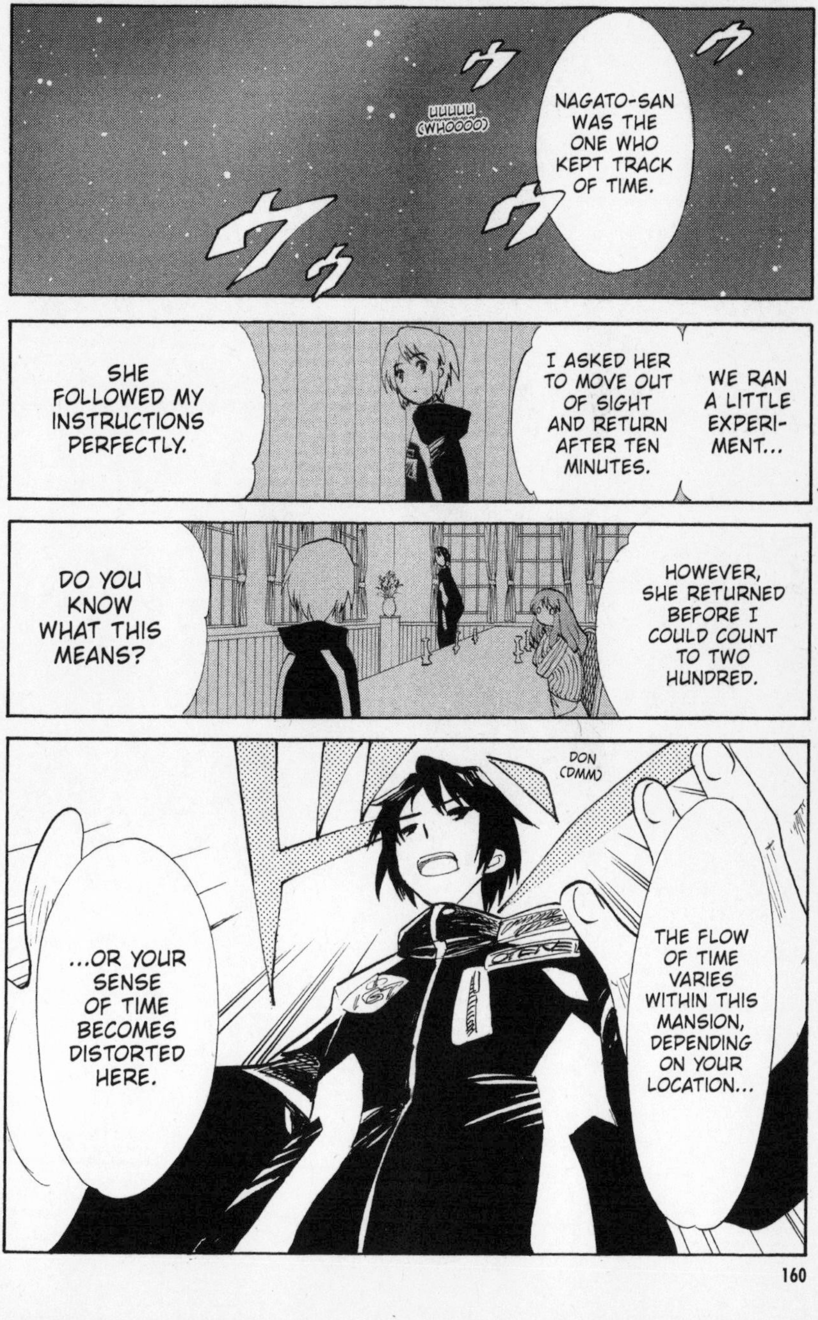
NAGATO-SAN WAS THE ONE WHO KEPT TRACK OF TIME.
UUUUU (WHOOOO)
WE RAN A LITTLE EXPERI-MENT...
I ASKED HER TO MOVE OUT OF SIGHT AND RETURN AFTER TEN MINUTES.
SHE FOLLOWED MY INSTRUCTIONS PERFECTLY.
HOWEVER, SHE RETURNED BEFORE I COULD COUNT TO TWO HUNDRED.
DO YOU KNOW WHAT THIS MEANS?
DON (DMM)
THE FLOW OF TIME VARIES WITHIN THIS MANSION, DEPENDING ON YOUR LOCATION...
...OR YOUR SENSE OF TIME BECOMES DISTORTED HERE.

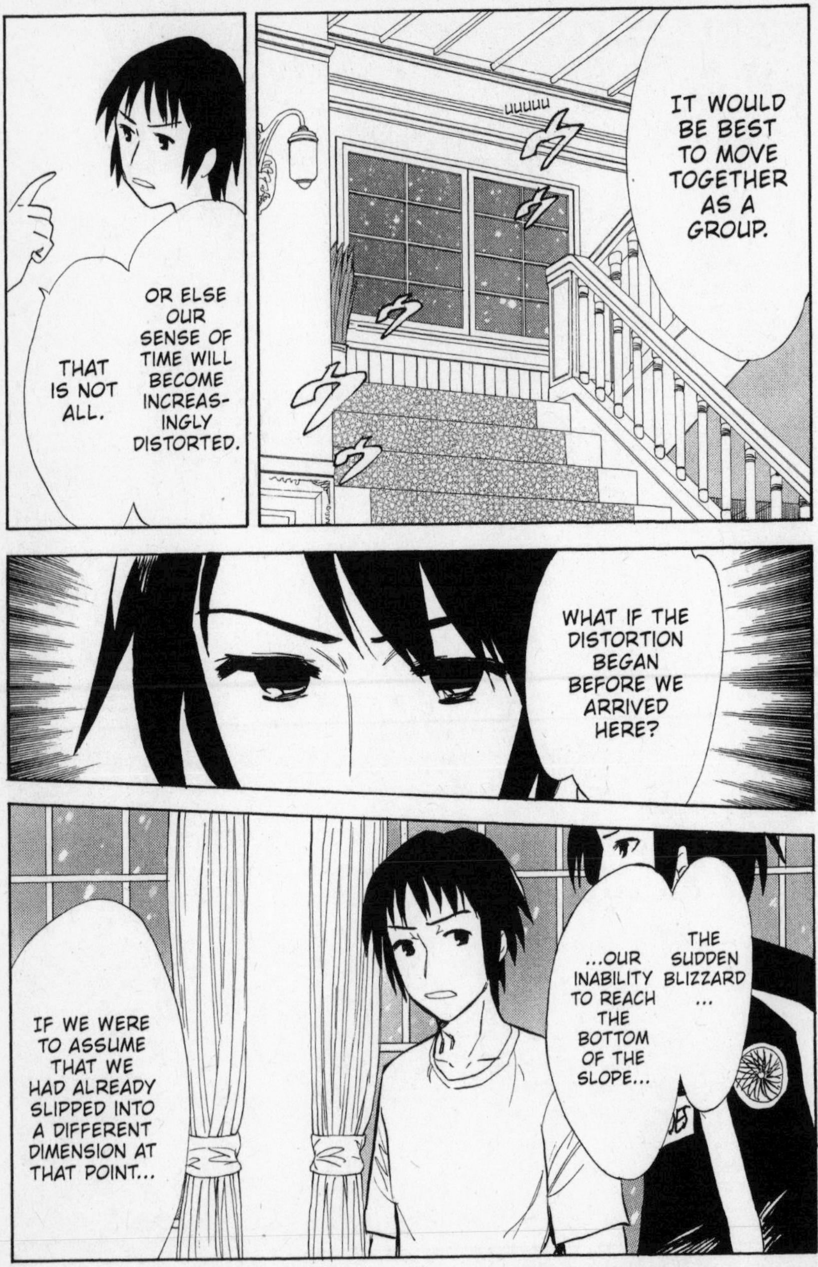
IT WOULD BE BEST TO MOVE TOGETHER AS A GROUP.
uuuuu
OR ELSE OUR SENSE OF TIME WILL BECOME INCREAS-INGLY DISTORTED.
THAT IS NOT ALL.
WHAT IF THE DISTORTION BEGAN BEFORE WE ARRIVED HERE?
THE SUDDEN BLIZZARD...
...OUR INABILITY TO REACH THE BOTTOM OF THE SLOPE...
IF WE WERE TO ASSUME THAT WE HAD ALREADY SLIPPED INTO A DIFFERENT DIMENSION AT THAT POINT...

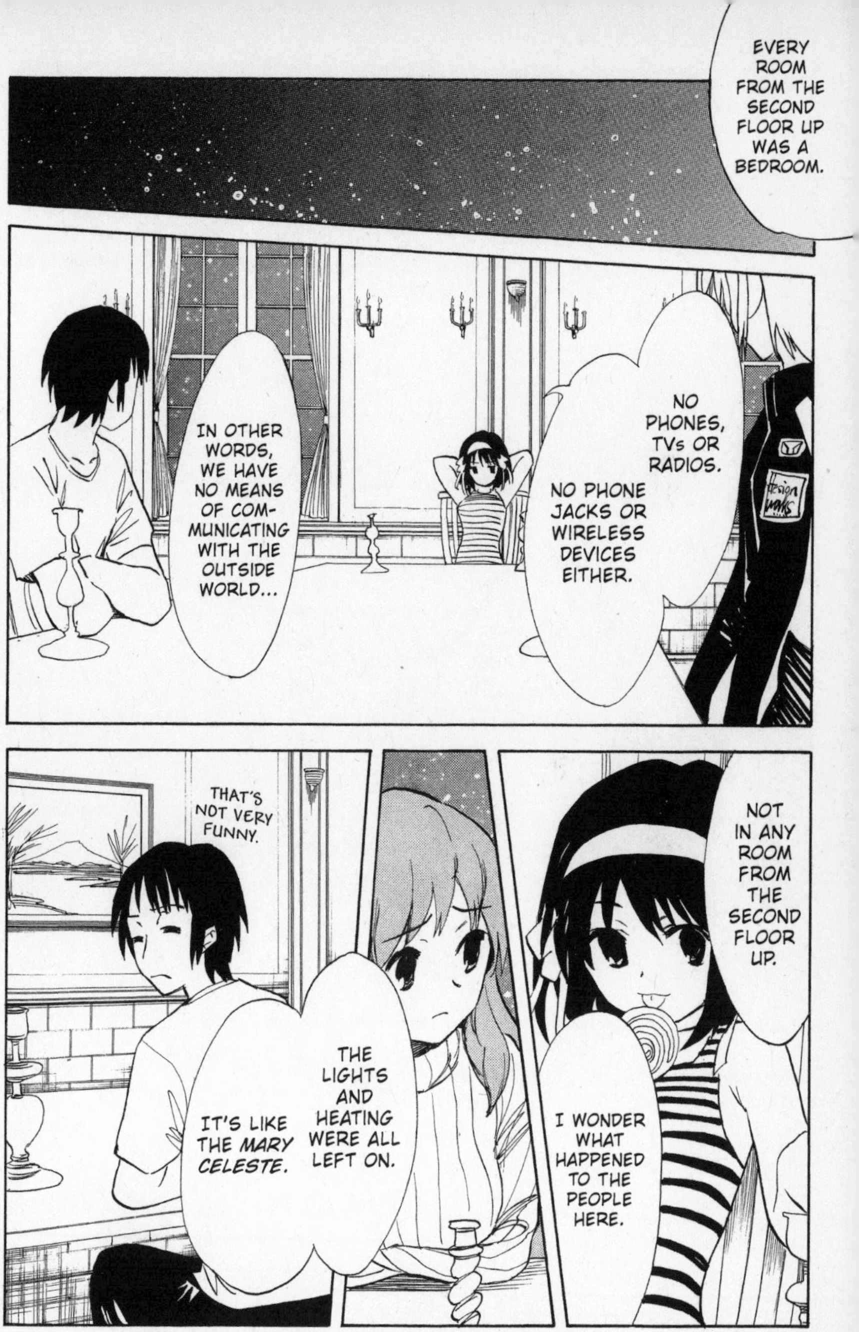

EVERY ROOM FROM THE SECOND FLOOR UP WAS A BEDROOM.
NO PHONES, TVs OR RADIOS.
NO PHONE JACKS OR WIRELESS DEVICES EITHER.
IN OTHER WORDS, WE HAVE NO MEANS OF COM-MUNICATING WITH THE OUTSIDE WORLD...
NOT IN ANY ROOM FROM THE SECOND FLOOR UP.
I WONDER WHAT HAPPENED TO THE PEOPLE HERE.
THE LIGHTS AND HEATING WERE ALL LEFT ON.
IT'S LIKE THE *MARY CELESTE*.
THAT'S NOT VERY FUNNY.

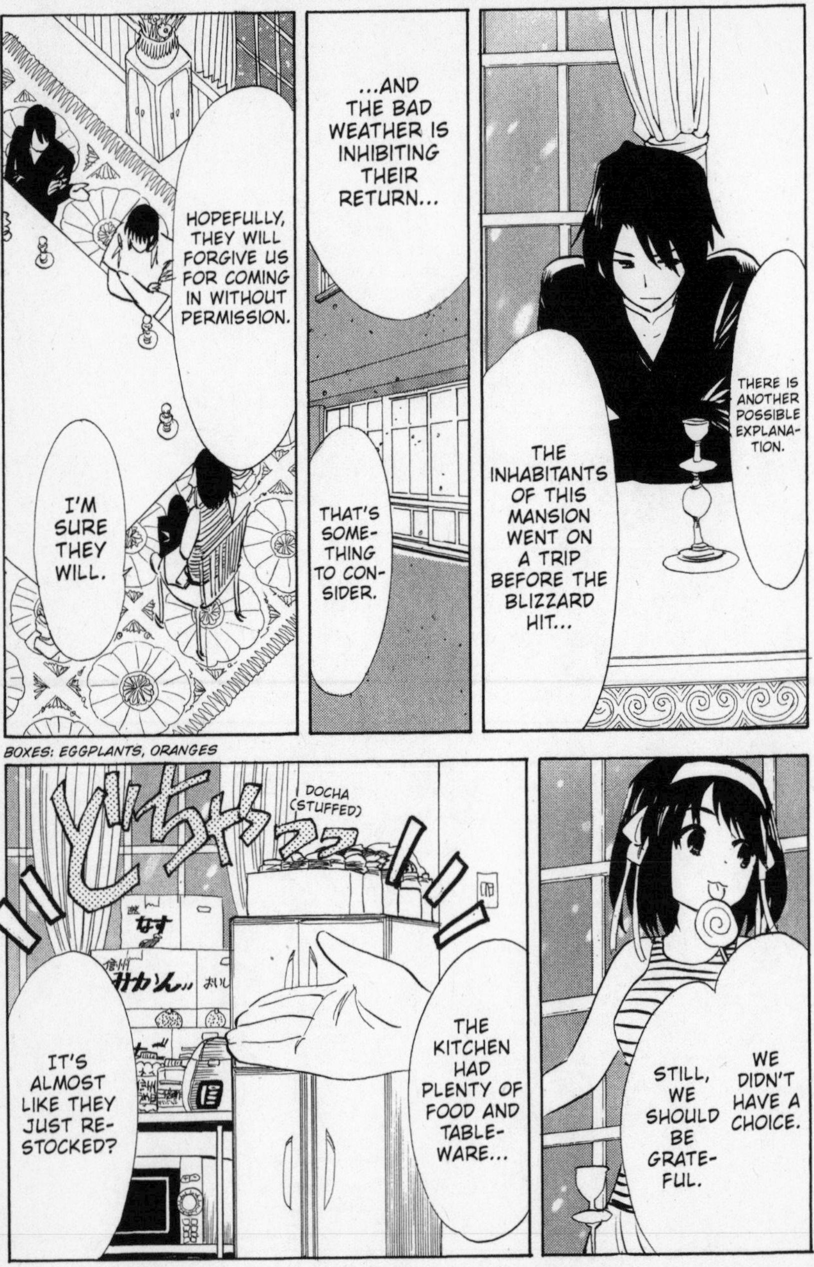
THERE IS ANOTHER POSSIBLE EXPLANATION.
THE INHABITANTS OF THIS MANSION WENT ON A TRIP BEFORE THE BLIZZARD HIT...
...AND THE BAD WEATHER IS INHIBITING THEIR RETURN...
THAT'S SOMETHING TO CONSIDER.
HOPEFULLY, THEY WILL FORGIVE US FOR COMING IN WITHOUT PERMISSION.
I'M SURE THEY WILL.
BOXES: EGGPLANTS, ORANGES
WE DIDN'T HAVE A CHOICE.
STILL, WE SHOULD BE GRATEFUL.
DOCHA (STUFFED)
THE KITCHEN HAD PLENTY OF FOOD AND TABLEWARE...
IT'S ALMOST LIKE THEY JUST RE-STOCKED?

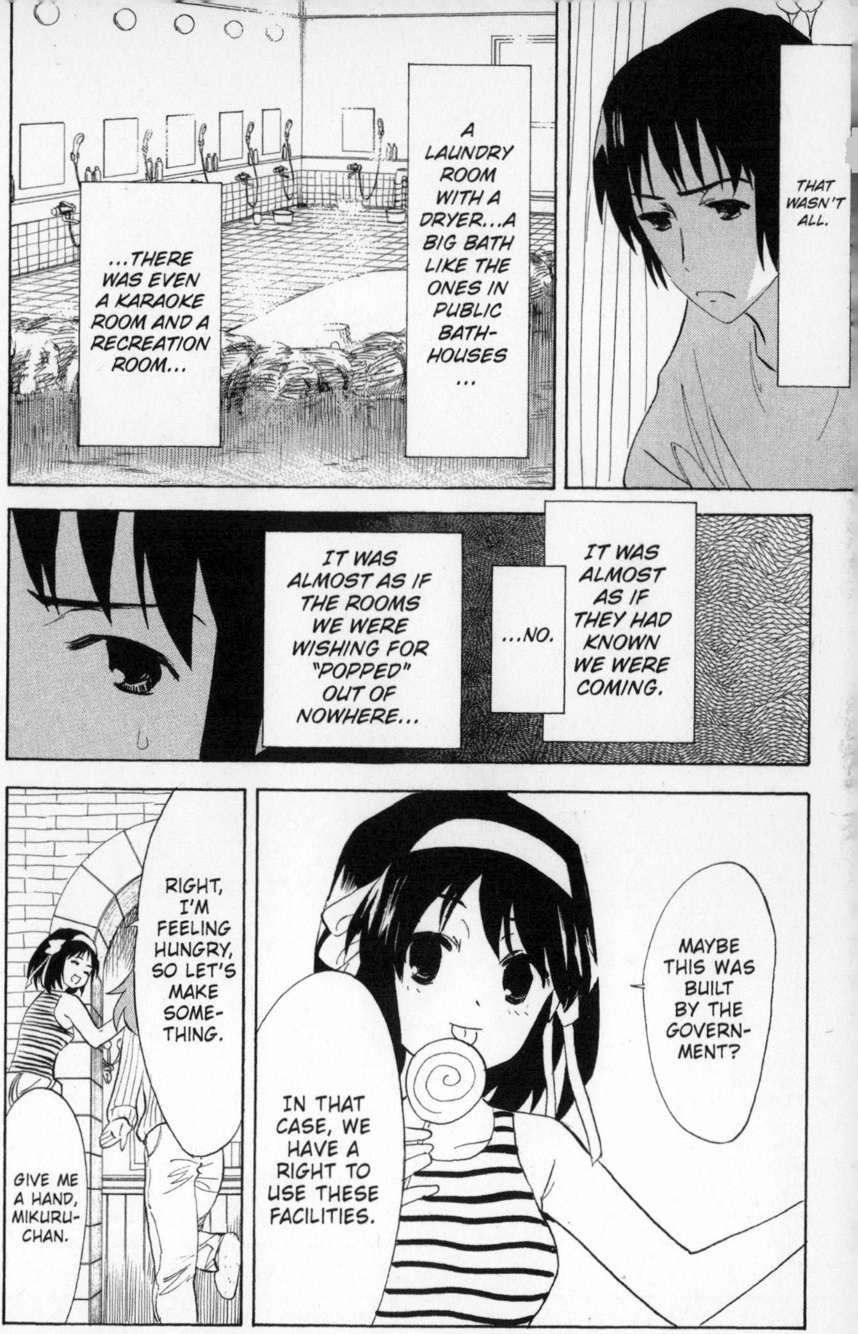
THAT WASN'T ALL.
A LAUNDRY ROOM WITH A DRYER...A BIG BATH LIKE THE ONES IN PUBLIC BATH-HOUSES ...
...THERE WAS EVEN A KARAOKE ROOM AND A RECREATION ROOM...
IT WAS ALMOST AS IF THE ROOMS WE WERE WISHING FOR "POPPED" OUT OF NOWHERE...
...NO.
IT WAS ALMOST AS IF THEY HAD KNOWN WE WERE COMING.
MAYBE THIS WAS BUILT BY THE GOVERN-MENT?
IN THAT CASE, WE HAVE A RIGHT TO USE THESE FACILITIES.
RIGHT, I'M FEELING HUNGRY, SO LET'S MAKE SOME-THING.
GIVE ME A HAND, MIKURU-CHAN.

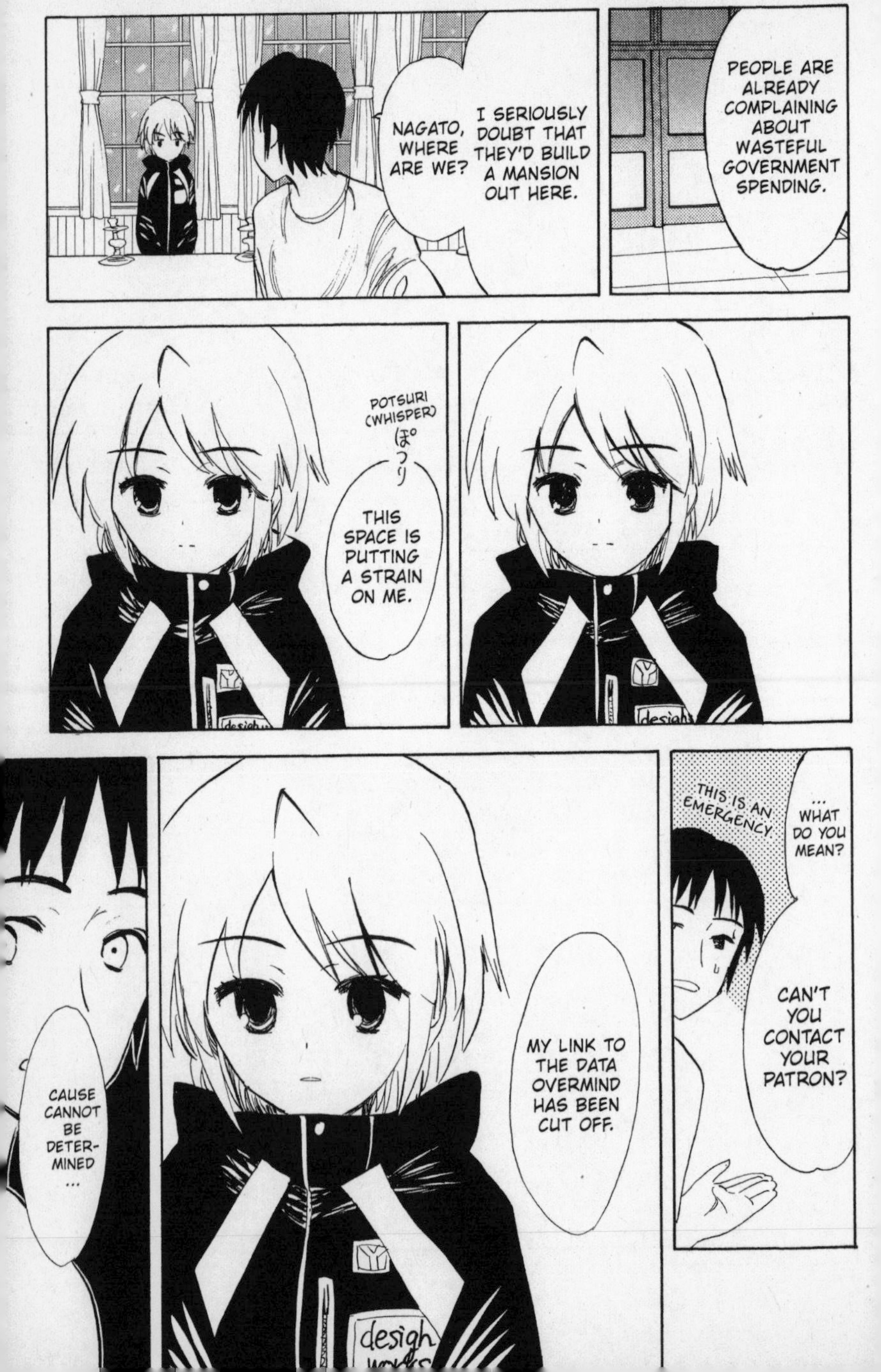
PEOPLE ARE ALREADY COMPLAINING ABOUT WASTEFUL GOVERNMENT SPENDING.
I SERIOUSLY DOUBT THAT THEY'D BUILD A MANSION OUT HERE.
NAGATO, WHERE ARE WE?
POTSURI (WHISPER)
ぽつり
THIS SPACE IS PUTTING A STRAIN ON ME.
... WHAT DO YOU MEAN?
THIS IS AN EMERGENCY.
CAN'T YOU CONTACT YOUR PATRON?
MY LINK TO THE DATA OVERMIND HAS BEEN CUT OFF.
CAUSE CANNOT BE DETERMINED ...

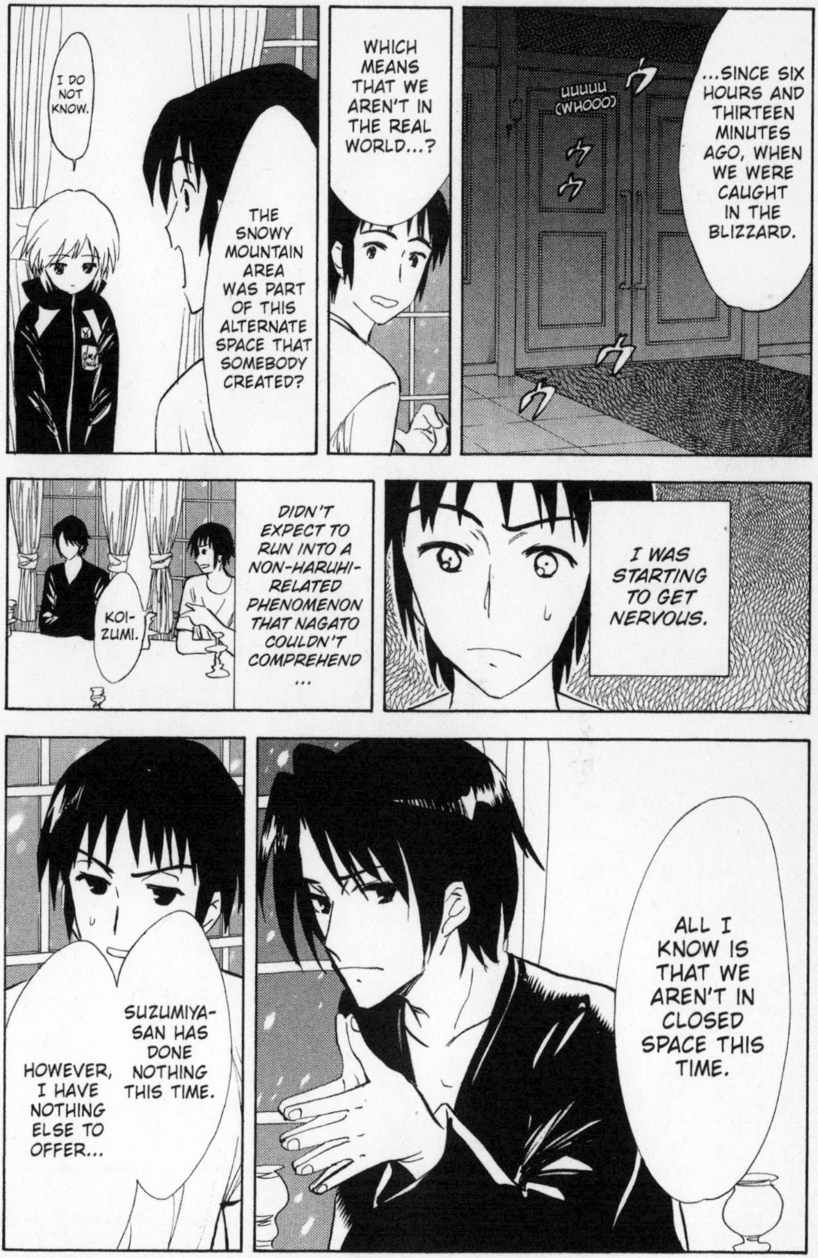
...SINCE SIX HOURS AND THIRTEEN MINUTES AGO, WHEN WE WERE CAUGHT IN THE BLIZZARD.
ウ ウ ウ ウ ウ
UUUUU (WHOOO)
WHICH MEANS THAT WE AREN'T IN THE REAL WORLD...?
THE SNOWY MOUNTAIN AREA WAS PART OF THIS ALTERNATE SPACE THAT SOMEBODY CREATED?
I DO NOT KNOW.
I WAS STARTING TO GET NERVOUS.
DIDN'T EXPECT TO RUN INTO A NON-HARUHI-RELATED PHENOMENON THAT NAGATO COULDN'T COMPREHEND...
KOI-ZUMI.
ALL I KNOW IS THAT WE AREN'T IN CLOSED SPACE THIS TIME.
SUZUMIYA-SAN HAS DONE NOTHING THIS TIME.
HOWEVER, I HAVE NOTHING ELSE TO OFFER...

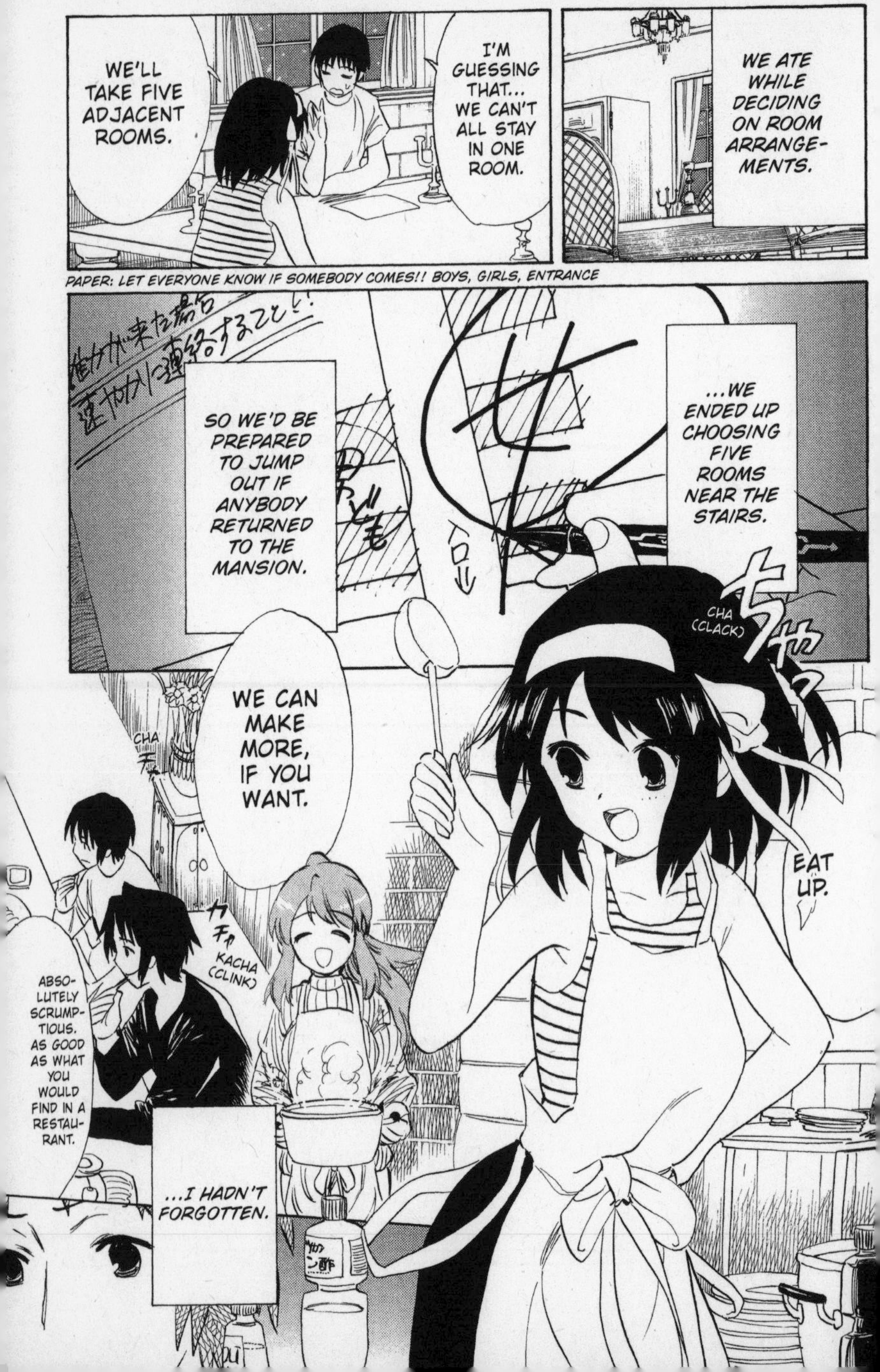
WE ATE WHILE DECIDING ON ROOM ARRANGE-MENTS.
I'M GUESSING THAT... WE CAN'T ALL STAY IN ONE ROOM.
WE'LL TAKE FIVE ADJACENT ROOMS.
PAPER: LET EVERYONE KNOW IF SOMEBODY COMES!! BOYS, GIRLS, ENTRANCE
...WE ENDED UP CHOOSING FIVE ROOMS NEAR THE STAIRS.
SO WE'D BE PREPARED TO JUMP OUT IF ANYBODY RETURNED TO THE MANSION.
誰かが来た場合
速やかに連絡すること!!
CHA (CLACK)
WE CAN MAKE MORE, IF YOU WANT.
EAT UP.
KACHA (CLINK)
CHA
ABSO-LUTELY SCRUMP-TIOUS. AS GOOD AS WHAT YOU WOULD FIND IN A RESTAU-RANT.
...I HADN'T FORGOTTEN.

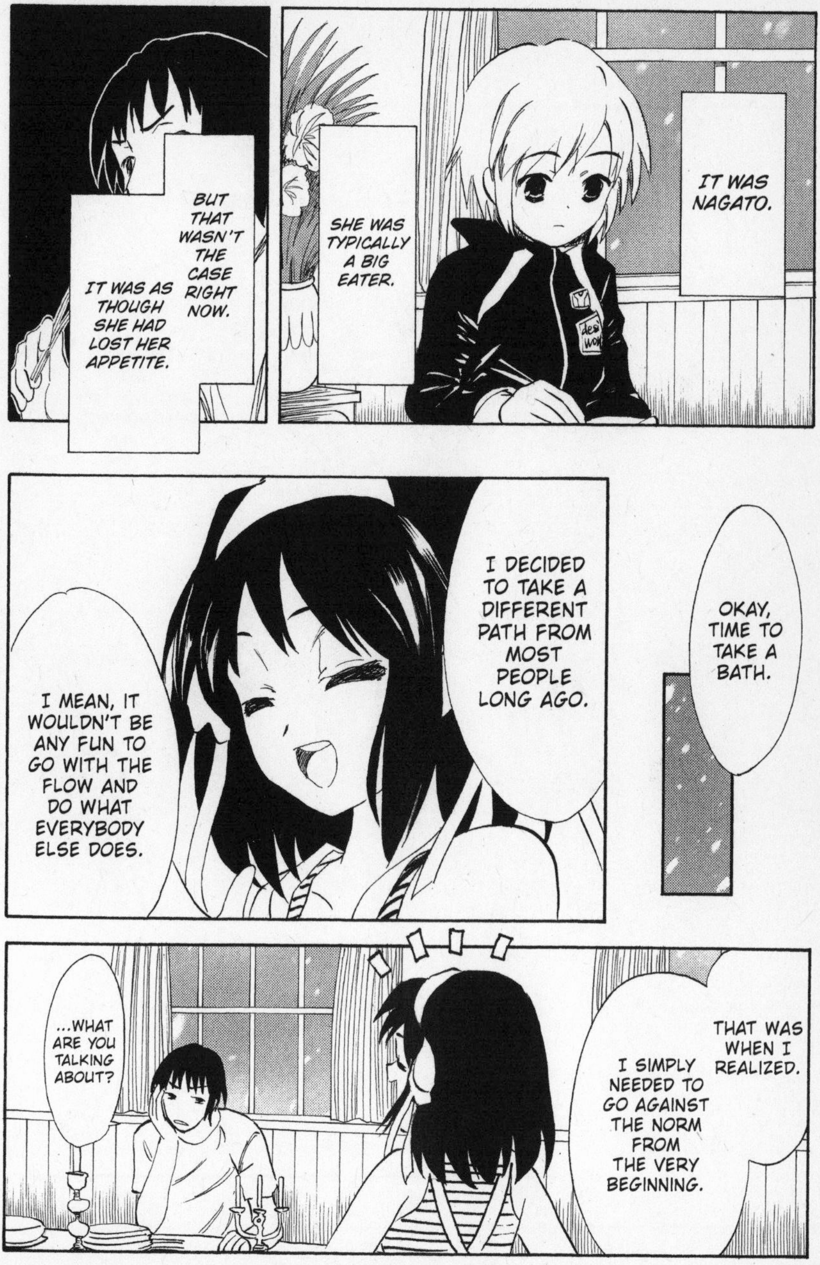
IT WAS NAGATO.
SHE WAS TYPICALLY A BIG EATER.
BUT THAT WASN'T THE CASE RIGHT NOW.
IT WAS AS THOUGH SHE HAD LOST HER APPETITE.
OKAY, TIME TO TAKE A BATH.
I DECIDED TO TAKE A DIFFERENT PATH FROM MOST PEOPLE LONG AGO.
I MEAN, IT WOULDN'T BE ANY FUN TO GO WITH THE FLOW AND DO WHAT EVERYBODY ELSE DOES.
THAT WAS WHEN I REALIZED.
I SIMPLY NEEDED TO GO AGAINST THE NORM FROM THE VERY BEGINNING.
...WHAT ARE YOU TALKING ABOUT?

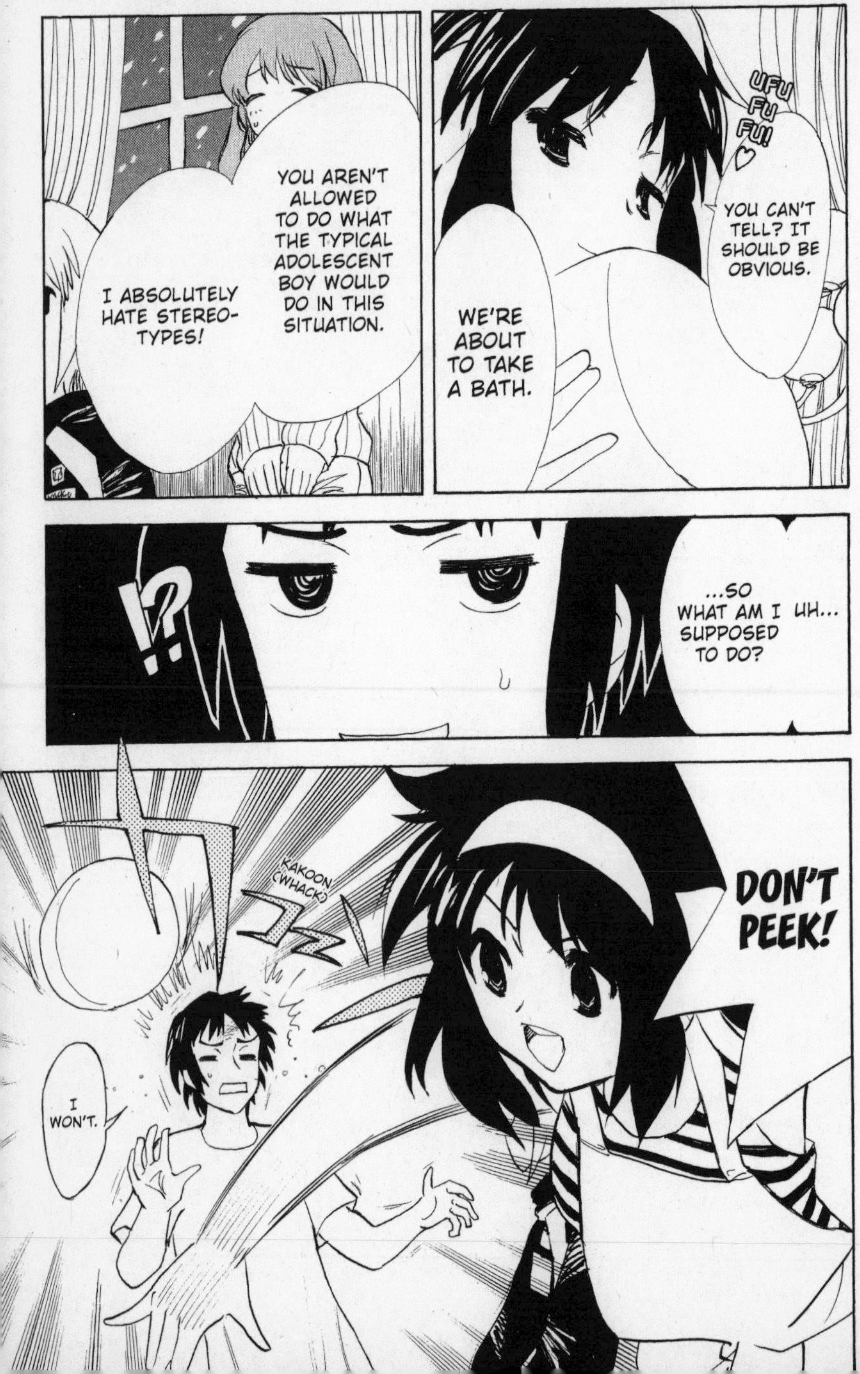
UFU FU FU! ♡
YOU CAN'T TELL? IT SHOULD BE OBVIOUS.
WE'RE ABOUT TO TAKE A BATH.
YOU AREN'T ALLOWED TO DO WHAT THE TYPICAL ADOLESCENT BOY WOULD DO IN THIS SITUATION.
I ABSOLUTELY HATE STEREO-TYPES!
...SO WHAT AM I UH... SUPPOSED TO DO?
!?
DON'T PEEK!
KAKOON (WHACK)
I WON'T.

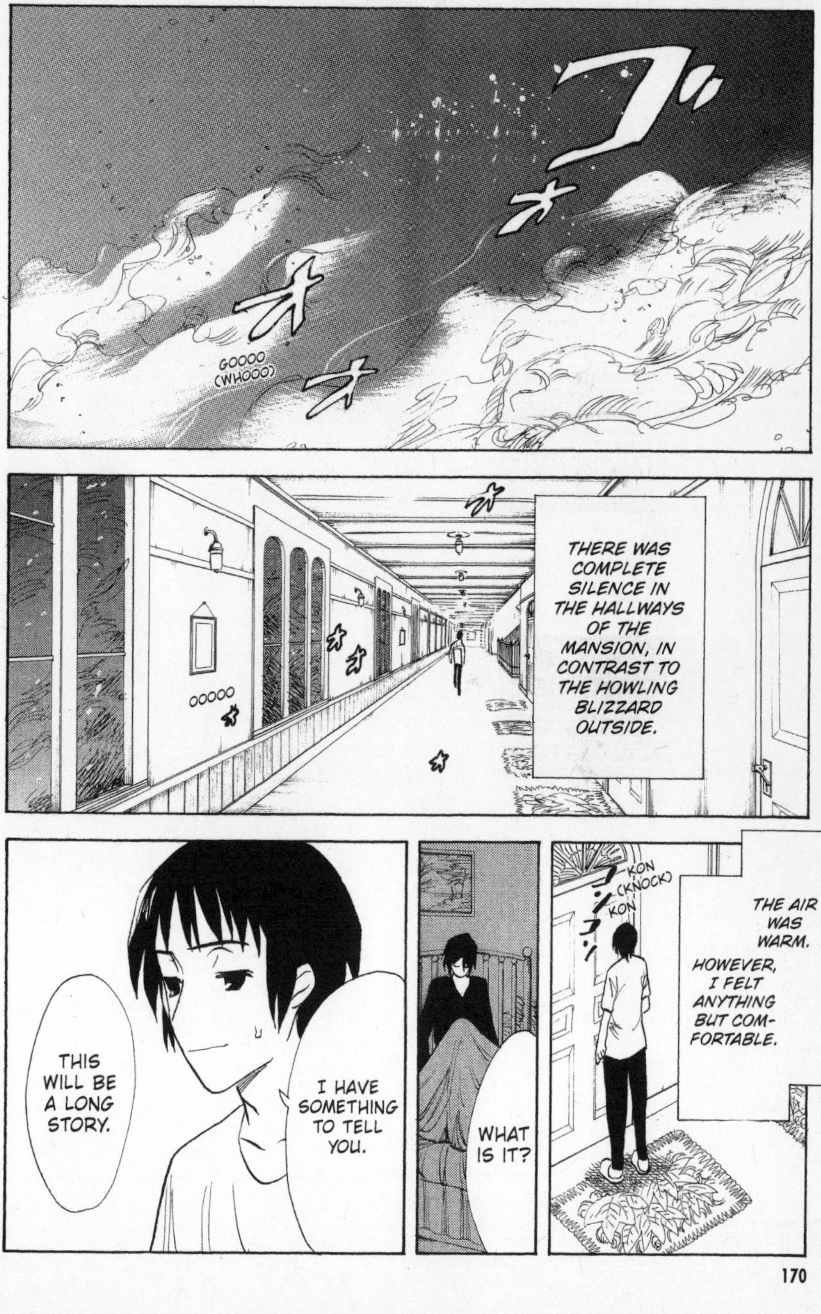
GOOOO (WHOOO)
THERE WAS COMPLETE SILENCE IN THE HALLWAYS OF THE MANSION, IN CONTRAST TO THE HOWLING BLIZZARD OUTSIDE.
OOOOO
THE AIR WAS WARM.
HOWEVER, I FELT ANYTHING BUT COM-FORTABLE.
KON (KNOCK) KON
WHAT IS IT?
I HAVE SOMETHING TO TELL YOU.
THIS WILL BE A LONG STORY.

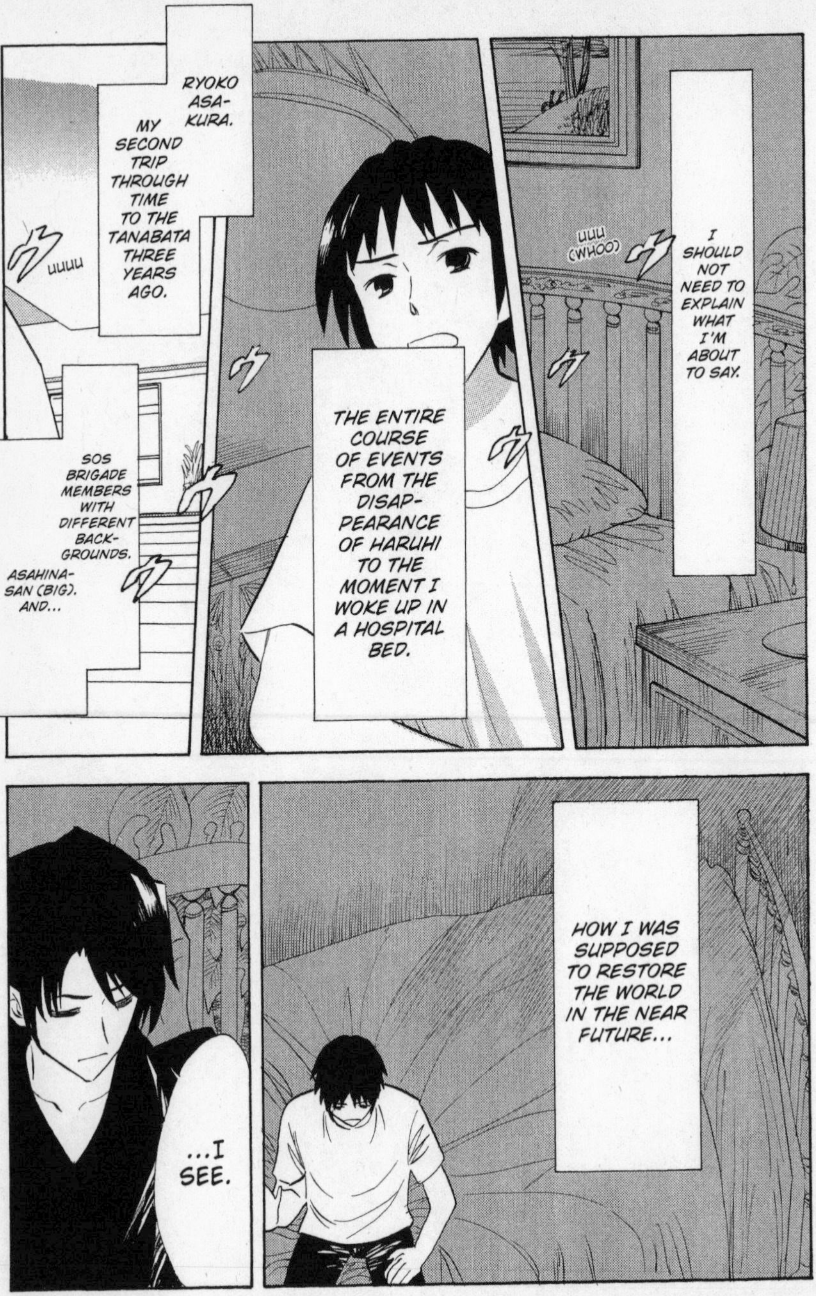
I SHOULD NOT NEED TO EXPLAIN WHAT I'M ABOUT TO SAY.
UUU (WHOO)
THE ENTIRE COURSE OF EVENTS FROM THE DISAP-PEARANCE OF HARUHI TO THE MOMENT I WOKE UP IN A HOSPITAL BED.
RYOKO ASA-KURA.
MY SECOND TRIP THROUGH TIME TO THE TANABATA THREE YEARS AGO.
UUUU
SOS BRIGADE MEMBERS WITH DIFFERENT BACK-GROUNDS.
ASAHINA-SAN (BIG). AND...
HOW I WAS SUPPOSED TO RESTORE THE WORLD IN THE NEAR FUTURE...
...I SEE.

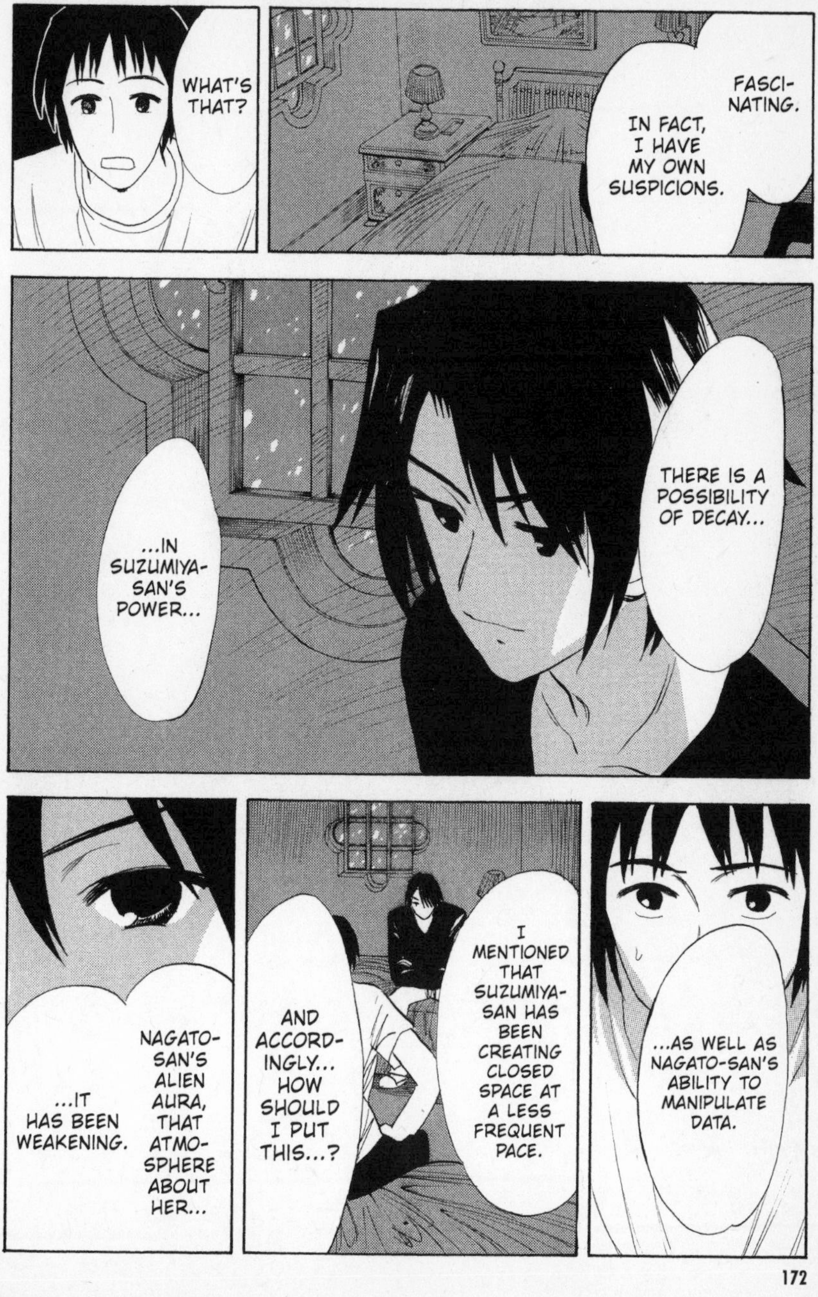
FASCINATING.
IN FACT, I HAVE MY OWN SUSPICIONS.
WHAT'S THAT?
THERE IS A POSSIBILITY OF DECAY...
...IN SUZUMIYA-SAN'S POWER...
...AS WELL AS NAGATO-SAN'S ABILITY TO MANIPULATE DATA.
I MENTIONED THAT SUZUMIYA-SAN HAS BEEN CREATING CLOSED SPACE AT A LESS FREQUENT PACE.
AND ACCORDINGLY... HOW SHOULD I PUT THIS...?
NAGATO-SAN'S ALIEN AURA, THAT ATMOSPHERE ABOUT HER...
...IT HAS BEEN WEAKENING.

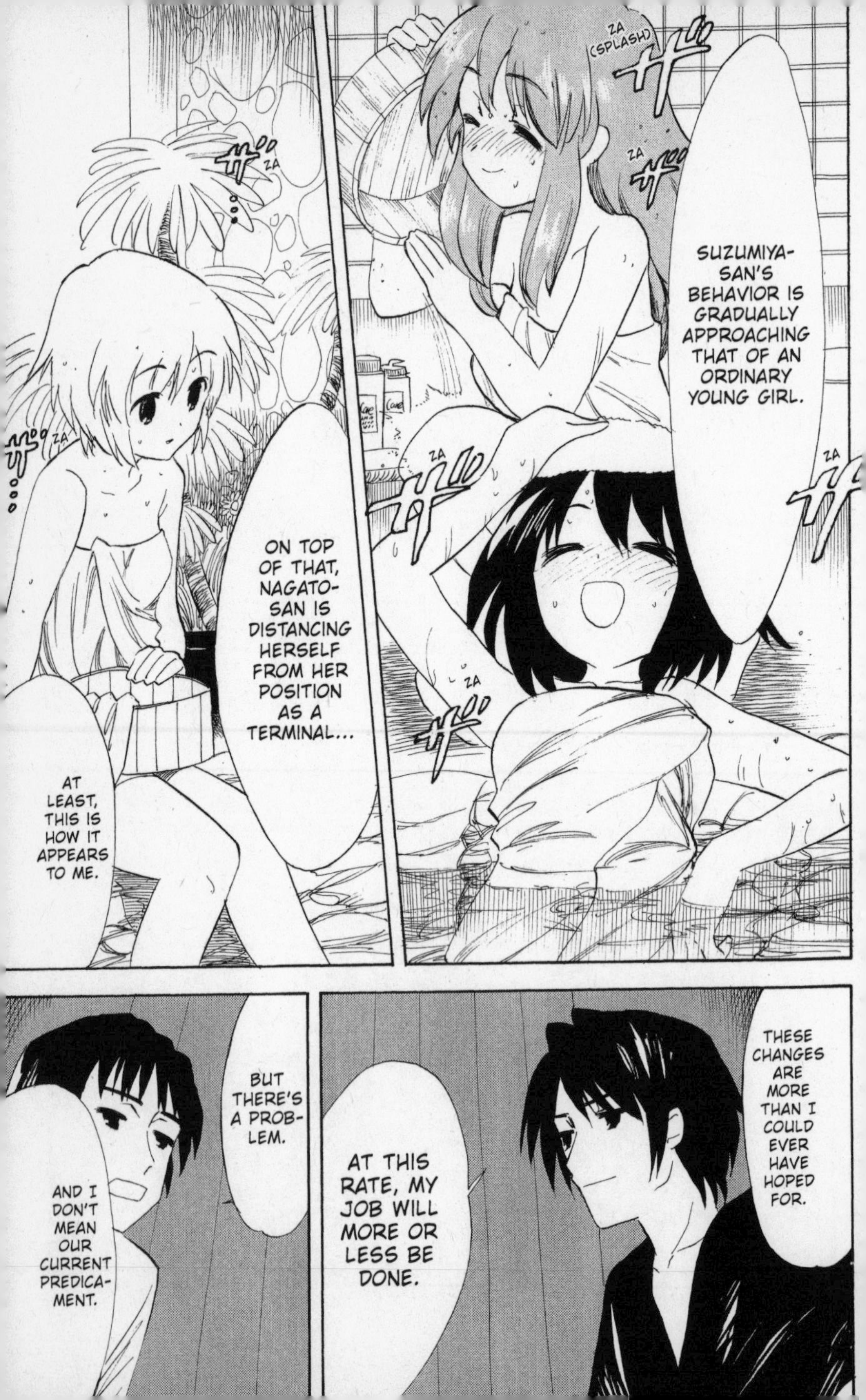
ZA (SPLASH)
ZA
SUZUMIYA-SAN'S BEHAVIOR IS GRADUALLY APPROACHING THAT OF AN ORDINARY YOUNG GIRL.
ZA
ZA
ZA
ON TOP OF THAT, NAGATO-SAN IS DISTANCING HERSELF FROM HER POSITION AS A TERMINAL...
ZA
ZA
AT LEAST, THIS IS HOW IT APPEARS TO ME.
THESE CHANGES ARE MORE THAN I COULD EVER HAVE HOPED FOR.
AT THIS RATE, MY JOB WILL MORE OR LESS BE DONE.
BUT THERE'S A PROB-LEM.
AND I DON'T MEAN OUR CURRENT PREDICA-MENT.

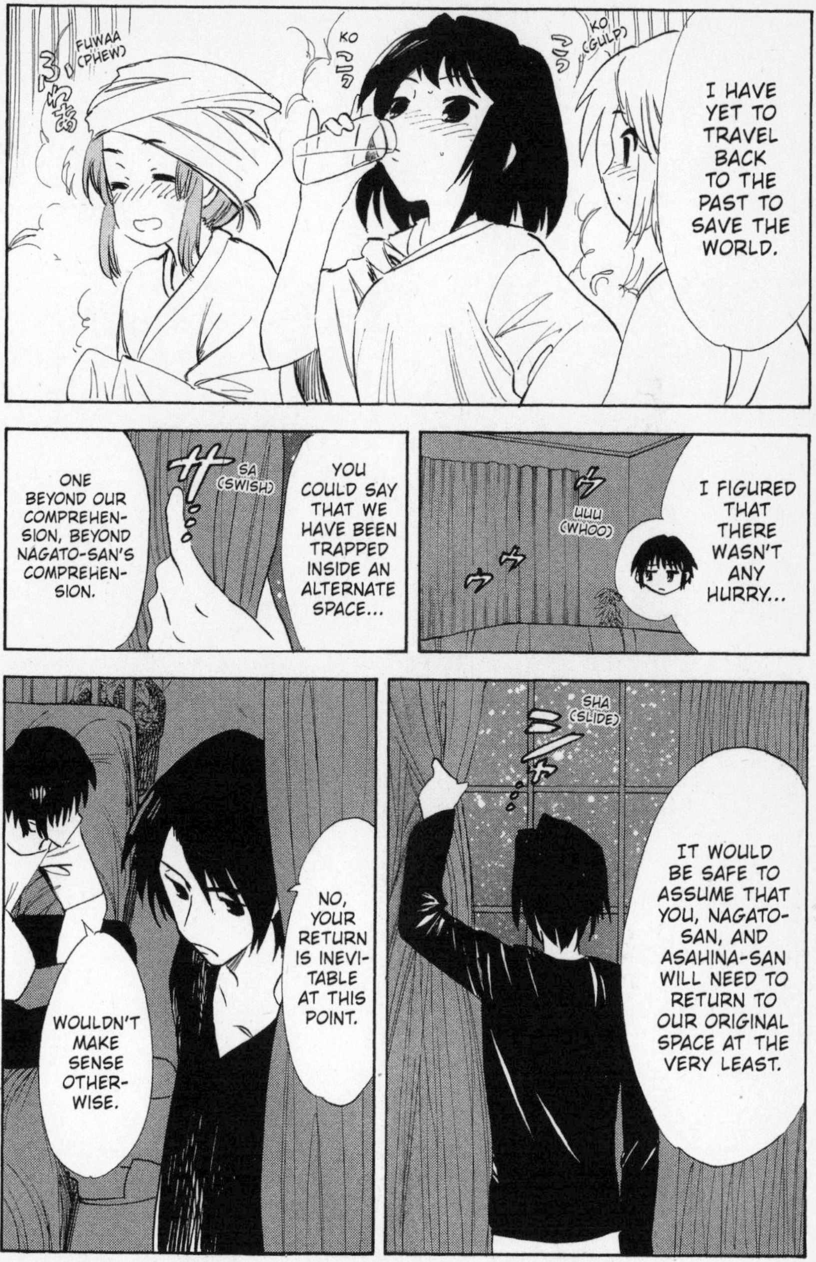
KO (GULP)
I HAVE YET TO TRAVEL BACK TO THE PAST TO SAVE THE WORLD.
KO
FUWAA (PHEW)
I FIGURED THAT THERE WASN'T ANY HURRY...
UUU (WHOO)
YOU COULD SAY THAT WE HAVE BEEN TRAPPED INSIDE AN ALTERNATE SPACE...
SA (SWISH)
ONE BEYOND OUR COMPREHENSION, BEYOND NAGATO-SAN'S COMPREHENSION.
SHA (SLIDE)
IT WOULD BE SAFE TO ASSUME THAT YOU, NAGATO-SAN, AND ASAHINA-SAN WILL NEED TO RETURN TO OUR ORIGINAL SPACE AT THE VERY LEAST.
NO, YOUR RETURN IS INEVITABLE AT THIS POINT.
WOULDN'T MAKE SENSE OTHERWISE.

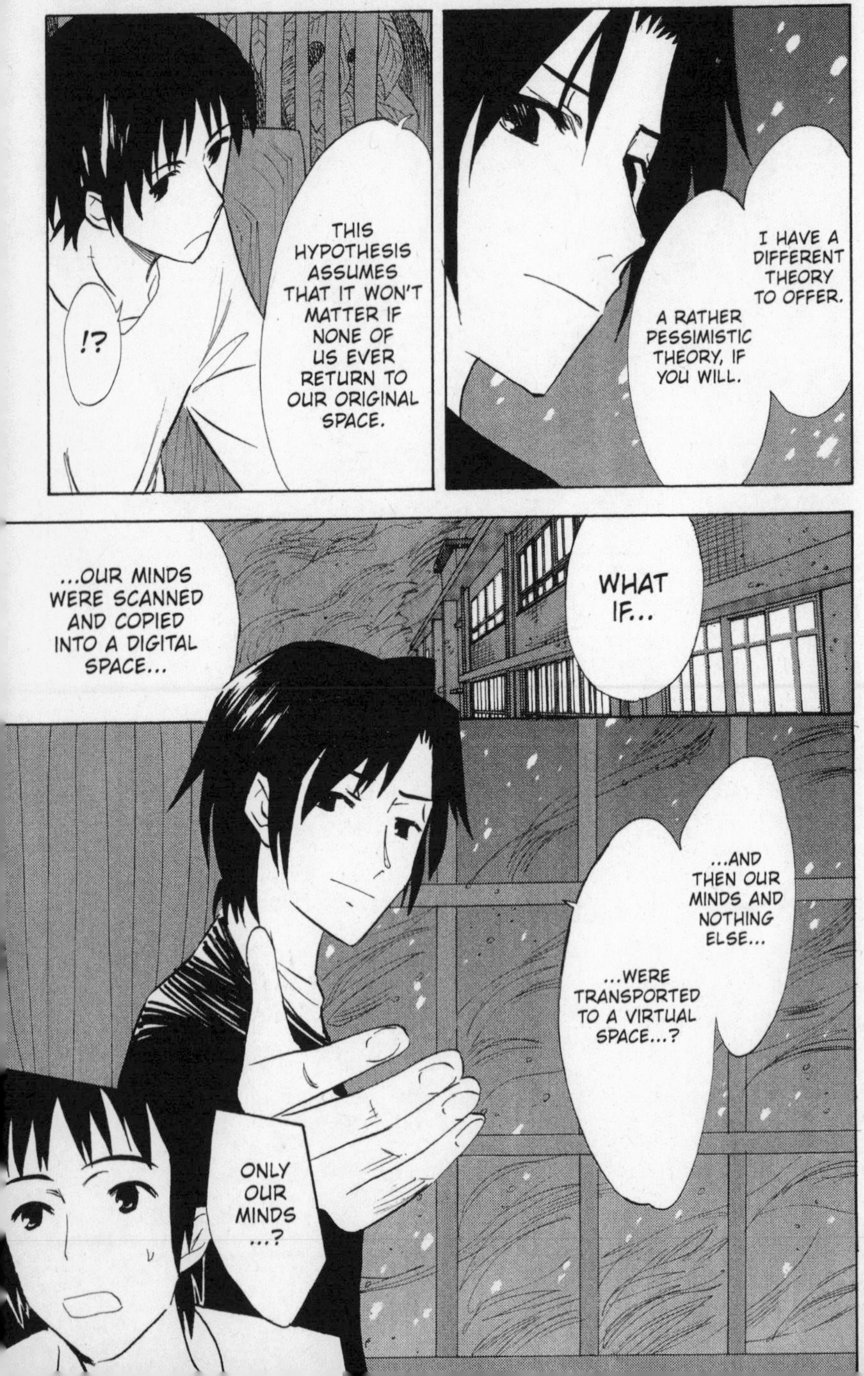
I HAVE A DIFFERENT THEORY TO OFFER.
A RATHER PESSIMISTIC THEORY, IF YOU WILL.
THIS HYPOTHESIS ASSUMES THAT IT WON'T MATTER IF NONE OF US EVER RETURN TO OUR ORIGINAL SPACE.
!?
WHAT IF...
...OUR MINDS WERE SCANNED AND COPIED INTO A DIGITAL SPACE...
...AND THEN OUR MINDS AND NOTHING ELSE...
...WERE TRANSPORTED TO A VIRTUAL SPACE...?
ONLY OUR MINDS ...?

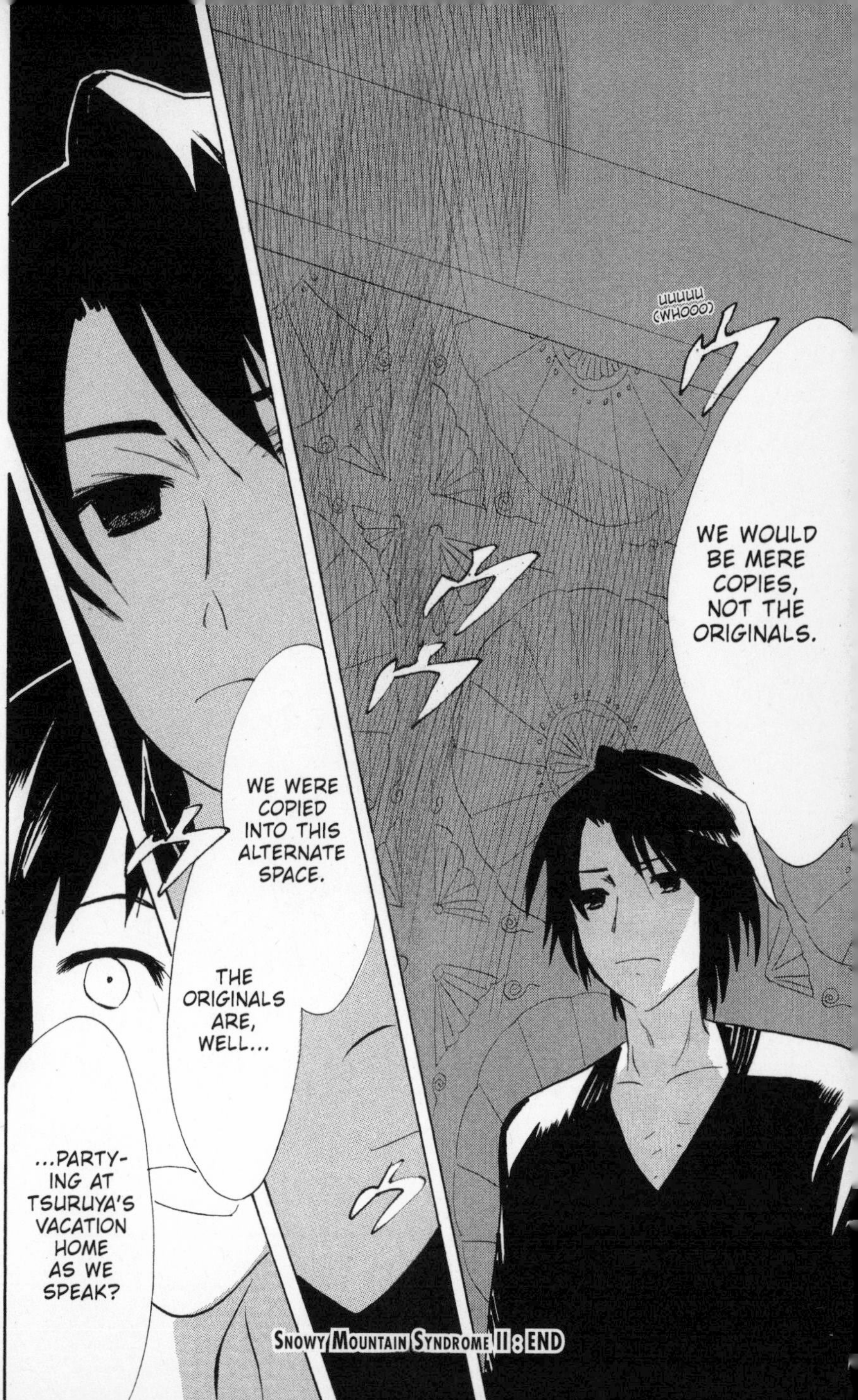
uuuuu (WHOOO)
WE WOULD BE MERE COPIES, NOT THE ORIGINALS.
WE WERE COPIED INTO THIS ALTERNATE SPACE.
THE ORIGINALS ARE, WELL...
...PARTY-ING AT TSURUYA'S VACATION HOME AS WE SPEAK?
SNOWY MOUNTAIN SYNDROME II: END

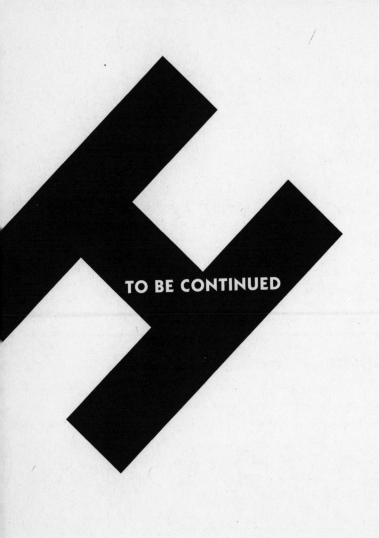

TO BE CONTINUED

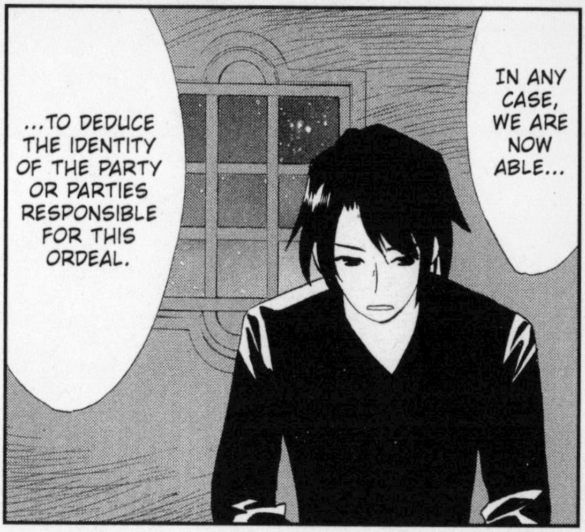
IN ANY CASE, WE ARE NOW ABLE...
...TO DEDUCE THE IDENTITY OF THE PARTY OR PARTIES RESPONSIBLE FOR THIS ORDEAL.

KYON AND KOIZUMI CONTINUE TO INVESTIGATE THE CIRCUMSTANCES BEHIND THEIR ORDEAL IN THIS MYSTERIOUS MANSION.

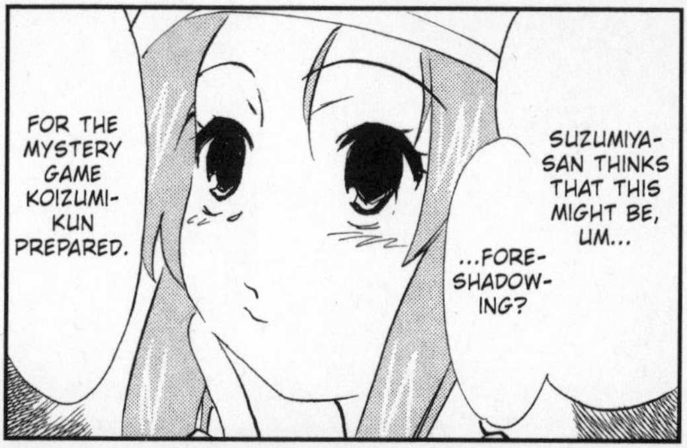
SUZUMIYA-SAN THINKS THAT THIS MIGHT BE, UM...
...FORE-SHADOW-ING?
FOR THE MYSTERY GAME KOIZUMI-KUN PREPARED.

HOWEVER, THEY TURN IN FOR THE NIGHT WITHOUT REACHING A SOLUTION...

THAT WAS WHEN IT HAPPENED!

"SNOWY MOUNTAIN SYNDROME" & "WHERE DID THE CAT GO?"

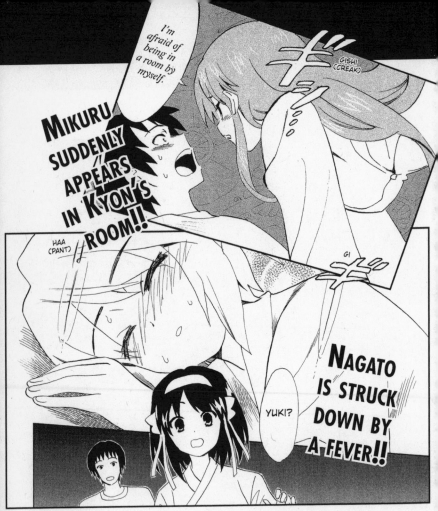

I'm afraid of being in a room by myself.

ギ (GISHI (CREAK))

MIKURU SUDDENLY APPEARS IN KYON'S ROOM!!

HAA (PANT)

GI ギ

NAGATO IS STRUCK DOWN BY A FEVER!!

YUKI?

AND WHAT IS THE MEANING OF THIS METAL PANEL THAT LOCKS THE ENTRANCE OF THE MANSION...?

$$x - y = (D - 1) - z$$
$$x = \quad y = \quad z =$$

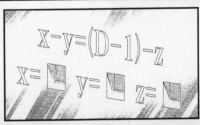

THE NEXT VOLUME INCLUDES THE CHAOTIC CONCLUSION OF

THE MELANCHOLY OF HARUHI SUZUMIYA

Original Story: Nagaru Tanigawa
Manga: Gaku Tsugano
Character Design: Noizi Ito

Translation: Chris Pai for MX Media LLC
Lettering: Alexis Eckerman

SUZUMIYA HARUHI NO YUUTSU Volume 10 © Nagaru TANIGAWA • Noizi ITO
2009 © Gaku TSUGANO 2009. First published in Japan in 2009 by KADOKAWA
SHOTEN CO., LTD., Tokyo. English translation rights arranged with KADOKAWA
SHOTEN CO., LTD., Tokyo through TUTTLE-MORI AGENCY, INC., Tokyo.

English translation © 2011 by Hachette Book Group, Inc.

Yen Press
Hachette Book Group
237 Park Avenue, New York, NY 10017

www.HachetteBookGroup.com
www.YenPress.com

Yen Press is an imprint of Hachette Book Group, Inc. The Yen Press name and
logo are trademarks of Hachette Book Group, Inc.

First Yen Press Edition: November 2011

ISBN: 978-0-316-18639-1

10 9 8 7 6 5 4 3

OPM

Printed in the United States of America